Centre and Provinces

Studies on Contemporary China

The Contemporary China Institute at the School of Oriental and African Studies (University of London) has, since its establishment in 1968, been an international centre for research and publications on twentieth-century China. *Studies on Contemporary China*, which is edited at the Institute, seeks to maintain and extend that tradition by making available the best work of scholars and China specialists throughout the world. It embraces a wide variety of subjects relating to Nationalist and Communist China, including social, political, and economic change, intellectual and cultural developments, foreign relations, and national security.

Series Editor
Professor Frank Dikötter, Director of the Contemporary China Institute

Editorial Advisory Board
Dr Robert F. Ash

Professor Hugh D. R. Baker

Professor Elisabeth J. Croll

Dr Richard Louis Edmonds

Mr Brian G. Hook

Professor Christopher B. Howe

Professor Bonnie S. McDougall

Professor David Shambaugh

Dr Julia C. Strauss

Professor Lynn T. White III

Dr Jonathan Unger

Centre and Provinces: China 1978–1993

Power as Non-Zero-Sum

LINDA CHELAN LI

CLARENDON PRESS · OXFORD
1998

Oxford University Press, Great Clarendon Street, Oxford OX2 6DP

Oxford New York
Athens Auckland Bangkok Bogota Bombay
Buenos Aires Calcutta Cape Town Dar es Salaam
Delhi Florence Hong Kong Istanbul Karachi
Kuala Lumpur Madras Madrid Melbourne
Mexico City Nairobi Paris Singapore
Taipei Tokyo Toronto Warsaw
and associated companies in
Berlin Ibadan

Oxford is a trade mark of Oxford University Press

Published in the United States
by Oxford University Press Inc., New York

A catalogue record for this book is available from the British Library

Library of Congress Cataloging in Publication Data
Li, Linda Chelan.
Centre and provinces—China 1978–1993 : power as
non-zero-sum / by Linda Chelan Li.
p.   cm.—(Studies on contemporary China)
Includes bibliographical references and index.
1. Central-local government relations—China. 2. China—Politics
and government—1976–   I. Title. II. Series: Studies on
contemporary China (Oxford, England)
JQ1506.S8L5 1998   320.951'09047—dc21   97–39265
ISBN 0–19–829361–5

1 3 5 7 9 10 8 6 4 2

Typeset by Alliance Phototypesetters, Pondicherry
Printed in Great Britain by
Bookcraft (Bath) Ltd, Midsomer Norton, Somerset

For Johnny

Preface

This project was first conceived in spring 1989, before the traumatic events in Beijing unfolded to a tragic climax. The original thinking was to contribute towards the identification of factors which underlie the 'cyclical' pattern of national integration and disintegration throughout Chinese history, and thereby to explore the possibilities of qualitative change in political processes.

The main body of the book, which is based on my doctoral thesis at the School of Oriental and African Studies, University of London, has, however, a narrower focus and a humbler objective. It examines how two apparently atypical provincial-level governments, Guangdong and Shanghai, have sought to achieve their objectives in investment expansion and economic development since 1978 within the constraints of the central government. The findings of this examination have, however, indicated that the central–provincial interface may be the locus where qualitative changes in political processes will first occur in China.

I have benefited from the assistance and guidance of numerous individuals from the initial stage of pondering to the actual production of the book. I am indebted to David L. Shambaugh, supervisor of the thesis, and the members of the examination board, Peter Ferdinand and Robert Ash, for their critical advice, warm support and many valuable suggestions. David Goodman, Jae Ho Chung and Paul Wilding read through the entire book manuscript and offered very constructive comments regarding both presentation and substantive arguments. Lynn White III, George W. Jones, Kuan Hsinchi, Brantly Womack, Julia Strauss and Sung Yun-wing, among others, reviewed earlier versions of various chapters. When this book was at its stage of fermentation, Audrey Donnithorne, John P. Burns and Yuan Cheng gave much food for thought. Jane Duckett, J. Wibowo Wibisono and S. B. Ko, fellow doctoral candidates at London, rendered gratifying intellectual as well as emotional support during both writing and research in the field. I must thank Andrew Schuller, the commissioning editor, and many others at Oxford University Press for their hearty effort in the production of this work, and the Contemporary China Institute of SOAS, particularly Robert Ash, Richard Louis Edmonds and Frank Dikötter, for making this publication possible.

This list of acknowledgements could be at least quadrupled in length, if it were not for the need for prudence regarding the unpredictable political circumstances in China. The many discussions I have had with Chinese scholars and officials during my stay in London and in China have given me an insider's view of the picture and greatly enriched my understanding of the very complicated issues. The brevity of these acknowledgements and the absence of many Chinese names greatly understate the gratitude I feel to these individuals who inspired me through the process of this work.

A good number of close friends, in Hong Kong as well as in London, have provided the tacit encouragement at various difficult times during the long period of gestation of this book. My family has been the reliable source of support to which I have always turned during times of stress. My mother, sisters and brothers, and above all, my husband, Johnny, have stood firmly with me throughout these years, when my career underwent twists and turns, and a new-born baby joined the family. My gratitude for their understanding is beyond words.

Linda Chelan Li
City University of Hong Kong
Hong Kong
November 1997

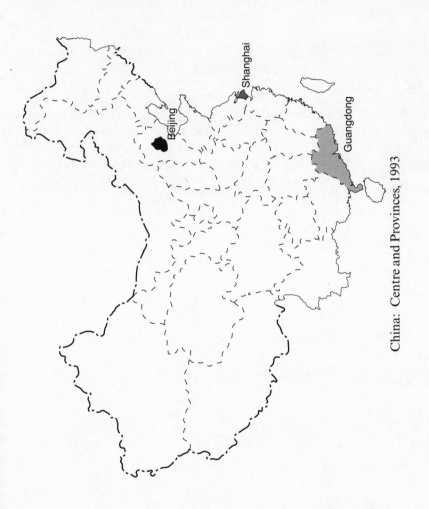

China: Centre and Provinces, 1993

Contents

List of Figures

List of Tables

Introduction

This book examines central–provincial politics regarding investment implementation in post-Mao China. Tensions between the centre and the provinces have been riding high since the commencement of economic reform in the late 1970s. Central government officials blamed provinces for their 'Machiavellian' shrewdness in getting around, if not ignoring, central directives and policies. Provincial officials, on the other hand, complained that the centre was often unreasonable in its demands and unsympathetic to their needs and difficulties. The consequence was that both parties blamed one another for their difficulties, and in the process various problems in the economy were aggravated. The pursuit of economic gain led to 'trade wars' between different provinces as well as massive wastage as a result of inefficient investment. The centre was largely ineffective in its efforts in controlling the problems, as its control instruments, outdated relative to the new requirements of reform, were increasingly evaded and ignored by the provinces. The extent of the crisis was so great that at times the very integration of the Chinese state was called into question.

It is worth remembering, however, that the relationship between the national and subnational levels of government is not an issue peculiar to China. The spatial dimension of politics has been a perennial and persistent issue within political systems worldwide, though the substantive content and degree of concern may vary among different countries. Underlying the interest in spatial politics within the national boundaries of different political systems is the generic concern regarding the gap between policy formulation and implementation or, simply, the 'implementation gap'. Governments exist to rule and perform. The existence of substantial differentials between policies as formulated and what is eventually implemented raises the question of effective governance.[1] The policy–implementation gap also invites questions as to what the process of governance actually consists of. What impact does the structure of state institutions have on what and how things are done? What is the dynamic between the national and subnational levels of government affecting where and how political agendas are struck, policies decided and implemented?[2]

In China, however, the concern for spatial politics goes beyond the concern over the 'implementation gap'. The historical experience of disintegration results in a heightened sense of concern among students of Chinese politics and Chinese political actors regarding the political ramifications of an implementation gap.[3] This concern over the spectre of national disintegration provokes questions as to *why* the fear should have arisen in the first place. What is the linkage between the observation of an implementation gap and the fear of national disintegration? Is it because the gap is so 'large' in China that we are led to feel that centrifugal tendencies are verging on secession and disintegration? How then can we measure the gap, in comparison with the gaps in other political systems? Alternatively, are there other issues associated with the implementation gap that may cause the concern?

This book argues for the latter position. The contention is that underlying the concern for national disintegration lies the as yet unresolved historical problem of power distribution and institutionalization within the Chinese political system. Policy implementation gaps in the post-Mao period of a magnitude to cause alarm at the prospect of possible disintegration of the Chinese state, it is argued, resulted from the failure of the Chinese political system to institutionalize any system of power distribution between the centre and the provinces, and to provide a regularized avenue of reconciliation and arbitration when conflicts arose. Likewise, this book argues that the crisis in the central–provincial relationship in reform China poses an opportunity to resolve this historical problem.

Against the background of heightened tension between the centre and the provinces, this book maintains that the central–provincial interface can become the breakthrough point whereby qualitative change regarding power distribution and institutionalization within the Chinese state may occur. Unlike the conventional wisdom among China analysts on this issue, which sees central–provincial relations as constituting a zero-sum game, this book identifies an interactive, non-zero-sum relationship between the centre and the provinces. This work thus departs from the static view of power which sees the centre and the provinces as trapped in endless cycles of centralization and decentralization. A unilinear conception of central–provincial relationships is unable, it is argued, to reconcile the apparent contradiction of central predominance and provincial power. It is also incapable of anticipating the circumstances whereby changes in the relationship may take place. The non-zero-sum view adopted here stresses the interdependence and thus mutuality of power between the centre and the provinces as constituent parts of the state. When both parties are

mutually dependent upon one another, conflicts necessitate compromise on both sides. The more intense the conflicts, the 'bigger' the compromise is required to be, resulting in, eventually, qualitative change in
the relationship.

Employing a non-zero-sum view of power, this book enquires into
the ways which provincial governments manoeuvred their way within
the constraints and opportunities provided by the institutional context to achieve their agendas. More specifically, it examines how leaders
of Guangdong and Shanghai bargained with central leaders regarding the formulation of central policies which had a bearing on investment and the allocation of centrally controlled resources so as to make
the institutional context work to their advantage. It examines the
strategies which provincial officials used to stretch the 'loopholes' in
established institutions and practices to make them work far beyond
their original limits. Provincial leaders were found to be remarkably
active political agents who engaged in a wide range of discretionary
behaviour in order to advance their objective of investment expansion. The picture shown is not, however, one of one-sided activism by
the provinces. Provincial governments were always constrained by
central policies, which explains their eagerness to bargain with the
centre for a more favourable institutional context.

The focus of this work is on the *linkage* between institutional context and discretion. It aims to explore the relationship between the
constraining/facilitating power of the centre and the ability to engage
discretion on the part of the provinces. Accordingly, the research
questions undertaken in this book can be grouped into two categories.
The first group concerns the institutional context which is largely set
by central policies. What parameters did the centre set for the provinces regarding investment? What were the substantive central policies
involved? In what ways did the centre influence, whether it be to *facilitate* or *constrain*, the discretionary behaviour of the provinces? The second group of questions targets the discretion of the provinces. How
did provincial governments manage to manoeuvre under, and regardless of, central government constraints? What strategies did they employ? To what extent did the provinces participate in formulating the
central policies which in turn constituted their institutional context?
In an interactive relationship, these two groups of questions obviously
criss-cross one another.

RESEARCH DESIGN

Investment as the political arena

Unlike most previous works on Chinese spatial politics, which have largely focused on the resource, or input, aspect of policy processes, such as fiscal revenue allocation and personnel control, this book has adopted a substantive policy as its focus: investment. Taking a substantive policy as the arena of analysis means starting the enquiry into the political dynamics from the output end of policy. The idea is to discern discrepancies between central policy and provincial implementation in the substantive output of a policy area, and then work through the process whereby the discrepancies evolved. In this way the study identifies factors which gave provincial governments room to manoeuvre, and conversely, the instruments through which the centre exerted its influence over the provinces. As it turns out, the fiscal system is, among other things, a major institutional factor shaping the provinces' discretionary behaviour over investment.

The advantages of starting from the output end, rather than the input side, of policy processes are two-fold (Chung 1995*b*). First, starting from the output end focuses attention on the 'implementation gap'. It is then possible to pinpoint the input factors which contributed to such a gap. This approach ensures that the analyst always relates what is observed in the interaction between the central and provincial actors, in the institutional context, and in whatever other information is considered relevant to the study to the original phenomenon of an implementation gap in the chosen policy area. The study is thereby process-oriented. Input factors and institutional arrangements will be studied in the search for an explanation of the implementation gap. Their relevance and role with respect to how the provinces manoeuvre their discretion or how the centre sustains its control will then be clearly defined.

Secondly, working from the output side of 'an implementation gap' back to the input institutions in identifying its causes safeguards analysts from falling into the analytical trap of static institutional analysis. For instance, it is common for studies focusing on fiscal arrangements to conclude that, as a result of the significant transfer of fiscal resources and authority from the centre, there has been a substantial loss of central power *vis-à-vis* the provincial governments since the 1980s. The linkage between the transfer of fiscal authority and resources on the one hand, and the loss of central power on the other, is assumed to be direct and straightforward. This assumption is itself problematic, since, as Chung (1995*b*) has noted, the fiscal status of a province can 'cut both ways of having a stronger (or weaker) say in policy-making and, at the same time, of being placed under tighter (or looser) control by the centre'. A static institutional focus also fails to illuminate the rich shades of interaction between the central and provincial actors— i.e. the process by which actors *interact* within the institutional context to bring about the implementation gap or its absence.

Amongst the various substantive policy areas, investment is the most important policy output of the socialist Chinese state in terms of the amount of resources devoted to its use. While class struggle still dominated political life prior to the Third Plenum in December 1978, investment as an item in the state budget was always the most important single issue, accounting for up to 56 per cent of total annual fiscal expenditure.[4] Since 1978, with the shift of national focus in political life from class struggle to economic construction, investment activities have gained greater significance in the task of fulfilling the national goal. The materialistic emphasis of socialist ideology as well as the nationalistic bent of central leaders have made investment the most important expenditure item of the state, at both central and provincial levels. As an important activity of both the central and provincial governments, investment therefore provides the best vantage point from which to view political processes in China, most particularly central–provincial politics. *Prima facie* evidence also suggests that investment is a mature policy area through which to explore the politics between centre and provinces. Reports referring to difficulties experienced by the centre in attempting to rein in the excessive investment enthusiasm of provincial governments abounded. Provincial governments consistently sought to increase the level of investment activities beyond the limits imposed by the centre, often resulting in lacklustre economic efficiency. Localistic orientation in investment and market protection by provincial governments has demonstrated the increasing contradictions between the centre's preferences and policies on the one hand and provincial incentives and policy outcomes on the other.

The provincial level as the level of analysis

In this book I have chosen the provincial level as the level of analysis. The reasons are threefold. First, the provincial level, with its size and command of substantial resources, has the potential of posing a

political challenge to the centre which is impossible in the case of more
localized units. As Whitney (1969: 79–80) has written on this point,
'the diminutive size of the lowest echelon units precludes them from
acquiring too much power. It is the units of the intermediary tiers with
their more extensive span of control and resource base that are most
likely to challenge the centre.' Studies of the more localized levels,
especially with respect to the township and the village, and their relations with the centre are essential in order to understand the extent of
state penetration into society, and vice versa, within a state–society
analytical framework. In order to tackle the recurrent concern over
national disintegration and the threat to central power in the political
system, however, one has to start from the main candidate for potential power contention with the centre: the provinces.

Secondly, the importance of the provincial level and its equivalent
in the Chinese political system has been underlined by its persistent
historical continuity, despite frequent attempts by the centre to manipulate provincial boundaries. The provincial level of administration
has formed a stable and nearly permanent intermediate link in the
chain of command between the centre and the districts for more than
a thousand years of Chinese history (Whitney 1969: 119).[5]

It is true that the boundaries of the provincial level have often been
changed but this should be taken to reflect, to an extent, the perceived
threat of this intermediary level of government to the centre (Whitney
1969: 120). The argument is that as the imperial bureaucracy developed,
more power came to reside in the province, it being the intermediary
level of state bureaucracy. The centre, however, became uneasy about
the growth in power of the intermediary level and periodically attempted to constrain its power by gerrymandering its boundaries.
However, the need for an intermediary level of government as a means
of enabling the centre to retain its hold over the more than one thousand units of county government meant that the provincial level
would nevertheless continue to exist.[6] Moreover, despite the repeated
central manipulations of provincial borders, and the creation and
abolition of entire provinces, there has been a relative continuity of
provincial sizes over time,[7] and occasionally the centre had to abandon
its attempts at gerrymandering.[8] This suggests that provincial-level
government has long been a potent political force within the Chinese
political system, and therefore deserves serious attention.

Thirdly, the provincial level has been chosen as the level of analysis
because it has not been adequately covered in existing literature on

Chinese politics.[9] Most previous works on Chinese spatial politics
have focused on the lower echelons. The reason for this focus can be
traced to the development of the field of Chinese political studies in
the West.[10] Research at county and township levels offered analysts a
peek into the triangle of forces between the centre, the local officials,
and the rural society over which the local officials have direct jurisdiction and of which they are a part.[11] The findings of this research
refine one's view as to the extent of state power in society, and as such
constitute an important critique of the previous, and still implicitly
pervasive, totalitarian model. While the implementation gap has been
the subject of a good number of works in this area, and explanations
have been sought within the state apparatus, there has not been similar
scrutiny at the provincial level.[12] The gap in the literature is obvious,
thus the pertinence of a provincial focus of analysis.

The choice of case studies

The arguments set forth in this book are based on the findings of two
case studies: Guangdong and Shanghai. These case studies permit an
in-depth examination of the political dynamics on which generaliza-
tions can be built. As comparative case studies they also provide an
additional dimension which single-case studies do not give.

But why have Guangdong and Shanghai been chosen? What does a
comparison of this pair highlight? What can a study drawing on a
comparison between Guangdong and Shanghai, probably the two
most atypical areas in China since the 1980s, tell us about central–
provincial relations in China as a whole? In other words, to what extent are the findings and conclusions drawn from the comparative case
studies of Guangdong and Shanghai generalizable? Moreover, since
Shanghai is actually a municipality, albeit of provincial-level administrative status, and Guangdong is a 'province proper', are the two areas
comparable?

What the pair can highlight

Guangdong and Shanghai make a good pair for comparative study
with respect to their relations with the centre because it is possible to
'isolate' the effect of central policies on the behaviour of two provincial-
level governments. The isolation of independent variables in real-life
observation requires a substantial level of *relevant* similarity between
the objects of analysis in other aspects. The first precondition of a good

pair for comparison is, therefore, that the areas be sufficiently similar in those aspects which may have an effect on the dependent variable but which are not the subject of the current study.[13] In the arena of investment and economic policy implementation, Guangdong and Shanghai in the late 1970s were situated, in relative terms, at a similar baseline regarding their *potential* in attracting foreign investment and developing an export-oriented, internationalized economy ahead of the rest of the country. Both Guangdong and Shanghai are situated along the coast of China. Historically both areas are commercial centres with substantial experience in doing business with foreigners. Guangzhou (then known as Canton) was the earliest port opened to foreign trade in the nineteenth century, and Shanghai was the largest industrial and economic centre of the country as well as the hub of foreign commercial and industrial activity in the early 1920s. Both have extensive overseas linkage. This linkage means that both areas already had a large reservoir of overseas Chinese capital and management expertise to tap when the Open Door Policy took effect in 1979, and gives both areas—relative to the inland provinces—a similar edge in terms of being able to take advantage of the reforms since 1979.

The second requirement for a good pair for comparison is a large difference in the independent variable: the central policies. The Guangdong government obtained very favourable preferential policies early in 1979 which allowed the provincial government an unprecedented latitude in manoeuvres and control over local resources. In contrast, the Shanghai government was stuck with the old centralized system for nearly the whole of the 1980s. The imposition of tight central control over a resourceful and wealthy area highlights the impact of central policies on provincial behaviour. The marked differences in central policies towards the two areas suggests that the dynamics between the two provincial governments and the centre may be substantially different. Interesting comparisons can then be made to reveal the discrete effect of central policies on the discretionary behaviour of the two provincial-level governments.

Implications for the general picture

Guangdong and Shanghai are atypical areas. Guangdong was the favoured site of the centre for pioneer reform experiments. As a result, for a considerable period in the 1980s the provincial government enjoyed a degree of leverage which was the envy of other provinces. Meanwhile, as the most important economic centre of China this century, Shanghai has always topped the list of provincial-level units in terms of national income per capita and fiscal revenue per capita.[14] The huge gap between the 'affluence' of Shanghai and the relative poverty of some of the interior provinces made the municipality look as much like 'the other China' as it was in the treaty-port period in the 1920s and 1930s.[15] The question therefore arises: how do findings on Guangdong and Shanghai reflect the dynamics of central–provincial politics in China in general?

Guangdong and Shanghai may be too 'peculiar' to make findings on them a representative case relevant to every other province in China. However, the atypicality of the pair is perhaps an advantage. After all, the generalizability of an apparently typical case is often assumed rather than demonstrated. For instance, does 'typicality' refer to the median, the mode or the average? What do we mean when we describe a certain province as being the 'typical' province? It may be justifiable to use a 'typical' measure, however arrived at, if the differences which are averaged out and thus erased from the analysis are irrelevant or un-important. More often, however, an average measure is used when we do not know whether or not the differences are relevant, or because the differences are incomprehensible to us. Against this background, the apparent unrepresentativeness of Guangdong and Shanghai in fact has the desirable effect of requiring the analyst to confront squarely the wider implications of the case studies, and to explicate what is otherwise often assumed.

Guangdong and Shanghai had experiences at opposite extremes with respect to central economic control in the late 1970s and most of the 1980s. Guangdong was exempted from implementing of some national policies, and in fact given a new set of custom-made policies allowing a large degree of provincial discretion. On the other hand Shanghai's huge resource base continued to be tightly controlled by the centre, the level of extraction remaining continuously high. Their extreme treatment by the centre makes them two poles of a continuum, between which the positions of other provinces are likely to fall. Here the differential central policies are the independent variable, and the provincial reactions and behaviour the dependent variable.

The choice of two resourceful areas along the coast, rather than one rich and one poor province, enables this study to minimize the number of independent variables and focus on the variable of central policies. More importantly, it serves to highlight the conflict, and the political dynamics therein, between the demands and constraints posed by the centre on the one hand, and the opportunities for discretion allowed by provincial socio-economic conditions on the other. The larger resource base the Guangdong and Shanghai leaderships had at their disposal, relative to many other more 'typical' and, therefore, poorer interior provinces, is indicative of the extent of *choice* of provincial leaders in the face of often contradictory pressures from the centre. The Guangdong–Shanghai comparison, therefore, leads to the core question concerning central–provincial politics: would provincial leaders comply with central policies if they had the means not to do so?[16] By ruling out the possibility that provinces comply simply because they have to as a result of absolute deprivation, the pair provides a clear-cut test case regarding the choice of provincial discretionary behaviour. In this process it may be possible to identify additional variables which serve to mediate the interaction between central policies and provincial behaviour.

Comparability

Another issue which arises when comparing Guangdong and Shanghai is whether they are comparable at all. Guangdong is a province with a sizeable rural hinterland, while Shanghai, as a municipality, is an essentially urban area, albeit with a number of suburban counties. This geographical difference means that Shanghai has been much more dependent on other provinces for raw materials and food supplies than has Guangdong. An implication is that Shanghai relies more on the centre for co-ordinating planned supplies from other provinces, and for adjudicating conflicts with their suppliers. The larger span of control required for the Guangdong government relative to Shanghai's is also likely to have an effect on their differential treatment of subprovincial delegation. The question therefore arises: is the spatial politics in the case of a municipality comparable to that of a province at all?

The answer lies in the basis of comparability of Guangdong and Shanghai. The objective here is to illuminate the political relationship between the central and provincial levels of government. Guangdong and Shanghai are both provincial-level governments. This single fact firmly establishes their comparability in a study of central–provincial politics. The fact that Shanghai is a provincial-level municipality, rather than a 'province proper', may have implications as regards its relations with the centre. But this does not disqualify Shanghai from being the object of a study of central–provincial politics. The reason is obvious. In a central–provincial study, the focus of analysis is obviously on, first, the different ways in which the centre deals with different provincial-level governments, with all their varieties of provincial conditions. A second focus is the ways in which the different kinds of central treatment affect the behaviour of different provincial-level governments. In other words, the differences between the relationship between the centre and Shanghai on the one hand, and between the centre and other provinces on the other, arising due to Shanghai's municipal characteristics constitute a valid part of what requires explanation.

This rationale of comparability is based on the political/administrative status of the Shanghai government within the Chinese political hierarchy. The assumption is the relevance of formal hierarchical status in Chinese politics. While fully acknowledging the importance of the personal status of leaders in the political processes of the Chinese system, a good number of works have underlined the importance of formal hierarchical status.[17] Communication within the state system is very much regulated by the structure of the hierarchy. In one particular instance, the Ministry of Education was upgraded in 1985 to a supra-ministerial rank of the State Education Commission in order to confer on it a higher bureaucratic standing enabling the former ministry to issue instructions to other ministries concerning educational matters in their 'systems' (Lieberthal and Oksenberg 1988: 144). Instead of sending an influential and powerful official to head what was then the Ministry of Education, the centre had to raise the rank of the entire ministry. This aptly demonstrated the relevance of formal bureaucratic ranking in regulating interactions between state agencies. The provincial-level ranking of Shanghai municipality, therefore, accords the same formal avenue of communication and interaction between the Shanghai government and the centre as in the case of other provinces. This fact is the basis of the comparability between Shanghai and Guangdong in this study.

ORGANIZATION OF THE STUDY

This book has a total of eight chapters. Following this introduction Chapter 1 provides a theoretical statement of the study. The chapter elaborates the ways in which this study seeks to advance our understanding of China's spatial politics, and of political processes in

12 Introduction

general. It outlines the development of the central–provincial literature, identifies the gaps this study strives to fill, and explicates the approach taken to achieve this task. It points to the need for an alternative concept of power and an alternative approach to the issue of central–provincial relationships.

Chapter 2 provides a background discussion of the failure of central control over provincial investment implementation during the post-Mao period. The discussion proceeds in two parts. The first section explicates the problem of investment administration and weakening central control. The second section seeks an explanation. To what extent is the problem a result of the economic reforms in the 1980s, and *which* reforms are the most crucial? This chapter argues that the centre itself is part of the story in causing its present problems.

Chapters 3 to 6 cover the details of the two case studies. Chapters 3 and 4 serve a dual purpose. First, the two chapters provide background information regarding investment in Guangdong and Shanghai, and identify the presence or absence of a provincial implementation gap regarding investment policies. Secondly, the chapters outline the institutional context of provincial investment behaviour. Specifically, two institutional arrangements, the fiscal system and the investment planning system, are identified as being of crucial significance to the implementation of investment policy. Their development in Guangdong and Shanghai since 1949, and especially since 1978, is outlined.

Chapters 5 and 6 describe the discretionary behaviour of the Guangdong and Shanghai governments in their pursuit of investment expansion. The chapters show how the provincial leaders manoeuvred within the institutional constraints of central policies to bargain for more favourable central policies as well as to redefine and bypass the institutional rules. A typology of discretionary behaviour classifies provincial discretion according to the relative dependence of discretionary behaviour on the centre. The findings of these two chapters reveal the rich varieties of discretionary behaviour of the Guangdong and Shanghai governments, thus demonstrating the vitality of the provincial-level government as a political actor.

Chapter 7 concludes the case studies with an explicit discussion of the *linkage* between institutional constraints and actors' choice, and in particular between central influence and provincial discretion. The influence of the centre on the discretionary behaviour of provincial governments is undeniable. The model of central–provincial relations this study puts forward is, however, not a Centre-led model with the

provincial governments relegated to agents passively reacting to stimuli from the centre, but an interactive and dialectical model which sees
the policies of the centre, the attitudes and role perceptions of provincial officials, and the discretion of provincial governments as constituent parts of a dynamic and interactive process. The argument can be
boiled down to one statement: provinces are also the forces of changes
at the centre. The resources and authority once delegated by the centre
to the provincial governments become part of provincial resources
and authority, which the entre may find very difficult to withdraw.[18] In
fact every wave of delegation gives the provinces additional leverage to
enable them to enhance their position in the political system.

In conclusion, Chapter 8 identifies the emerging trends of central–
provincial relations since the reform period. The chapter argues that
the changes have resulted from compromises by the centre *and* the
provinces to improve their respective situations. It is impossible for the
centre totally to 'eliminate' the power of the provincial governments
as an intermediary level in the state hierarchy. From the perspective of
provincial governments, other than at times of extreme secessionism,
they have to live with the power of a central government. The mutual
indispensability of the central–provincial relationship forces both
parties to learn to live with one another. As conflicts became protracted
and bargaining more intense, both the centre and the provinces gradually came to acknowledge the necessity for a better institutionalization of their relationship. Ambiguity was giving way to clarity as
the defining characteristic of central–provincial interactions, albeit
gradually. The trend towards increasing institutionalization in the
spatial arena between Centre and provinces could signal the development of a politics of compromise and co-existence, which would
radically change the character of Chinese politics.

NOTES

1. This book employs the notion that politics is *both* a matter of allocation of
   'who gets what and how' and a matter of domination, rule and governance,
   of 'us versus them'. That these two views of politics, derived from David
   Easton and Der Begriff Schmitt, actually complement one another is cogently argued in Poggi (1978: 2–12). Vivienne Shue (1988: 19) has also recognized the utility of the notion of politics as governance, *vis-à-vis* the
   dominant notion of politics as allocation in most Western studies of Chinese politics.

2 As a background note, these questions regarding the internal dynamics of
   the state structure have not always been considered 'fashionable'. When
   pluralism dominated political studies in the West, the emphasis on inputs to
   the political system relegated the dynamic political processes within the
   state apparatus to the status of the 'black box' of politics. See Dunleavy and
   O'Leary (1987: 108). The 'black box' has only been 'opened' with the return
   of the state institutions as a focal subject of political studies since the 1970s
   and the 1980s. There have been disagreements, however, as to when the state
   again became the focal point of Western political studies, or indeed whether
   there was any departure from the study of the state at all. One cause of such
   differing perceptions is the variety of conceptions of the 'state' as a subject
   of study which disputing parties had in mind. Those arguing for a break in
   such study were thinking in terms of the study of state structures and the
   constituent parts and institutions of the state, while those arguing against a
   break thought in terms of the state as the 'polity', of the state as a whole.
   For examples of the former view, see Evans *et al.* (1985) and Krasner (1984).
   For the latter view, see for instance Migdal (1988: 10 n. 1) and Dunleavy and
   O'Leary (1987).

3. David Goodman (1986: 4) noted the persistent concern of China scholars
   in the West and Chinese politicians about the centrifugal tendencies and
   threat of national disintegration in China. The increasingly reported
   occurrence of the implementation gap in post-Mao China as a result of
   subnational discretion has attracted wide attention among Western students of Chinese politics. Many describe the discrepancies between central
   policy prescriptions and local implementation as the reflections of region-
   alistic tendencies, and some even ponder the possibilities of national disintegration. See, for instance, Segal (1994), Chang (1992), Joffe (1994), and
   Goodman (1994).

4. The highest proportion was attained in 1958, the year of the Great
   Leap Forward. See Ministry of Finance (1992: 116). For more discussion
   see Chap. 2

5. This can be traced back to 756 AD, which is the middle of the Tang Dynasty.

6. The number of county-level governments has varied from exactly 1,000 in
   the Qin Dynasty (221 BC) to around 1,400 units in the Ming and Qing Dynasties (1368–1911 AD). The number stood at around 1,600 in the early
   years of the People's Republic of China, albeit with drastic reductions by
   over 300 units during the communization and Great Leap Forward campaign in the late 1950s. See Whitney (1969: Table 6).

7. Whitney (1969: 129) argues that if the size of provinces were to be ration-
   ally decided in order to facilitate optimum control from a management
   point of view, size should be inversely correlated with the population
   density of the area. His findings show that the designation of provincial
   boundaries more closely conformed with this rational management

principle in earlier times than in more recent years, suggesting that there was substantial inertia and continuity in the size of provinces, and a relative inability of the centre to change them radically.

8. One such instance occurred in 1906, when an attempt of the Qing central government to divide Jiangsu Province into two was aborted as a result of widespread resentment (Whitney 1969: 121).

9. This is recognized and noted by China scholars, who have called for more work to be done on the spatial aspect and on the provincial level in particular. See for instance Harding (1993: 30).

10. For a discussion of the development of the field, see Shambaugh (1993). See also Perry (1994). Perry attributes the focus of previous research on the state–society interface and the lack of attention to the interrelationships between political actors within the state and within society to China studies being a 'consumer field' borrowing analytical constructs from elsewhere, rather than a 'producer field' drawing insights from China's historical experiences and generating original analyses of interest to comparativists in general.

11. Some seminal works in this category are Shue (1988), Oi (1989) and Siu (1989).

12. See for instance Lampton (1987, ed. 1987); Lieberthal and Oksenberg (1988); Lieberthal and Lampton (1992). In disaggregating the state institutions, most of these works focus on the bureaucratic vertical 'systems' in explaining variations between policy intentions and implementation.

13. The similar potential of Guangdong and Shanghai in economic development and expanding investment enables this study to avoid the problems of isolating the effect of multiple independent variables on provincial behaviour. See Goodman (1986).

14. As of 1990 Shanghai's national income per capita amounted to 4,822 yuan and fiscal revenue per capita to 1,180 yuan, a long way ahead of Beijing, in second place at 3,577 yuan and 702 yuan respectively. Guangdong was at only 1,842 yuan and 206 yuan due to its much larger population. See Ministry of Finance (1992: 336, 348).

15. For the notion of 'the other China', see Bergère (1981).

16. In Goodman (1986) it is concluded that both provincial conditions and national policies determined provincial discretion. While this must be true, what the case of Guizhou, an extremely poor province, illuminates is at best indeterminate. The extremely deprived conditions in a province might have literally deprived the provincial leaders of the ability to follow central policies, as Goodman has concluded. Alternatively, however, the difficult provincial conditions might have the effect of increasing bottom-up pressure on the provincial leaders to stand up against inappropriate central policies. The 'unsatisfactory' performance of the provincial government, which caused its leader to be sacked, might thus be attributed to

entirely different reasons. The implication is that the case of a poor province is not able to highlight the difficult choices provincial leaders have to make between their agency role for the centre and their representative role for the province.

17. See for instance Barnett (1967: 72), Lieberthal and Oksenberg (1988: 142–8) and Shirk (1993).

18. Gerald Segal (1994: 3, 11, 54) has made a similar observation.

1 Towards a non-Zero-Sum Analytical Framework

What degree of power does the provincial government command within the Chinese political system, and what is the nature of this power? This is the fundamental question which runs through the literature on central–provincial relations in contemporary China. In trying to understand this power relationship, analysts have often dwelt on the roles of provincial leaders and the nature of the political system within which they operate. This chapter reviews how the existing literature has addressed and answered the following questions in the context of contemporary China. To what extent do provincial leaders act as the loyal agents of the centre, and, conversely, as representatives of their province? How can we make sense of the prevalence of bargaining behaviour between the centre and the provinces, and the intensity of conflicts in their interactions? Do the instances of China's previous disintegration and the emergence of separatist movements in some provinces signal a trend towards independence for the provinces? Or do they represent the reaction of provincial forces to a weak centre? How should these tensions between the centre and the provinces be interpreted? Moreover, by what approach may changes in the balance of power between the centre and the provinces be better understood?

This chapter argues that the literature has, by and large, failed to reconcile the co-existence of two apparently contradictory phenomena: on the one hand, complex bargaining activities between the centre and provinces with the latter often succeeding in winning concessions from the former; on the other hand, the undeniably superior power of the centre as witnessed during occasional 'crackdowns'. The major shortcoming of the existing literature stems from its interpretation of the concept of power. One recurring problem has been whether the asymmetrical relationship between the centre and the provinces is of a zero-sum nature.

THE DEVELOPMENT OF CENTRAL–PROVINCIAL STUDIES

The development of Western studies on China's post-1949 central–provincial relations has been heavily influenced by Western studies on

the Chinese political system in general.[1] This was true of the totalitarian literature of the 1950s and 1960s, the 'pluralist' and 'conflict' approach of the late 1960s and 1970s, and the reform studies of the 1980s.

Totalitarian literature: provincial leaders as agents of the centre

From the 1950s to the early 1960s, the prevalence of the Soviet model
of totalitarianism within China studies resulted in a threefold image
of the post-1949 political system. It was characterized by the per-
vasiveness of Marxist-Leninist-Maoist ideology, a high level of centralization of political power, and an unprecedented penetration of
the state into society. This early literature attempted to explain the success of the Chinese revolution in terms of ideology, leaders and organization. As such the literature saw the central–provincial relationship
as one between the superordinate and the subordinate. The provincial
government, as the major intermediate level between the centre and
the vast rural expanse, was perceived as the centre's agent.

This literature did not, however, deny that the intermediate level of
government was granted some discretion in policy decisions. For instance, A. Doak Barnett (1967: 72), when describing the post-1949
Chinese system as totalitarian, admitted that the degree of autonomy
granted to provincial departments by central ministries was at times
substantial. Similarly, Franz Schurmann (1968) recognized the importance of decentralization even when power in the 1950s was generally considered to be highly centralized.

The nature and extent of provincial power as envisaged in totalitarian literature was, however, pretty limited. The literature assumed a
hierarchy in the formulation and implementation of policy (Schurmann 1968: 216; Barnett 1967: 74). Policy formulation was *by definition* the job of the centre, with provinces allowed to exercise initiative
and innovation only when implementing these policies. Analysts
argued that accusations of localism in Chinese politics often merely
camouflaged changes within the centre.[2] According to this argument,
provincial leaders accused of 'localism' often only fell prey to the
'house-cleaning purges' of the new central leadership, having implemented the central policies of an earlier time. In the final analysis,
since the source of power was at the centre, the provinces were seen as
completely at the mercy of the centre, and enjoying 'no inviolable
autonomy' (Barnett 1968: 73). In essence, the totalitarian literature
sees a centralized state in which power distribution is essentially an

issue exclusively concerning the centre. The provinces are regarded as passively abiding by decisions of the centre as to whether more or less discretionary power should be left to them.

Pluralist literature: the province as a coerced and responsive entity

The outbreak of the Cultural Revolution revealed the vast mix of interests within the Chinese political system. The experience of the Cultural Revolution demonstrated that actors outside the centre could influence events. In order to explain the new phenomenon, a new theory, and a new set of concepts, was needed. After the pioneering steps of Soviet studies, China scholars turned to pluralistic theory for new tools to understand the dynamics of the Cultural Revolution.[3] Provincial leaders were analysed as an interest group with interests of their own to advance.[4] Others disagreed with the notion of interest groups,[5] and a wide range of models were developed in the effort to search for an explanation of central–provincial relations.[6]

The search for an explanation focused on the question whether provincial officials acted on behalf of the centre or the provinces. To what extent did provincial leaders work with the centre on a basis of mutual support within an insecure and volatile political environment? To what extent were provincial leaders advocates and spokesmen of provinces advancing provincial interests? If the various provincial leaders possessed similar interests, did they undertake collective actions similar to a typical interest group in the West?

Some studies in this period emphasized the success of provincial manoeuvres against central demands,[7] the existence of provincial 'autarchical' tendencies, and the limits of central control (Skinner 1964–5; Donnithorne 1969, 1972). Most works, however, argued for the dominance of the centre over the provinces, where the balance of the dual provincial roles of central agent and provincial spokesman weighed in favour of the former.[8] Frederick C. Teiwes (1966, 1972), for instance, argued that provincial leaders were purged during the 1950s because, as a result of the ascendancy of different groups of central leaders, the policies at the centre had changed too rapidly for provincial leaders at a distance from the power centre to follow. Teiwes found a lower level of elite turnover in richer provinces and interpreted this as a possible confirmation of the view of a predominant centre over the provinces. Provincial leaders were 'basically' responsive to the

centre, because 'the rules of the game stressing provincial responsiveness to the center are clear' (Teiwes 1972: 177). Those that could more
successfully respond to central demands enjoyed a better chance of
political survival.

Similarly, in his case studies of Sichuan and Guizhou during the
period preceding the Cultural Revolution, David Goodman found
little evidence for provincial power. Provincial variations were often
centrally mandated flexibilities and policy experiments, rather than an
'exercise of provincial political power' (Goodman 1986: 23). Provincial conditions might have affected the form of these variations, but
their effect was primarily either to *constrain* or *facilitate* the ability of
provincial leaders to respond to central policies. Therefore, according
to Goodman, Guizhou's provincial first secretary, Zhou Lin, was removed in 1965 because he had been ineffective in carrying out the expected job of central agent. The poverty and lower degree of social
integration of Guizhou constrained the ability of provincial leaders to
act as central agents, whilst Sichuan's relative wealth and social homogeneity enhanced its leaders' ability to respond to the demands of the
centre (Goodman 1986: 20).

The unanswered question is: why were provincial leaders 'responsive' to the centre? What led these studies to conclude that central predominance prevailed, when the ability of provincial leaders to engage
in various strategies of self-protection and enhancement against unwelcome central control had been so thoroughly exposed during the
conflicts of the Cultural Revolution? Why should provincial responsiveness be a sign of provincial weakness, as the 'central predominance
thesis' implied, rather than of provincial strength?[9]

An explicit answer was given by Victor Falkenheim (1972*b*: 202),
who stated that 'The case for provincial power . . . requires that it be
shown to be autonomous. This case is difficult to make in the face of
the historically clear ability of the central government to exact compliance . . . and to remove [provincial leaders] from office when necessary.'
Therefore, the centre's command of coercive force, in the form of the
power to hire and sack provincial leaders, and, as a last resort, the ability to deploy the military to suppress opposition, clearly prescribed
the 'rules of the game' under which provincial leaders were seen to be
responsive to the centre in order better to advance their own interests.

The dominant view was, therefore, of an authoritarian unitary state
where the centre might freely impose its coercive force to extract compliance. Provinces were in an inherently inferior and disadvantaged

position. Local requirements would affect the behaviour of provincial leaders only because provincial leaders could not ignore local conditions in their efforts to implement national policy. The dominance of the centre was, therefore, a foregone conclusion. According to this view, the ability of provincial leaders to engage in a wide range of self-preservation strategies in conflict situations merely demonstrated the responsiveness of provincial leaders to shifts in policy and power configurations at the centre. The literature did not deny the existence of 'parochial' provincial interests, which could be the self-interest of provincial leaders for political advancement and physical survival, or provincial leaders' perceptions of the interest of the province.[10] But these 'local requirements' were not considered as constituting autonomous provincial power. They were no match for the coercive power commanded by the centre. The emergent dominant image of provincial leaders was, therefore, of a group of agents responsive to the centre, albeit through coercion.

Reform implementation studies: the province as the unequal bargaining 'partner'

The 1980s saw an unprecedented relaxation within the research environment as a concomitant of economic liberalization. The move towards 'new institutionism' in the discipline renewed interest in the effect of state structures on the formulation and implementation of policies. As a result, China scholars turned to studying the importance of institutions in addition to their previous emphasis on leadership and elite preferences.

The resultant literature has highlighted the complex and multi-faceted relationships between bureaucratic actors in the political system in the formulation and implementation of policies.[11] Not only did analysts find it necessary to account for the obvious gaps between reform policies as formulated and the results of their implementation, they also found it difficult to define exactly what constitutes 'failures of implementation' (Lampton ed. 1987: 5–7). Indeed, if there is no clear chain of command in the political system, any clear distinction between policy formulation and implementation is inevitably elusive.

The literature, nevertheless, persevered with the traditional conception of policy formulation and implementation, albeit with multiple qualifications and redefinitions. The centre was considered as the locus of policy formulation, and the provinces that of implementation.

Central–provincial relations were pictured as involving intense inter-agency bargaining. The image was one of 'a center forced to bargain with very powerful localities' (Goldstein 1988: 228), who were able to distort central policies to their advantage. Barry Naughton (1987: 52–3) has, for instance, described the Chinese system as characterized by a strong 'implementation bias', as central policies were distorted in ways advantageous to their implementers. Similarly, when discussing tax policy reforms, David Bachman (1987: 144) noted the rule of an 'iron law of autarky' as local authorities deliberately withheld revenues that should, in theory, have gone to the central coffers. The prevalence of bargaining behaviour and the propensity of lower-level authorities to abort and distort central reform policies led Lieberthal and Lampton (1992: 8, 20) to characterize Chinese politics, as situated below the apex and above grassroots level, by a 'fragmented authoritarianism' model. While the Chinese system was portrayed as necessarily authoritarian, such authority was nevertheless seen as highly fragmented in the 'no-man's land' between the very top and the very bottom.

This model of Chinese politics as 'fragmented authoritarianism', and its implication of a potent province, has to a large extent opposed the previously dominant 'central predominance' thesis. Indeed, Lieberthal (1992: 10–11) regarded the approach as an attempt to synthesize two competing models: one focusing on elite preferences and positing a centralized and top-down view of central–provincial relations, the other arguing for a decentralized and 'cellular' socio-economic structure. The former has been more dominant among scholars but as Vivienne Shue (1988) has elaborated, the central state never had effective control over the vast rural expanse at the periphery. The socio-economic-political structure of Maoist China was 'honeycombed and cellular'; and in the post-Mao period, it has been 'fragmented'.

This continuity in the incompleteness of central control over time applies also to actors' behaviour. The wider policy context differed in Maoist China and post-Mao China: class struggle versus economic reform. However, the manner in which ostensibly disparate actors tailored their behaviour so as to maximize their perceived interest was remarkably similar.[12] Provincial leaders during the Cultural Revolution and during the post-Mao reforms were equally 'Machiavellian' in their substantive stances. During the Cultural Revolution, provincial leaders emulated the revolutionary rhetoric of the centre, cultivating 'royalist' rebel groups whilst suppressing those hostile to them. They 'waved the red flag in order to oppose the red flag'. During the reform period, provincial leaders have both supported and opposed reforms. They have supported those reforms which advance their perceived interests and opposed those working against them. Moreover, when opposing unwanted reforms, provincial leaders have manipulated the language of reform in the same way as their precedessors manipulated the language of political struggle. They have stressed, for example, the adverse effects of the unwelcome reforms on the 'enthusiasm' of the lower levels to increase production. During the Cultural Revolution, provincial leaders suppressed 'hostile' rebel groups by declaring them 'counter-revolutionaries'. The events of both periods show that provincial leaders have not been passive actors. Rather than merely responding to central demands, provincial leaders have mobilized substantial resources for their own use. Their lower status in the state hierarchy might have made them the weaker partner in the bargaining relationship with the centre. However, despite the disparity in theoretical power, the provinces have shown themselves to possess no small measure of power in their own right.

UNRESOLVED QUESTIONS

Indeterminacy of provincial power

Through the successive models of 'central agent' to 'responsive province' to asymmetrical bargaining with the centre, China scholars in the West have deepened their understanding of the position of the provinces within the Chinese political system. It has been recognized that provinces did, in fact, wield power. However, this conclusion on provincial power has often been based on observations of discrepancies between pronounced central policy objectives and the outcome of implementation, as well as on the frequent expositions of 'localistic behaviour' of provincial and lower-level officials by central officials during the post-Mao reform period. While discrepancies *of some kind* undoubtedly existed, a suitable approach regarding the interpretation of the *meaning* of such discrepancies has remained elusive. How should we assess the significance of the prevalence of provincial bargaining behaviour in the context of central–provincial power relations? What is meant when provinces are described as powerful *but* unequal bargaining partners? Did the implementation literature and, in particular, the 'fragmented authoritarianism' model imply that provinces were *in the process* of gaining more power, *but still had not approached a level* which would make them equal bargaining partners with the centre?

The fact that these important questions are as yet unanswered suggests an indeterminate element in the understanding of the central–provincial relationship. On the one hand, the implementation literature has made a strong case for provincial power. Provincial leaders were undoubtedly not *merely* central agents. On the other hand, the literature maintained that the central leadership continued to play a dominant role. It found that, in many instances, 'higher-level leaders were able to impose their will on lower levels without serious institutional constraints' (Lieberthal 1992: 16). Therefore, the power of the provinces during the reform period might still only amount to another form of 'delegated provincial flexibilities'. The decline of central control, according to this argument, was but the result of voluntary self-restraint by the centre in its exercise of power over the provinces. For instance, Naughton (1987: 78) once argued that the central leadership 'have shown themselves willing to accept a dramatic decline in their own control over investment resources in the pursuit of the elusive goals of "reform". The struggles between the Center and locality for control . . . thus remain fundamentally unequal because the Center fights with one hand tied behind its back.' The apparent conclusion on the central–provincial relationship is that the substantial power which the provinces enjoyed was merely a result of central policy. As and when the centre decided otherwise, and as long as the central leadership was not weakened by divisions among its own ranks, the will of the centre would invariably prevail.[13]

It is, however, tenuous entirely to attribute the power of provinces to the decision of the central leadership not to impose its will. To suggest this immediately leads one to ask: why have the central leaders not acted sooner and more decisively in curbing the 'power' of the provinces about whom they frequently and openly complain?

It is ironic that after the documentation of numerous instances of 'localistic' behaviour, and subsequent rejection of the earlier view of a highly centralized political system (at least for politics within the state bureaucracy below the apex), the understanding of central–provincial relations has turned full circle. The difficulty is that, apparently, both ways of understanding central–provincial relations—central predominance and provincial power—stand on similarly slippery ground. A conclusion acknowledging provincial power disputes the obvious superiority of central power, particularly taking into account the centre's power to appoint and dismiss provincial leaders, and when necessary, to deploy the army to obtain compliance. However, a conclusion arguing for continued central predominance is equally unsatisfactory. It is unsatisfactory because *it is almost tautologically true*, other than in the extreme case of secessionist movements and the breakup of China as a unified nation. Moreover, if one concludes that provincial discretion makes no substantive difference to the central–provincial relationship, it is still necessary to state precisely what differences discretion does make.

The inability to explain change

As a result of this failure to make sense of the meaning of bargaining activities and increasing provincial discretion, the literature has been unable to account for changes within the central–provincial relationship. It might reasonably be surmised that bargaining activities have significance, and that they do make some difference. But the question is: what kind of difference? Some scholars have attributed the difficulty of identification and explanation to data deficiency (Lieberthal 1992: 25–7). It has been argued that inadequate access to information on the pre-reform period (before 1978) has prevented analysts from assessing the full extent of continuity and change before and after post-Mao reform. However, data deficiency is not the only problem. The failure in explaining change lies more in the literature itself. This can be shown by imagining a hypothetical situation. Suppose it were possible to obtain enough data on the Maoist period to compare the extent of provincial power during both periods. Two crucial problems would remain unresolved. First, by what yardstick can we compare the power of provinces and the power of the centre, and thereby arrive at a view of their relative balance of power? The root of the question is: what constitutes 'power'? The literature on central–provincial relations has so far tended to be ambivalent on the question of what constitutes the power of the provinces, whilst unanimous in stressing the importance of the coercive power of the centre over the provinces. With this predisposition, the balance of power will inevitably tilt in the centre's favour.

Secondly, comparison is likely to show variations over different periods. The problem is how to make sense of the variations. Does this mean that the development of provincial power may be conceived on some sort of continuum? Also, if there is a greater occurrence of provincial discretion during the reform period, does this then amount to an incremental accumulation of provincial power *vis-à-vis* the power of the centre? The implementation literature has apparently answered in the affirmative, and the assumption of some kind of unilinear, evolutionary framework of central–provincial relations is evident within the literature.[14]

The simplicity of a linear model is disturbing. It is disturbing because it suggests, implicitly at least, that as the forces of fragmentation accumulate, the forces of centralization will *in due course* be overwhelmed. The unanswered question is how this 'overwhelming' can be effected. On this aspect the evolutionary framework remains silent. As Lieberthal himself rightly noted, the gap between fragmentation and legitimate autonomy is huge and of a qualitative kind. More fragmentation will *not* automatically bring about legitimate autonomy. The literature, however, provides no room to explore the question of how qualitative change could ever take place, even though it acknowledges, somewhat intuitively, the possibility of qualitative change.

TOWARDS AN INTERACTIVE FRAMEWORK

The failure of the literature on central–provincial relations to explain the meaning of provincial discretionary behaviour and to account for change are the result of theoretical failures in the conception of power. First, confusion has arisen over the role of coercion within a power relationship. This lies behind the tautology of the thesis of 'continued central predominance'. Secondly, most studies of central–provincial relations see power as zero-sum and adopt a centrist perspective. The result is a static picture of central–provincial relations where the centre and the provinces are in a seemingly endless cycle of conflict. We need to identify the implicit concept of power within the central–provincial literature, and to suggest an alternative concept which provides a better analytical tool for understanding central–provincial relations.

Coercion and power

A central question in this discussion is: what is the relationship between coercion and the concept of power? Scholars writing on China's central–provincial relations have generally been less than explicit about their specific concept of power. In most cases when reference was made to the sources of the power of the centre or the provinces, it has been based on Robert A. Dahl's notion of power 'between the lines'.

It should be recalled that Dahl (1969: 80) understands 'power' in terms of its four aspects: the base of power, means of power, amount of power, and scope of power. The base of an actor's power 'consists of all the resources, acts, objects, etc. that he or she can exploit in order to affect the behaviour of another' (Dahl 1969: 81). A major characteristic of the base of power is that it is 'inert, passive'. To activate the base, therefore, an actor has to engage in some actions. Such actions engaged in are the 'means of power'. For instance, while the ability to exercise patronage, and the option of a veto, are amongst the bases of power available to the President of the United States over the Senate, the President nevertheless has to pledge *promises* of patronage, or indicate a *threat* of veto in his attempt to influence the Senate. Therefore 'the means is a mediating activity by A between A's base and B's response' (Dahl 1969: 81). Meanwhile, the 'scope' of A's power refers to the reach of A's means of power, and what possible responses B might make. The resultant ability of A to bend B to its will constitutes the 'amount' of power which A has.

The similarity between Dahl's concept of power and that employed by the literature on central–provincial relations is obvious. In the literature, the sources of central control are often identified as: (1) the power of the centre to appoint and dismiss provincial leaders, (2) the centre's effective control of physical forces of coercion, specifically the military, (3) the centre's control over the propaganda apparatus, and (4) the centre's control over key economic resources (Lieberthal and Oksenberg 1988: 347–8). Meanwhile, the sources of provincial autonomy are (1) the sheer size of the country, (2) the cumulative result of temporary grants of authority by the centre in the past, and (3) its intermediate position within the state hierarchy, which makes the province 'the gatekeeper guarding and providing access [for the centre] to local levels' (Lieberthal and Oksenberg 1988: 349–50). A shift in terminology reveals that these 'sources of power' are actually Dahl's 'bases of power' by another name.

The strength of Dahl's concept of power lies in its distinctions between the different aspects of power. Since the 'base of power' is inert and passive, it is *irrelevant* to the 'amount of power' A is able to exert on B unless it is effectively activated by some 'means of power'. Therefore, while the 'base of power' encompasses *all* resources A may *potentially* employ in order to affect the behaviour of B, the extent of power A eventually exercises over B depends very much on what means of power A possesses, and how effective these are. There is hence a significant gap between one's *bases* of power and the *amount* of power one actually has over others, the gap depending on the *means*, which is the mediating process, and the variables which affect it.

The danger of employing Dahl's concept of power is the greatest when one is not sensitive to these distinctions. This is the major problem in the literature on central–provincial relations.[15] In such cases the base of power is often confused with the amount of power actually exercised. The lists of sources of central and provincial power noted above include all identifiable sources of *potential* power upon which the centre and provinces may draw in their interactions with one another. However, analysts have neither identified nor explained the mediating process whereby the extent of applicability of the sources of power in an actual situation is specified. Rather than being a dependent variable in accordance with Dahl's concept, the base of power has been taken as an independent variable through which to interpret the meaning of bargaining activity between the centre and the provinces. On taking the base of power as the *actual* power in force, the literature tends to compare two 'lists' of power, one for the centre and one for the provinces, and somehow arrive at a judgement on the balance of power.

Mistaking the base of power for actual power has serious implications for the understanding of the central–provincial relationship. By definition, provincial governments are in a subordinate administrative position *vis-à-vis* the centre, which commands superior control over vital resources through its superior organizational status. As a result, an empirical analysis of the process of bargaining behaviour and policy making appears immaterial to an understanding of central–provincial relations. A simple calculation of the balance of military and other resources between the centre and provinces should suffice.

Yet that is plainly unsatisfactory. A solution is found in Talcott Parsons' concept of power. The major difference between Parsons and Dahl is that while coercion is clearly one of those resources forming the base of power in Dahl's concept, according to Parsons (1969: 257), 'securing compliance . . . simply by threat of superior force is not (in itself) an exercise of power.' This does not mean that coercion has no place. Power for Parsons is a phenomenon of *both* coercion and consensus, but coercion is not the crucial variable in the exercise of power in a complex society. Coercion in *any* exercise of power, according to Parsons (1969: 260), is the 'ground', or the basis, of power. It is akin to the role of gold metal within a gold-based monetary system. The value of the precious metal gives some kind of security to the exchange value of money, but the value of money as a medium of exchange is not reducible to the total value of gold in the market. Likewise, while any exercise of power by A over B embodies coercion as the 'ground' of power, the amount of power, in Dahl's terminology, is not reducible solely to the amount of power of coercion A possesses. For power to be assessed solely in terms of coercion potential, the system would need to be very primitive, 'just as a monetary system resting entirely on gold as the actual medium of exchange is a very primitive one' (Parsons 1969: 260). Given the limited amount of coercion possessed by any actor in any system, it is the ability of the actors to obtain compliance via symbolic means which reflects the power of the actor.

Parsons' concept of power carries significant implications. Unlike Dahl, and others, who treat coercion as one of the bases of power, and see the exercise of power as *sometimes* relating to the use of coercion, and *at other times* to consensus, Parsons insists that power is a phenomenon which essentially integrates both coercion and consensus. By seeing power as oscillating between different 'forms of power', Dahl's concept when applied to China posits an indeterminate picture of power relations between the centre and the provinces. As the literature on China's central–provincial relations has shown, provinces are sometimes portrayed as powerful actors, and at other times as passive and virtually helpless. The 'superiority' of the coercive form of power has also cast doubt on the significance of other forms of power, for instance economic power in economic policy bargaining. By rejecting this eclectic concept of different forms of power, and by specifying the role of coercion as the ground of power, Parsons has successfully clarified the essence of a power relationship as well as the focus of power analysis (Parsons 1969: 251, 256–7, 280). Parsons' concept of power has particular utility in the analysis of power relationships in which the distribution of coercive resources is inherently unequal. As the national level of government, the centre is in a superior organizational position. By specifying the role of coercion and focusing on the manipulation of 'symbols' in the study of power, Parsons avoids the tautological trap of Dahl's concept, which leads analysts to conclude that the centre is powerful *because it is the centre.*

Power as a non-zero-sum game

The dominant assumption in the literature on central–provincial relations is that power between the centre and the provinces is a zero-sum game. This assumption pre-dates the post-Mao reform period, but has been reinforced by the concentration of research attention on the fiscal system in the reform period.[16] The simplicity of the fiscal relationship, as expressed in percentage terms of provincial remittance and retained revenue, easily projects a 'zero-sum' image of central–provincial relations (Chung 1995*b*). However, the implications of these fiscal changes in relation to the respective powers of the centre and the provinces over policy formulation and implementation have been largely overlooked.

The prevalence of the zero-sum perception of the central–provincial relationship is attributable to the dominance of the centrist perspective in the literature. Central-provincial relations have been studied primarily as a phenomenon of declining central control and weakening state capacity.[17] This is especially the case in the more recent body of literature focusing on the post-Mao period. The focus of analysis of these works is invariably on the factors and processes which lead to the apparent decline of central control over policy implementation by the provinces. The insistence on posing the issue for research as an implementation problem leads researchers to view the relationship between the centre and the provinces as an issue of central control and provincial compliance. Moreover, this image of a zero-sum game of politics has been reinforced by the absence of a regularized and institutionalized system of conflict resolution within the Chinese political system. As Tang Tsou (1991: 266) has noted, political conflicts throughout Chinese history have been characterized by a 'total victory versus total defeat' situation in which the winning side retains 'all real power to make decisions, whereas the other side is totally defeated.' Because of the low level of institutionalization of power and the absence of a regularized framework to resolve conflicts within the system, political struggles in China have been notable for their ferocity. If there was a prospect of total victory, it was often argued, the actor with the upper hand in the conflict would not hesitate totally to smash its opponent. The target was total victory, and the defeated opponent would be totally 'eliminated' from the scene. In Tsou's words, although 'at times there were compromises, concessions, admissions of defeat, negotiations, and even co-operation with . . . opposing forces, . . . those were tactical measures' in search of a better opportunity to strike the final blow (Tang Tsou 1991: 319). Actors might temporize but not compromise. The tradition of political authoritarianism from imperial times has forestalled the development of 'a politics of compromise' in China.

Trying to understand central–provincial relations as a zero-sum game poses insoluble questions. It prevents the analyst from envisaging the *circumstances* whereby the rules of the game might be changed. While analysts agree that the ferocity of previous political struggles in China was due to the authoritarian nature and the low level of institutionalization of the political system, their zero-sum analysis of the central–provincial relationship suggests a static picture of power in which centralization and decentralization occur in an endless cycle. As a result they have been unable to discern any possibility of change within this cyclical pattern, other than through the mutual good will of central and provincial leaders to reach a 'historical compromise' (see Jia Hao and Lin Zhimin 1994: 10). While analysts recognize that successive decentralizations have resulted in a dispersion of authority and resources from the centre, and feel intuitively that the system *might* evolve towards genuine autonomy for the provinces, the literature has been silent about the possible circumstances under which this 'qualitative' change in the nature of the central–provincial relationship could come about. The Chinese system, it would seem, has been stuck in its historical tradition of authoritarianism and in endless cycles of decentralization and centralization. The only possible way out, as the literature has implicitly suggested, is through the emergence of 'enlightened' leaders.

To escape from such pessimistic determinism it is necessary to depart from the centrist perspective and the state capacity paradigm. Instead of posing the research question in terms of the decline of central control over unruly provinces, we need a reconceptualization of central–provincial relations as an interactive process in which both the centre and the provinces struggle hard in order to attain their respective objectives. The asymmetry of the relationship means that changes in institutional rules have to be agreed to and formally laid down by the centre. However, the centre does not have *carte blanche* in this respect. Nor is it the case that what is laid down by the centre is invariably subverted by the provinces. It is rather pressure from the provinces which leads the centre to prescribe the rules in such a way that they protect its interests as well as those of the provinces.

An illustration of this interactive process between the centre and the provinces is found in Susan Shirk's study of economic reform. In studying the decision made in 1979 to implement nationwide fiscal reform, Shirk (1993: 163) found that reform was a means employed by the central bureaucracy to 'divest [themselves of] responsibility', as opposed to being a preconceived plan to decentralize fiscal autonomy to the provinces, as had previously been assumed by Western scholars. The centre was constrained in the options it could take. Given the dispersion of resources in the early 1970s, central officials at the Ministry of Finance concluded that the only way to improve the interests of the central coffers at that time was through the further step of decentralization. The 1980 nationwide fiscal reform was thus the result of a compromise between the centre and the provinces. From the perspective of the centre, further decentralization of fiscal authority was the only possible way to improve its fiscal situation. It was then considered impossible to recentralize enough resources from the provinces and to reimpose the centralized fiscal regime of the early 1950s. The centre, with its shrinking share of resources, could not, however, cope with its share of responsibility. The major fiscal problem for the centre on the eve of fiscal reform was thus one of arresting the decline in central revenue whilst delegating more spending responsibility to the provinces. By signing a multiple-year contract with the provinces guaranteeing a fixed share of central revenue, the centre therefore 'clarified the responsibilities as well as resources of each tier of government and guaranteed central income at current levels' (Shirk 1993: 163).[18] Shirk's account reveals, therefore, a dynamic picture of central–provincial relations. Rather than seeing the relationship as one between a weakening but 'all-powerful' Centre and the subordinated, responsive, yet 'undisciplined' parochial provinces, Shirk sees the centre responding to powerful provinces whilst seeking to strike the best deal to enhance its interests. Power between the centre and the provinces is therefore not one of control versus disobedience, but one of calculated compromise on both sides.

But how could a politics of compromise be possible at all if, according to the 'conventional wisdom' in the prevailing literature, most political struggles in Chinese history have taken on a zero-sum nature? Is the fiscal reform decision of 1980 merely an exception to the general rule? If not, and if as a general rule the centre has to compromise with the provinces, from where do the provinces derive their strength? If the ground of the centre's power, in Parsons' terminology, lies in its superior command of coercive force, what is the ground of provincial power? Why should the centre feel compelled to reach a compromise with the provinces? Why does the centre not 'smash' all provincial resistance and emerge as a 'total victor'?

The answer to these questions is found in the intermediate position of the province in the state hierarchy. Existing works in the literature have also stressed the power of the province as the intermediary. But in such studies the power of the intermediary is always seen as double-edged. On the one hand, it gives the province substantial discretion and control over resources, whilst, on the other, making it the object of central manipulation and control. So if the ground of provincial power lies in its intermediate position, in what does this strength of the intermediary consist?

At this point it is important to note that Tang Tsou, when commenting on the zero-sum nature of political struggles in Chinese history, also noted that there were limits to the application of the logic of total victory versus total defeat. In Tsou's own words, political conflicts acquire the zero-sum nature only 'if one side believes that it can win in a final confrontation and is willing to pay the necessary price' (Tang Tsou 1991: 320). In other words, where there is a 'mutual perception that a stalemate will continue indefinitely into the future, . . . the expectation that there will be a final confrontation and settlement of accounts' will gradually change (Tang Tsou 1991: 320–1). With no prospect of total victory for oneself, one is therefore forced to compromise with one's opponent.

Herein lies the strength of the intermediary. It is impossible for the centre to win a total victory over its intermediary. Provincial governments are an indispensable ally of the centre in governance. The centre has to rely on provincial leaders and lower-level officials to govern society. As individuals, provincial leaders may be purged and replaced, *but* as a group and an institution, provincial leaders and the provincial-level government are here to stay. Tsou's thoughts on the limits of the zero-sum nature of political conflicts is set out in the context of state–society confrontation in the Tiananmen tragedy of 1989. In that case, the state could still rely on coercive power as the last resort in order to achieve an apparent 'total victory', although the excessive use of naked force revealed the weakness of the centre and damaged its legitimacy (Tang Tsou 1991: 316).[19] The hands of the centre in its struggles with the provinces are more constrained. As power-holders, provincial leaders possess more resources which they can use to protect themselves against the encroachment of the centre than are normally available to private individuals in the case of a state–society confrontation.

Consequently, the centre may win in specific instances of central–provincial confrontation, but the necessity of ruling *through* an intermediary dictates that its victory will be short-term and incomplete. An ideal example is the cycles of centralization and decentralization since 1957. Each round of recentralization reclaimed only part of the power and resources which had been decentralized earlier, and each subsequent round of decentralization brought the provinces control over more resources and broader room for manoeuvre.[20] The organizational position of the province therefore guarantees that it cannot be 'totally eliminated' by the centre in any central–provincial conflicts. As the stalemate persists, the centre is forced to compromise with the provinces, as in the case of the 1980 fiscal reform decision. Rather than seeing the course of economic reform as a process through which central policies are distorted by provincial implementation, this new picture of central–provincial relations shows a process of accommodation and compromise. As neither the centre nor the provinces can decisively win over and eliminate the other, *both* are forced to accommodate the interests of the other and to compromise.

This non-zero-sum framework of the central–provincial relationship can be portrayed as in Fig. 1.1.

FIG. 1.1 CENTRAL-PROVINCIAL RELATIONS: A NON-ZERO-SUM
    FRAMEWORK

1. Both the centre and provinces have *irreducible* power over one another
2. Irreducible basis (ground) of Centre's power over provinces: coercion
3. Irreducible basis of provinces' power over the centre: Its intermediary role
4. Mutual interdependence and indispensability ⟶ protracted conflicts ⟶ a situation of total victory/total failure not feasible ⟶ a politics of compromise and a non-zero-sum game situation

The implication of the non-zero-sum nature of central–provincial power is significant. It envisages change. In a zero-sum framework, any possibility of change awaits the wisdom of the victor after all accounts have been settled and its opponent eliminated. This suggests a heavy reliance on *ad hoc* factors of an idiosyncratic nature for changes ever to occur. In a non-zero-sum framework, the forces of change are built in to the system through the power of the actors over one another.

The amount of power at the disposal of the centre and of the provinces differs, but their interdependence and long-term co-existence requires both parties to compromise. A strong Centre during the 1950s, for instance, still found it necessary to decentralize power to the provinces in order better to implement its policies. Something has to be given out in order to get back something in return. Consequently, as provinces gather more and more resources as a result of successive decentralizations, their bargaining power *vis-à-vis* the centre increases. With increased power, the provinces are in a position to demand more concessions from the centre than before. The result is the increased occurrence of central–provincial conflicts, as manifested during the reform period. In these circumstances, if increased institutionalization of the distribution of power is the way out of protracted conflicts, it will *not* come into being as a result of the wisdom of some enlightened leaders. Rather, the leaders, central and provincial, will become aware of the need to institutionalize when they see this as the only way out of such protracted conflicts and as the best means available through which to protect their interests, given the constraint of their opposite number.

METHODOLOGY

Rational-choice institutionalism

An institutional approach means that the thrust of analysis is placed on institutions and the effect of the institutional context on behaviour. Individual actors, whether at the centre or in the provinces, are studied in terms of their interaction with the institutional context. The prefix 'rational-choice' emphasizes that actors in central–provincial politics exercise choice over their behaviour in a rational manner. Acting within a host of rules and norms does not rob the actors of their freedom to choose, by rational articulation, those specific courses of action which can best serve their interest.[21] Institutions and rules prescribe certain limits to behaviour, but actors can nevertheless exercise considerable choice within the limits. In fact this possibility of choice within institutional rules represents the basis of the very existence of discretion.

Taking 'rational choice' and 'institutional' together, the 'rational-choice institutional' approach can have two alternative meanings.

First, it can refer to an approach in which the rational behaviour of actors is analysed in terms of the structure of incentives built in to the institutions of a system. That is, the emphasis is on the institutional *context* of rational choice. This approach stresses the impact of institutions on the rational choices of actors. The prefix 'rational-choice' is meant as a minor qualifier. It is the definition used in Susan Shirk's (1993) rational-choice institutional study of economic reform. The second meaning of the term 'rational-choice institutionalism' stresses the *co-existence* of actors' rational choice and of institutions setting the basic parameters and rules for the exercise of such choice. The emphasis is on what institutions do *not* constrain. The message is that, notwithstanding the impact of institutions on the choice of actors, institutions are not so 'totalitarian' that they leave no room at all for choice. This second meaning of 'rational-choice institutionalism' therefore presupposes and builds on the first meaning.[22] Whilst, in the first meaning, rational choice is subsumed under an institutional approach, in the second meaning the two are regarded as complementary to each other. The second meaning does not negate the first meaning, but questions its claim regarding the scope of the impact of institutions on behaviour. In this sense the term could be modified to read 'rational-choice-cum-institutionalism' to identify more clearly the fundamental complementarity of rational choice and institutions.

This book adopts the second meaning of rational-choice institutionalism and focuses on the *linkage* between institutions and actors' choice. In studies of Chinese politics it is being increasingly recognized that institutional rules and choices of individual actors together determine the course of events.[23] Institutions and actors' choices respectively form the focus of analysis of two major approaches of China political studies—the institutional approach and the elite model. Despite the recognition of the limitations and partiality of both approaches by their proponents, there have been no conscious efforts to reconcile the two and incorporate their perspectives (see Goldstein 1988: 231). By studying both the institutional context and actors' choices, this book attempts a synthesis. The centre and the provinces impose formidable constraints on each other. The task is to identify the choices made by provinces under the institutional constraints posed by the centre and vice versa, as well as to illuminate the processes through which these choices are made.

A Provincialist perspective

This book focuses on the choices of provinces under the institutional constraints of the centre. Relatively more research has been done from the perspective of the centre. I therefore believe that more light may be shed on the central–provincial relationship by a study focusing on the provincial side of the story.

There are more deep-seated considerations for a provincialist perspective.[24] The literature on China's central–provincial relations, as discussed above, has adopted a primarily top-down, state capacity paradigm. This is, in part, the result of the relatively greater visibility and accessibility of the top levels of the political system, and, in part, the result of the influence of theoretical constructs such as the centre–periphery paradigm on the analytical framework of the commentators. The centre–periphery paradigm starts with the simple idea that 'societies have a centre to which their members orient themselves and which influences their conduct' (Shils 1975: p. xxxi) (1975: 3). As Shils explains, 'The centre, or the central zone, is a phenomenon of the realm of values and beliefs. It is the centre of the order of symbols, of values and beliefs, which govern the society.' But values and beliefs have to be acted upon. Therefore 'the centre is also a phenomenon of the realm of action. It is a structure of activities, of roles and persons, within the network of institutions.'

It is very important to note that the construct itself is not a spatially delimited concept. The central zone in different societies may reside in different actors and different institutions, and within a society the locus of 'the centre' may well differ according to different subjects of concern (Shils 1975: 3). However, the authority of the national government has often led analysts to *assume* that the national government is 'the centre' in the society. This bias towards the authority of the national government has profound significance in terms of how the central–provincial relationship is understood. As the 'central zone', from where values flow to the periphery, the central government becomes by definition the source of authority and the originator of policies. The provinces, as the 'periphery', are the object of rule and of integration by the centre. The occurrence of non-compliance signals the refusal of the 'periphery' to integrate with the 'centre' and is a deviational and dysfunctional phenomenon, leading to a 'weakening' of the capacity of the 'centre' to govern. Any notion of local autonomy in this analytical framework is thus anomalous. To the extent that

autonomy assumes some kind of legitimacy and discretionary independence of the lower levels, there is no place for local autonomy in
this conception of the political system.

A provincialist perspective helps to avoid the pitfalls of this assumption regarding the locus of the 'central zone'. By focusing research
attention on the behaviour and choices of provincial actors, this perspective highlights the activism in parts of the political system other
than the national centre. Specifically, it calls attention to the possibility that the province, as well as the national centre, could become the
'central zone' of values, beliefs and actions. Provincial autonomy is
not some kind of residual sphere which exists beyond the reach of the
centre.[25] It is the product of compromise between the centre and the
provinces based on the insurmountable power of both over the other.
It is noteworthy that previous works have noted the multiplicity of
'centres' within the political system, and that the lower-level units of
the state could be, and have been, the 'fountain of political ideas and
administrative techniques' (White 1976*a*: 490).[26] A provincialist perspective facilitates a better elaboration of these insights and observations, and, consequently, a deeper understanding of their significance.

CLARIFICATIONS AND DEFINITIONS

The centre

Unless otherwise specified 'the centre' in this study means the na-
tional-level government *vis-à-vis* the subnational levels. The national-
level actors in this study of central–provincial relations are primarily
the State Council and the various central government ministries and
agencies subordinated to it. Given the heterogeneity of interests
amongst these constituent units of 'the centre', the concept of 'the
centre' does not assume the existence of a unified entity acting coher-
ently in its interaction with the provinces. It is acknowledged that there
are often contradictions and inconsistencies in the instructions and
guidelines issued by different centre actors to the provinces. Provinces
have often benefited from such inconsistencies within the centre by
playing one centre actor against another. To the extent that a different
policy matter involves a different group of centre actors, the locus of
'the centre' also shifts in accordance with the contexts and issues being
discussed. When the context of discussion is non-specific, 'the centre'

in this study generally refers to the top central leadership of the State Council.

The province

'The province' means the provincial-level government, including provinces, provincial-level municipalities and autonomous regions. Specifically, 'the province', as in the case of 'the centre', refers basically to the provincial leadership. As in the case of 'the centre', 'the province' is composed of various provincial departments and agencies. Horizontally there are numerous provincial departments; vertically the choices and preferences of the 'provincial level' are in part a function of the choices and preferences of the subprovincial levels, i.e. the cities, counties and townships. Within each provincial department there is also a heterogeneity of actors, from the head of department to working-level officials. However, as in the case of the centre, there is a hierarchy amongst the actors of the province, and this makes it possible to speak of the province as a single actor in its relationship with the centre. The heterogeneity of the province forms part of the story of how strategies and courses of actions are formulated in its relations with the centre.

The subprovincial-level actors

The subprovincial levels enter this study as variables that help to explain behaviour at provincial level. These actors include the subprovincial levels of government, namely, the city, the county and the township. They also include the actors in the semi-governmental sectors: the state enterprises (budgetary or extrabudgetary) and the collective enterprises. The dominant role of the state in the public sector, and in the economy in general, enables us to regard state and collective enterprises in the province as somewhat also part of the state at subprovincial levels. In particular, this study shows how the extrabudgetary sector has enabled the Guangdong and Shanghai governments to outmanoeuvre the centre in respect of revenue and investment policies. Moreover, as a result of extensive subdelegation of investment authority and decentralization of fiscal resources to the subprovincial levels of government, Guangdong's provincial government has been able to sustain a rapid growth of investment in the face of repeated pressures from the centre to contain investment.

In existing literature on Chinese politics the term 'local' has been used to refer to different subnational levels of government. Depending on the level of analysis of the study, the term 'local government' could mean the provincial level or the more grassroots level of the county or township, and sometimes of the village. The former has been the predominant usage in literature on central–provincial relations within China, and in literature written by Western-trained scholars from the Mainland. The identification of the term 'local government' or, in Chinese, *difang*, with the provincial level as opposed to 'the centre' or, in Chinese, *zhongyang*, reveals the importance accorded by Chinese scholars to the provincial-level government in China's spatial politics. Conversely, the more frequent use of the term to refer to the grassroots level of government amongst Western scholars reflects their greater interest in the interface of state and society at the grassroots level.

To avoid confusion about the referent of the term 'local', this study seeks to avoid its use as far as possible. Wherever possible more specific terms such as 'provincial-level', 'subprovincial' and 'municipal' are used. The term 'lower level' is often used to refer to subprovincial levels of government in the context of discussing the province and, at times, to all subnational levels as opposed to the central level. However, when discussing investment in Guangdong and Shanghai, as well as nationally, the normal usage of central as opposed to local investment will be followed. This also applies to the discussion about 'local' fiscal revenue in the two areas. In both cases 'local' means 'provincial/municipal' as a whole, encompassing the subprovincial grassroots levels, rather than referring to the grassroots levels only.

Investment

In this book the term 'investment', unless specified otherwise, is taken as the synonym and diminutive for 'fixed asset investment'. It refers to the total value of fixed asset investment undertaken within a specified territorial jurisdiction, as reflected in the statistics on 'total investment', alternatively described as 'societal investment' in Chinese statistical books. 'Total investment', or 'societal investment', comprises the sum total of investment made in the state and non-state sectors, and includes both projects which are included and those not included in the state investment plans. As a summary statistic of the total value of investment within a jurisdiction (a province, city etc.), it includes investment financed by various kinds of funding channels. In other words, the term 'investment', unless specified otherwise, includes budgetary investment, which is financed by funds from the state budget, as well as extrabudgetary investment, which is financed by 'own funds' of various units, foreign capital, and bank loans.

Historically, investment projects in China have been classified into two major categories: capital construction and technical renovation investment. Capital construction refers to new projects of construction or major additions to existing enterprises or projects. Technical renovation refers to relatively minor upgrading or renovation works to existing projects and enterprises. Different accounting and planning procedures are prescribed for the two, which historically are financed by quite different funding channels. These differences have, however, been decreasing in the post-Mao years. The concept of 'fixed asset investment' encompasses both of these categories, as well as some other, minor categories of miscellaneous investment. A thorough understanding of the concept of 'investment' in China, and of the complications involved in the accounting of investment activities, requires no small probing into the webs of the planning, budgeting and financing systems of the People's Republic. A more detailed discussion is given in Chapters 2 to 4.

Total scale of investment: central control figures

A key concept in the discussion of investment politics is that of the control figures of the total scale of investment imposed by the centre. These control figures are an administrative instrument used by the central government since the mid-1980s to put a ceiling on the total value of investment spent by each province and other units on an annual basis. The figures are issued every year, and each provincial government is responsible for ensuring that the total value of investment completed within the provincial jurisdiction in the year does not exceed the ceiling prescribed. As a control instrument the control figures supposedly cover investment made in both the state and non-state sectors, and investment financed by both the budgetary and extrabudgetary funds. However, as a result of the proliferation of investors and financing channels, detailed in Chapters 3 and 4, the control effect of these figures has been more symbolic than real, and is highly reliant on the voluntary restraint of the provincial and lower-level units. How a provincial government treats the central control figures, therefore, reveals much of the dynamics of its relationship with the centre.

Provincial discretionary behaviour

The concept 'provincial discretionary behaviour', or simply 'discretion', refers to actions and inactions of provincial governments without the formal endorsement of the centre. The term 'formal endorsement' refers to written affirmation by the centre through the issue of formal central, State Council or ministerial documents. Such 'endorsements' are, however, often not clearly defined. Very often the behaviour of the centre has been first to acquiesce, only to criticize or give explicit endorsements to the contrary at a later stage. It is arguable that acquiescence itself constitutes some kind of *de facto* endorsement, especially when seen from the provincial perspective. Such 'approval', however, is of an unstable and transient nature. It is thus not considered in this book as constituting formal endorsement.

Discretionary behaviour takes two forms, bargaining and implementation deviations, which provincial leaders may employ during different stages of policy formulation. Bargaining occurs normally during the deliberation stage of a policy yet-to-be formulated. The target of bargaining may be certain major central policies which, in the eyes of the provincial leadership, may affect provincial interests. In addition, bargaining may be directed to more 'mundane' concerns of a day-to-day sort. A typical example of the former type, which may be described as 'macro-bargaining', is that of the bargaining and articulation of interests which occurred in April 1979 at the Central Work Conference. The bargaining between the central and the Guangdong/Fujian leaders led to the centre's agreement that Guangdong and Fujian should receive preferential treatment, thus significantly enhancing their fiscal and economic planning autonomy. Macro-bargaining is particularly important for the provinces since, if they win, they will enjoy enlarged room for manoeuvre in an altogether more favourable policy environment.

The other type of bargaining focuses on the day-to-day interpretation of policies already formulated, and the allocation of centrally controlled resources. Although apparently routine, this is nevertheless just as important as the first type of bargaining for two reasons. First, central policies are generally laid down in vague and flexible terms, so that central ministries have a great deal of power of interpretation. Secondly, central ministries control a substantial amount of the resources on which provinces depend. Provinces might seek, for instance, a higher annual quota of investment and more central investment projects, as well as a greater say in the design of detailed implementation prescriptions of central policies.

Apart from bargaining, the other form of discretionary behaviour, 'implementation deviations', refers to discretion operating during the implementation phase of central policies. Whether or not provinces have successfully influenced the formulation of central policies by means of bargaining, they can always affect the ultimate outcome of the policies through implementation. Different strategies of implementation deviation may be adopted to suit different situations.[27]

The relationship between bargaining and implementation deviations is complex, and the distinction between them is far from clear. The analytically clear-cut stages of policy formulation and implementation are, in practice, part of a continual process through which policies are initially formulated, implemented and tried out before being adjusted and reformulated. Bargaining and implementation deviations, being forms of discretionary behaviour employed during this process, are not, therefore, clear-cut and separate activities. They interact. Provinces first bargain with the centre as it 'sets the scene', within which they make their own decisions on exactly which directives to implement and in what manner. The conditions resulting from such implementation deviations subsequently constitute an altered environment in which provincial leaderships may again bargain with the centre on new policies as they arise, or on revisions of existing policies. The entire process is characterized by a high degree of continuity.

This suggests that it may be misleading if we proceed with the discussion of provincial discretion under a classification of temporal developments. A more viable way is to discuss provincial discretion in terms of its differential degree of dependence on the centre, whilst bearing in mind the possible forms the discretion may take. This approach has the advantage of focusing squarely the discussion of provincial discretion on its relationship with central policies.

Fig. 1.2 shows a typology of provincial discretion. The x-axis classifies provincial discretion in terms of the degree of interaction with centre actors. Provincial autarchy indicates that the discretionary behaviour is done with little reference to and interaction with the centre. On the other hand, central orientation suggests a situation whereby provincial discretion is largely directed towards the lobbying of, and bargaining with, central leaders for more favourable policies and more central resources. The y-axis measures the degree of involvement of the local plans and the 'market' in the discretionary behaviour, *vis-à-vis* central plans and policies. Some provincial discretionary moves are directed towards central policies and plans, while others are concerned with local plans and the market situation. The five categories of discretionary behaviour in the cells are:

1. *Bargaining with the centre for more favourable policies.* The objective of this behaviour is for the provincial governments to obtain more authority and greater room for manoeuvre regarding investment.
2. *Bargaining with the centre for more direct central support,* in the form of injection of central resources, such as budgetary or extrabudgetary fiscal resources, bank finance and larger investment scale quotas.
3. *Flexible implementation of central policies*—provinces using feigned compliance as the 'cover' whilst engaging in various 'creative' interpretations of central policies in order to attain provincial objectives.
4. *Developing the 'new horizon' of investment expansion*—provincial governments moving beyond the state budget and the conventional state sector towards the burgeoning market (the non-state sector as well as the 'extrabudgetary state enterprises') in their pursuit of investment expansion.
5. *Internationalization*—the provincial effort to attract external resources from beyond the national borders; a new pretext used by provincial government to demand greater autonomy from the centre.

It is clear from Figure 1.2 that discretionary behaviour in quadrant C has the highest degree of provincial independence: participation by the centre and the relevance of central plans/policies are both low. At the opposite end is quadrant B, which includes discretionary behaviour heavily directed towards the central government and involving central plans/policies. Bargaining with the centre for more favourable central policies and resources involves a high degree of participation by central officials as well as having central plans and/ or policies as the focal point of the entire exercise. At the intermediate range of provincial independence are acts of discretion in quadrants A and D. In the case of quadrant A, one very famous type of provincial discretionary behaviour particularly in Guangdong, is that of flexible implementation of central policies. Such behaviour represents a very

Fɪɢ ɪ.2 Pʀᴏᴠɪɴᴄɪᴀʟ Dɪsᴄʀᴇᴛɪᴏɴ: ᴀ Tʏᴘᴏʟᴏɢʏ

Relevance of   *Degree of participation by the Centre*
central/provincial plans

	Provincial autarchy	*Central dependency*
Central plans or policies	–Flexible implementation of central policies (A)	–Bargaining for more favourable central policies –Bargaining for direct central support (e.g. budgetary resources, larger investment control figures) (B)
Provincial plans or markets	–Develop 'new horizon' beyond the budget: expansion into the market –Internationalization (C)	–Bargaining for direct central support (e.g., extrabudgetary resources of central ministries) (D)

considerable degree of provincial independence and critical analysis as to the applicability of central policies in local circumstances. It also requires careful judgement regarding the changing limits of such manoeuvres as the boundary of central tolerance alters over time. On the other hand flexible implementation is focused on the manipulation of central policies, and notwithstanding the autarchic character of this behaviour the shadow of the centre looms large. In the case of quadrant D, centre actors are involved but not central plans or policies. This is the situation, for instance, when provinces seek investment capital from the extrabudgetary resources of various central units. Unlike the case of budgetary resources, the rules of the game regarding extrabudgetary resources are set more by the 'market' and the economic strength of the provinces concerned.

NOTES

1. For practical reasons, this discussion will concentrate mostly on studies done in the United States, Britain, and to a lesser extent Australia. The discussion of the China studies literature draws heavily on Shambaugh (1993), Nee and Stark (1989), Oksenberg (1987), and Harding (1984b).
2. See for instance Teiwes (1966: 14–32).

3. For a pioneering Soviet study using the pluralist theory to analyse the Soviet political system, see Griffiths and Skilling (1971).

4. The first explicit attempt in China political studies to borrow the analytical tools of pluralism and interest-group literature on the Western political system is Goodman (ed. 1984), followed by Falkenheim (1987).

5. A notable opponent was Lucian Pye (1981*a*), who maintained that it is inappropriate to try to understand Chinese politics, and therefore central–provincial relations, as bureaucratic politics. Provincial leaders form part of the vertically organized factions, instead of part of the horizontally organized interest groups.

6. The search for appropriate conceptions of the role of provincial leaders in the political system was part of a larger search for appropriate conceptions of the classification and alignment of actors when the homogeneous image of totalitarianism broke down. For a discussion of the models, see Harding (1984*a*) and Starr (1976).

7. See for instance Parris Chang (1972*b*), Shambaugh (1984) and Goodman (1981*a*).

8. In David M. Lampton's case studies of six upwardly mobile leaders, half of whom had strong territorial power bases, it is concluded that the six secured their advancement in the political system largely by serving as followers (Lampton 1986: 294).

9. An alternative view favouring an interpretation of provincial strength is put forward by Chang (1972*a*); but this is a relatively lonely voice. An example of the 'mainstream' opposing view is found in Falkenheim (1972*a*). Similarly, Donnithorne's view of a cellular socio-economic structure with decentralized political authority in the provinces has been disputed by other economists: see Lardy (1975, 1976).

10. For an insightful discussion of the meaning of 'provincial interest', see Ferdinand (1984: 18–19). Ferdinand argues that since it is impossible to determine with any certainty the motives of any individual's action, it is immaterial to attempt to limit the definition of provincial interest to the 'self-interest' of individual leaders, or to leaders' subjective perception of what should be in the 'public interest' of the province. In other words, provincial interest simply means a *conscious* desire on the part of provincial leaders to have public policy move in a specific direction. The motives of the leaders, whether they are acting for themselves or the public interest, are irrelevant because the two are often mixed and indistinguishable in real terms.

11. Major works taking the institutional approach include: Lampton (1987, ed. 1987), Lieberthal and Oksenberg (1988), Zhao Suisheng (1990), Lieberthal and Lampton (1992) and Shirk (1993).

12. Reference to the framework of bargaining in post-Mao China is found in Shirk (1992). Details of the 'Machiavellian' strategies of provincial leaders

and how they usurped the language of Maoist leadership in the effort of self-preservation during the 1966–8 period are found in an illuminating article by Parris Chang (1972*b*).

13. In this connection see Zweig (1987). Zweig argues that elite constancy, commitment and attention were crucial factors for the successful implementation of agricultural responsibility policy.

14. This is pointed out by Goldstein (1988: 231). Lieberthal was clearly thinking in unilinear terms when he wrote, 'The fragmentation [of the political system] has not reached the point where its constituent parts have the legitimate autonomy characteristics of a pluralist system' (Lieberthal 1992: 12).

15. For an example of commentators focusing on the analysis of the 'bases of power' of political actors in attempting to explain their success and failure at political survival, disregarding the gap between the *potentiality* of such power and the actual power wielded, see Dittmer (1978).

16. This concentration on one aspect of central–provincial relations—the *fiscal* relationship—is largely a reaction to the course of events during reform. Some examples of these works are: Oksenberg and Tong (1991); Tong (1989); Shirk (1990); Wang Shaoguang (1994); Lin Zhimin (1994); Wong (1991); Kojima (1992); and Bachman (1987).

17. Two works which explicitly employ the state capacity paradigm are Jia Hao and Lin Zhimin (1994) and Zhao Suisheng (1990).

18. The fact that the centre *subsequently* felt that it, again, was losing out to the provinces after the implementation of the 1980 fiscal reform is, however, a separate story. It shows the success of the provinces in outmanoeuvring the centre and the *shifting perceptions* of both the centre and the provinces regarding their interests.

19. On this point, Tsou's remark bears a remarkable affinity to Parris Chang's on the Cultural Revolution, and Parsons' on the role of coercion in the concept of power in general.

20. For discussions on the 'diminishing returns of repeated recentralization' and the cumulative effect of successive decentralization–recentralization cycles in the provinces' favour, see Zhao Suisheng (1990: pt. 2, p. 55); Lieberthal and Oksenberg (1988: 349); Riskin (1991: 143).

21. The complementarity of the institutional and rational-choice approaches is cogently discussed in Ostrom (1991). Susan Shirk (1993) also employs the rational-choice institutional approach, but her focus is more on the institutional context of the rational choices of actors, that is, how rational choices of actors can be explained by incentive structures built in to the institutional context, rather than emphasizing *the room for* active choice within the constraints of institutions.

22. Indeed, the second meaning is an improvement on the first in the sense that the re-emergence of institutionalism as a major analytical framework

in political science in the 1970s has led to debates regarding its scope and relation to the earlier rational-choice approach. See Ostrom (1991) for an excellent exposition of institutional analysis in this latter sense.

23. For instance, towards the end of her work Shirk notes the limitation of the institutional approach. She writes, 'I often found myself unable to explain changes in policies by the institutional context and fell back on *ad hoc* explanations instead.' The 'ad hoc' explanations are, in a 'rational-choice-cum-institutional approach', the roles played by actors' choices within the constraints of the institutional context (Shirk 1993: 339).

24. A distinction must be made between the provincialist perspective and the provincial perspective. The corresponding distinction is between the centralist perspective and the centrist perspective. Both the provincialist and centralist perspectives assume an interactive framework of central–provincial relations, their differences being their differing emphases on the subject of analysis—in other words, whether the story is about the choices of provinces in the context of central constraints (the provincialist perspective), or about the choices of the centre in the context of provincial constraints (the centralist perspective). An example of the latter is Shirk (1993). On the other hand, both the provincial and centrist perspectives assume not an interactive framework but a unilinear one, either bottom-up or top-down. Most previous studies in central–provincial relations, as this chapter has pointed out, assume an implicitly centrist perspective.

25. Nor should be the power of society in the state–society paradigm. However, most works in the state–society paradigm have assumed a statist perspective, and tend to regard the state as the 'centre' and society as the 'periphery' in a centre–periphery analytical framework. Shue's analysis of state–society relations in Maoist China is an example of a work that makes this assumption. See Shue (1988: 42, 54–69).

26. On the multiplicity of centres, see Ferdinand (1984: 21). On Guangdong and Shanghai serving as the sources of inspiration for national economic reform policies during the post-Mao reforms, see Jia Hao and Lin Zhimin (1994: 5).

27. Yang Xiaohui in his study of the Guangdong Government describes five types of implementation deviations: passive implementation or feigned compliance, 'native' policies, evasion of central policies, acting without asking, and explicit contravention of central directives (Yang Xiaohui 1990: 61–5).

2 The Decline in Central Control Over Investment

The importance of investment within the agenda of the post-1949 Chinese government makes it an ideal medium through which to observe the dynamics of political processes. Notwithstanding changes in their political agenda, the Chinese leaders have, since 1949, sought to build up the economic strength of the country by increasing investment. From 1950 to 1978, the average percentage of fiscal expenditure spent on investment was 35 per cent, whilst the peak figure for a single year stood in 1958 at 56 per cent.[1] When the national agenda was shifted to modernization and economic development in 1976, and particularly after the Third Plenum in 1978, the linkage between investment and the attainment of the national goal became still more direct. However, as a result of the decentralization reforms of the 1980s, the percentage of fiscal expenditure spent on investment, has, ironically enough, declined conspicuously. For instance, in 1979 it stood at 40.4 per cent. By 1991 it had more than halved to 19.4 per cent. Investment has, nevertheless, remained the largest expenditure item in the state budget (Ministry of Finance 1992: 116–19).[2]

The decline of investment expenditure as a proportion of total fiscal expenditure since the 1980s by no means denigrates its importance as a function and a task of the Chinese state. It rather reflects the changes in the relationship between the central and the provincial governments over investment since the reforms in the 1980s.[3] These changes include, briefly, a dispersion of investment resources and authority in the state apparatus from the central to the provincial and lower levels, and the apparent weakening of central control as reflected in the phenomenon of 'excess investment' over successive years.

This chapter looks into this dispersion of investment resources and authority on a national level. Dispersion at a provincial level, within Guangdong and Shanghai, will be discussed in Chapters 3 and 4 respectively. This chapter has two specific purposes. The first is to provide a working definition of the major investment issues in the context of central–provincial relations. The second is to examine and explain these issues.

DISAGGREGATING THE INVESTMENT

A prerequisite for analysing central–provincial interactions in investment policy is having a clear idea of what the investment issue is about. By identifying the crux of what is really meant when we mention the 'decline of central control over investment', this section serves to provide a clear focus for subsequent discussion on the causes of such a weakening in control. There are two dimensions to this decline in central control: first is the decline in control over the total amount of investment, and second, the decline in control over the direction and allocation of investment resources. It is argued here that these two dimensions of investment control intersect one another.

The weakening in central control over the investment total made each year since reform is obvious. The annual planned quotas of total investment prescribed by the centre, described by Chinese economists as 'central control figures', have, as a rule, been surpassed rather than observed by provincial governments. The amount of investment implemented over and above these prescribed annual quotas constitutes the amount of 'excess investment' made. 'Excess investment' is thus a *prima facie* measure of the level of provincial non-compliance regarding the centre's policy on investment.

The other dimension of central control refers to control over the allocation of investment resources to various industrial sectors and projects. As a result of decentralization in the investment planning system during the reform period, as detailed later, the centre has lost control over the allocation of the bulk of investment resources. The consequence is that although discussions about investment control have often revolved around the size of investment, what is actually of significance is the allocation of investment resources and the efficiency of such decisions by provinces. Often, for instance, the centre publicly blamed excess investment at provincial level for causing 'overheating' in the economy, and for diverting the supply of raw materials and energy away from more desirable projects. While the blame was explicitly to do with the size of total investment, the fundamental concern of the centre was that a substantial portion of investment taking place in the provinces had been spent on projects regarded by the centre as of questionable benefit from the national perspective—so that more investment resulted in more waste.[4] In other words, the concern over the scale of investment in practice *subsumed* and *presupposed* the concern over investment direction and efficiency.[5]

That the total scale of investment *per se* is not the issue is supported by the fact that, during some historical periods, exceeding the planned quotas of investment was regarded as desirable. This was particularly so during the First Five-Year Plan period (1953–7), when surpassing the planned targets of production and investment was commended as an achievement.[6] Investment efficiency was, at that time, relatively high and, more importantly, the direction of investment was then basically controlled by the centre. After that, however, investment gradually moved away from the control of the central government, and the efficiency of projects declined.[7]

In the final analysis, therefore, the decline of central control over investment refers to the decline in the centre's ability to direct appropriate levels of investment resources to those sectors it sees fit. The scale of investment has remained, however, the major indicator of central control as well as the focus of discussion among China analysts and political actors within China on the subject of central–provincial investment relations. Its resilience is due to two factors. First, it is a relatively simple indicator amenable to measurement and comparison across provinces; whereas the level of inefficient investment is more difficult to ascertain and more subject to dispute.[8] Secondly, and perhaps more importantly, central–provincial *interactions* over investment have largely been conducted around the issue of investment scale and the control of excess investment. Investment scale thus provides an apt focus for an analysis of central–provincial politics in this respect. Throughout this study, therefore, the efforts of provincial leaders to increase the *quantity* of investment will be the focus of analysis.[9]

Successive excess investment: loss of central control

As the operational indicator, the scale of investment presents a picture of unambiguous decline, if not total loss, of central control since the 1980s. A report on investment by the State Planning Commission describes the situation as follows: 'Over the years there have been very obvious gaps between the amount of investment planned and that eventually spent. In practice, the value of investment completed each year was, almost invariably, in excess of the value in the plan' (State Planning Commission and State Statistical Bureau 1991: 18) Table 2.1 shows the extent of excess investment over and above centrally prescribed quotas: the total value of investment completed was roughly

TABLE 2.1. *Excess Investment in Total Investment* (billion yuan)[a]

Period	Quotas[b]	Actual investment	Excess investment (%)
1981–5	360[c]	532[c]	47.8
1986–90	1,296[d]	1,974[e]	52.3

[a] Total investment refers to total 'societal investment', which comprises all investment in a defined geographical jurisdiction irrespective of the ownership relations of the units responsible for the investment, or the funding channels of the investment. It is a standard statistical measure in official statistical yearbooks. The concept is a product of the economic reforms of the 1980s. Prior to the reform, investment was basically monopolized by the state sector and most projects were included in the state investment plan. Since the 1980s more investment has been conducted outside the state sector and, in particular, outside the state plan. It has therefore been necessary to use a new concept to measure the total value of investment. Since then, the value of societal investment for the pre-1980 years has been reconstructed. However, coverage of the quotas was only extended to the non-state sector from the mid-1980s. In order appropriately to reflect the percentage of excess investment in relation to the quotas, the figures of actual investment in different periods were chosen to align with the coverage of the quotas for the period. The figures in the table correspondingly have different coverages: figures for 1981–5 cover investment in the state sector only; those for 1986–90 also include the non-state sector.
[b] Figures for both periods are quotas originally prescribed at the beginning of the five-year plan periods, prior to amendments and adjustments being made in the interim.
[c] See Xie Minggan and Lou Yuanming (1990: 187).
[d] Ibid 189.

1.5 times that of the value originally set by the centre as the limit. In fact, not only were the quotas successively surpassed, the centre was also often forced, in the middle of the financial year, to raise the limits originally set by the planned quotas. In this way a portion of the excess investment was recognized as legitimate and 'legal'.

Table 2.2 gives more details to the picture. While Table 2.1 shows the gap between central quotas of investment and the actual value of investment implemented, Table 2.2 shows that during the four years for which the original and revised planned quotas are available, quotas were usually revised substantially upwards in order to approach the level of the actual value of investment. Consequently, after the revisions, percentages of excess investment could often be slashed by more than half from the level depicted in Table 2.1. In 1983, to cite a

TABLE 2.2. *Excess Investment in Total Investment: Original and Adjusted Quotas* (billion yuan)[a]

Year	Quotas	Actual investment	Excess investment (%)[b]
1981	(30) 38[c]	44.3[d]	(47.7) 16.6
1982	(38) 44.5[e]	55.6[d]	(46.3) 24.9
1983	(36.2) 58[f]	59.4[d]	(64.1) 2.4
1984	65[g]	74.3[d]	14.3
1985	(140) 150[h]	168.0[d]	(20) 12
1986	228[i]	302.0[j]	32.5
1987	287[h]	364.1[j]	26.9
1988	330[l]	449.7[m]	36.3
1989	n/a	413.8[m]	n/a
1990	455[n]	444.9[o]	−2.2
1991	500[p]	550.9[o]	10.2
1992	570[q]	785.5[r]	37.8
1993	800[s]	1245.7[t]	55.7

[a] As mentioned in Note *a* in Table 2.1, the quotas issued by the centre had different coverages, hence the appropriate coverage of actual investment is cited in these two tables in order to reflect the percentage of excess investment: For 1981–4, all figures refer to capital construction investment in the state sector; for 1985, investment in the state sector; for 1986 onwards, total investment comprising the non-state sector.

[b] The excess investment percentages are calculated from the figures in the other two columns of the table. For some years the original figures of the quotas and the subsequently adjusted figures are available. The original quotas, and the corresponding excess investment percentages, are listed in brackets. Figures for the other years are adjusted figures of the quotas.

[c] See Xie Minggan and Lou Yuanming (1990: 187).

[d] See State Statistical Bureau (1986: 9).

[e] See 'Report on the 1983 National Economic and Social Development Plan', in *Nanfang Ribao*, 20 Dec. 1982.

[f] See 'Report of the Sixth Five-Year Plan', in *Nanfang Ribao*, 30 Nov. 1982.

[g] See 'Report on the 1984 National Economic and Social Development Plan Bill', in *Nanfang Ribao*, 16 May 1984.

[h] See Wu Jinglian and Wu Ji (1988: 38).

[i] Calculated from data on total investment completed and the amount of excess investment. For the former source see note j below. For the latter see *China Capital Construction* 10 (1988): 14.

[j] See State Statistical Bureau (1989): 12.

[k] See *China Capital Construction* 2 (1988):9

[l] See *China Investment and Construction* 3 (1989): 22.

[m] See State Statistical Bureau (1991: 13).

[n] Calculated from State Planning Commission and State Statistical Bureau (1992: 1). The figure is the quota in the adjusted plan.

[o] See State Statistical Bureau (1993: 16).

[p] See State Planning Commission and State Statistical Bureau (1992: 1). See also Ma Hong and Sun Shangqing (1992: 2, 207).

[q] See Ma Hong and Sun Shangqing (1993: 207).

[r] See *Statistical Yearbook of China* (1993: 146).

[s] See *Ming Pao* (Hong Kong), 30 Oct. 1993: 13, quoting the vice-director of the Construction Commission for the Three Gorges, Guo Shuyan.

[t] *Statistical Yearbook of China* (1994: 143).

more conspicuous case, the planned quota was revised upwards by 60 per cent. As a result the percentage of excess investment was reduced from the original 64 per cent to a negligible 2.4 per cent. This demonstrates the success with which provincial governments could make the centre adjust its criteria of control and legitimize what would otherwise have been illegitimate. However, the fact that the extent of excess investment often remains substantial, even after the central control figures have been significantly revised upwards, reflects again the ineffectiveness of the centre's control over the actual level of investment.

The question is: who should be held responsible for the excess investment? It should be noted that central government ministries, independently of provincial governments, also implemented investment and had their own investment budgets. They were, therefore, responsible for part of the excess investment. The trend since the 1980s, however, has been that provincial governments were the more important actors on the investment scene. Table 2.3 shows that the percentage of total investment resulting from decisions by the central government has been shrinking during the 1980s. The implication is that the excess investment statistics reflect, to a large extent, the degree of non-compliance of provincial governments.

Table 2.3 indicates that the share of total investment arising from the decisions of provincial and lower-level governments rose from an already high percentage of 59 per cent in 1980 to over 70 per cent in the early 1990s. In view of the fact that an absolute majority of investment was the result of decisions made within provincial boundaries, it was no surprise that the centre was largely unsuccessful in carrying through its control measures over investment. When the centre sought to reduce the scale of investment, a tactic often used by provincial governments was to reduce investment in less profitable but much more necessary sectors, for instance transport and energy. The centre was therefore left to fill the gaps, thus defeating the purpose of the original clampdown.[10]

EXPLAINING THE PHENOMENON

Why was the centre unable to control investment in the provinces? To what extent was the failure of control a result of the decentralization reforms in the 1980s? What did this decline in investment control tell us about central–provincial relations in China? To answer these ques-

TABLE 2.3. *Percentage Share of Centrally Decided Investment in Total Investment*

Year	Share
1980	41
1981	34
1982	40
1983	32
1984	36
1985	32
1986	31
1987	32
1988	30
1989	32
1990	33
1991	27
1992	24
1993	28

Notes:1 Centrally decided investments cover (1) those capital construction and technical renovation projects in the state sector which are subordinate to the central ministries, in other words, central investment projects; and (2) those 'above ceiling' locally subordinated capital construction and technical renovation projects, thus requiring the approval of the State Planning Commission at the centre.
2 From 1979–84 the 'ceiling' was 10 million yuan; from 1985 it was 30 million yuan.
3 The value of the second part, that is local projects which are above the ceiling, is estimated by taking 35% of the total value of medium-sized to large projects in the state sector for 1980–4, and 25% since 1985.

Sources: Information from 1980 to 1990, as well as the notes, is adopted from State Planning Commission and State Statistical Bureau (1992: 30); information from 1991 to 1993 computed from *Statistical Yearbook of China* (1992–4).

tions we need to look at both the socio-historical and institutional dimensions. More importantly, this issue is more than a mere question of the centre exerting control over the provinces. On the one hand, resource misallocation and subsequent waste on a massive scale were sometimes the result of investment initiatives by the centre. The most spectacular example is the Great Leap Forward of 1958–60, during which enormous quantities of resources were misused and wasted in the blind pursuit of rapid heavy industrialization. On the other hand, waste and inefficiency at a micro-level had always existed prior to investment administration being substantially decentralized in the 1980s. The fact that investment control had not been a problem regarding only the provinces had important implications for the relationship between the centre and the provinces. It explained why the centre was so ineffective in exerting control over the provinces in the 1980s.

The socio-historical background: the urge for national strength and glory

The Chinese socialist revolution was, to a large extent, the action of a country to reassert itself after decades of foreign invasion and humiliation. The desire for rapid modernization and ascendancy underlay the waves of 'radicalism' during the Maoist period. The impact of such radicalism for investment policy was that little consideration was paid to objective constraints posed by resource availability when investment decisions were made. The belief was that all difficulties could be overcome by human effort. Limitations of resources were considered secondary. Planning within the limits of available resources and acting within the bounds of plans were seen as deplorable, as these would reduce achievements, thus unnecessarily lengthening the road to prosperity and modernization. A casual look at press reports during the 1960s and early 1970s reveals numerous instances in which substantial amounts of materials and equipment were saved by the initiatives of the people. Indeed, it was argued that plans with 'gaps' were a tactic of central leaders within an economic system devoid of effective incentives—in order to extract more productivity out of a 'slack' workforce (Wu Ruyin 1992: 163).

While radicalism gradually receded in the political arena after the 1978 Third Plenum, the urge to develop the economy remained the goal of the post-1978 leaders. Investment, therefore, remained a priority item on the national agenda. A very important feature of this nationalistic urge was that the central leaders, as the representatives of the nation, were themselves very aware of the importance of investment. This made the centre traditionally the driving force in successive investment waves. The centre demanded more investment because it felt the most pressure to strengthen the national economy and guarantee prosperity for the population. Through its dealings with the international community, on both political and economic issues, the central leadership was convinced of the importance of a strong economy for its international status and bargaining leverage. As the People's Republic entered its fourth decade during the 1980s, the central leaders knew that they did not have much time in which to prove to the population that socialism could produce a better standard of living. Economic growth and prosperity was central to the political legitimacy of the regime. This urgency was particularly felt when communist regimes in the Soviet Union, in Mongolia and in Eastern Europe collapsed during the years 1989–91. Deng Xiaoping's comments in 1990 aptly reflect why the central leadership was always so concerned about investment:

We have to pay special attention to the drop in the economic growth rate. I am worried about it. . . . Some countries have encountered problems, in the final analysis, because their economy is failing. . . . Why do the people support us now? Simply because there has been progress in the economy over the last decade, and obvious progress. . . . This question [about economic development] is, therefore, not only an economic issue. It is in fact political. . . . If only we successfully attain the objective [of improving the living standard of the population], we will be safe regardless of what changes take place internationally.[11]

At the time of making these remarks Deng was concerned about whether or not central leaders had set off at the right rate of growth. Was it too low? How could the momentum of economic growth in the 1980s be sustained in the 1990s? Deng was obviously unconvinced that the 6 per cent annual growth planned by Premier Li Peng for the 1990s was fast enough. He encouraged central leaders to explore new development opportunities, and in particular the development potential of China's largest economic centre, Shanghai:

What is proper growth? The criterion is: that which can guarantee a doubling of our economy in the next decade, at constant prices, discounting inflation, and taking population growth into account. At what rate does the economy have to grow per annum in order to achieve this objective? Is our present calculation correct and reliable? Can an annual 6 per cent growth rate really bring us the second doubling [of economic wealth] in the coming second decade of reform? We really need to apply our mind to this . . . People are very sensitive about their well-being, and we cannot cheat on this . . . We have to grasp opportunities and make timely decisions. We have to identify places having more potential for development . . . for instance Shanghai. This would be a big move . . . Developing Shanghai could be a quick route to achieving our object-ive.[12]

In the end, after some delay and considerable intra-elite debate,[13] in 1992 the planned growth rate was raised from the original 6 per cent per annum throughout the 1990s to 9–10 per cent, following Deng's Southern Tour early that year.[14]

Nationalism was not the motive for investment of the central leaders only. Provincial leaders might also share this urge for modernization as a result of political socialization, in which nationalism and patriot-ism played an important part. The importance of modernization was moreover reflected in performance appraisal 'yardsticks' for provin-cial leaders, whereby the centre sought to ensure that provincial leaders worked towards the same goal as the centre. Although the yardsticks were not institutionalized, it was clear that from 1978 par-ticularly, the levels of provincial economic development and social stability constituted two major yardsticks in the assessment criteria for the performance of provincial leaders. Economic development was often measured in terms of the growth rate of societal produc-tion,[15] and social stability often hinged on job opportunities. Both could be achieved through expanding investment and building more factories. Provincial leaders were thus effectively motivated to launch investment projects which could increase the level of production, and provide more jobs for the local population.[16]

The institutional base and facilitation

In addressing the institutional base of the investment phenomenon, there were two levels of analysis which reinforced and sustained the nationalistic motives for investment as described above. The first is the more fundamental level regarding the effects of the public ownership system, and of the 'soft constraints' and 'iron bowl' characteristics de-riving from the public ownership system.[17] The public ownership system is the *definitive* institution in Marxist economics. Investment expansion is, in the final analysis, rooted in the nature of this funda-mental institution of the socialist economy. The second level of ana-lysis refers to the *specific* forms of the economic management system within the public ownership system. The questions addressed at this level include how public ownership was actually effected in practice, and how this in turn affected investment behaviour. This second level serves to explicate the ways in which the public ownership system, *through* its specific forms and via specific policies, has brought about investment expansion. The central–provincial interface enters the picture at this second level.

The public ownership system and soft constraints

There has been a growing body of literature which addresses the linkage of the public ownership system in socialist countries with the phenomenon of investment expansion as well as other economic problems.[18] Some analysts attribute economic problems commonly found in socialist systems to the excessive demand for consumer and investment goods. Others argue that the system is incapable of supplying goods of appropriate quality. In other words, these interpretations disagree on whether investment expansion *per se* does or does not constitute the key to solving economic difficulties. These arguments between economists, however, are not the subject of concern here. Rather, the interest of this study is in the circumstances wherein investment expansion as a phenomenon occurred and, in particular, in the ways through which provincial governments achieved such expansion regardless of central efforts at control. In this respect, it should be noted that, notwithstanding their disagreements regarding the *significance* of investment expansion, there is nevertheless wide agreement amongst economists regarding what *causes* investment expansion in socialist economies.

This explanation focuses on one point: the public ownership system, as it has been practised in China and other socialist countries, is unable to define clear boundaries of property ownership or to specify responsibility for investment decisions. Ownership signifies rights as well as responsibilities. An owner of property enjoys the right to use and dispose of the property, as well as shouldering all liabilities in this connection. The clear assignment of responsibility inevitably imposes restraint on the owner. It necessitates careful consideration as regards investment plans, and provisions whereby the adverse effects of any failures may be mitigated. In a society dominated by public ownership, such a natural restraint mechanism is conspicuous by its absence.

Ownership by all of the people, as public ownership is described in China, denotes that all the means of production in society are collectively owned by all the people in that society. As regards any single individual, he or she owns all means of production in society, but *only* as a member of the entire community. In practice, public ownership has led to a paradox of ownership relations: an individual is both an owner and a 'non-owner'. The public ownership system should in theory render the very concept of 'ownership' redundant and useless to the practical needs of individuals, who are required to 'contribute according to capability, and take according to need'. In practice, rights and responsibilities must be defined. Since the state has taken up the role of guardian of public ownership, it is therefore the representative of 'all the people' in exercising its rights and bears all responsibility in its capacity as the owner of the means of production. The individual, though still the ultimate owner in name, only takes up, in practice, the roles of worker and consumer.[19]

Consequently, the individual, although the ultimate owner, does not have to shoulder responsibility for the use, reproduction or accumulation of the means of production. That is the work of the state. However, the state is not itself a monolithic whole. Different tasks must be done by different departments and enterprises at different levels. This gives rise to a paradoxical situation. On the one hand, each unit of the state is entrusted with responsibility over a certain segment of the means of production on the behalf of the public. In this sense units are expected to act *like* the owners of the segment of public property under their jurisdiction. On the other hand, each of these units is but an administrative arm of the state. As ownership by all the people is a 'collective ownership' and is not to be distributed amongst individuals, so ownership when entrusted to the state as a whole is, in theory, not amenable to division between the various state organs. The implication is that any state unit, be it a government department or a state enterprise, does not have a clear-cut boundary of ownership and responsibility for the property under its control. Moreover, the picture is further complicated by the fact that responsibility is not only porous but shared. As part of the state *and* in a sense the state itself, a government department or a state enterprise can claim the right to deploy resources entrusted to *other* units, based on the argument that this will be beneficial to the common interests of all. Conversely, therefore, this unit is also vulnerable to 'intrusion' from other units.[20] The implication of such flexible boundaries of 'ownership' has been that should one unit suffer loss in an investment, that unit would be able to diffuse the losses through other units. The responsibility of any actor under the public ownership system is thus 'softly' delineated and subject to all kinds of manipulation.[21]

It is therefore obvious that, although discussions since the 1980s on the 'departmentalization' and 'regionalization' of public ownership suggested a fragmentation of public ownership within the state,[22] such a compartmentalization phenomenon did not actually entail *clear-cut* ownership relations between the various actors. Compartmentalization became a major phenomenon primarily as a result of the decentralization reforms of the 1980s. The decentralization reforms tightened the hold of state units—provinces, government departments and state enterprises—on resources and therefore had the effect of *encouraging* investment expansion behaviour. However, insofar as the reforms strengthened the *de facto* ownership rights of provincial governments over local resources, the reforms did not in themselves lead to an insatiable appetite for investment. It was the *interaction* between quasi-ownership rights and flexible boundaries of responsibilities on the one hand, and the latent modernization drive previously discussed on the other, that led to the investment expansion phenomenon. The fluidity of any demarcation of responsibility meant that provincial governments were not required squarely to bear the risks of their investment decisions. All internal checks on investment expansion were, therefore, rendered ineffective.

The above discussion indicates that the difficulty in controlling investment pre-dated the decentralization reforms of the 1980s, and explains to a large extent why the centre was so ineffective in forestalling provincial non-compliance over investment policy. In other words, the fact that China's investment problem is not solely an issue concerning central–provincial relations accounts to some extent for the central–provincial conflicts in the investment arena.

The economic management system: decentralization in the 1980s

The decentralization reforms of the 1980s changed the economic management system from one which was basically top-heavy to one which placed more power and responsibility at the provincial level. Provincial governments were, subsequent to these reforms, given more powers and incentives with which to make, and benefit from, investment. Consequently, the problem of investment control, previously a basically Centre-led issue, has, since the 1980s reform, become increasingly one in which the provincial level has played an important part.

The Fiscal Reform   The fiscal reform instilled in 1980 was central in this process. The fixing of revenue shares for five years and the autonomy to arrange local spending intensified the local economy orientation of provincial governments and reinforced the provincial officials' sense of proprietorship over provincial enterprises. As this fiscal reform allowed provincial governments to retain all local revenues, after remittance of a prearranged sum/percentage to the centre and with the added security of a five-year arrangement, they consequently became more motivated towards developing the local economy, thereby increasing local revenue.

In 1980 the State Council announced that all provincial levels, with the exception of three provincial-level municipalities, should practise a contractual fiscal system in which the level of remittance or subsidy would be fixed for five years.[23] Two crucial features of the 1980 reform set it apart from the previous numerous changes made to the fiscal system, and account for the significance of the changes in 1980. First, the level of provincial remittance or central subsidy was to be fixed for a period of five years. This was a feature which appeared briefly in the 1958 fiscal reform, but which did not persist long due to the chaos of the Great Leap Forward.[24] Secondly, the sectoral expenditure control figures imposed by the central government ministries on provincial governments were abolished, allowing the latter unprecedented leeway in allocating resources within the provincial budgets. Again, this had been a feature of the aborted 1958 system.

It is true that the decentralization of fiscal power and resources from the central to the provincial and lower levels did not begin in 1980 but dated back to the Cultural Revolution. Michel Oksenberg and James Tong (1990) have pointed out that, in this respect, the Cultural Revolution was the turning point in the history of the People's Republic, when the highly centralized system established in the 1950s gave way to a highly decentralized and even fragmented system. Due to the virtual paralysis of the state apparatus between 1966 and 1968 and the emphasis on local radicalism thereafter, central control over the collection and spending of local revenue in the provinces simply collapsed. There was no annual economic plan for 1967 and 1968, and nine central government agencies in economic planning and management were merged into one in 1970, when only 11.6 per cent of their combined total establishment remained in operation.[25]

The decentralization of fiscal resources during the 1966–76 decade was a *de facto* result of the radical opposition to bureaucratic control and management which caused the paralysis of the centre at that time.[26] The design of the fiscal system was reduced to a bare minimum whereby the continual running of the state, however shattered, could be ensured and the dispatch of necessary expenditures carried out. The following quote from an official in the Ministry of Finance explicates the nature of the decentralization of the period:

The fiscal management system during the decade of the Cultural Revolution could hardly be described as forming any sort of model. The system kept changing all the time, almost annually. There was hardly any mechanism as such; the purpose was simply to muddle through, and to survive, the chaos. (Song Xinzhong 1992: 48).

Decentralization in the late 1960s and early 1970s was, therefore, a convenient expedient and *de facto* consequence of the chaos of the Cultural Revolution. Provincial governments enjoyed substantial autonomy, not because the system explicitly allowed them the authority to do so, but because the system of control had fallen apart. Provincial governments, as the level of the state apparatus responsible for policy implementation and the collection and spending of most state revenues, simply filled the vacuum of power.

The decentralization of fiscal authority in the 1980s was both a break with and a continuation of the situation in the 1970s. Unlike the *de facto* dispersion of fiscal resources during the decade of the Cultural Revolution, the 1980 fiscal decentralization reform signalled a deliberate decentralization of fiscal responsibility, as well as resources, to the provincial level and below. Whilst the autonomy of provincial-level governments was, in the earlier period, largely the result of the failure of control by a divided centre, the enlarged provincial fiscal authority in the 1980s was part of a larger programme of economic reform of a relatively unified centre. Notwithstanding the incremental manner whereby reform programmes were tested in the 1980s, there was an unambiguous sense of direction when contrasted to the 'muddling through' mentality of the early 1970s. However, on the other hand, there was also an obvious continuity of the 1980 decentralization decision with developments in the previous decade. As noted in Chapter 1, the decision of the 1980 fiscal reform, from the centre's point of view, was largely a reaction to the financial difficulties which resulted from the extensive diffusion of fiscal resources to provinces during the previous decade (see Shirk 1993: 163). The *status quo* as of 1979 was perceived by central leaders as leaving them little choice but to decentralize fiscal authority further in order to arrest the decline in central fiscal revenue.

The significance of the 1980 fiscal reform for provincial investment behaviour is *not* solely manifest in the fact that provincial governments could obtain a larger share of national fiscal revenue, and therefore more budgetary revenues to spend on investment.[27] The significance rather lies in two other aspects. First, the security of a five-year contract, in which all above-quota revenue could be retained for local discretionary use, reinforced the *incentive* of provincial governments to increase investment and thereby increase revenue. Under the soft constraints of the public ownership system, the provincial government could easily transfer the risks of investment to other entities whilst retaining all the benefits, such as the new tax and profit revenue arising from new enterprises, the additional job opportunities, and the glamour brought about by big investment projects. In other words, the contractual fiscal system brought more benefits to provincial governments as regards additional investments, but did nothing to change the lack of financial accountability and responsibility associated with the public ownership system. Consequently, the symptoms of 'investment hunger' became intensified, and the enthusiasm of provincial governments for new investment became greater than ever before.

The other implication concerns the supply of a relatively independent source of finance. The new fiscal system led indirectly to the explosion of the extrabudgetary part of public finance, which ensured the provincial governments a secure and 'private' source of revenue for their investment plans. Extrabudgetary finance (*yusuanwai*) used to be a marginal feature of fiscal finance intended to supplement the rigidity of a highly centralized system. It originated as early as 1951, when the State Council issued an administrative notice authorizing the imposition of local surcharges by county-level governments amounting to 15 per cent on top of state taxes in order to finance discretionary local expenses. City governments were also authorized to levy public utilities surcharges in order to raise funds for the construction and maintenance of urban infrastructure (Song Xinzhong 1992: 42). During the 1970s extrabudgetary finance grew to a substantial portion of total fiscal finance, reflecting the dispersion of resources and loosening of central control during the decade of the Cultural Revolution. Yet the most spectacular growth was in the 1980s. From 1966 to 1976, total extrabudgetary finance, as a proportion of budgetary finance, increased from 15.1 per cent to 35.5 per cent. In 1980 this figure stood at

53.5 per cent, rising to 83.3 per cent in 1985 and 94.5 per cent in 1991 (Ministry of Finance 1992: 186–7).

Behind the spectacular growth of extrabudgetary finance were the deliberate tactics employed by provincial governments in order to maximize retained local resources under the fiscal contractual system. Revenues and resources from the budgetary sector were diverted to the extrabudgetary sector. This diversion slowed down the growth of local budgetary revenue, and therefore reduced the exposure of provincial coffers to the enroachment of the centre via the adjustment of contracted remittance. The means by which provincial governments achieved their purpose is discussed in detail in Chapters 5 and 6. At this point it is sufficient to note that whilst fiscal reform enabled provincial governments to get hold of more resources with which to finance investment projects independently, extra revenue nevertheless came only indirectly from extrabudgetary finance. The availability of a huge pool of extrabudgetary funds enabled provincial governments to disregard the bulk of central directives.

Investment Administration While fiscal reform strengthened the provinces' *incentive* to invest and indirectly provided, through extra-budgetary finance, the *resources* with which to invest, the decentral-ization of investment administration authority *facilitated* investment expansion by putting the bulk of investment decisions within the juris-diction of provincial authorities. Major changes took place in two areas. First was the abolition of sectoral control figures previously as-signed by the central ministries. This enabled the provincial govern-ments to arrange their own investment priorities with unprecedented flexibility. The other was the decentralization of project approval authority and the simplification of approval procedures, with the effect that provincial governments had much more control over whether or not individual local investment projects might proceed.

Sectoral control Sectoral control figures are the detailed mandatory prescriptions of investment for each 'administrative system' (xitong) which are determined at central government level and then passed down to the provinces for implementation. They symbolize the tight control of the central government over investment and were a major feature of the investment administration system prior to the 1980s. The abolition of this control instrument in the reform period was pertinent to the centre's eventual loss of control over the allocation of investment resources, and its subsequent concern over the problematic efficiency of many investment projects launched by provinces.

Ironically, as also in the case of many other reform measures, the abolition of sectoral control was repeatedly attempted by the central government. As early as 1958, and later in the 1970s, the centre had sought to do away with sectoral control figures on provincial investment. These earlier efforts failed either because the economic situation changed too rapidly (as in the case of the 1958 reform), or because any possible effects were swamped by the inertia of central dominance in a politically charged climate (Zhao Xiaomin 1985: 40).

The centralized system was in place early in 1952, when the procedure of investment planning was formalized and the rules promulgated. The central government, through the various ministries, was responsible for the prescription of investment control figures for the lower levels of government. Unlike the central control figures of the 1980s, which were only lump-sum figures for the total investment scale in a province, control figures from the 1950s to the 1970s were disaggregated into specific industrial sectors and administration systems. The lower-level governments were required to propose specific investment projects within the control figures for screening and approval, as well as for inclusion in the state investment plan. Provinces themselves had very little discretion in the allocation of resources across sectors (Dangdai Zhongguo Congshu Bianji Bu 1989a: 19). The central government exercised tight control over the size of total yearly investment, as well as over which specific investment projects were launched or dropped from the plan. As a result the centre controlled both the amount and the allocation of investment. Provinces were merely delegated the tasks of detailed planning and implementation.

In 1958 the control figures were nearly axed under the decentralization of the Great Leap Forward. According to the reform design, the entire planning system was to be shifted to a province-based one. Instead of central ministries assigning specific mandatory targets for the provinces, investment plans were to be based on suggestions from the provinces. Provinces would also enjoy more discretion as regards the allocation of resources *across* sectors, provided that the overall spending limit was not exceeded (Dangdai Zhongguo Congshu Bianji Bu 1989a: 26).

The 1958 reform failed, and with recentralization setting in, the old control figures were resurrected. Then in 1965, when the economy was back to normal, a limited degree of decentralization was again launched. The sectoral investment control figures for eighteen non-industrial sectors were replaced by one single lump-sum control figure. The purpose was obvious. It was beyond doubt that the existing system was too centralized. The 1958 experience, however, reminded the central leadership that steps needed to be cautious. The eighteen sectors chosen were the smaller and more localized economic sectors which, in any case, could not be efficiently planned from so far away as Beijing. Another sector was added in 1966 (Dangdai Zhongguo Congshu Bianji Bu 1989*b*: ii. 472).

In the 1970s, as still more emphasis was placed on strengthening local autonomy, the discretion of provincial governments in investment planning was enlarged. The dual system existing from 1965 was replaced by a system whereby each level of government would be awarded discretionary control for projects within their jurisdiction. In other words, instead of central ministries issuing investment control figures to all sectors, or to all except the nineteen designated sectors after 1966, central ministries would issue mandatory control figures for central investment projects only. However, because of instabilities in the economic and political situation, the changes did not fully materialize, and on the eve of reform in 1980, central ministries were still issuing mandatory investment figures to the provinces (Dangdai Zhongguo Congshu Bianji Bu 1989*b*: ii. 473; see also Zhao Xiaomin 1985: 40).

Eventually, the sectoral control figures were successfully abolished in 1980 when the fiscal system was changed to that of a contractual system.[28] Thereafter provincial governments were allowed, in principle, to allocate resources to local investment projects in different sectors according to their own priorities, instead of, as previously, merely providing the resources with which to implement the priorities of the central government ministries. Provincial governments thus became more or less independent actors regarding investment decisions. They had both the power to plan investment projects and a relatively secure and independent access to resources with which to finance their plans.

Decentralization of project approval In China every investment project, irrespective of ownership types and finance channels, and covering projects both within and outside of the state investment plan, has to be screened and approved by the government. Historically the power to approve projects was highly centralized. However, since the 1980s this authority has been decentralized on a substantial scale, resulting in the bulk of projects having been approved within the provincial boundaries.

Fiscal reform and the abolition of the sectoral control figures in 1980 gave provinces the freedom to plan, to propose and to spend. However, in between the planning and actual spending, there is still an intermediate step: that of having the plans and the specific projects approved. Two issues are involved here. First is the approval of yearly investment plans, a power firmly vested in the centre. The other is the approval of individual investment projects on a case-by-case basis. The two are interconnected because, as a rule, the yearly plans only list the projects requiring the approval of the central government. For projects which can be approved within the province, only the lump-sum total of investment is listed.[29] Therefore, if provinces are allowed to approve more projects, they can then invest more without reference to the centre.

This detailed mechanism works in the following manner. The control instruments used by the centre have always been targeted at *yearly* investment. The annual investment plan submitted to the centre for approval lists the planned value of investments in the coming year. The total investment control figure assigned to each province by the central government refers to total investment *for the year*, as do the control figures for bank finance issued to the banks. There has been basically *no* measure to ensure that the central government controls the total amount of *committed* investment, as expressed in the total accumulated planned investment of all the approved projects. At times when the central government discovered that yearly investment was running out of control, the provinces would be told to examine critically the total scale of approved projects, and some projects would be dropped to cut down the commitment. Such an exercise depended, however, on the co-operation of the provinces, which quickly faded as soon as political pressure from the centre subsided. The recurrent cycle of clampdowns and excess investment over previous decades suggests that this manner of control was largely ineffective.

The extensive decentralization of approval authority was central to such failure in control. As provinces were authorized to approve more projects, they could easily expand the total commitment of investment and use this as a bargaining chip when negotiating the yearly control figures with the centre. By approving more projects and allowing construction to commence, a province increased the committed cost to the central government in case of retrenchment, since the central government was less likely to abandon projects under construction than projects existing only on paper. After all, under the public ownership system most of the resources are 'state' resources, and provincial governments could always justify investment projects in terms of the public interest. The province was thus likely to be able to retain more investment projects, despite retrenchment, and to expand the yearly investments by starting from a larger base. This also explains why 'outside plan' (*jihuawai*) investment was so resilient a feature. No matter how often and how strongly the central government issued orders to stamp out these 'illegitimate' investment projects, provinces nevertheless knew that 'outside plan' projects were their best guarantee for winning a bigger share in total investment nationwide. Some central officials thus came to the conclusion that as long as the central government did not control the level of investment *commitment*, its battle on the yearly investment front would be doomed to failure.[30]

Due to its importance, project approval authority has historically been centralized. From the early 1950s, investment projects were classified into various categories in accordance with their design production capacity or investment value. Provinces were, generally speaking, allowed to approve only small projects.[31] During 1953–8, projects under provincial approval authority amounted to only 13.5 per cent of total investment. The central government, through the State Council and the various ministries, controlled the planning as well as the detailed scrutiny of the vast majority (86.5 per cent) of investment projects. During the 1958 reforms, provincial approval authority was briefly extended to medium-sized and large projects (Dangdai Zhongguo Congshu Bianji Bu 1989a: 26).[32] As a result of the chaos in investment and production between 1958–60, powers which had been decentralized were recentralized again after 1960. In 1962, approval authority for *all* medium-sized to large investment projects was placed with the State Planning Commission. In 1963, a regulation was issued stating that ministries and provinces should be responsible for approving investment projects of less than 0.5 million yuan only (State Planning Commission 1987a: ii. 61–3).

The approval authority of provinces saw several up-and-down adjustments during the 1970s. The provinces' power was enlarged in 1972, when it was announced that provinces could approve those medium-sized and large projects which had been included in the state's long-term investment plan.[33] In 1978, the situation again reverted to centralized control.[34] However, centralized control apparently did not last long because evidence available indicates that, on the eve of the 1984 decentralization, provincial governments already had the authority to approve projects below 10 million yuan.

In 1984, in another major decentralization move, provincial approval authority was trebled from 10 million yuan to 30 million yuan.[35] The screening and approval procedures for provincial projects still requiring the centre's approval were also simplified. Provinces were also entrusted with the formulation of implementation plans for these projects, once approved.[36] The consequence was that the participation of provincial governments in investment decisions was further enhanced. A further move was made in 1987 when, in order to encourage local investment in 'bottleneck' sectors, the central government enlarged the approval authority of provincial governments in the energy, transportation and raw materials sectors to up to 50 million yuan.[37] No further decentralization has formally been made since then. Many provincial governments during late 1992 to 1993 were, however, by their own initiative approving projects up to 200 million yuan as a result of the relaxation of the macro-policy environment after Deng Xiaoping's Southern Tour in spring 1992.[38] This meant that nearly all investments other than those over 200 million yuan, which fell, officially, under the jurisdiction of the State Council, were being approved by provincial governments on their own. Notwithstanding the effect of price rises, the scale of decentralization, from 0.2 million yuan to a *de facto* authority of 200 million yuan, was very extensive indeed. Authority was similarly delegated with respect to foreign investment projects.[39]

This extensive decentralization of project approval authority made it possible for provincial governments to control the bulk of investment activities within the boundaries of their provinces. Its consequences on provincial investment autonomy were twofold. First, the annual investment plan was no longer effective as a central control instrument on provincial investment. As noted earlier, provincial governments were required to submit annual investment plans to the centre for approval. However, the design of the plan was such that only those projects which fell within the approval authority of the central government would be individually listed. The rest of the projects, those approved within the provincial boundaries, were only reflected in a lump-sum figure. As most investment projects within the province were approved by provincial governments, the yearly investment plan was increasingly uninformative, inhibiting the centre from conducting a close scrutiny of the appropriateness of the bulk of investment decisions within the plan. Secondly, provinces were able to swell the total scale of *committed* investment by approving more and larger projects, thus strengthening their bargaining power with the centre in the event of retrenchment. The fact that a substantial part of provincially approved investment was often 'outside plan' investment—that is, it often fell beyond the centrally endorsed annual quota—was immaterial.

Investment expansion: central and provincial facets

This chapter has so far argued that investment control in China has been a problem for both centre and provinces. It has been a problem for the centre because the quest for more investment is ultimately grounded in a nationalistic desire to regain national glory and to raise the international status of the nation. Given the historical context of the formation of the People's Republic, the success or failure of the modernization program could affect the political legitimacy of the regime. Investment and economic development have therefore always been a major concern of leaders at the centre.[40] Moreover, the institutional context which has facilitated excess investment over and above prescribed quotas over the years is part and parcel of the socialist system of public ownership. Consequently, the issue of investment control is endemic to the socialist system, and, given the bias toward centralization within such a system, the local factor of implementation bias was, until the 1980s, only secondary.

The decentralization reforms of the 1980s gave enough power and resources to provincial and lower levels to change the scene, however. The fiscal reform in 1980 in particular resulted in a situation whereby the provincial governments had a built-in incentive to increase investment. In the political language of the central leadership, fiscal reform successfully built up a second source of 'enthusiasm' at the provincial level, as 'back-up' to the source of enthusiasm at the centre.[41] The changes outlined in this chapter demonstrate that the provincial government became an increasingly independent actor in investment decisions, so that the problems of investment since the 1980s increasingly merged into an issue of central control over decisions made at provincial level. In other words, the reforms of the 1980s added a local dimension to the issue.

The nature of the investment problem, however, remained unaltered. The problem was bound up in the nationalistic drive for rapid modernization and in the failure of the public ownership system to impose an effective self-monitoring efficiency mechanism. The dual nature of the investment problem beginning with the 1980s explained its complexity. In particular, it explained the recurrent phenomenon whereby after each round of central control and investment contraction, there would be a new round of investment expansion, often sanctioned by the central leadership itself. Instances showing the contribution of central leaders to investment expansion abound. Zhao Ziyang, former premier and general secretary of the Chinese Communist Party, was slack in the enforcement of control instruments and policies, and ignored the excessive expansion of bank credits which first started in the south and which became serious in the mid-1980s.[42] Eager to develop the economy, Zhao apparently believed that inflation was not a serious issue, and did not bother, therefore, to revise the original quotas of credits so as to make them approach the actual level.[43] The system simply fell into disuse. The consequent unconstrained growth in investment finally led to retrenchment, which started in late 1988 and lasted until 1991. The Southern Tour of Deng Xiaoping in 1992 represented another central intervention. Provincial governments interpreted the tour as signalling a change in the 'political wind' at the centre and accordingly readjusted their plans and strategies. As a Guangdong official commented in 1993, 'control over the scale of investment, stringent once again since 1989, is no longer working. There has, however, been no explicit change of policy or rules. The climate is simply different, and any attempts at control in this situation would have been futile.'[44]

The recurrent cycles of expansion and contraction suggest that central control, or effective central control, was at best an intermittent phenomenon. Although there were regulations, rules and policies prescribing the proper scale of investment and the proper procedures for project approval, provincial officials knew that it was safe to ignore, or pay only lip service to, the rules 'when the climate is right'. The fact that central leaders themselves were eager to increase *viable* investment and to launch good investment projects enabled provincial leaders to argue for exceptions to the various central control measures by appealing directly to the desires and inclinations of the central leaders.[45] In fact, because of such inclination on the part of the central leadership, a 'relaxed' environment, meaning that rules and regulations might be ignored or bypassed with relative safety, had become the 'normal' state. The 'stringent' climate whereby the centre demanded strict enforcement of existing rules was regarded, by provincial officials, as 'extraordinary' if not 'abnormal'.

The centre's control on the provinces was ineffective because the situation had never been merely one of control and compliance in the first place. Provincial government officials had always argued, and justifiably so, that their investment plans were of help to the centre in its task of developing the national economy. By speaking the same language of nationalistic modernization, a motivated provincial government official could frequently convince an equally motivated central government official that certain local investment projects were good and well worth the resources, even though the original, centrally prescribed investment quotas would necessarily be exceeded as a result.

NOTES

1. Calculated from Ministry of Finance (1992: 116–19). The average percentages have been arrived at by averaging the annual percentage shares.
2. By 1991, however, expenditure on education, science and health had caught up and, at 18.6%, was only marginally below the share of capital construction investment.
3. In this respect, Barry Naughton (1987) has documented the inability of the centre to impose its will on investment, which has increasingly become an 'internalized', and thus independent, activity of subnational governments.
4. In a survey by the Construction Bank of China on the 275 medium-sized to large capital construction projects completed between 1984 and 1986, it was discovered that overspending amounted to 28% of the total original estimates. A total of 174 projects did not attain the originally designed production capacity—74% of the total number of projects. 206 projects, or 87.7% of the total, spent more than they were originally budgeted. 70% of this overspending is attributable to mismanagement and faults in the original plans while the remaining 30% may be due to inflationary factors or upward adjustment of the spending standards of the original plans. See Wang Haibo (1990: 430, 432).
5. There are, broadly speaking, two schools of thought among economists in China on what is the major issue in investment. The predominant school places emphasis on the *scale* of investment, and argues that excessive demand for investment relative to available resources is the major problem. The other school focuses directly on the inefficiency problem of the supply side, and argues that the major problem rests with the *inefficiency* of investment decisions rather than the level of investment *per se*. It is clear that in the first school, the efficiency issue is in fact taken for granted. The line of argument becomes this: given that there is inefficiency, if there is less

investment, there is less waste. Members of the former school, the 'de-mand-generated' theory, include Wu Xiaoqiu (1991) and Fan Gang *et al.* (1990). For a full-fledged exposition of the views of the latter school, the 'supply inefficiency school', see Wu Ruyin (1992).

6. This attitude is obvious in Xie Minggan and Lou Yuanming (1990: 170–1). When discussing investment over the decades of the People's Re-public, excess investment beyond the targets of the First Five-Year Plan was regarded as a 'victory', while excess investment in later periods was described as causing wastage and reflecting the loss of central control.

7. For an authoritative discussion by the State Planning Commission of the investment efficiency issue of the various periods, see Lin Senmu and Jiang Guangxin (1992: 653–62). Altogether seven indicators were identi-fied which reflect investment efficiency. The First Five-Year Plan period has the highest rating for most of the indicators.

8. This is reflected in the discussion on investment efficiency in Lin Senmu and Jiang Guangxin (1992). Multiple indicators do not always tally with one another and this injects an element of indeterminacy and ambiguity into the exact level of investment efficiency for a year.

9. The concern here is to find a relatively simple and easily amenable indic-ator to measure and reflect the extent of non-compliance of provincial governments *vis-à-vis* central orders on investment since the 1980s, and then to explain how they managed to avoid compliance to that extent. This choice of an operational indicator should not be taken to imply that the author supports the 'demand-generated theory' of investment.

10. This is a comment frequently made by respondents from the central gov-ernment (author's interviews). An indirect piece of evidence for the move is the growing 'similarity' of industrial structure in the provinces in the 1980s, as a result of the inclination of all provincial governments to con-centrate investment in more profitable processing industries. See State Planning Commission and State Statistical Bureau (1992: 23).

11. Deng Xiaoping, 'The International Situation and Economic Issues', 3 Mar. 1990, in Deng Xiaoping (1993: 353–6, 354–5). This is part of a con-versation between Deng and several 'third-generation' central leaders.

12. Deng Xiaoping, 'The International Situation and Economic Issues'.

13. Despite the reservations of Deng in March 1990, the rate of growth for the 1990s was still planned at 6% per annum in the Ten-Year Plan and the Eighth Five-Year Plan submitted by Premier Li Peng in March 1991 to the National People's Congress. See Li Peng, 'A Report on the "Ten-Year Plan for National Economic and Social Department" and the Eighth Five-Year Plan Outline', speech to the Fourth Session of the Seventh National People's Congress, 25 Mar. 1991, printed in Zhonggong Zhong-yang Wenxian Yanjiushi (1991–3: iii. 1486). The 6% rate of growth was in-sisted upon even in the immediate aftermath of Deng's Southern Tour.

When Li Peng made the government report to the National People's Congress in March 1992, he reiterated that the planned growth rate for the coming year, that is 1992, would be 6%. See Li Peng, 'The Government Report', 20 Mar. 1992, in Zhonggong Zhongyang Wenxian Yanjiushi (1991–3: iii. 1993).

14. See Jiang Zemin, 'Deeply Understand and Fully Implement the Spirit of Deng's Talks, to Develop the Economy and Carry On Reform and Opening in a Better and Faster Way', 9 June 1990, in Zhonggong Zhongyang Wenxian Yanjiushi (1991–3: iii. 2063).

15. For instance, at both the Twelfth and Thirteenth Party Congresses, the target of the economic work of the country was expressed in terms of the total value of agricultural and industrial production. At the Twelfth Party Congress in September 1982, the target was to quadruple this value from 710 billion yuan in 1980 to 2,840 billion yuan in 2000. See You Lin *et al.* (1993: 114–15). Moreover, back in 1958 the centre had issued a document to provincial officials explicitly requiring them to increase their industrial production capacity so that the value of industrial production output could exceed that of agriculture. See Fang Weizhong (1984: 210).

16. This paragraph is deduced from the author's various interviews. The yardstick of production level is a feature both before and after 1978, but social stability was less a concern for the pre-1978 decades, when the ideological mobilization of the population meant that stability was not an issue. In fact the more social instability there was in the engineered direction of the central leadership, the more 'revolutionary' and the better the work of the local leadership was thought to be.

17. The phenomenon of 'soft budget constraints' was first discussed in the classic work by Janos Kornai, *The Economics of Shortage*, in which Kornai identifies the soft budget constraints of a socialist firm as sufficient cause for the constant phenomenon of insatiable investment and investment tension in socialist economies (Kornai 1980: 210).

18. In this section, I draw mainly on the following literature on China: Fan Gang *et al.* (1990); Wu Ruyin (1992); Liu Guoguang *et al.* (1988); and Wu Xiaoqiu (1991). I have also consulted Kornai (1980) and Gregory and Stuart (1990), which are on the Soviet and Eastern European experience.

19. See Fan Gang *et al.* (1990: 24–8) for an exposition of this paradox of ownership status in societies with public ownership as the dominant system. Some colloquial catchphrases on such a paradoxical situation are: 'One has everything, and at the same time has nothing'; 'Everybody is the owner, nobody is the owner.' Reflecting the indivisibility of ownership rights and the confusion arising there is the saying: 'Mine is yours, and yours is mine.'

20. The situation whereby the administrative units of the state exercise an incomplete degree of ownership rights over the 'public property' under

their administrative jurisdiction is described as the 'proliferation of the public ownership system' in Quan Zhiping and Jiang Zuozhong (1992: 23–7). Each level of the state hierarchy and each administrative unit of the party-state has become the *de facto* owner of the slice of public property under its administrative custody, although the exercise of its power is subject to control and manipulation by the superior levels and ultimately by the centre.

21. Janos Kornai (1980: 306–7) identifies several conditions, any one of which in his view would be sufficient to make the constraints 'soft': (1) firms as price-makers instead of price-takers; (2) a 'soft' tax system, meaning both that the formulation of tax rules is influenced by firms—firms may be granted exemption or postponement of payment as an individual favour—and that the collection of taxes is slack; (3) free stage grants, in the form of *ad hoc* or recurrent state subsidies, and injection of investment capital; (4) a 'soft' credit system: credit is granted even if there is no full guarantee of repayment.

22. See, for instance, Granick (1990) and Shirk (1993).

23. See 'State Council Document on Implementing the "Dividing Revenues and Expenditures, Contracting at Various Levels" Fiscal Management System', 1 Feb. 1980, in State Planning Commission (1987: 629–31).

24. During 1971–3 a somewhat similar fiscal system was practised, whereby remitting provinces were required to remit a certain amount of revenue to the centre, retaining wide discretionary powers regarding the utilization of the retained revenue. Such lump-sum transfers in 1971–3 were, however, single-year arrangements only, meaning that provinces had to renegotiate the lump-sum payments or subsidies every year. Provinces whose financial situation improved one year were then often obliged to increase their remittances the following year.

25. Oksenberg and Tong (1990: 8 nn. 12, 13), quoting Gao Shanquan *et al.* (1984).

26. This fact is also briefly noted in Oksenberg and Tong (1990: 5), where they write that 'the long-term trend since 1949 has been toward an expansion of the fiscal powers of provincial governments. To a considerable extent this trend is the result of default rather than design.'

27. Retained local fiscal revenues nevertheless generally increased, as provincial governments generally succeeded in ensuring that changes in the system worked in their favour. See Song Xinzhong (1992: 52).

28. See 'State Council Document on Implementing the "Dividing Revenues and Expenditures, Contracting at Various Levels" Fiscal Management System'.

29. Interview, respondent no. 5, Guangdong, Sept. 1993.

30. Hence some officials of the State Commission on Economic System Reform have suggested mandatory controls on the total committed

investment scale for projects approved both at the central and provincial levels. See Xie Minggan and Lou Yuanming (1990: 194).

31. There were four categories. Category A projects, projects of over 10 million yuan, were to be screened and approved by the State Council. Category B projects, those with an investment under 10 million yuan, would have their project design documents screened by the relevant central government ministry for subsequent approval by the State Council. Projects of a value between 200,000 yuan and the 10 million yuan ceiling were in Category C, screened and approved by the relevant central government ministries or the regional governments. Category D projects, under 200,000 yuan, were approved by provincial governments. See Dangdai Zhongguo Congshu Bianji Bu (1989 a: 14–15). Later the categories were simplified. Categories A and B became the near-equivalents of large and medium-sized projects, and Categories C and D became the small projects.

32. The new authority allowed provincial governments to approve *all* Category C projects and, under two circumstances, projects in Categories A and B as well. First, provinces were made responsible for screening the design and budgetary documents prior to submitting the Category A and B projects to the centre for approval. Secondly, if the Category A and B projects did not require co-ordination from the centre either during construction or after production, the provinces themselves would be allowed to approve them, reporting to the centre for record thereafter.

33. Regulation issued by the State Council on 31 May 1972. See State Planning Commission (1987a: ii. 63).

34. According to the 'Regulation on Procedures of Capital Construction' issued by the State Planning Commission, State Construction Commission, and Ministry of Finance on 22 April 1978 printed in State Planning Commission 1985: 121–8), all medium-sized to large projects, irrespective of subordination relations, were to be approved by the State Planning Commission, and small projects were to be approved in accordance with their subordination relations.

35. State Council Notice no. 138 (1984) 'Temporary Regulations on Improving the Planning System', 4 Oct. 1984, in State Planning Commission (1985: 1–12).

36. State Planning Commission, 'Notice on Simplifying the Approval Procedures of Capital Construction Projects', 18 Aug. 1984, in State Planning Commission (1985: 21–5).

37. State Council Notice no. 23 (1987), 'On the Extension of Project Approval Authority of Fixed Asset Investment and the Simplification of Approval Procedures', 30 Mar. 1987, printed in State Statistical Bureau (1992a: 111–17).

38. Interview, respondent no. 31, Beijing, Jan. 1994.

39. In 1979, it was announced that as long as provinces could find their own supplies of raw materials and balance their foreign exchange without assistance from the centre, they could approve export-oriented projects and other forms of foreign investment up US$1 million. See State Council Notice no. 202 (1979), 'On Approving the Regulations on Promoting Foreign Trade and Increasing Foreign Exchange Revenue', 13 Aug. 1979, in State Commission for Economic System Reform (1983: 481–7). In 1982 this ceiling was raised to US$3 million for provincial-level governments, other than the three provincial-level municipalities, Shanghai, Beijing and Tianjian, and apart from Guangdong and Fujian, who enjoyed greater power under the 'Special Policy'. These five provinces could approve foreign investment of up to US$5 million (see Central Committee Notice no. 6 (1982), 'On Approving the Notes of Meeting on the Foreign Trade-Related Work in the Nine Coastal Provinces and Municipalities', 15 Jan. 1982, in State Commission for Economic System Reform (1983: 577). In 1984, the jurisdiction of Guangzhou, together with that of Dalian, was increased by 100% to US$10 million and Shanghai's power was raised to US$30 million (see State Council Notice, 'Temporary Regulations on Improving the Planning System'). Guangdong's power was further raised to US$30 million in 1987 (see Guangdong Provincial Party Committee 1986–88: iv. 388).

40. This is despite the fact that leaders of different periods have made widely differing assessments of the economic situation of the country, as well as having divergent ideas regarding development strategies. Mao Zedong opted for a mobilization approach, whereby the enthusiasm of the masses was used to provide extra inputs of resources at a time when the international exclusion of China prevented it from obtaining additional resources from external sources. This strategy required a more optimistic assessment of China's strength, so that the enthusiasm of the masses could be maintained and reinforced (see Fang Weizhong 1984: 205). The excesses of optimistic radicalism forced the post-Mao leadership under Deng Xiaoping to adopt a more realistic assessment of the situation. The warming up of Chinese–US relations from 1972 also provided a favourable international environment for the change.

41. The reference to provinces and localities as the second source of enthusiasm, the centre being the first and primary source, was made by Mao Zedong in his famous speech, 'Lun Shida Guanxi' (On the Ten Great Relationships), 15 Apr. 1956, printed in Mao Zedong (1977: 275).

42. Interview, respondent no. 39, Beijing, June 1994. An official in Guangdong revealed that during 1987 and 1988, the banks relaxed the control over credits, and many bank officials at that time had to 'knock on the doors' of local government departments and enterprises for loan applications (interview, respondent no. 1, Guangzhou, May 1993).

43. Interview, respondent no. 39, Beijing, June 1994.
44. Interview, respondent no. 4, Guangzhou, May 1993.
45. One tactic used by the Guangdong provincial government to bargain for higher investment quotas from the centre, and to legitimize excess performance, was to convince the central leadership of the desirability of specific investment projects (interview, respondent no. 9, Guangzhou, Dec. 1993).

3 Investment in Guangdong: Central Policy and Provincial Implementation

The objective of this chapter is to provide the context for answering the question: what does investment implementation in Guangdong tell us about central–provincial relations? Two sets of questions are involved here. First, what characterized Guangdong's investment after 1980? Was there an 'implementation gap' in investment policy in the centre-Guangdong interface, and what were its characteristics? Secondly, with respect to the factors behind the investment problem identified in Chapter 2, in particular the reforms in the fiscal system and in the administration of investment, what were the developments in Guangdong? This discussion of the institutional context is a prerequisite to understanding the politics of the process, the subject of discussion in Chapters 5 to 7.

INVESTMENT IN GUANGDONG

The investment scene in Guangdong after 1980 was characterized by two phenomena. One was the proliferation of investment funding channels and investment actors. The other was the rapid growth of the total size of investment from a relatively low base. The two were closely related. On the one hand, the rapid growth in total investment was the result of the proliferation of investment funding channels and investment actors. On the other hand, such a plurality of actors and funding sources had evolved in the first place due to a strong demand for more investment.

Rapid growth from a low base

Historically Guangdong had not been a preferred recipient of state investment. The proportion of national income utilized in the province for accumulation purposes prior to 1979 was low compared to the national average and that of industrial centres such as Shanghai. At that time there were few large and medium-sized investment projects in the province, most of the investment having been in the light and

TABLE 3.1. *Accumulation Ratios (%)[a]*

Year	National average	Guangdong	Shanghai
1952	21.4	13.9	25.6
1957	24.9	17.2	34.6
1962	10.4	6.6	n/a
1965	27.1	17.1	12.4
1970	32.9	21.9	28.3
1975	33.9	26.1	41.0
1978	36.5	28.4	41.0

[a] The accumulation ratio is the ratio of utilized national income used for working capital stock, and fixed asset investment.

Source: Guangdong Statistical Bureau (1989*a*: 197–9).

TABLE 3.2. *Ranking of Accumulation Ratios*

year	Guangdong	Shanghai	Total number of rank[a]
1952	16	4	24
1957	26	5	27
1962	12	n/a	22
1965	24	26	26
1970	24	17	25
1971	21	6	25
1978	23	4	24

n/a = not available

[a] The total number fluctuates each year and is not necessarily equal to the total number of provinces, as some provinces may have identical accumulation ratios. The higher the number of ranking, the lower the accumulation ratio in the province.

Source: Computed from Guangdong Statistical Bureau (1989*a*: 197–8).

processing industries. Tables 3.1 to 3.3 show the low level of investment in Guangdong before the reform decade commenced in 1979.

Tables 3.1 and 3.2 show that Guangdong's accumulation ratios prior to 1979 were, for most of the years shown, at least 7 per cent lower than the national average. Compared with the 28 other provincial-level administrations, its ranking was always at the bottom end of the scale.[1]

Its ranking was particularly poor when compared to Shanghai, which was, with the exception of 1965 and 1970, amongst the upper ranks.

As a result of its below-average accumulation ratio, Guangdong's yearly investment also fell below the national average. From 1950 to 1978, Guangdong's investment in the state sector amounted to a total of 21.3 billion yuan, as Table 3.3 shows.

TABLE 3.3. *State Sector Investment, 1950–1978* (billion yuan)

	National	Guangdong	
		Total	% of national
Total	768.8	21.3	2.8
Annual average	26.5	0.7	2.6

Source: Guangdong Statistical Bureau (1989*a*: 158–61); State Statistical Bureau (1986: 9).

The small share of Guangdong's investment in the national total before 1979 indicates how much has changed since then. In 1993 Guangdong's total societal investment amounted to 13.1 per cent of the national total (*Statistical Yearbook of China* 1994: 146). In 1991, 1992 and 1993, Guangdong ranked first among the 30 provincial-level administrations in terms of the value of total investment, with Shanghai ranking sixth, seventh and then sixth again (ibid.; see also State Statistical Bureau 1992: 19). Guangdong's yearly average investment during the 1979–93 period amounted to 59.1 billion yuan, more than 73 times the average during the 1950–78 period, as shown in Table 3.4.

This 'great leap forward' in Guangdong's investment ranking suggests a higher than average growth rate of investment during the post-1978 period. Table 3.5 contrasts the annual investment growth rates of Guangdong with the national average.

TABLE 3.4. *Guangdong: Total Investment*, (billion yuan)

Period	Total	Annual average
1950–78	22.6	0.8
1979–93	887.2	59.1
1950–93	909.8	20.7

Source: *Statistical Yearbook of Guangdong* (1993: 236, 1995: 269).

TABLE 3.5. *Growth Rate of Total Investment* (%)

Year	Guangdong	National average
1979	3.9	n/a
1980	35.4	n/a
1981	57.7	n/a
1982	40.3	28.0
1983	4.7	16.2
1984	47.0	28.2
1985	41.6	38.7
1986	17.3	18.7
1987	16.0	20.6
1988	40.9	23.5
1989	−1.8	−8.0
1990	7.3	7.5
1991	28.3	23.8
1992	92.8	42.6
1993	76.8	58.6
1979–93	33.9	24.9[a]

n/a = not available

[a] The cumulative average for the national figure is for the period 1982–93 only.

Sources: *Statistical Yearbook of Guangdong* (1992: 145, 1993: 236, 1995: 269); Guangdong Statistical Bureau (1989a: 176); State Statistical Bureau (1986: 8, 1991: 13); *Statistical Yearbook of China* (1994: 269).

Table 3.5 shows that for most years since 1979, total investment has more often than not grown more rapidly in Guangdong than nationwide. The average annual growth rate in Guangdong for the 1979–93 period was 33.9 per cent, whilst nationally during the 1982–93 period the growth rate stood at 24.9 per cent. This continual growth throughout the fifteen-year period was interrupted in 1989, when investment throughout the country was hampered by severe retrenchment measures and the national growth figure dived to minus 8 per cent. However, investment in Guangdong's collective sector nevertheless rose by 1.7 per cent in 1989, indicating that the 1989 austerity programme failed to suppress entirely the investment drive in Guangdong. Investment projects undertaken during the 1980s were also on a much larger scale than those prior to 1980, when Guangdong was assigned only a small number of medium-sized to large investment projects. Guangdong topped the national league into the 1990s in the number of medium-sized to large projects completed.[2]

As a result of its high rates of growth, Guangdong's total investment has consistently surpassed the control figures agreed with the centre, and by very large margins. Table 3.6 shows that during the 1980s control figures passed down by the central government were consistently and substantially surpassed. The retrenchment years of 1989, 1990 and 1991 were no exception. The investment level for 1989 in the provincial plans made according to central directives prescribed a decrease of 20.5 per cent from the planned level in 1988.[3] However, actual total investment for the year 1989 surpassed the control limit by 150 per cent.

Complicating the picture is the fact that the coverage of the control figures and of the investment statistics differ and the figures are thus not, strictly speaking, entirely comparable. The investment statistics purportedly measure all investments undertaken in the province which have been reported to the authorities concerned.[4] Such statistics include investment in the state and non-state sectors and all funding channels, including those of both central and local investment projects. The control figures, on the other hand, have a narrower scope due to multiple exclusion categories as detailed below. Coverage has also varied over the years. For instance, in 1980 control figures cover

TABLE 3.6. *Differentials Between Plans and Performance in Guangdong* (billion yuan)

Year	Control figures[a]	Actual total investment	Excess investment (%)
1980	5.1	3.8	–25.5
1985	5.5	18.5	236.4
1988	12.8	35.4	176.6
1989	14.0	34.7	147.9
1990	20.7	37.3	80.2
1991	23.6	47.8	102.5
1992	34.5	92.2	167.2

[a] Figures for 1980, 1985 and 1988 and control figures calculated at the beginning of the year. Adjusted figures calculated at the end of the year, which are usually larger, are not available. Figures for the other years are year-end adjusted figures.

Source: Personal communication.

capital construction investment in the state sector only, but as from 1988 capital construction in the non-state sector is also included. Since 1990 investment in commodity housing projects has been included due to its increasing share in total investment. However, central investment projects in either sector have always been excluded, as have direct foreign investments. And in 1992 the central government assigned specific control figures to Shenzhen and Guangzhou, whose investments have since also been excluded from the Guangdong provincial control figures.[5]

In a sense the different coverage is due to differences in the nature of the two. Investment statistics are meant to be a factual reflection of the total amount of investment activity taking place in the province, irrespective of whether the investments are authorized or 'illegal', or whether the investments have a subordination relationship within or outside the province, or whether the funding comes from inside or outside the state coffers, or from inside or outside of China. On the other hand, the planning control figures are a tool of the central government to control investments undertaken by Guangdong. As a result, investments undertaken in Guangdong but not by the enterprises and authorities of Guangdong, for instance those by the central ministries and other provinces, are excluded from the planning figures.[6]

Certain categories of investment may also be excluded from the planning figure as a result of central policy. Direct foreign investments, for example, are excluded so as to encourage Guangdong province to attract more foreign investments. In 1982 and 1985, eleven and five categories of investment respectively, such as the repair of existing equipment, the building of roads, schools, hospitals and museums, and staff hostels using extrabudgetary or 'own funds' were excluded so as to avoid these socially desirable projects from being crowded out by more profit-oriented projects (Dangdai Zhongguo Congshu Bianji Bu 1985: 237).

If investment in central projects is deducted from the total investment figure, thereby eliminating a major source of coverage incompatibility, excess investment ratios fell but are nevertheless still significantly high (Table 3.7).

Their different coverages notwithstanding, the substantial differentials between the control figures and actual investment give some idea as to the extent of investment activity taking place beyond the scope of planning control. This is indicative of the waning control of central government over the province via the traditional planning system, and

TABLE 3.7. *Differentials Between Plans and Performance (adjusted) in Guangdong* (billion yuan)

Year	Control figures	Total investment[a]	Excess investment (%)
1980	5.1	3.0	−42.0
1985	5.5	15.6	184.4
1988	12.8	35.4	139.8
1989	14.0	30.0	113.7
1990	20.7	31.5	52.0
1991	23.6	41.3	75.4
1992	34.5	82.5	139.2

[a] The adjusted figures are arrived at by deducting central projects (state sector) investments from the total investment figures. (For sources see Table 3.8.) Because investment in the non-state sector is normally of local subordination relations, the difference should all be locally subordinated (state and non-state) investment.

of the increasing irrelevance of the state plan as an indication of actual investment activities at provincial and lower levels.

Proliferation of actors

The proliferation of actors in investment during the 1980s occurred on two interrelated fronts. First, there was a diversification of investment funding channels, which had the effect of bringing in more actors as lenders and investors in the undertaking of investment activities than ever before. Consequently the state, and in particular the central government, could no longer dominate the investment scene by controlling the supply of funds. Secondly, investment became more diffuse within society and was no longer the sole privilege of the state sector. The non-state sector, comprising the collectives and the private sector, grew at a much faster rate than the traditionally mighty state sector. Within the state sector itself decentralization of investment authority made subprovincial governments at city, county and township levels independent investors. The authority of the central government was, as a result, appreciably marginalized.

Declining central investment

The most significant phenomenon resulting from the proliferation of funding channels in Guangdong was the marginalization of central investment in Guangdong's investment.

As shown in Table 3.8, during the early 1950s investment by the central government accounted for over 70 per cent of the total. This share declined drastically during the 1960s and 1970s, when a large number of central enterprises were decentralized to provincial and lower levels. The share of central investment again rose to 66 per cent in 1978, when many large enterprises resumed their former subordination relationship. A new cycle was started with decentralization once more during the 1980s. By 1993 the share of central investment amounted to less than 10 per cent of the total.

It should be noted that the percentage shares in Table 3.8 are calculated according to the subordination relations of each investment project. The entire value of a centrally subordinated investment project is calculated as central investment. The same applies conversely to locally subordinated projects. However, it appears from data made available during the 1980s that there have been substantial cross-overs

TABLE 3.8. *Central and Local Investment in Guangdong's State Sector* (%)

Year	Central investment	Local investment
1952	72.0	27.9
1957	64.0	36.0
1962	31.6	68.4
1965	37.6	62.4
1970	12.2	87.8
1975	17.4	82.6
1978	66.4	33.6
1980	32.6	67.4
1981	27.8	74.2
1984	25.8	74.2
1987	29.7	71.4
1988	16.4	83.6
1989	23.9	76.2
1990	23.4	76.6
1991	21.3	78.7
1992	19.5	80.5
1993	9.7	90.3

Source: For 1952–78: *Statistical Yearbook of Guangdong* (1984: 217). For 1979–83: Guangdong Statistical Bureau (1989a: 172). For 1984–92: Guangdong Statistical Bureau (1985–93). For 1993: *Statistical Yearbook of Guangdong* (1994: 219).

of funds from one government level to a project subordinated to another government level.[7] It is thus possible to know more precisely the share of central/local investment in terms of actual monetary contribution. The movement of funds also indicates the underlying central–provincial dynamics. Details are shown in Tables 3.9 and 3.10.

Table 3.10 shows that in Guangdong between 1984 and 1992 the total cross-over of funds amounted to some 2.2 per cent of the total

TABLE 3.9. *Guangdong: Local Investment Share* (%)

Year	By subordina-tion relations	By funding source
1984	74.2	68.2
1985	79.1	77.6
1986	80.7	80.7
1987	71.4	74.2
1988	83.6	n/a
1989	76.2	75.5
1990	76.6	76.3
1991	78.7	78.4
1992	80.5	81.1
1984–92	78.2	76.5

n/a = not available

Source: Guangdong Statistical Bureau (1985–93).

TABLE 3.10. *Guangdong: Fund Cross-overs* (million yuan)

Year	Central funds to local projects	Local funds to central projects	Cross-over % of total
1984	379.9	26.4	5.1
1985	81.9	54.7	1.1
1986	0.0	n/a	n/a
1987	47.7	113.5	0.9
1988	n/a	n/a	n/a
1989	151.5	169.3	1.6
1990	185.0	117.2	1.2
1991	333.6	260.5	2.0
1992	150.2	554.4	1.4
1984–2	1329.8	1296.0	2.2

n/a = not available.

Source: Guangdong Statistical Bureau (1985–93).

value of investments. Table 3.9 shows that, after accounting for the cross-over of funds as detailed in Table 3.10, the share of local investment during the 1984–92 period dropped slightly, but still remained at more or less the same level as the subordination figure. It is interesting to note that in Table 3.10, the cross-over of local funds to central projects is not much less than vice versa. And in 1987 and 1992, Guangdong's injection into central projects was between two and three times the value of the inflow of funds from the centre.

The information shown in Table 3.10 represents only part of the scale of fund movement which actually took place. To disaggregate entirely the source of funding, a detailed breakdown of every channel of funds is necessary. In other words, the general category of 'budgetary funds' needs to be broken down into central budgetary funds and local budgetary funds. 'Own funds' should be differentiated in accordance with the source, namely, whose own funds. As a portion of bank loans was financed directly from the central coffers, this part should be differentiated from the balance of loans which were financed by local bank deposits. Thus each category of funding source and its allocation of funds to central/local investment projects will be clearly identified.[8]

Due to data limitation, Table 3.10 is primarily based on the cross-over of 'own funds'. A breakdown of budgetary funds is available for technical renovation investment in 1984 only. This piece of information, however, indicates that the budgetary channel was a major channel of inflow of central funds to local projects.[9] Thus the extent of the inflow of central funds over the years might well be substantially under-reported due to the lack of available data in this area. Meanwhile, the fact that there was a substantial outflow of local funds to centrally subordinated projects in Guangdong should not be interpreted as skill on the part of the centre in extracting local resources from Guangdong. The phenomenon was more likely the result of Guangdong's successful 'fishing' for central investment in the province. By agreeing to contribute capital to central projects located *in* the province, the Guangdong government could increase the total value of investment projects in the province, particularly when central investment projects were not taken into account in the centrally prescribed quotas of total local investment. As a planning official put it, 'since these projects are all located in Guangdong, they contribute towards the multiplier effect of economic development in the province regardless of their subordination relations and where the direct taxes and profit of the projects go'.[10]

It must be recalled that Tables 3.8 to 3.10 refer to investment in the state sector only. As most investment in the collective sector, and virtually all in the private sector, was local investment, the share of local investment in total investment would be larger than the percentage shares indicated in these tables. This was especially so for the 1980s, when non-state sector investment grew to a substantial share.

Decline in budgetary investment

Underlying the shrinking share of central investment in Guangdong was a greater shrinkage still of the share of investment using budgetary resources. The state budget, whether at the central or provincial level, used to be the major source of funding for investment. Before 1978 over 80 per cent of state sector investment in Guangdong was funded by the state budget. After 1980 the percentage share of investment funded by the state budget dropped drastically and continuously, until it was no more than 2 per cent of the total. Table 3.11 gives the details.

The gap left by the rapid shrinking of budgetary investment was filled by investment financed by bank loans, by 'own funds' of enterprises and departments, by foreign investment and, from the early 1990s, by societal capital gathered through the issue of shares via the developing securities market. Table 3.12 shows the distribution of state investment by funding channels.

TABLE 3.11. *Share of Investment Financed by the State Budget in Guangdone* (%)

Year	Total investment	State investment
1978	46.3	62.9
1979	49.0	69.0
1980	30.0	44.6
1981	15.1	26.4
1985	7.2	10.2
1988	3.1	4.3
1989	n/a	4.4
1990	3.2	4.4
1991	2.5	3.7
1992	1.3	1.9
1993	1.2	1.9

Sources: Guangdong Statistical Bureau (1989*a*: 88–9); *Statistical Yearbook of Guangdong* (1992: 231 and 233, 1993: 237, 1994: 219).

TABLE 3.12. *Funding Channels of State Sector Investment in Guangdong, 1979–1988* (%)

State budget	Bank loans	Foreign capital	Own funds	Other
13.3 ·	25.2	13.7	34.2	13.6

Source: Guangdong Statistical Bureau (1989a: 12).

Table 3.12 shows that during the 1979–88 decade, the state budget became the least important channel of investment funding for state sector investment in Guangdong. More investment in the state sector was financed by money from abroad than by money from the state.

Before proceeding further it may be useful to consider the significance of this budgetary investment statistic and its relevance to this study. In order to do so it is necessary to know precisely what this statistic comprises. *Prima facie*, it is a measure of the total value of investment financed by the state budget, central or local, in a given year. (This is the definition given in the explanatory notes of official statistical publications and other reference materials on investment statistics) However, when looking at the breakdowns of local fiscal expenditures and comparing the figures covering investment expenditure with those projects within the state plan measured by the 'budgetary investment' statistic, it is plain that the two have very different coverages. Table 3.13 gives the details.

Table 3.13 shows a cumulative discrepancy between the two statistics, whereby fiscal expenditure exceeds the budgetary investment figure for the five years between 1987 and 1992 by nearly 140 per cent. According to interviews in Guangdong, this was more than a mere discrepancy in statistics. The value of budgetary investment within investment statistics covers the amount of investment included in the state plans, having been approved by the centre and which, in accordance with the plan, is to be financed from the state budget. However, the figures for fiscal expenditure on investment, as they appear within government finance statistics, refer to the actual amount of local budgetary funds spent on investment. In theory any outlay from local coffers should be strictly in accordance with state investment plans, and as such, local fiscal expenditure would be expected to be smaller than or at most equivalent to the value of investment financed by the state budget. This is because budgetary investment might be financed by state budget resources from the central budget as well as from the

TABLE 3.13. *Budgetary Investment and Local Fiscal Investment Expenditure in Guangdong* (billion yuan)

Year	Budgetary investment[a]	Fiscal expenditure	Discrepancy[b]	%[c]
1987	1.26	2.05	0.85	70.2
1988	1.09	2.62	1.53	141.1
1989	1.10	2.64	1.54	140.2
1990	1.20	2.96	1.76	146.8
1991	1.26	3.62	2.36	186.8
Total	5.91	13.89	8.04	137.3

[a] State sector only.

[b] The amount of local fiscal, that is, budgetary, investment expenditure over the value of budgetary investment as appeared in the statistics of investment by types of funding.

[c] Absolute discrepancy value as a percentage of budgetary investment.

Sources: Ministry of Finance (1992: 157); *Statistical Yearbook of Guangdong* (1988–92).

provincial budget. The existence of such a disproportionate discrepancy in favour of local fiscal expenditure suggests, therefore, that 'outside-plan' (*jihuawai*) investments were conducted by the provincial government, financed from provincial fiscal resources. To what extent the discrepancy was equivalent to that portion of outside-plan investment would depend on the amount of budgetary investment that was funded from the central rather than provincial budget.[11]

The budgetary investment statistic is not, therefore, a measure of the total value of investment financed with budgetary funds, as was originally intended and formally defined in official publications. From the way the statistic has been compiled, it could be seen to be rather a measure of the portion of total investment which is included in the centrally endorsed investment plans and financed with budgetary funds.[12] Those outside-plan investments financed with local budgetary funds have been categorically excluded from the budgetary investment statistic. They have been largely included in the 'own funds' category.[13]

The implications of this disclosure of the vagaries of the budgetary investment statistic are threefold. First, there is now not only hard evidence of the existence, but also a partial indication of the extent, of outside-plan investments in the provinces other than records of the centre's complaints on the issue. Secondly, it demonstrates that the Guangdong provincial government had been very actively involved in such supposedly 'illegal' activities. Findings detailed above show that

more than half the provincial fiscal outlay for investment in Guangdong during 1987–91 was assigned to projects not endorsed by the
centre. One can only imagine the Guangdong government's attitude
towards similar 'illegal' activities by enterprises using their own funds.
Third, the relevance of the budgetary investment statistic to the present
study is now clear. Since the statistic is actually a reflection of the state
investment plan, its utility in a study of central–provincial relations is
greater than that of a comprehensive statistic of investment financed
with budgetary funds.[14] In other words, the significance of the discrepancy between the two statistical measures is that it exposes the discretionary behaviour of provincial governments regarding the financing
of outside-plan investment with fiscal resources. To the extent that the
central government had traditionally used the plan and the supply of
money to keep its grip on the provinces and society in general, the
budgetary investment statistic measured how much hard-core control
the centre actually retained. Table 3.14 illustrates the position in the
early 1990s.

If bank loans and 'own funds' are to an extent transferred resources
from the state,[15] foreign capital, on the other hand, represents a source
of funding which is external to the state. It is thus worth noting that,
between 1979 and 1991 cumulatively, the share of foreign capital in
Guangdong's total investment funding rose to a substantial 25 per cent
(Zhang Hanqing 1992: 120). Moreover, the 'other' category accounted
for an even bigger share, and was the largest single category of funding in 1992. The fact that an ostensibly miscellaneous category had
acquired such prominence demonstrated the extent of funding proliferation.[16]

TABLE 3.14. *Guangdong: Funding Channels of Total
Investment* (%)

Year	Budget	Bank loans	Foreign capital	Own funds	Other
1990	3.2	18.1	14.9	32.1	32.2
1991	2.5	21.1	13.0	32.0	31.0
1992	1.3	20.4	12.0	31.7	34.3
1993	1.2	19.8	16.4	37.5	25.1

Note: Percentages do not add up to 100 as one minor channel of
funding, the 'coal for oil fund', is not listed here.

Source: *Statistical Yearbook of Guangdong* (1991: 193, 1992: 231
1993: 237 1994: 219).

Rise of the non-state sector

Prior to the 1980s investment in Guangdong and in China overall was largely confined to investment in the state sector. Investment in Guangdong's non-state sector, that is, in urban collective enterprises, rural communes and communal workshops, in small private businesses, and in the building of houses in the countryside, amounted to only 6 per cent of the total investment for the 29 years from 1950 to 1978. Between 1979 and 1993 the share rose to a significant 30 per cent. Table 3.15 details the escalation.

Table 3.15 shows that by 1993, just under 30 per cent of total investment in Guangdong took place in the non-state sector. This leap in the relative share within little more than a decade was indicative of the high rate of growth in the non-state sector, as shown in Table 3.16.

From Table 3.16, it can be seen that during the 15 years from 1979 to 1993 the growth rates of investment in the non-state sector exceeded those of the state sector for nine years. The other six years, during

TABLE 3.15. *Guangdong: non-State Sector Investment* (million yuan)

Period	Collective	Private	% share of total investment		
			Collective	Private	Collective + private
1950–2	—	—			
1953–7	—	—			
1958–62	348	4	8.2	0.1	8.3
1963–5	254	—	1.3	—	1.3
1966–70	—	—			
1971–5	—	—			
1976–80	346	2,452	2.7	19.1	21.8
1981–5	7,219	12,255	13.2	22.3	35.5
1986–90	21,838	20,902	14.2	13.6	27.8
1991	7,121	6,398	14.9	13.4	28.3
1992	20,932	10,914	22.7	11.8	34.5
1993	30,571	16,781	18.8	10.3	29.1
Total					
1950–78	686	639	3.0	2.8	5.8
1979–93	87,944	69,066	16.6	13.1	29.7
1950–93	88,630	69,705	22.2	17.5	39.7

Sources: For 1950–85: Guangdong Statistical Bureau (1989a: 158–61). For 1986–92: *Statistical Yearbook of Guangdong* (1993: 236). For 1993: *Statistical Yearbook of Guangdong* (1994: 219).

TABLE 3.16. *Investment in Guangdong: Annual Growth Rates* (%)

Year	Total	State sector	Collective	Private	Collective + private
1979	3.9	0.1	13.1	14.9	14.5
1980	35.4	28.2	76.8	49.6	52.7
1982	40.3	49.6	79.4	10.7	105.2
1981	57.7	34.6	281.6	78.0	27.8
1983	4.7	8.0	3.6	–2.7	–0.005
1984	47.0	44.2	52.8	51.0	51.7
1985	41.6	62.6	32.9	–7.0	7.6
1986	17.3	21.0	7.0	9.4	8.3
1987	15.9	12.9	31.4	18.8	24.4
1988	40.9	42.1	52.9	25.6	37.9
1989	–1.8	–1.8	1.7	–5.5	–1.7
1990	7.3	9.0	1.9	3.9	2.8
1991	28.3	26.0	32.3	37.3	34.6
1992	92.8	75.9	194.0	53.3	135.6
1993	76.8	48.4	46.0	53.8	48.7
Average, 1979–93	34.0	30.8	60.5	26.1	36.7

Source: Computed from *Statistical Yearbook of Guangdong* (1993: 236, 1994: 219).

which growth rates in the non-state sector slowed down, were those when the centre demanded retrenchment action from the provinces. This suggests that the non-state sector was not altogether impervious to interference from the state. Nonetheless, investment in the non-state sector quickly rebounded once political pressure had died down. At 36.7 per cent the average growth rate of investment in the non-state sector was also well above that of the state sector at 30.8 per cent, illustrating that the non-state sector was, on balance, more prone to investment growth than the state sector.

The increasing importance of investment in the non-state sector marked an important development in China since the commencement of the economic reform programme in 1979. This ostensibly socialist country was no longer solely dominated by 'socialist' modes of production. For instance, in 1980 the state sector in Guangdong produced over 60 per cent of the total production output value of the industrial sector. By 1993 the percentage had dropped by half to 30 per cent (*Statistical Yearbook of Guangdong* 1994: 175). Moreover, what had previously constituted the collective sector had also changed considerably. What had been a 'para-state' sector gradually took on characteristics of an autonomous private sector. The number of collective enterprises within the non-state sector was inflated as a substantial number of private enterprises were registered as collective enterprises in order to qualify for lower tax rates and easier access to bank finance. Nevertheless, the relationship between the non-state sector and the state remained 'close', with the state, especially at local levels, exercising a pervasive influence, a point to be discussed in greater detail in later chapters.

This growth in the non-state sector is material to comprehending the decline of central and budgetary investment in Guangdong. The previous dominance of the state budget and therefore of the central government in investment existed in a social context in which the state sector was supreme and central planning was the main mode of economic management. Even though there has always been a collective sector in the cities, and state ownership has never been the dominant mode of production in the countryside, the ideological orthodoxy before the 1980s nevertheless specified that the collectives were the younger brothers of the state sector. When a collective enterprise had achieved notable results, the enterprise would subsequently be 'upgraded' and become state-owned. Investment in the collective sector was, therefore, definitely on a small scale. Into the 1980s, economic reforms worked to loosen central control on the lower levels of government, enabling the growth of a relatively autonomous non-state sector outside the scope of control of the traditional system of administration. The consequence of this was a relative decline in central investment.

INSTITUTIONAL BACKDROPS

It was noted in Chapter 2 that changes in the economic management system from the 1980s were central to the increasing conflicts between the centre and the provinces over investment. Fiscal reform and decentralization of investment authority were two such major changes. This section looks at the specific changes in Guangdong, and how, generally, they worked to result in the investment expansion phenomenon as mentioned above.

Fiscal reform

Fiscal reform in Guangdong was arguably the most important single change in central–Guangdong relations. Fiscal reform had profound effects regarding the degree of provincial control over investment in Guangdong. It also represented the juncture at which developments which would affect future investment activity began.

Reform content and developments

The *dabaogan* fiscal system approved by the State Council in 1979 allowed Guangdong to retain all fiscal revenues collected from provincial sources after remitting an annual sum of 1.2 billion yuan, which would remain unchanged for five years (State Commission for Economic System Reform 1983: 471). When compared to the nationwide reform of 1980, Guangdong's 1979 reform was not only 'one step ahead' in terms of the timing of approval, but also in terms of its aggressiveness. In other provinces, what was fixed was often the ratio of fiscal remittance, instead of the absolute sum as in Guangdong (Oksenberg and Tong 1991).[17] Moreover, this sum was subsequently reduced. It was cut to 1 billion in 1980, then further to 778 million yuan for the period 1985 to 1987, on the premise that a number of Guangdong enterprises hitherto under the jurisdiction of the provincial government were converted to central enterprises, thereby shrinking the revenue base of the provincial coffers (Dangdai Zhongguo Congshu Bianji Bu 1991: i. 687).

In 1988, the system was adjusted in order that the central government might extract more revenue from Guangdong. Instead of fixing a lump-sum payment for a number of years, the central government fixed a base figure with a percentage increase each subsequent year. The base figure was fixed at 1.413 billion for 1988, and the percentage increase for 1989 and 1990 set at 9 per cent (Dangdai Zhongguo Congshu Bianji Bu 1991: i. 687).

On balance, however, the fiscal reform started in 1980 had increased the pool of fiscal revenue retained by the provincial government for its discretionary use. From 1980 to 1987, for instance, Guangdong's total net remittance to the centre amounted to 12.2 billion and accounted for 26.5 per cent of the provincial fiscal revenue for the period.[18] This figure compared favourably with Guangdong's fiscal remittance for the entire 1950–87 period, which amounted to a full 37 per cent of Guangdong's total fiscal revenue (Dangdai Zhongguo Congshu Bianji Bu 1991: i. 673).[19] The fiscal system did not constitute a stable contract, however. During the retrenchment years of 1989, 1990 and 1991, Guangdong was obliged to raise its remittance substantially in order to supplement the national coffers. In 1991, for instance, when the fiscal scheme was renewed for another three years, the base figure was reportedly increased by 360 million yuan, though the annual increment percentage remained unchanged at 9 per cent.[20] According to senior Guangdong leaders, the net remittance in the retrenchment years of 1990 and 1991 was respectively 5.2 billion and 7 billion yuan, amounting to about 40 per cent of the provincial budgetary revenue. Total fiscal remittance to the centre from 1980 to 1991 amounted to 31.5 billion yuan (Zhang Hanqing 1992: 7; Guangdong Provincial Party Committee 1993: 43, 59). The amount of net provincial remittance in 1991 was 7.2 times as great as that of 1979 (7 billion yuan as compared to 850 million yuan), representing an annual average growth rate of nearly 17.6 per cent (Guangdong Provincial Party Committee 1993: 59).

Notwithstanding the fact that Guangdong was repeatedly obliged to remit more than the agreed sum, provincial officials were nevertheless very keen to retain the *dabaogan* system for Guangdong. In this connection, it should be recalled that, as noted in Chapter 2, the significance of the 1980 fiscal reform for investment went beyond the increase in fiscal revenue as retained in the provinces. In 1992, Guangdong succeeded in its negotiations with the centre to retain its system until the year 2000. The terms of the deal were that, from 1994 to 1997, the yearly remittance would be based on the existing base figure plus an annual increment figure, which would remain at 9 per cent, whilst the increment percentage from 1998 to 2000 would be negotiated at a later stage.[21] This agreement was, however, curtailed when towards the end of 1993 the centre announced its decision to replace nationwide the fiscal contractual system with a tax-sharing system starting in 1994. At that time, Guangdong's officials were still unambiguous about their preference for the *dabaogan* system.[22] As they had failed to retain the system, their objective was to tailor the new system in such a way that Guangdong's existing financial autonomy would not be jeopardized.

Enhanced financial security and investment drive

What was, then, the significance of the fiscal system of 1980 and its relevance to the phenomenon of investment expansion? First, there is evidence showing that the mere increase in retained revenue was not the issue. As Table 3.17 shows, more of the additional local fiscal revenue Guangdong retained as a result of the fiscal reform was assigned to social expenditure such as education and health than to investment, both in absolute as well as in percentage terms.[23]

TABLE 3.17. *Share of Major Expenditure Categories in Guangdong's Budgetary Expenditure* (%)

Expenditure	1987	1988	1989	1990	1991
Investment	21.3	22.7	18.7	19.7	19.8
Education and health	23.7	22.6	23.5	23.4	21.8
Price subsidy	14.0	12.3	12.4	11.8	6.6
Agriculture	7.8	7.5	7.8	7.3	7.1
Law and order	n/a	3.2	3.9	4.1	3.9

n/a = not available

Source Ministry of Finance (1992: 157).

Table 3.17 suggests that the rapid growth in investment in Guangdong in the 1980s was not a result of more budgetary revenue being allocated for investment purposes. In fact, a much smaller portion of budgetary expenditure went to investment in the 1980s than previously. During the 1970s 30 per cent of Guangdong's total budgetary expenditure was spent on investment. During 1980–91 this figure fell to only 18 per cent (Dangdai Zhongguo Congshu Bianji Bu 1991: i. 673). The influence of fiscal reform on investment growth was apparently far more subtle than the straightforward supply of budgetary funds.

The argument here is that the fiscal system formed the core of a new environment which as a whole was conducive to the rapid growth of investment activities in Guangdong. The key features of the new environment were as follows:

1 The provincial government had a clear and focused target and agenda, namely economic development and pioneering in reforms.
2 Repeated and high-level assurances from the centre during the 1980s reinforced the sense of security and direction first conferred by formal arrangements and policies.
3 There was a rapid diffusion of such clarity of direction and purpose from the provincial government to subprovincial levels and to the community, so that a self-generating momentum of change and development eventually developed in society at large.

This momentum, in turn, served to provide the pressure and impetus needed for further initiatives within the provincial government. In other words, the *dabaogan* fiscal system was not the direct cause for the investment phenomenon in Guangdong. Its effect was also not linear.

The *dabaogan* system allowed Guangdong to retain all provincial revenue over and above its lump-sum remittance. As a result, Guangdong could obtain conspicuous benefit from new investments, themselves being an expansion of the provincial revenue base. On the other hand, negative sanctions remained minimal, as provincial governments could, as previously, 'transfer' the costs of poor investment decisions to other state units and to the centre. Consequently, more investment was not made possible simply because the Guangdong government was allowed to retain more fiscal revenue locally, thus having more funds to finance investment projects. Investment grew immensely in Guangdong because the provincial government felt reasonably secure, due to the *dabaogan* fiscal system and other central policy concerns, that most of the additional revenue generated from the new projects would remain in the province.

Extrabudgetary finance

It was noted earlier in this chapter that most investment since the 1980s has been financed by funds outside the state budget. The growth of extrabudgetary finance in the 1980s was, however, partly a consequence of the 1980 fiscal system. One implication is that, although as noted above, the increase in retained local fiscal revenue in Guangdong since the 1980s did not lead to a corresponding increase in investment expenditure within Guangdong's provincial budget, it would be misleading to conclude that the Guangdong government no longer played a major role in investment financing. The role merely shifted outside the budgetary avenue.

Table 3.18 compares the total value and the yearly growth rates of Guangdong's budgetary/extrabudgetary fiscal revenue in the 1980s. In 1990, Guangdong's extrabudgetary fiscal revenue amounted to just under 10 billion yuan, ten times that of the original budgetary remittance value agreed with the central government in 1980, and equivalent to over 75 per cent of the budgetary revenue for the same year. In 1990, 47 per cent of total extrabudgetary expenditure was spent on investment. In absolute terms this is nearly 20 per cent more than the amount drawn from the budget (Ministry of Finance 1992: 157, 232). As shown in Table 3.19, the cumulative value of investment financed by extrabudgetary fiscal revenue for the period 1986–90 was almost one-quarter more than that financed from the official budget.

The existence of a parallel fiscal system external to the budget at all levels of government provided a second coffer from which to finance

TABLE 3.18. *Guangdong: Fiscal Revenue*

Year	Budgetary (billion yuan)	Growth (%)	Extrabudgetary (billion yuan)	Growth (%)
1982	4.2	—	2.9	—
1983	4.4	5.0	3.2	9.2
1984	4.9	11.4	3.7	16.7
1985	6.5	32.7	4.6	8.6
1986	8.2	26.2	5.2	14.2
1987	9.6	17.2	6.7	29.2
1988	10.8	12.2	8.4	25.2
1989	13.7	27.2	9.1	7.9
1990	13.1	−4.3	9.8	8.4

Sources: Ministry of Finance (1986a: 144, 1992: 78, 204); *Statistical Yearbook of Guangdong* (1984: 295, 1986: 291, 1987: 367).

TABLE 3.19. *Guangdong's Investment: Budgetary and Extrabudgetary Fiscal Funds* (million yuan)

Year	Budgetary[a]	Extrabudgetary[b]	Extrabudgetary over budgetary (%)
1986	2,053	2,536	23.5
1987	2,616	3,097	18.4
1988	2,644	3,573	35.1
1989	2,964	3,774	27.3
1990	3,617	4,293	18.7
Total	13,894	17,273	24.3

[a] Budgetary investment figures amalgamate the following categories as listed in the original source: (1) capital construction; (2) enterprise funds for technical renovation; (3) three funds for scientific development.
[b] Extrabudgetary figures amalgamate (1) fixed asset investment; (2) the Repair Fund; (3) miscellaneous construction; (4) Road Maintenance Fee Fund expenditures; (5) three funds for scientific development.

Source: Ministry of finance (1992: 157, 232).

investments other than those specified within the state budget. The phenomenal rise of the importance of extrabudgetary finance was itself, in turn, largely a result of provincial discretionary behaviour, which will be discussed in detail in Chapter 5. With such substantial growth in extrabudgetary finance, provincial and lower-level governments in Guangdong and elsewhere were able to finance their investment projects with a source of revenue which was less noticeable and therefore less subject to scrutiny and control from the centre.

Decentralization in investment administration

Along with the 1980 fiscal reform came the devolution of planning
authority in various areas, including investment administration, to the
Guangdong provincial government. Fiscal and planning reforms
went hand in hand. The *dabaogan* system required Guangdong to be
responsible, in theory, for all provincial expenditures, including investment expenditure. As Guangdong's more 'aggressive' fiscal system
gave it a higher degree of fiscal autonomy than most other provinces,
the effect of planning reforms was correspondingly more conspicuous
in Guangdong than elsewhere.

From 1980, with the institution of the *dabaogan* fiscal system, the
entire planning system between Guangdong and the centre became a
'province-based' system. A major difference from the previous centralized system was that the central ministries, as noted in Chapter 2, ceased
issuing detailed and mandatory orders instructing provincial governments to invest how much at what time and in what area. From the
central government's point of view, the slackening of sectoral control
represented an adjustment in the relative power of the ministries (*tiao-
tiao*) and the provinces (*kuai-kuai*), which was, after all, the essence of
the post-1978 liberalization reforms. Nevertheless, decentralization
did not mean total withdrawal of central control. The central government did not intend to abandon control entirely and the State Planning Commission continued to prescribe quotas of yearly investments
for provinces, and Guangdong's investment plans, like those of other
provinces, were still required to be submitted to the centre for approval. The central government also controlled the total amount of
bank finance via mandatory control figures issued every year. One new
rule of the game under the new system was, however, that the centre
was expected to accept the investment plans proposed from below.[24]
In other words, the province became the major player and the formal
power of the central government receded by a considerable extent.

In addition to the abolition of the sectoral control figures, the extensive devolution of project approval authority to the provinces also
played an important role in the constitution of a 'province-based'
planning system. Specifically, as discussed in Chapter 2, it was this
aspect of decentralization that enabled provincial governments to
circumvent central control on the scale of investment. As provincial
governments were authorized to approve more and ever larger-scale
investment projects, the centre was confronted with ever more *fait*

accompli situations whereby it was forced to recognize the legitimacy of projects which had been approved by provincial and lower-level governments but which fell outside the state plan and central quotas on the scale of investment.

Prior to the nationwide decentralization of approval authority in 1984, which increased the ceiling of provincial approval authority to projects of up to 30 million yuan, Guangdong's authority had already been enlarged under the auspices of the central government's preferential policy for Guangdong. In 1981, to complement the enhanced authority conferred on Guangdong and Fujian under the 1979 Special Policy,[25] the two provincial governments were authorized to approve medium-sized and large projects, which had previously required the approval of the State Planning Commission (as was then still the case in other provinces), other than projects which still required the State Council's approval. The only precondition of this authority was that the two provinces be solely responsible for all aspects of investment, from funding to construction materials, exclusive of assistance from the centre.[26] In November 1982, Guangdong and Fujian were further authorized to approve investment projects of up to 30 million yuan. This was a full two years ahead of the nationwide decentralization move in 1984.[27]

Then, shortly after the nationwide decentralization in October 1984, Guangdong and Fujian again received preferential treatment when, in March 1985, the Special Policy for the two provinces was extended for another five years. The Centre was apparently quite satisfied with developments in Guangdong and Fujian, and the power of Guangdong and Fujian provincial governments to approve investment projects was raised from 30 million yuan to 200 million.[28] This meant that the entire jurisdiction of the State Planning Commission was delegated to the two provincial governments, a privilege which was only conferred on Shanghai in 1992 for projects in Pudong, and which no other provincial-level governments had ever been granted.[29] Apart from investments in 'bottleneck' sectors, namely, the energy, transportation and raw materials sectors, for which the authority of all provincial governments was raised to 50 million yuan in March 1987,[30] the jurisdiction for other types of investments in provincial governments other than Guangdong and Fujian remained unchanged at the 30 million yuan limit.[31]

The extent of the delegation of project approval authority is vividly reflected in the volume of planning documents submitted annually by

Guangdong to the central government. As an informed source described the situation, previously whole cartons of materials were sent to Beijing for scrutiny and approval each year. These were gradually reduced to only a few volumes by the late 1980s.[32] Apparently, since more investment projects had had their planning and approval procedures completed within the province, there was increasingly less to be reported to the centre.

Extensive subdelegation of authority

An important feature of Guangdong's reforms in the 1980s was the extent of delegation to the subprovincial levels. Extensive subdelegation to lower levels had the effect of magnifying the impact of the original decentralization at the central–provincial nexus. Although delegating authority to cities and counties might appear to be a measure which would deplete the power of the provincial government, in the final analysis it could not but work to strengthen further the position of the provincial government *vis-à-vis* the central government. The dynamics of subdelegation strongly suggest that power between governments at different levels is not of a zero-sum nature.

The Fiscal System

The 1980 fiscal reform at the central–provincial interface initiated a wave of subprovincial fiscal reforms which to a large extent mirrored the reform at the central–provincial level. By the late 1980s, the majority of governments at grassroots administrative level, in townships and villages, had entered into some kind of fiscal contractual arrangement with their county superiors, who, in turn, had similar arrangements with the cities.[33] Whilst the details of fiscal systems differed across the many localities within the province, the spirit of the reform was nevertheless the same: to instil a sense of financial security and responsibility at the local level so as to give it the incentive to solve its own financial problems and develop the local economy.

Such extensive subdelegation of fiscal autonomy was not, however, the product of some preconceived grand plan of the provincial government. Initially after 1980, the fiscal system at subprovincial levels was still operating along traditional lines, whereby the provincial government would negotiate a certain percentage share of the fiscal revenue collected at the lower levels. Although more discretionary money was granted to counties and cities, the fiscal system between

the provincial government and the cities, and between the cities and
the counties, was still that of the 'common bowl'. There was no financial security at subprovincial levels, and therefore no incentive to increase revenue. Between 1980 and 1984 total provincial fiscal revenue
grew at only half the rate of national income. This apparently alarmed
the provincial government and forced it to admit that it, too, had to
allow its lower levels more financial autonomy, as it had been allowed
by the centre. In 1985 five new fiscal arrangements were introduced at
subprovincial levels. The counties and cities were, in turn, authorized
and encouraged to subdelegate authority to the townships (Wang
Yaming 1989: 14).[34]

As a result of this subdelegation, local governments' remittances to
the provincial coffers dropped from a 33 per cent share of total provincial fiscal revenue in 1980 to only 20 per cent in 1988 (Wang Yaming
1989: 15). In other words, while Guangdong's *dabaogan* contract with
the central government effectively retained more fiscal revenue within
the province, a large portion of that retained fiscal revenue was in fact
retained at city, county and township levels. The extension of the fiscal
contractual scheme to the subprovincial levels thus accentuated the
diffusion of financial resources. As fiscal reform at the central–
provincial level strengthened the autonomy of the provincial government, the replication of such reform at subprovincial levels meant
that, as regards centre–Guangdong relations, the central government
was dealing not only with the provincial government, but also with a
multitude of local actors, each claiming their own interests and jealously guarding their autonomy and jurisdiction.

Investment administration

Decentralization of investment approval authority to cities and counties dates back to 1980. In 1980 Guangdong provincial government
announced that as long as the general policy on foreign investment
was complied with, and as long as the various production and marketing requirements of the projects did not affect the provincial overall
balance, then cities, districts and counties would be authorized to
approve foreign investment and outward processing projects. The
allocation of jurisdiction was: Guangzhou, US$5 million or below;
Hainan, US$3 million; all other districts, cities and bureau-level units,
US$1.5 million; counties, US$0.5 million (Guangdong Jingji Xuehui
1986: 121).

Power to approve domestic investment was also delegated. Before 1979, all investment projects of over 300,000 yuan had to be approved by the provincial government.[35] After 1979, when the provincial government was authorized to approve medium-sized to large projects as long as the province arranged the investment funds and materials for construction and subsequent production, the power of the subprovincials was also enhanced: Guangzhou could approve projects of up to 10 million yuan; Foshan, Jiangmen, Shantou, Zhuhai and Zhanjiang could approve projects of up to 5 million yuan, while for other district-level cities, the figure stood at 3 million yuan; for county-level cities, it was 1.5 million yuan; and for counties, 1 million yuan (Guangdong Jingji Xuehui 1986: 122). By September 1992 the extent of delegation reached the uppermost limit. City-level governments were authorized to approve projects of up to 30 million yuan, so long as no direct capital injection was required from the superior government.[36] This meant that the entirety of the jurisdiction of the provincial government which had been delegated by the centre was 'passed on' to the city level.

Authority to approve foreign-related investment was similarly delegated, and occurred at an even earlier time. In March 1992, the Guangdong government announced that it would delegate its authority in foreign investment projects entirely to city governments and departments directly subordinated to it. The counties would, in turn, be delegated the authority originally assigned at city level. As a result the cities and provincial bureaux were empowered to approve foreign investment projects of up to US$30 million, and county governments to approve foreign investment projects of up to US$15 million.[37] The consequence was that a large portion of investment activity would take place further away from the scrutiny of the central government. Successive delegation of approval authority for investment projects meant that most of the investment projects could be (and were) approved at city, county and even township level. Table 3.20 shows that for the period 1985–92, the share of subprovincial investment in Guangdong's state sector investment amounted to 62 per cent. Moreover this share exclusive of central investment amounted to a staggering 80 per cent.

The 'beauty' of subdelegation

It should be noted that such extensive subdelegation was not in line with directives from the centre. In a regulation issued by the State

TABLE 3.20. *Proportion of Subprovincial Investment in Guangdong's State Sector Investment* (%)[a]

Year	Proportion of subprovincial investment in local investment[b]	Proportion of subprovincial investment in total investment[c]
1985	86.0	66.9
1986[d]	64.9	48.0
1987	75.5	55.8
1988	81.6	65.4
1989	77.0	58.7
1990	77.6	59.4
1991	79.9	62.8
1992	82.2	66.1
1985–92	82.2	61.9

[a] These figures cover capital construction investment and technical renovation, and do not include other miscellaneous investments such as single-item purchases. Calculations are in accordance with the subordination relationship of the investment project, and do not take into account injection of provincial/central funds or the outflow of subprovincial funds to central/provincial projects.

[b] Local investment = provincial and subprovincial investment.

[c] Total investment = local investment plus central investment.

[d] 1986 figures include capital construction investment only.

Source: Guangdong Statistical Bureau (1985–93).

Planning Commission in 1978, it was announced that subsequent to the delineation of project approval authority between central and provincial governments, such authority should not be subdelegated to lower levels.[38] This was tersely reiterated in 1981 and 1983. The 1981 directive specified that approval authority was to remain at central government and provincial level only. Therefore subprovincials did not in theory have the power to approve investment plans and projects.[39] The 1983 statement made the reason for the official disapproval explicit: subdelegation contributed to runaway investment. As and when approval powers were delegated to levels below the province, and where the extent of delegation was more extensive, it was often much more difficult to control the level and allocation of investment.[40] This, of course, was exactly why subdelegation of authority had been so keenly expedited, and was so pertinent a factor in central–provincial politics in investment administration.

On the surface it is surprising that the centre could find it difficult to estimate how much investment was being carried out in the country. In theory, the planning authority of capital investment resided at only two levels: first, the central government, i.e. the level of the State Planning Commission and State Council; and secondly, the provincial-level government, and the central ministries.[41] Moreover, all investment projects should have been included in the state investment plans, which required the centre's approval. In practice, each level of administration would add its own projects to the plan approved at the higher levels. The widespread existence of outside-plan projects made the plan, and the original control figures, irrelevant. Not only were the control figures issued by the centre substantially exceeded, as Table 3.6 shows, but investment plans drawn up by the provincial government were utilized as the base upon which the subprovincial levels would plan their own additional projects, rather than as an authoritative document for implementation.[42]

Extensive subdelegation of provincial fiscal and planning authority to the subprovincial levels in Guangdong thus enabled the provincial government to multiply the benefits originally conferred by central policies. Fiscal subdelegation nurtured the incentive to invest, while planning decentralization allowed subprovincial governments a free hand to spend the new resources. Although such delegation was, strictly speaking, 'illegal' from a central point of view, the formal and open way in which subdelegation had occurred provided strong protection for outside-plan investments made under subdelegated powers. The Guangdong provincial government found it easy to ward off central pressure to cut provincial investment by claiming that a substantial portion of provincial investment had in fact been approved by the cities and counties, thus beyond its immediate sphere of control.[43] In this way, whilst outside-plan investment served as a tool with which to bargain for a higher control figure, subdelegation of fiscal and planning authority was a means to a defence of excess investment, as well as providing a venue for investment.[44]

NOTES

1. Prior to 1988 there were only 29 provinces (including provincial-level municipalities and autonomous regions) in China. In 1988 Hainan was separated from Guangdong and made a province of its own.
2. A total of 19, 22 and 23 projects were completed for 1990, 1991 and 1993 respectively, compared with 9, 4 and 8 projects in Shanghai; data for 1992 are not available (State Statistical Bureau 1992*b*: 27; *Statistical Yearbook of*

China 1994: 160). Before 1980, the total value of medium-sized to large investments in Guangdong had steadily accounted for a low percentage of the national total of around 3%. The share then rose, with some fluctuations during the 1980s, to over 10% in 1990 and 1991, and 7% for 1993 (calculated from Guangdong Statistical Bureau 1989*a*: 197; *Statistical Yearbook of Guangdong* 1991: 151, 1992: 153; *State Statistical Bureau* 1986: 70, 1991: 60; *Statistical Yearbook of China* 1994: 160).

3. See extracts from 'Report on Guangdong's 1989 Economic and Social Development Plan' by the director of Guangdong's Provincial Planning Commission, published in *Jihua Yu Fazhan* 1 (1989): 7.

4. Some investments, usually at local levels, were not reported to superiors and therefore were not included in the statistics. A former central official told the author that in his visits to the localities, he had discovered some 'unreported' investment projects which had never gone through the formal planning and approval procedures and were supposedly 'non-existent' in the state investment plans and in the investment statistics (interview, respondent no. 5, Guangzhou, Sept. 1993).

5. Interview, respondent no. 9, Guangzhou, Sept. 1993.

6. See State Planning Commission, State Economic Commission, and Finance Ministry, 'Supplementary Regulations on Domestic Joint Investments', 19 Dec. 1984, printed in State Statistical Bureau (1992*a*: 326).

7. It should be noted that before 1980 it was customary to have substantial inflows of central funds to locally subordinated investment projects. This was because under the traditional fiscal and planning system, revenues were highly centralized and the central government was responsible for the planning approval as well as the funding of the larger investment projects. However this has changed since 1980, especially in Guangdong which, with the new *dabaogan* system, has become responsible, in principle, for the planning and funding of most investment activities within the provincial borders. This must be taken into account when looking at statistics on central and local investment calculated according to subordination relations before and after 1980 (see Chap. 4 for more discussion on this point). In accordance with the new principle of division of responsibilities between centre and provinces, the amount of local investment by subordination is purportedly the same as the amount by source funding. This sets the scene for the following discussion on the cross-over of funds.

8. The necessity of such disaggregation was confirmed in an interview with respondent no. 4 (Guangzhou, Sept. 1993). Respondent no. 36 (interview, Beijing, May 1994) made it clear that foreign loans which were centrally co-ordinated did not imply a central injection of funds. The distinction between centrally or locally co-ordinated foreign loans referred to the method of arranging the loans. Centrally co-ordinated loans might enjoy a lower interest rate because of the type of loans normally dealt with by the centre

and its superior bargaining power with the lending parties. Nevertheless the loans would still be repaid by the user units, albeit via the centre, to the lending parties.

9. This pattern of capital inflow from the centre was also confirmed by respondent no. 4 (interview Guangzhou, Sept. 1993).

10. Interview, respondent no. 9, Guangzhou, Dec. 1993. It should be noted that before the 1994 tax reform, indirect taxes, for instance turnover taxes, of all central and local enterprises went to the local coffers where the enterprises were situated. After the reform 75% of the turnover taxes of all enterprises went to the central coffers, and 25% to the local coffers. See State Council Notice no. 85 (1993), 'State Council's Decision on Implementing the Tax-Sharing Fiscal Management System', printed in *Caizheng* 2 (1994): 18–20.

11. Interviews with respondents no. 4 and 6, Guangzhou, Sept. 1993. Interestingly, Guangdong officials did not seem very worried about the fact that the discrepancy between the two statistics revealed that the provincial government had been launching and financing outside-plan investments with money from the state coffers. Moreover, as the amount of inflow of central budgetary funds to Guangdong was very small, the discrepancy could be regarded as a fairly accurate indication of the portion of outside-plan investment directly conducted by the provincial government with budgetary money.

12. The statistic is calculated from data provided by the Provincial Planning Commission. The data basically cover the yearly investment plans endorsed by the centre. Hence it does not include 'budgetary investment' in projects which are not listed in the plans (interview, respondent no. 4, Guangzhou, Sept. 1993).

13. This was confirmed by respondent no. 4 (interview, Guangzhou, Sept. 1993). This classification was considered to make sense although fiscal revenues had been used. Given the *dabaogan* fiscal system in Guangdong, local fiscal revenues from the provincial budget had been regarded as 'own funds' of the provincial government from the provincial planning perspective. A research report by the State Planning Commission in Beijing also stated that the 'own funds' in the source of investment funds mainly included two types of funding: (1) fiscal investment expenditure coming from the budgets of the local governments, and (2) funds raised from society by various means. See Li Fan and Zheng Xiao-he (1991: 83).

14. Provincial governments have had much more autonomy in the allocation of local budgetary funds since the 1980 fiscal reform, so that a comprehensive statistic of investment financed with budgetary funds would not be able to highlight the differences between centre and provinces over investment decisions, unless the statistic could be further disaggregated into those investments financed by central budgetary funds and those

financed by provincial budgetary funds. On the other hand, the state investment plan, both before and since the 1980s, has always required the approval of the central government, with investment projects not included in the plan being outside-plan investment. By reflecting the latter measure, the budgetary investment statistic highlights the conflicts between a control instrument of the centre and investment implementation by the provinces.

15. This statement is made on the basis that state banks were closely associated with state finance and were not therefore independent of the state. 'Own funds' of enterprises were boosted in the first place because the state cut taxes, the amount being arbitrarily decided by the government. Also, as noted above, some of the 'own funds' were actually budgetary funds of provincial and lower-level governments.

16. Respondent no. 4 (interview, Guangzhou, May 1993) revealed that there remained irregularities and 'diversities' in the collection of data for the 'other' category. This aggregated category was often used as a dumping ground for 'illegal' and unorthodox funding so as to evade supervision and queries from superior levels. The sudden increase in investment capital obtained through the securities market was included in the 'other' category in some localities, and in 'own funds' in others.

17. This was the case until 1988.

18. This amount included the amount of fiscal remittance as defined by the fiscal system, as well as the part of fiscal revenue extracted by the centre in addition to the agreed sum, for instance, in the form of intergovernmental 'loans', Treasury bonds and new taxes.

19. Total Guangdong fiscal revenue means the total amount of fiscal revenue collected from Guangdong. This includes revenue collected by the provincial government as well as that collected directly by the central government, e.g. from central enterprises in Guangdong and from tariffs and customs.

20. Figures reported in *Wen Wei Po* (Hong Kong), 9 Mar. 1991.

21. Speech given by the director of Guangdong's Finance Bureau on 16 Jan. 1993 during a provincial financial conference, reported in *Guangdong Caizheng* 1 (1993): 7.

22. Interview, respondent no. 6, Guangzhou, Sept. 1993.

23. It should be noted that in Chinese accounting, fiscal expenditure on education and health, etc. normally does not include those fixed asset investment expenditures spent on the construction of schools or hospitals. These investment expenditures are entered under the categories of capital construction, technical renovation or miscellaneous investment. Guangdong's fiscal expenditure on education and health from 1987 to 1991, in billion yuan, was 2.29, 2.60, 3.32, 3.53 and 3.98 respectively, while fiscal expenditure on investment for the same period was 2.05, 2.62, 2.64, 2.96 and 3.62 billion yuan. See Ministry of Finance (1992: 157).

24. Interview, respondent no. 1, Guangzhou, May 1993.

25. The Special Policy is discussed in more detail in Chap. 5.
26. Central Committee Document no. 27 (1981), 'Approving the Notes of Work Conference of Guangdong, Fujian and the Special Economic Zones', 19 July 1981, printed in State Commission for Economic System Reform (1983: 558–66). See also Dangdai Zhongguo Congshu Bianji Bu (1989*b*: ii. 481).
27. Central Committee Report, 'On the Implementation of the "Special Policy" in Guangdong and Fujian, and the Operation of Special Economic Zones', 15 Nov. 1982, in Guangdong Provincial Party Committee (1986–88: i. 406).
28. State Council Notice no. 46 (1985), 'On Approving the Notes of Meeting on Extending the Special Policy of Guangdong and Fujian', 28 Mar. 1985, printed in Guangdong Provincial Party Committee (1986–88: ii. 377–85).
29. The question here is whether or not the central government has ever conferred formal authorization. The 'contraction' of delegated powers during the retrenchment years is not the issue. It was revealed during field interviews that most provincial-level governments, if not all, had been exercising *de facto* approval power of up to 200 million yuan since the second half of 1992, without formal endorsement and authorization from the centre.
30. State Council Notice no. 23 (1987), 'On the Extension of Project Approval Authority of Fixed Asset Investment and the Simplification of Approval Procedures', 30 Mar. 1987, printed in State Statistical Bureau (1992*a*: 111–17). See also the discussion in Chap. 2.
31. Shanghai has been excluded here, as Shanghai's authority was formally raised to 200 million yuan in 1992. See the discussion in Chap. 4.
32. Interview, respondent no. 1, Guangzhou, May 1993.
33. Over 70% of rural townships in Guangdong entered into some kind of fiscal contractual arrangements with the counties in 1988, indicating the thoroughness of the extension of the *dabaogan* fiscal system throughout the province. See Wu Yixin (1990: 127).
34. See also Wu Yixin (1990: 127) for a description of the five types of fiscal regimes which the provincial government entered into with five groups of cities/districts in 1985. These five types were: (1) Shenzhen, Zhuhai and Swatow Special Economic Zones: to retain all fiscal revenue for local use; (2) Guangzhou, the provincial capital: to retain 60% of the surplus revenue after remitting a fixed lump sum; (3) Foshan and four other cities with a surplus in local revenue: a base figure of remittance and incremental increase for subsequent years, ranging from 4% to 7%; (4) the 'deficit' areas: a fixed lump-sum as subsidy; (5) minority areas: a fixed lump-sum as subsidy, to be increased by 10% per annum.
35. Guangdong Planning Commission, Economic Institute, 'Guangdong Touzi Lingyu de Jihua yu Shichang' (Plan and Market in the Investment Arena of Guangdong), in State Planning Commission (1992: 69).

36. See Guangdong Provincial Government Notice no. 131 (1992), in *Guangdong Zhengbao* 9 (1992): 46.

37. *Nanfang Ribao*, 5 May 1992, 1. The extract of the formal government notice, Guangdong Provincial Government Secretariat Notice no. 36, is published in *Guangdong Zhengbao* 5 (1992): 11.

38. 'Notice by the State Planning Commission, State Construction Commission, and Ministry of Finance on Regulations (Trial) on the Procedures of Capital Construction', 22 Apr. 1978, printed in State Planning Commission (1985: 121–9).

39. State Council, 'Regulations on Strengthening the System of Capital Construction Administration and Controlling the Level of Investment', 3 Mar. 1981, printed in State Planning Commission (1987*b*: 556–8).

40. State Planning Commission, 'Report on Controlling the Level of Investment and Reducing the Number of Investment Projects under Construction', 22 Oct. 1983, printed in State Planning Commission (1987*b*: 584–6).

41. The provincial level and the sectoral central ministries are of the same administrative ranking; their jurisdiction in investment project approval is therefore the same in most cases.

42. An informed respondent told the author that very often even the provincial governments themselves did not know how much investment was actually taking place within the provinces. For instance, Shunde city was supposed to have 100 million yuan of investment in Guangdong's 1992 provincial investment plan. The total amount of investment undertaken in Shunde that year was actually more than 1 billion yuan, ten times the province's planned value (interview, respondent no. 2, Guangzhou, May 1993).

43. In one provincial report on Guangdong's industrial structure, the author grouped the investments planned by the centre and by the provincial government together as one category, as opposed to the 'local investments' by the subprovincial governments. In this way the provincial government put itself in the same camp as the centre, thus being able to put the blame for problematic local investment on the lower-level governments. See The Project Group, 'The Adjustment of Guangdong's Industrial Structure and Deepening of Economic System Reform', in Xiao Ruchuan (1991: 267).

44. Guangdong and some other provinces argued for a higher quota at a time when the central government was pushing for austerity. The argument put forward was that outside-plan investment which had been completed earlier in the year had already used up a substantial portion of the central quotas to the provinces. Such investment being *fait accompli*, there would be great hardship if projects within the state plan and considered essential were to be discontinued. Therefore it was necessary to adjust the central control figures upwards (State Planning Commission, 'Report on Controlling the Level of Investment').

4 Investment in Shanghai: Central Policy and Provincial Implementation

The industrialization and commercialization of the Shanghai economy earlier in the century has led to descriptions of Shanghai as the 'other China'. Its modern and cosmopolitan orientation was a stark contrast to the agrarian and inward-looking orientation of most parts of the country. Its wealth also caused hostility and suspicion within both the bureaucratic and the revolutionary forces of China, especially since its economy flourished largely under the protection of the foreign treaty powers (Bergère 1981). After 1949, this 'one-step-ahead' economic development nevertheless gave Shanghai a peculiarly important place in the construction of a socialist economy. As a result of the nationalization of Shanghai's industry between 1955 and 1956,[1] this previously most developed hub of capitalism and private enterprise had became the centre of gravity of the central planning system.[2]

Until the 1990s Shanghai was the highest contributor of national revenue amongst the provincial-level administrations and generated roughly one-seventh of the total national fiscal revenue. From 1953 to 1980, Shanghai generated over 280 billion yuan, or 14 per cent of the cumulative total national fiscal revenue, while Guangdong generated only 43 billion yuan, 2.7 per cent of the national total and less than one-sixth that of Shanghai.[3] The total profit and tax submitted by Shanghai's enterprises from 1949 to 1989 amounted to six times that of the total value of their fixed assets at original prices, and its export trade accounted for one-quarter of the national total (Shanghai Statistical Bureau 1989: 77). Politically, its leaders have always been part of national politics. Shanghai's leaders in the early years, for instance Chen Yi and Ke Qingshi,[4] were all central government figures posted in Shanghai. Later Zhang Chunqiao, Yao Wenyun and Wang Hongwen became central leaders during the Cultural Revolution. And in the 1990s Shanghai's leaders, Jiang Zemin, Zhu Rongji, Wu Bangguo and Huang Ju, all rose to national power.

It has been argued that, given Shanghai's importance in the national economy, its leaders were more subject to the pull of central politics than leaders of other provinces were.[5] Did the historical importance of Shanghai affect its relations with the centre in the era of decentralization and reform beginning in 1979? How did the new environment of the post-Mao reform era affect Shanghai's relationship with the centre? How did Shanghai compare with Guangdong as regards central–provincial relations? These are the general questions which this case study of Shanghai seeks to answer. This chapter will first discuss the contextual information regarding investment implementation in Shanghai. The purpose is to map out the institutional context of central-Shanghai political processes to prepare the way for a discussion of Shanghai's discretionary behaviour and central-Shanghai interactions in Chapters 6 and 7.

INVESTMENT IN SHANGHAI

On the eve of reform in the late 1970s Shanghai's investment was at a higher base than that of Guangdong, but thereafter grew at a sluggish rate. Funding for investment had become diversified, in line with the nationwide trend, but throughout the 1980s Shanghai was remarkably more reliant on central investment than was Guangdong, and the share of investment financed by the state budget in Shanghai was also significantly larger.

Trailing performance

At the beginning of the 1980s, Shanghai's investment was at a much higher base than Guangdong, Shanghai having invested 30 per cent more during the previous 30 years than had Guangdong, as Table 4.1 shows.

TABLE 4.1. *Total Investment in Shanghai and Guangdong, 1950–1980* (billion yuan)

Period	Shanghai	Guangdong
1950–2	0.29	0.16
1953–7	1.93	1.28
1958–62	5.56	4.26
1963–5	2.03	1.99
1966–70	3.48	2.60
1971–5	9.58	6.12
1976–80	15.14	12.87
1950–80	38.01	29.28

Sources: Statistical Yearbook of Shanghai (1980: 271);
Guangdong Statistical Bureau (1989a: 158–61).

Table 4.1 also shows that between 1950 and 1980 Shanghai had a consistent lead over Guangdong and by 1980 the cumulative difference amounted to 30 per cent of Guangdong's total investment. This was despite the fact that many factories in Shanghai were moved inland during the 1950s under a central policy at that time to develop the inland economy.[6] Its industrial infrastructure and highly educated workforce apparently led the centre to inject more resources into its industries than into those of Guangdong.[7]

However, during the 1980s, when the central government's experimental reforms gathered momentum in the southern provinces, the small lead which Shanghai had previously enjoyed was reversed. Shanghai's cumulative investment during the period 1981–93 was just over 50 per cent of Guangdong's. Table 4.2 shows that in 1993, Guangdong's total annual investment amounted to 2.5 times that of Shanghai.

This situation resulted from slower growth rates in investment during the 1980s, as indicated in Table 4.3. Table 4.3 shows that in ten of the fourteen years between 1980 and 1993, Shanghai's total investment grew more slowly than that in Guangdong. Investment in Shanghai grew at an annual average rate of 25 per cent, which was on a par with the national average, but substantially below that of Guangdong. More notably, despite having obtained a more favourable fiscal arrangement with the centre in 1988, and the centre having announced the Pudong policies in 1990, the rate of investment growth in Shanghai in 1991 and 1992 was still far short of the national average, not to mention that of Guangdong. Guangdong's investment performance

TABLE 4.2. *Total Investment in Shanghai and Guangdong, 1981–1993* (billion yuan)

Period	Shanghai	Guangdong
1981–5	41.28	54.88
1986–90	102.04	154.10
1991	25.83	47.82
1992	35.74	92.18
1993	65.39	162.99
Total	270.28	511.97

Sources: Statistical Yearbook of Guangdong (1993: 236, 1994: 219); *Statistical Yearbook of Shanghai* (1989: 271, 1990: 260, 1992: 281, 1993: 244, 1994: 72).

TABLE 4.3. *Shanghai's Total Investment: Annual Growth Rates* (%)

Year	Shanghai	Guangdong	National
1980	28.8	35.4	n/a
1981	20.2	57.7	n/a
1982	30.7	40.3	28.0
1983	6.4	4.7	16.2
1984	21.5	47.0	28.2
1985	28.5	41.6	38.7
1986	23.9	17.3	18.7
1987	26.8	16.0	20.6
1988	31.7	40.9	23.5
1989	−12.4	−1.8	−8.0
1990	5.7	7.3	7.5
1991	13.7	28.3	23.8
1992	38.4	92.8	42.6
1993	83.0	76.8	58.6
Average, 1980–93	24.8	36.0	—
Average, 1982–93	24.8	34.3	24.9

Source: *Statistical Yearbook of Shanghai* (1989: 271, 1990: 238, 1991: 260, 1992: 280, 1993: 244, 1994: 72).

in 1992, the year of Deng Xiaoping's Southern Tour, was particularly spectacular. That year total investment grew by 93 per cent, more than double the growth rate in Shanghai and nationally. Moreover, investment in Shanghai contracted on a larger scale during the 1989 national retrenchment drive (at minus 12.4 per cent) than was the case nationally (minus 8 per cent) and when compared with Guangdong's modest dive (minus 1.8 per cent). This suggests that, contrary to what happened in Guangdong, Shanghai's investment during the 1980s was more prone to contract than expand, even when the stimuli for both growth and contraction came from the same origin: the centre.

Table 4.4 gives a brief summary of Shanghai's investment performance *vis-à-vis* Guangdong's. It shows that the lead Shanghai enjoyed over Guangdong prior to 1980 was thereafter reversed. Guangdong tops the list of provincial-level jurisdictions as regards the value of its total investment since 1988, whilst Shanghai trails far behind between fourth and seventh positions. From 1988, Shanghai has moved down

TABLE 4.4. *Shanghai and Guangdong: Total Investment Compared* (billion yuan)

Period	Shanghai (S)	Guangdong (G)	Lead
1950–80	38.0	29.28	(S over G) 8.73
1981–93	270.28	511.97	(G over S) 241.69
1950–93	308.29	541.25	(G over S) 232.96

Source: Calculated from data in previous tables.

in the ranking one position annually, having been overtaken by Shandong, Zhejiang, Jiangsu, Sichuan and, recently, Liaoning.[8]

Lingering state dominance

The proliferation of actors in the field of investment was a nationwide phenomenon. Nonetheless Shanghai's investment had three particular characteristics. First, the state sector continued its predominance, with the non-state sector growing more slowly than in Guangdong and nationally. Secondly, the central government played a far more active part in Shanghai's investment than in Guangdong. Third, whilst funding for investment had diversified substantially, money from the state budget still accounted for a higher proportion of total funding than was the case in Guangdong, and the eventual drop in this proportion was not until much later. All these factors point to the conclusion that the grip of the central state via the traditional planning mechanism on investment and other economic activities was much stronger and more persistent in Shanghai than in Guangdong.

Continuing central dominance

In contrast to the marginalization of central investment in Guangdong from the 1980s, central investment in post-1980 Shanghai was resilient. Table 4.5 depicts the different proportions of central and local investment in the state sector since 1950.

Table 4.5 shows that from 1981 to 1985 the share of central investment in Shanghai surged nearly 20 percentage points to account for half of state sector investment before subsiding in later years. During the 1981–93 period central investment accounted for 36 per cent of total investment in the state sector, as compared with a 31 per cent share during 1950–80. It was interesting that central investment should have

TABLE 4.5. *Central and Local Investment in
Shanghai* (% share)[a]

Period	Central investment	Local investment
1950–2	52.1	47.9
1953–7	70.0	30.0
1958–62	15.8	84.2
1963–5	29.2	70.8
1966–70	27.1	72.9
1971–5	24.0	76.0
1976–80	30.4	69.6
1981–5	49.8	50.2
1986–90	29.3	70.7
1991	36.1	63.9
1992	27.3	72.7
1993	24.2	75.8
Total		
1950–80	31.3	68.7
1981–93	36.4	63.6

[a] Statistics for 1950–77 include capital construction only, as capital construction accounted for the bulk of state sector investments (from more than 80 per cent in the 1950s to more than 60 per cent in the 1970s) and no data of this kind are available for technical renovation.

Source: Computed from *Statistical Yearbook of Shanghai* (1993: 248 and 259, 1994: 72).

become more important to Shanghai during the 1980s when the national trend elsewhere was towards decentralization of power and resources to the provinces. When looking more closely at the capital construction portion of investment, it becomes clear that the part played by the central government increased, and that the upward trend of central participation in Shanghai's capital construction investment persisted through to the end of the 1980s (as shown in Table 4.6).

When this issue of the heavy share of central investment was raised with Shanghai officials during interviews, they invariably cautioned against too simplified an interpretation of the statistics. First, they stressed that the calculation of proportions according to the subordination relations of the projects might be misleading as regards the extent of central influence over Shanghai's investment activities. This was because other factors, such as the planning system and the

TABLE 4.6. *Central Investment in Capital Construction*

Year	% share
1981–5	66.0
1986	49.6
1987	55.3
1988	62.8
1989	60.5
1990	61.0
1986–90	58.6
1991	50.5
1992	34.7
1993	30.1
1991–3	35.6

Source: *Statistical Yearbook of Shanghai* (1991: 264, 1993: 248, 1994: 74).

funding arrangement of investment, also had a significant effect on the pendulum of power between the centre and the municipality. Secondly, it was suggested that a substantial part of local investment had not been included in the official statistics, so that the share of central investments was artifically inflated.[9]

As regards the first point, the shares of central and local investment calculated according to the subordination relations of projects undertaken are undoubtedly only a rough indication of the balance of central/provincial influence over investment in a province. Subordination relations assigned the detailed management of projects to different levels of the government. The extent of power the government department-in-charge had over projects was, however, dependent also on a host of other factors. This point is also apparent in the case of Guangdong. Discussion in Chapter 3 regarding the effect of the extensive decentralization of investment powers in the 1980s suggested that one should not interpret the heavy share of local investment in Guangdong after 1958 in the same way as one would interpret the similar situation in the 1980s and 1990s. The centralized planning and fiscal systems before 1980 ensured that even though projects and enterprises had been delegated to local administration, the centre still retained a high degree of control over planning and approval of investment, as well as over the allocation of resources which made investment possible in the first place. Caution is therefore necessary when interpreting Tables 4.5 and 4.6. As one respondent explained to the author, due to changes in funding channels the extent of central control over central investment projects had changed considerably since the early to mid-1980s. The proliferation of funding channels towards the end of the 1980s had reduced the centre's grip even when the project concerned was a central project, as the local economy and the Shanghai government played a more active role in 'supporting' central investment projects.[10]

Caution and prudence notwithstanding, it is important not to under-estimate the significance of these statistics. First, given the national policy of decentralization in the 1980s and the nationwide trend of proliferation of investment actors, it is noteworthy that such a high percentage of Shanghai's investment was under the administrative jurisdiction of the central government. The high percentage of central funds in Shanghai's investment is an indication of the high degree of central involvement in Shanghai's investment activity. Secondly, evid-ence exists that most central investment projects in the 1981–5 period were directly financed by the central government budget, whether in the form of central budgetary funds or planned loans under the quotas of the central ministries. This means that for the first half of the 1980s at least, the high percentage shares of central investment are a fairly accurate reflection of the extent of central control over investment in Shanghai.

Under-reporting was probably a common practice nationwide and its extent is, therefore, difficult to gauge. Under-reporting actually en-compassed three types of situation. First was the conscious decision of provincial governments deliberately to conceal information from the centre. In such cases data for projects was actually available in the provincial government files, but these data were not included in yearly investment plans and reports submitted to the centre, or in official stat-istics. The second type was a development corresponding to the first type at subprovincial levels *vis-à-vis* the provincial level: subprovincial governments did to the provincial governments as provincial govern-ments did to the centre so as not to appear to be disobeying orders and flouting planning limits assigned from above. Such a practice might exist at every level of the hierarchy from the lowest grassroots level of enterprise. The third type of under-reporting was due to the methods of collection of statistics and data on investment activities. Owing to a lack of personnel or inadequacy in management, some investment activities, usually those small in scale or occurring in remote places where management standards were the weakest, never entered the statistical books or files at any level of government.[11] It is obvious that the largest area of under-reporting within provincial statistics was that of local investment. One respondent explicitly stated that official statistics were compiled in accordance with the planning control figure of total investment handed down from the centre every year. The total value of investment as shown in the statistics would be made to appear roughly equivalent to the value endorsed by the centre, allowing a reasonable, though not too wide, margin to account for the narrower coverage of the planning control figures.[12]

The magnitude by which local investment was under-reported is difficult to ascertain. Obviously no such data would be made available whilst the provinces and lower levels still felt the need to engage in such a practice. Nonetheless, by comparing the absolute amount of central investment in Shanghai and Guangdong, it is beyond doubt that Shanghai had far more central investment in absolute terms (Table 4.7).

TABLE 4.7. *Central Investment in the State Sector: Shanghai and Guangdong* (billion yuan)

Year	Shanghai	Guangdong
1981		0.94
1982		1.33
1983	16.10	1.42
1984		1.99
1985		8.32
1986	4.22	3.25
1987	6.06	4.02
1988	8.29	4.40
1989	7.79	4.78
1990	7.54	5.84
1991	7.37	6.49
1992	7.01	9.86
1993	12.20	15.64
Total	76.58	62.60

Sources: Guangdong Statistical Bureau (1989*a*: 172); Guangdong Statistical Bureau (1985–93: 1989–92 vols.); *Statistical Yearbook of Guangdong* (1994: 219); *Statistical Yearbook of Shanghai* (1991: 264, 1993: 248 and 259, 1994: 72).

There is a connection between the resilience of central investment in Shanghai and the apparent use of under-reporting in the compilation of investment statistics within Shanghai. The fact that Shanghai was more reliant than Guangdong on central investment suggests that Shanghai officials were more obliged than their Guangdong counterparts to report an investment total which did not far exceed the central control figure.[13] The concern was that central investment was, in theory, more subject to central control than was local investment. In the event of an investment clampdown, Shanghai could thus be hit harder than other provinces where central investment was less important.[14] One way of avoiding such a scenario was to under-report investment in official statistics, by under-reporting those investment projects which did not require planning permission from the centre, namely, local investment.

Funding channels

Funding of investment in Shanghai was characterized by a relatively high proportion of budgetary funds, foreign capital and bank loans and, in contrast to Guangdong, a lower share of 'own funds' and other miscellaneous sources. Table 4.8 shows the cumulative position from 1983 to 1992.

Table 4.8 shows that although the cumulative value of Shanghai's state sector investment was only three-fourths of Guangdong's, the absolute value of investment using budgetary funds and domestic bank

TABLE 4.8. *Funding Channels of State sector Investment in Shanghai, 1983–1992*

Channel	Billion yuan		%share	
	Shanghai	Guangdong	Shanghai	Guangdong
Budget	14.74	12.72	8.50	5.48
Bank loans	58.56	57.46	27.29	24.76
Foreign capital	30.54	35.15	19.02	15.15
Own funds and others	71.50	126.72	44.52	54.61
Total	175.34	232.05	100.00	100.00

Sources: *Statistical Yearbook of Shanghai* (1983–93); Guangdong Statistical Bureau (1989*a*:89); *Statistical Yearbook of Guangdong* (1991: 195, 1992: 231, 1993: 237).

loans was 3 billion yuan more than that of Guangdong. The proportional share of foreign capital is also almost 4 percentage points higher, despite the fact that Guangdong took the lead in the Open Door Policy and had been successful in attracting direct foreign investments. A more detailed look at the figures suggests that the higher share of investment using budgetary funds, foreign capital and bank loans is related to the high proportion of central investment (Table 4.9).

Table 4.9 shows that Guangdong started off with a higher share of budgetary investment in 1983, but that this share rapidly and consistently declined over the years. Five years later in 1987, the share of budgetary investment in Guangdong was only about one-third that of 1983. On the other hand, budgetary investment in Shanghai was resilient. Between 1983 and 1987, the share of budgetary investment was generally on an upward trend, climbing from 13.6 per cent in 1983 to 17.8 per cent in 1987—more than 10 percentage points higher than Guangdong's 7.6 per cent share the same year. It was only in 1989 that the budgetary investment share declined, abruptly, falling 7.5 percentage points to the same level in Guangdong at 5.5 per cent.

Tables 4.5 and 4.9 together show that the period during which Shanghai's budgetary investment increased was precisely the time when central investment surged in Shanghai. Table 4.10 provides the

TABLE 4.9. *Budgetary Investment in the State Sector* (% share)

Year	National	Shanghai	Guangdong
1983	34.9	13.6	22.6
1984	34.2	15.2	17.0
1985	23.9	12.9	10.6
1986	22.1	15.0	11.7
1987	20.5	17.8	7.6
1988	14.8	13.0	4.8
1989	13.3	5.5	5.5
1990	13.1	5.6	4.4
1991	10.1	4.5	3.3
1992	6.2	4.0	1.9
1993	6.0	n/a	1.9

Sources: Guangdong Statistical Bureau (1989*a*: 89); *Statistical Yearbook of Guangdong* (1991–4); *Statistical Yearbook of Shanghai* (1983–94); *Statistical Yearbook of China* (1993: 146 and 149, 1994: 144); State Statistical Bureau (1986, 1989, 1991, 1993).

data suggesting the extent of the contribution from the central government to Shanghai's budgetary investment.

Comparing Table 4.10 with Table 3.13, it can be seen that the overall discrepancy ratio in Guangdong during 1987–91, 137 per cent, is much higher than the 22 per cent in Shanghai. Table 4.10 thus conveys

TABLE 4.10. *Discrepancy Between Budgetary Investment and Local Fiscal Investment Expenditure in Shanghai* (million yuan)

Year	Budgetary investment[a]	Local fiscal investment expenditure	Discrepancy[b] Total	%[c]
1952	141	91	−50	−35.5
1957	330	132	−198	−60.0
1962	169	145	−24	−14.2
1965	283	336	53	18.7
1970	521	731	210	40.3
1978	1,139	1,601	462	40.6
1980	1,222	890	−332	−27.2
1981	1,008	887	−121	−12.0
1982	733	914	181	24.7
1983	821	1,030	209	25.5
1984	1,063	1,620	557	52.4
1985	1,194	2,364	1,170	98.0
1986	1,777	2,773	996	56.0
1987	2,930	1,747	−1183	−40.3
1988	2,712	2,397	−315	−11.6
1989	945	2,291	1,346	142.4
1990	1,106	2,123	1,017	92.0
1991	1,044	2,107	1,063	101.8
1992	1,147	2,247	1,100	50.0
Total				
1981–92	16,480	22,500	6,020	36.5
1987–91	8,787	10,665	1,928	21.9

[a] State sector only, and prior to 1983, capital construction only.

[b] Amount of local fiscal, that is, budgetary investment expenditures over the value of budgetary investments as shown in the statistics of investment by types of funding.

[c] Absolute discretionary value as a percentage of budgetary investment.

Sources: Fiscal expenditure: *Statistical Yearbook of Shanghai* (1993: 56. Budgetary investment: before 1983, *Statistical Yearbook of Shanghai* (1986: 243); From 1983, *Statistical Yearbook of Shanghai* (1983: 219, 1984: 133, 1986: 242, 1987: 232, 1988: 244, 1989: 274, 1990: 239, 1991: 261, 1992: 281, 1993: 245).

two important pieces of information. First, it shows that, in Shanghai as in Guangdong, the amount of provincial budgetary revenue spent on investment was larger than the value of investment recorded in the official statistics as having been financed by budgetary funds. As discussed in Chapter 3, this indicates that the governments of both Guangdong and Shanghai were involved in outside-plan investment, although the more modest difference in the case of Shanghai suggested that the extent of such engagement might be smaller. Secondly, the relatively modest difference in Shanghai's figures is largely a result of two years' negative discrepancy in 1987 and 1988, which served to cancel out a substantial portion of the positive discrepancy in other years. When looking at the years 1990 and 1991, the discrepancy percentage in Shanghai was not much less than that of Guangdong, and in 1989 it even marginally surpassed Guangdong's.

In Chapter 3 it was noted that, in theory, a negative discrepancy was the norm. This was because if local fiscal resources were spent strictly in accordance with the state investment plan, and given that there was normally some inflow of central budgetary funds, the amount of local fiscal spending on investment would be only a portion of the investment financed with budgetary funds, the balance of the portion depending on the amount of central inflow. However, in practice the opposite was the case. Table 4.10 shows that for the entire decade of the 1980s, negative discrepancy occurred in only three years. Data available in the 1960s and 1970s also recorded the frequent occurrence of positive discrepancies of some magnitude. This demonstrates that the Shanghai government for a long period of time actively engaged in outside-plan investments, the extent of which increased still further in the 1980s. Given this historical trend, the fact that a negative discrepancy recurred in 1987 and 1988 indicated a very substantial inflow of central budgetary funds. Taking into account the underlying trend of a positive discrepancy, the actual amount of central budgetary inflow was likely to be in excess of the discrepancy value.[15]

A dominant 'central factor' is also indicated in data available on the composition and allocation of foreign capital. Such data reveal that there were three major ways in which foreign loans were raised and arranged in terms of the involvement of the central government. First, the central government would arrange both the raising and repayment of the loan. Secondly, the centre would arrange the raising of the capital, but the user would repay the loan directly. Thirdly, the user both raised and repaid the loan directly exclusive of direct involvement

with the central government. The centre had the highest degree of involvement in the first type of foreign loans, which were often described
as being 'centrally co-ordinated'. It should be noted that in all three
cases the users were responsible for repaying the loans. In the case of
centrally co-ordinated loans, repayment would be via the central government ministry concerned. The second type was probably the most
beneficial of the three from the provincial perspective, since it allowed
provinces to make use of the superior bargaining power of the centre
in securing the loans whilst retaining most aspects of loan management for the provincial users.[16] There was, however, no statistical breakdown available for the second and third type of arrangement. The two
are thus lumped together in the following discussion as symbolizing a
high extent of provincial involvement.

Table 4.11 shows that over one-third of foreign capital used in state
sector investment between 1987 and 1992 was centrally co-ordinated.
It can be seen that the percentage shares stood at a very high level, at
over 60 per cent in 1987 and over 40 per cent until 1989, before drop-
ping substantially in the 1990s. Although data for earlier years are not
available, the trend of the available data suggests a high percentage for
the pre-1987 years. A contrast with Guangdong better illustrates the
picture, as Table 4.12 shows.

A comparison of Tables 4.11 and 4.12 shows that the amount of centrally co-ordinated foreign loans in Shanghai between 1987 and 1992
was nearly ten times that in Guangdong. Shanghai was consequently
more dependent on the central government for the supply of foreign

TABLE 4.11. *Centrally Co-ordinated Foreign Loans in
Foreign Capital: Shanghai's State Sector Investment*
(billion yuan)

Year	Foreign capital	Centrally co-ordinated	
		Total	% share
1987	3.60	2.20	61.11
1988	4.62	2.04	44.16
1989	3.74	1.60	42.78
1990	3.54	1.01	28.53
1991	3.74	0.99	26.47
1992	3.01	0.001	0.03
Total	22.25	7.84	35.24

Source: *Statistical Yearbook of Shanghai* (1988–93).

TABLE 4.12. *Centrally Co-ordinated foreign loans In Foreign Capital: Guangdong's State Sector Investment* (billion yuan)

Year	Foreign capital	Centrally co-ordinated	
		Total	% share
1984	0.90	0.06	6.67
1985	1.74	0.18	10.34
1986	2.46	0.32	13.01
1987	2.69	0.26	9.67
1988	n/a	n/a	n/a
1989	3.90	0.24	6.15
1990	4.89	0.18	3.68
1991	n/a	n/a	n/a
1992	7.66	0.14	1.83
Total			
1984–92	24.24	1.37	5.65
1987–92	19.14	0.82	4.28

n/a = not available

Source: Guangdong Statistical Bureau (1985–93: 1984–92 vols.).

investment funding, whilst in Guangdong the portion in this area was less than 5 per cent. This indicates that Guangdong, due to its success in attracting direct foreign investment, has been more capable than Shanghai of raising foreign capital independently. More importantly, Shanghai has been much less successful in gaining control over resources provided by the centre. As Table 4.13 reveals, Guangdong was able to deploy the bulk of its 5 per cent of centrally co-ordinated loans on local investment projects, whilst the majority of such loans to Shanghai were used for central projects in Shanghai.

Table 4.13 shows that between 1984 and 1992, nearly 70 per cent of centrally co-ordinated loans in Guangdong were used for local investment projects. This share rose to over 80 per cent between 1989 and 1992, as compared to less than 4 per cent in Shanghai. It is, therefore, clear that although Shanghai had more than three times the amount of Guangdong's centrally co-ordinated loans, the amount that was used for local projects was only 15 per cent of the amount spent on local projects in Guangdong in absolute terms. The message is loud and clear: whilst the Shanghai government succeeded in 'pulling in' resources to the municipality,[17] such resources came with strings attached. The centre retained control over the resources by assigning them largely to

TABLE 4.13. *Distribution of Centrally Co-ordinated Foreign Loans in Local and Central Investment Projects in Guangdong and Shanghai* (million yuan)

Guangdong

Year	Total	Central projects		Local projects	
		Total	%	Total	%
1984	59.7	59.7	100.0	0.0	0.0
1985	175.2	87.5	49.9	87.7	50.1
1986	315.4	164.5	52.2	150.9	47.8
1987		n/a		n/a	
1988		n/a		n/a	
1989	236.6	158.6	67.0	78.0	33.0
1990	179.9	36.3	20.2	143.5	79.8
1991		n/a		n/a	
1992	142.5	3.5	2.5	139.0	97.5
Total					
1984–92	1,069.1	510.2	31.5	1,109.3	68.5
1989–92	559.0	198.4	18.6	870.7	81.4

n/a = not available

Source:Guangdong Statistical Bureau (1985–93).

Shanghai

Year	Total	Central projects		Local projects	
		Total	%	Total	%
1989	1,603	1,540	96.1	63	3.9
1990	1,013	958	94.6	55	5.4
1991	992	978	98.6	14	1.4
1992	1	0	0.0	1	100.0
Total	2,006	1,936	96.5	70	3.5

Source: *Statistical Yearbook of Shanghai* (1990–3).

centrally subordinated projects. Apparently, this is the price that Shanghai has paid for its reliance on central-originated funding.

A slow-growing non-state sector

Concomitant with the lingering dominance of central investment and the resilience of budgetary funds as a source of funding was the predominance of the state sector in investment and in the economy of Shanghai generally. As detailed in Table 4.14, as late as 1993 investment in the non-state sector accounted for just over 20 per cent of the total, with the state sector accounting for 80 per cent. For the entire 1981–92 period, the share of non-state sector investment cumulatively was only about 18 per cent, less than 8 percentage points higher than the share during the 1950–80 period.

When comparing Table 4.14 with Table 3.15, the sluggish growth of investment in Shanghai's non-state sector relative to Guangdong's is clear. In line with Shanghai's high base of total investment before 1980, and in particular due to the concentration of the country's private capital there in the early 1950s, both the absolute value and percentage share of non-state sector investment was larger in Shanghai than in Guangdong in the 1950–80 period. The absolute cumulative value was nearly four times as much, and the percentage share was almost double. During the 1981–93 period, however, investment in Shanghai's non-state sector was only 40 per cent that of Guangdong's,

TABLE 4.14. *Shanghai's non-State Sector Investment* (million yuan)

Period	Collective	Private	% share of total investment		
			Collective	Private	Collective + Private
1950–2	2	48	0.7	16.4	17.1
1953–7	15	315	0.8	16.3	17.1
1958–62	167	133	3.0	2.4	5.4
1963–5	149	97	7.3	4.8	12.1
1966–70	262	213	7.5	6.1	13.7
1971–5	615	305	6.4	3.2	9.6
1976–80	1,297	485	8.6	3.2	11.8
1981–5	3,616	3,323	8.8	8.1	16.8
1986–90	10,096	7,296	9.9	7.2	17.0
1991	2,782	1,487	10.8	5.8	16.5
1992	6,416	1,755	18.0	4.9	22.9
1993	12,056	746	18.4	1.1	19.5
Total					
1950–80	2,507	1,596	6.6	4.2	10.8
1981–93	34,966	14,607	13.5	5.6	19.1
1950–93	37,473	16,203	12.2	5.3	17.5

Source: *Statistical Yearbook of Shanghai* (1993: 244, 1994: 72).

and the proportion share of the total lower by, again, 40 per cent. The non-state sector became a relatively small component in Shanghai's economy, as compared with Guangdong and nationally, as shown in Table 4.15.

Table 4.16 details the annual growth rates of investment in the state and non-state sectors in Shanghai. When looking at Table 4.16 in tandem with Table 3.16 on Guangdong, the following observations may

TABLE 4.15. *Proportion of non-State Sector Investment in Total Investment, 1993* (%)

Sector	National	Guangdong	Shanghai
State	61.4	54.9	77.1
Non-state	38.6	45.1	22.9
Collective	17.9	18.8	18.4
Private	11.8	10.3	1.1

Sources: Table 4.14; Table 3.15; *Statistical Yearbook of China* (1994: 143).

TABLE 4.16. *Investment in Shanghai: Annual Growth Rate* (%)

Year	Total	State sector	Non-state sector		
			Collective	Private	Collective + Private
1981	20.2	11.8	51.9	163.1	86.1
1982	30.7	36.9	5.9	10.4	11.7
1983	6.5	5.5	21.3	2.8	12.5
1984	21.5	16.6	44.8	58.6	50.9
1985	28.5	26.6	16.2	62.2	37.2
1986	23.9	27.7	34.0	−14.1	8.1
1987	26.8	26.1	33.4	25.9	30.6
1988	31.7	28.6	55.6	33.1	45.8
1989	12.4	10.0	27.7	14.8	22.8
1990	5.7	7.5	−12.9	10.7	−3.1
1991	13.7	8.2	52.1	−10.2	22.5
1992	38.4	26.4	130.6	18.0	91.1
1993	83.0	91.6	87.9	−57.5	56.7
Average	24.5	23.4	37.0	23.3	32.9

Source: *Statistical Yearbook of Shanghai* (1989: 271, 1990: 238, 1991: 260, 1992: 280, 1993: 244, 1994: 72).

be made. First, in both Guangdong and Shanghai investment in the non-state sector grew at a faster rate than it did in the state sector. Secondly, in both places it was the collectives within the non-state sector that took the lead, and, despite the stronger presence of the state and the plan in Shanghai, the greater gap in growth between the collective and the private/individual was in Guangdong. Here, the gap was more a result of the high growth rates of the collective than of a low base in private investment. Table 4.17 gives a clear illustration of the loci of growth in Guangdong and Shanghai.

Between 1981 and 1993, Guangdong's investment in the collective sector grew at an average annual rate of 63 per cent, as against a rate of only 25 per cent in private investment. In Shanghai the respective rates were 37 per cent and 23 per cent, a much smaller difference. The largest gap in growth rates between Shanghai and Guangdong is in the collective sector, amounting to 26 percentage points. This recalls the early stage of development of the non-state sector in China, and the heavy involvement of the government in the economy and in investment decisions in particular. The non-state sector in China has never been simply the opposite of the state sector. Within the non-state sector the collective has always been favoured as a magnet for economic activities. Here is a large grey area outside the strict control of the central planning system yet still endowed with the label of public ownership, thus making the collective much more attractive and convenient politically than the capitalistic private sector.

TABLE 4.17. *Average Annual Growth Rates of Investment: A Comparison, 1981–1993 (%)*

Sectors	Shanghai	Guangdong	Gap[a]
Non-State Sector			
Collective	37.0	62.9	25.9
Private/individual	23.3	25.1	1.8
Total non-state sector	32.9	37.1	4.2
State sector	23.4	33.3	9.9
Total investment	24.5	35.0	10.5

[a] 'Gap' here means the excess of Guangdong's growth rates over Shanghai's. The 'gap' mentioned in the text means the differences in growth rates between the collective and private investments in a locality.

Source: Calculated from data in previous tables.

Why did the central government retain such a level of dominance in
Shanghai's investment, when the national catchwords for the 1980s
were 'decentralization' and 'reform'? The answer requires a closer examination of the institutional environment in Shanghai.

The fiscal system: strait-jacket

The most important constraint of Shanghai's development was arguably its tight financial situation resulting from a centralized fiscal
system in place almost throughout the 1980s. Burdened with a high extraction rate and left with little money to spare,[18] the Shanghai government was keen to fight for central investment as well as for all kinds
of other central support. In the eyes of Shanghai officials, the inflow
of central resources was but a partial refund of the huge contributions
which Shanghai had made to the central coffers in previous decades.

From 1980 to the eve of 1994, when the new tax-sharing fiscal system was adopted nationwide, the fiscal system in Shanghai went
through three stages. Whilst in 1980 nearly all provinces adopted some
kind of contractual fiscal system allowing them more autonomy and
resources, it was not until 1988 that Shanghai won its own kind of fiscal reform. Moreover, this belated change only came after two rounds
of unusual slides in Shanghai's fiscal revenue, in 1981–3 and 1986–7,
which convinced the centre that changes could no longer be delayed.

Developments 1980–1984

The most striking and, from the viewpoint of Shanghai, unfortunate
development in the 1980s was the central government's announcement of the adoption of a new contractual fiscal system nationwide in
February 1980, from which Shanghai, along with the other two
provincial-level municipalities, Beijing and Tianjin, was to be excluded.[19] Consequently, as Guangdong entered what has subsequently
proved to be an unprecedented period of local autonomy and development via the *dabaogan* system, Shanghai was stuck with the old-
style centralized system, which had been in operation since 1976.

The essence of the 1976 system was to enable central government to
take the bulk of local fiscal revenue, after leaving behind an agreed
sum to cover local budgetary expenditures and another small fixed

amount for discretionary use. Under this system the central government prescribed a revenue target for Shanghai, which in 1976 was set at 13.84 billion yuan. The centre also determined, after considering expenditure proposals from the province, the total level of fiscal expenditure to be financed by the retained local revenue. This total was in turn subdivided into categories of expenditures for each policy sector in accordance with prescriptions by the relevant central ministries. In 1976 planned total expenditure was 1.6 billion yuan. On top of that was a fixed sum of 0.15 billion yuan, known as the additional 'retention funds', which could be spent at the discretion of the municipal government. The balance of local fiscal revenue would go to the central coffers. If at the end of the year total budgetary revenue exceeded the prescribed revenue target, Shanghai would receive additional retention funds amounting to 30 per cent of the surplus revenue. If, however, the prescribed revenue target was not met, planned expenditure would be reduced proportionately.[20]

At face value the system was not entirely unfair to the municipal government. Shanghai could in theory retain more if more fiscal revenue was collected: a full 30 per cent of the portion of revenue exceeding the prescribed target would go to the coffers of Shanghai. In practice the target was so high that it was very difficult to overachieve. The fact that the revenue target was set every year also eliminated the possibility of a substantial surplus. Meanwhile if the target was not met, as in 1976, the centre would accordingly reduce the amount allotted for local spending, thus ensuring that remittances to the centre would not be significantly affected. This system put pressure on the municipal government to achieve the target as, in the event of a shortfall, municipal expenditure would be cut. The value of central remittance was thus guaranteed. In contrast with the contractual system in place in other provinces, which had the effect of fattening the local coffers at the expense of the centre, the system in place in Shanghai until 1984 was one that ensured that the centre got the best deal.

As a result of this arrangement, only 12 per cent of the total local budgetary revenue was retained in Shanghai to cover municipal expenditure during the 1980–4 period. As Table 4–18 shows, the retention rate in Guangdong was 82 per cent. Table 4.18 also shows that although the absolute value of Shanghai's fiscal revenue was more than four times that of Guangdong, given the much higher central extraction rate in Shanghai the value of revenue spent in the municipality was only just over half that of Guangdong.

TABLE 4.18. *Remittance Rates of Fiscal revenues in Shanghai and Guangdong*, 1980–1984

	Shanghai	Guangdong
Fiscal revenue (billion yuan)	82.3	21.3
Fiscal expenditure (billion yuan)	9.9	17.5
Remittance (%)	88.0	17.8

Sources: *Statistical Yearbook of Shanghai* (1993: 55); Guangdong Statistical Bureau (1989*b*). State Statistical Bureau (1986: 54, 92).

Developments 1985–1987

From 1981 to 1983, Shanghai's municipal fiscal revenue experienced its first ever slide since 1949. Municipal budgetary revenue decreased from 17.21 billion yuan in 1980 to 17.15 billion in 1981, then to 16.51 billion in 1982, and still lower to 15.37 billion yuan in 1983, a decline of minus 0.3 per cent, minus 3.76 per cent, and minus 6.9 per cent respectively (*Statistical Yearbook of Shanghai* 1993: 55). When the slide finally halted in 1984, the value of revenue at 16.1 billion yuan was still much lower than the level achieved in 1980. The causes of the slide are many: rises in industrial production costs not keeping up with rises in product prices, the reduction of taxes on enterprises, mismanagement resulting in losses of opportunity and an increase in waste and costs, and so forth.[21] Whatever the causes, the unprecedented slide in revenue in a place long renowned for its economic efficiency and ability to turn over revenue constituted a clear signal to the centre: some kind of change was necessary. As Shanghai had been complaining about the insufficiency of discretionary funds provided in the 1976 fiscal system, the central government finally agreed to increase Shanghai's local financial resources by means of a new system implemented in 1985.[22]

The 1985 system abolished the previous practice of dividing locally retained fiscal revenue into various portions for 'planned expenditure', 'fixed retentions', and 'additional retentions'. Instead Shanghai would get a fixed percentage of the total local fiscal revenue which would be used to cover all local expenditure. The percentage was fixed at 23.2 per cent in 1985 and would supposedly remain unchanged for six years. Shanghai could, therefore, retain a greater amount for local use and avoid the lack of security of the previous system, whereby the sum retained locally was subject to annual adjustment. Moreover, in order to improve Shanghai's financial situation, some 1.5 billion yuan was added to the actual expenditure of 2.2 billion in 1983, bringing the retention ratio up to 23.2 per cent. As a result the amount of fiscal revenue spent in Shanghai increased from 3 billion yuan in 1984 to 4.6 billion in 1985, a leap of over 50 per cent (Jiang Zemin 1989: 114). More importantly, with the new system the central prescriptions on spending in each policy sector ceased. Thereafter the Shanghai government could control the deployment of the entire amount of retained local fiscal revenue, rather than only the tiny portion as before (*Shanghai Economy Yearbook* 1987: 830). This amounted to a substantial enhancement of the autonomy of the municipal government, although this autonomy had been in place in Guangdong and other provinces since 1980.[23]

The new fiscal system had two important features which promised enhanced local financial autonomy. The first was the sense of security gained from the fixation of the remittance percentage for six years. This provided the Shanghai government with the means whereby it could make plans which had not previously been possible due to uncertainty regarding available resources for the following year. The second feature was the enhanced responsibility and autonomy of the municipal government as regards decisions on municipal expenditure. With the sectoral control targets gone, the Shanghai government was free to act more like a municipal government, and take responsibility for municipal policies and expenses, rather than behaving as the agent of the central government ministries. Moreover the immediate effect of the 1985 fiscal regime was the lowering of the remittance rate to 76.8 per cent, down 11 percentage points from the 1980–4 figure of 88 per cent.

However, it was later found that the challenge to Shanghai's economy required more than a mere adjustment in the fiscal system. The municipal coffers witnessed the second slide in local budgetary revenue in 1986–7. In 1986 Shanghai's budgetary revenue decreased by 3 per cent in absolute value from the level in 1985, and in 1987 further dropped by another 6.2 per cent (*Statistical Yearbook of Shanghai* 1993: 55). State enterprises which had long since adapted to operate under the traditional planning system, whereby low-priced raw materials were supplied through the allocation system and products were eventually purchased by the state, performed badly as state supplies of raw materials dried up and new markets for products had to be found. As the absolute amount of revenue fell, the original fixed retention percentage arrangement which had been intended to allow Shanghai to retain more revenue each year went seriously awry. According to the agreed sharing percentage, local retention in 1986 and 1987 would be 4.09 billion yuan and 3.51 billion yuan respectively, which was 0.52 billion and 1.1 billion less than the amount actually retained and used locally in 1985. The sharing percentage was thus not strictly applied. This 'funding fiasco' had, however, clearly demonstrated the need for further and more radical change in the system.

Developments 1988–1993

Whilst the 1985 system was intended to enhance the sense of financial security within the Shanghai government as well as to raise the retention share for Shanghai, the basic tenet of the design was nevertheless to ensure that remittances to central coffers would increase in line with local revenue increases. Since the percentage share was heavily in favour of the centre, the system ensured that only a minor portion of new increments of revenue would go to the municipal government. In other words, there would be security for Shanghai, but the gains, even in the best situation of rising total revenue, would be modest.

The 1988 fiscal system negotiated between the Shanghai government and the centre in the midst of the fiscal slide of 1987 effectively reversed previous systems.[24] Instead of fixing the portion to be retained for local use, be it the absolute amount or a percentage share, the 1988 contractual system fixed for five years the absolute amount that Shanghai would have to remit to the centre. In other words, as with the *dabaogan* system of Guangdong, Shanghai would be able to retain all its revenues upon fulfilment of its obligation to the central government. Initially, from 1988 to 1990, Shanghai would remit to the centre 10.5 billion yuan of its local budgetary revenue and retain the rest. The 10.5 billion figure was based on the actual performance in 1987, when local budgetary revenue amounted to 16.5 billion yuan. This sum was taken as the base figure. As actual budgetary expenditure in 1987 had been 5.3 billion yuan, some 6 billion yuan of local expenditure was allowed for, thus giving the 10.5 billion yuan remittance figure. As from 1991, however, Shanghai was to share the portion of revenue in excess of 16.5 billion yuan with the centre on a 50 : 50 basis.

The 1988 system was obviously designed to confer more financial resources on Shanghai. According to the calculations of Shanghai's officials, the new system would make Shanghai better off by 1.4 billion

yuan in 1988 alone (*Shanghai Economy Yearbook* 1989: 73). The remittance of 10.5 billion yuan was also substantially less than the
amount in the early 1980s.[25] Shanghai's benefits were, however, on a
far smaller scale than those of Guangdong's *dabaogan* system. First,
Shanghai's required remittance was the higher of the two. As seen in
Chapter 3, the total cumulative remittance from 1980 to 1987 in
Guangdong's case amounted to 12.2 billion, an amount Shanghai was
obliged to remit annually. Although Guangdong was required to
remit more in later years, its remittance in 1991 at 7 billion yuan was
nevertheless only 70 per cent of Shanghai's. Secondly, the 50 : 50 sharing ratio for revenue over and above 16.5 billion yuan effective from
1991 was much less favourable than the 9 per cent incremental growth
of remittance in operation in Guangdong from 1989 to 1993. Table
4.19 shows the remittance rates in Shanghai from 1980.

TABLE 4.19. *Remittance Rates of Shanghai's Local Budgetary Revenues*

Period (billion yuan)	Local revenue (billion yuan)	Local expenditure (%)	Remittance rate
1980–4	82.3	9.9	88.0
1985–7	52.2	14.8	71.6
1988–93	107.8	50.2	46.6
1980–93	242.3	74.9	69.1

Source: *Statistical Yearbook of Shanghai* (1993: 55), 1994: 21).

Consequences

Given the circumstances surrounding the birth of the 1985 and 1988
fiscal systems, it might be surmised that Shanghai's late entry into the
fiscal reforms and the consequently depleted state of its local coffers
would limit the amount the Shanghai government could afford to
spend on investments. However, the breakdown of fiscal expenditures
between 1987 and 1991, as detailed in Table 4.20, shows that this is not
strictly the case.

Shanghai spent almost as much budgetary resources on investment
as Guangdong, despite the fact that Guangdong's total local budgetary revenue for the period was more than double that of Shanghai.
Whilst Shanghai may have experienced financial difficulties, such
difficulties apparently did not inhibit the municipal government from
launching investment projects financed from budgetary resources.

TABLE 4.20. *Local Fiscal Investment Expenditures: Share of Total Local Fiscal Expenditure*

Year	Shanghai		Guangdong	
	million yuan	% share	million yuan	% share
1987	1617	32.2	2053	21.3
1988	2247	34.8	2616	22.7
1989	2291	31.3	2644	18.7
1990	2123	28.1	2964	19.7
1991	2107	20.8	3617	19.8
Total	10385	35.0	13894	20.3

Total fiscal expenditures, 1987–91: Shanghai, 29.7 billion yuan; Guangdong, 68.6 billion yuan.

Source: Ministry of finance (1992: 138, 147, 157).

It has been noted in Chapter 3 that the major significance of the *dabaogan* fiscal system did not lie in the increased amount of fiscal revenue the Guangdong government was permitted to retain. Liberalization policies and the opening up of the domestic economy to the international community made it impossible, in any event, for the state budget, central or local, to foot all the investment bills. In fact, as Guangdong's local revenue grew, the proportion that was spent on investment fell rather than rose. Likewise, the sluggishness of investment in Shanghai was not directly related to the tight financial situation resulting from the high remittance rate. Table 4.20 shows that it would be wrong even to deduce that potential financial difficulty was the inhibiting factor in local government investment activity.

The implication was rather that Shanghai leaders had, as a result of the tight financial situation, focused more on the day-to-day balancing of the local budget than on forward-looking long-term plans for the economy. As the extraction rate was high and Shanghai's previous supplies of low-priced raw materials and consumer goods from the planning channels dried up, the municipal government was caught in the double bind of having to reduce the burden of tax on enterprises to enable them to survive on the one hand, and having to hand out increasingly large sums of subsidy on the other. The two fiscal slides of 1981–3 and 1986–7 indicate fully how difficult the financial situation really was. The local financial situation was often described as 'catering finance', meaning that it was so tight that the budget could normally provide for only the most basic needs. The most important task for senior officials therefore became the routine balancing of the budget books. Attention focused on lobbying the central government to raise the local retention rate every year, and on closely confining expenses to those of immediate need. When survival was regarded as the paramount issue, there could be no place for long-term planning and development strategies.[26]

In other words, as in the case of Guangdong, the most important consequence of the fiscal system for Shanghai's investment was that in practice the fiscal system created an environment which, contrary to Guangdong's situation, led the municipal government to care more about the meticulous administration of the account books than about the development of the economy. The horizon of concern was largely restricted to the traditional boundaries of the state sector, and working methods accordingly followed the traditional style. Nevertheless, investment remained a high priority of the municipal government, as Table 4.20 has made clear. The municipal budget was, however, far too small to satisfy investment requirements. Shanghai consequently took the traditional route and turned its attention towards the centre as a means of increasing its investment resources. This explains why the percentage share of central investment in Shanghai in the 1980s was so high and, given the difficulty in local finance at that time, Shanghai's reliance on central investment was higher in the 1980s than during the previous full decade.

Investment administration

In its capacity as the largest port in China and until 1986 the top exporter,[27] Shanghai had been able to obtain more autonomy in the area of investment administration relative to the situation in the area of fiscal finance. The central government had in fact adopted a more even-handed approach to the decentralization of investment administration than it had to reform in the fiscal system. In the 1984 decentralization move, all provincial-level governments were awarded the power to approve investment projects up to a value of 30 million yuan.

Shanghai was, however, later than Guangdong in having the central ministries' mandatory sectoral control figures abolished. It was not until 1983, three years after central sectoral control figures of all kinds were abolished in Guangdong, that Shanghai was awarded the autonomy to decide its own fiscal investment expenditure.[28] As regards project approval authority, Shanghai was awarded, in 1985, the power to approve domestic investments forming part of a foreign investment project of under 30 million yuan. This came later than similar privileges to Guangdong, whose power had been enhanced in 1981 and again in 1982. There was then the boost in 1984, when the central government raised the ceiling for provincial-level jurisdiction of all domestic investments across the board. Subsequently, in March 1987, as noted in Chapter 3, the centre raised provincial-level jurisdiction nationwide on approving projects in the 'bottleneck' sectors to 50 million yuan. In this instance, Shanghai's authority had apparently been raised to 50 million yuan ahead of the national move.[29] In 1992, as part of the central policy to encourage the development of the Pudong area, Shanghai was authorized to approve projects in Pudong up to 200 million yuan. Shanghai thereby became the third provincial-level government, after Guangdong and Fujian, to whom such authority had been granted in 1985, to wield such power.[30]

As the historic hub of foreign commercial activity, Shanghai has been more successful in obtaining power to attract foreign investment. In 1983 Shanghai was authorized to approve foreign investment projects of up to US$10 million, which was twice the ceiling in Guangzhou.[31] In October 1984, the centre enlarged the power of the fourteen open coastal cities in relation to foreign investment, and Shanghai's jurisdiction, together with Tianjin's, was raised to cover foreign investment projects of up to US$30 million, three times more than the jurisdiction for Guangzhou.[32] If there was still some lag in investment administration between Shanghai and Guangdong, therefore, it was nevertheless minor as compared with the greater disparities of the fiscal system.

Having an enlarged power to approve investment projects might be necessary but not sufficient for a take-off in investment activities. For instance, the decentralization of investment administration from the centre had been fairly uniform nationally, but the performance of different provinces in investment and economic development was conspicuously uneven. In the words of an authoritative source in Beijing,

the devolution of investment authority to the provinces has had different effects in different provinces. The inland provinces complain that in any event they have little money to spend on investment and development, so enlarged powers for investment mean little to them. They are simply too constrained by survival matters to utilize the powers fully.[33]

It is necessary, therefore, to look at the basis on which new policy initiatives were made in order to have a clear idea of their effects.

In this connection local scholars and officials have criticized the system of administration in Shanghai, and its approval process for investment projects, as bureaucratic and inefficient.[34] The pace at which Shanghai utilized new powers delegated by the centre was also slow. Although Shanghai was awarded increased powers in 1984, along with other open coastal cities, the system within the municipality remained highly centralized for some years thereafter. For instance, it was only in 1987 that the power to approve investment projects, originally centralized at the municipal Planning Commission, was decentralized to other municipal departments. Vertical decentralization to bureaux and counties was also slow, finally gathering momentum as late as 1988.[35] Apparently one major factor behind the slow pace of subdelegation was simply that there had never been a central document specifically sanctioning the authority of provincial levels to delegate downwards![36] The cumulative effect of always being under the close scrutiny of the centre, and the internalized expectation of having to set an example for other provinces to follow, resulted in relatively rule-abiding behaviour amongst officials in Shanghai. Shanghai officials tended to follow more closely the rules and regulations laid down by the centre and were less inclined than counterparts in other provinces to venture into the unspoken grey areas, a practice for which Guangdong was famous. Consequently Shanghai in the 1980s was not able to enjoy the 'multiplier effects' conferred by the extensive subdelegation of powers to subprovincials as in Guangdong.

The Shanghai leadership eventually learned its lesson, albeit slowly. As from 1988 bureaux, districts and counties were authorized to approve domestic investments of a 'productive' nature of up to 10 million yuan, and up to 5 million yuan for non-productive projects such as hotels and real estate (*Shanghai Economy Yearbook* 1989: 85). As from 1992 they could also approve foreign investments of up to US$5 million.[37] In 1992 district governments were authorized to raise loans, foreign and domestic, for urban renewal projects, and to lease public land sites to investors. The rapid growth in investment activity from 1992 apparently convinced the Shanghai government of the utility of extensive subdelegation. In 1993 the foreign investment powers of the districts were further enhanced to US$10 million.[38] However, the shadow of central monitoring still exerted a pervasive influence on officials' behaviour and attitudes. As an official in Shanghai described the 'rule-abiding' behaviour of Shanghai officials,

Unlike their counterparts in Guangdong, the bank and auditing personnel in Shanghai were, and are, very 'conscientious' about their job. That is, they are much stricter in applying the rules. Officers in the banks are more concerned with the 'propriety' of the projects in loan applications, for instance: whether the projects are included in the state plans for investment and bank finance, and whether the projects' finance is strictly in order. Audit officials are most assiduous in their task of locating misdeeds in financial management within the units in question. The background of such behaviour can be traced back to the tight financial situation in Shanghai, and to the heavy extraction of revenue by the centre, so that traditionally the banks were more vigilant in their lending procedures for fear of missing the central remittance target, and auditing personnel were under pressure from the municipal leadership to ensure that every penny was duly collected for the local fiscal coffers. The resultant situation is in direct contrast to the 'hands-off' approach in the auditing and banking sectors of Guangdong. However, such behaviour and attitudes cannot be changed within a short time.[39]

If China could be said to be administered by the cross-cutting systems of *tiao-tiao* and *kuai-kuai*, then Shanghai might be characterized as a place wherein the *tiao-tiao* historically had the upper hand within the administration. This did not mean, however, that local interests were not important in Shanghai, but that the influence of the *tiao-tiao* became so strong that following central regulations was regarded as the best policy for safeguarding local interests. Since, in any event, there could be little room for manoeuvre under the high extraction rate and close scrutiny of the centre, it appeared better for Shanghai to exceed the expectations of the centre and earn the reputation of being a 'good boy'. In local official and non-official publications, therefore, the high percentage of remittance was traditionally hailed not as a burden, but as a positive contribution fulfilling Shanghai's obligation to the country as the 'elder brother'.[40] Shanghai thus strove for over-achievement of remittances to the centre, and was, ostensibly, happier to report a higher, rather than lower, extraction rate. Following the central rules or, in many cases, maintaining the image of following the rules, appeared to be the safest course to take, because in the event of any failure to accomplish targets assigned from the centre, the municipal government could point to the fact that every directive had been followed, thus enabling it to disclaim responsibility.

Such behavioural patterns gave rise to the conservative manner in which the Shanghai government utilized the new powers conferred by the centre during the 1980s. It took the Shanghai leadership almost a decade to recognize that the circumstances within which they had been operating had, in fact, changed radically, and, consequently, that their strategy of survival within the system also had to change. As economic reforms deepened in the 1980s, the state plan was no longer operating as before. Consequently, Shanghai's obedience and responsiveness could no longer be rewarded by supplies through the administrative system. As the centre did not have its previous leverage over other provinces, Shanghai could not rely on the influence of the centre in its dealings with other provinces. In fact, being the 'good boy' of the centre made Shanghai a mockery amongst the other provinces, since the centre could no longer 'deliver the goods' as effectively as in the past, and yet Shanghai was still stuck with its own obligations to the centre.[41] From 1988 Shanghai sought to reduce these obligations, but the city started from a high base, and changes in behaviour and attitudes took time. This process of behavioural change from the late 1970s through the stringent 1980s to the early 1990s will be the subject of discussion in Chapters 6 and 7.

NOTES

1. The Politburo discussed the 'Draft Resolution for Transforming Capitalist Industries and Commerce' on 16 December 1955. Within one month Beijing announced the completion of the transformation of all capitalist industries and commerce in the city. See Fang Weizhong (1984: 158, 163).
2. Interview, respondent no. 14, Shanghai, Jan. 1994. Other respondents have expressed similar comments on the changing face of the city before and after 1949. Lucian Pye (1981b: xii) noted that the Chinese Communist Party realized after gaining power that the economic strength of Shanghai, which they had previously tended to blacken as a model of foreign and capitalistic exploitation, could be usefully 'exploited' for the development of the rest of China. As a result Shanghai became more important strategically.
3. Calculated from Shanghai Statistical Bureau (1989: 78), *Statistical Yearbook of Shanghai* (1993), 14, Guangdong Statistical Bureau (1989b: 74), and *Statistical Yearbook of China* (1993), 229.
4. Chen Yi was the second First Party Secretary of Shanghai (1950–4) and Ke Qingshi the third (1954–65). Both were prominent figures in the Party and joined the revolution in its early years. Chen was regarded as one of the ten greatest generals of the Army and Ke had served as the General Secretary of the Party before the outbreak of the Sino–Japanese War, becoming a member of the Party Politburo in 1956. See Ma Qibing *et al.* (1989: 574).

5. This is the argument of David S. G. Goodman (1981*b*) and in a more complicated way of Lynn T. White III (1976). For an alternative view, see Parris Chang (1981).
6. See Howe (1971: 37) and Fang Weizhong (1984: 144). The latter source states that resiting was part of the exercise to alleviate the oversupply of workers and equipment in established industrial centres in the 1950s.
7. The policy of the central government towards the developed areas in the coastal region in the 1950s and 1960s can be described as one of 'utilization to the full'. In accordance with the central policy, the Party Committee of Shanghai formulated an investment policy which 'fully utilizes the existing capacities while reasonably developing new facilities'. See *Shanghai Economic Yearbook* 1982, Internal version: 844. As a result of this policy, although Shanghai had more investment than other coastal provinces, almost all investments were aimed at a quick return of revenue whilst infrastructure such as roads and residential buildings were seriously neglected.
8. See State Statistical Bureau (1992*b*: 19, 1991: 24); *Statistical Yearbook of China* (1994: 146).
9. Interviews, respondents no. 15, 22 and 17, Shanghai, Jan. 1994. The interviews were conducted separately. Although the precise words of the different respondents may have differed, they all suggested the same message concerning what should be concluded from the statistics on central investment.
10. Interview, respondent no. 15, Shanghai, Jan. 1994.
11. Interview, respondent no. 15, Shanghai, Jan. 1994. That local governments had indeed been manipulating statistical data was confirmed by the centre's move to ban such behaviour openly in May 1994, when in a national telephone conference with provincial governments Vice-Premier Zhou Jiahua announced a comprehensive inspection exercise regarding the accuracy of statistical information reported to the centre. See *People's Daily*, 27 May 1994, 3. The problematic behaviour Zhou pointed out in the conference included delays in reporting data, refusing to submit reports, hiding data and inflating data.
12. Interview, respondent no. 15, Shanghai, Jan. 1994. It was revealed in a study on local (provincial) government investment behaviour that in some provinces the provincial government had been keeping two separates sets of investment statistics. One set was the raw data recording the total amount of investment undertaken and known to the provincial government. The other set was a 'processed' version of the first for forwarding to the central government. According to the study, the existence of two different sets of statistics explained why there were often huge discrepancies between investment data released by the banks and the final official investment statistics released by provincial governments. See Zhong Chengxun

(1993: 448). From the interviews conducted in Shanghai, Shanghai was likely one of those provinces.

13. This was also reflected in the different responses by Guangdong and Shanghai officials to the question of which type of under-reporting was the most common in their locality. Guangdong officials mentioned the third type as the most common, and to a lesser extent the second type (interviews, Guangzhou, May and Sept. 1993). On the other hand, Shanghai officials listed the first type, that is, under-reporting by provincial level, as the most common (interviews, Shanghai, Jan. 1994).

14. Interview, respondent no. 15, Shanghai, Jan. 1994. It should be noted that, *in reality*, central investment was not necessarily more subject to retrenchment moves than was local investment. Since 'strategic' projects were not usually the targets of retrenchment, more often receiving additional resources released from other projects, and since central projects were more likely to be regarded as 'strategic', central investment projects were likely to be less affected than local investment during retrenchment. In fact this was the case in Shanghai, where central investment in 1989 shrank by less than 6% from the level of 1988, as against a 12.4% decrease for local investment (see *Statistical Yearbook of Shanghai* 1991, 1993). However, since central investment was directly under the control of the central government, the feeling in the locality was that this was a slice of investment subject to the mercy of the centre.

15. This interpretation of the negative discrepancies as signalling large inflows of central fiscal funds was confirmed with informed sources in the Shanghai municipal government (interviews, respondents no. 20 and 21, Shanghai, Jan. 1994).

16. This is the opinion of respondent no. 36, (interview, Beijing, Apr. 1994). Provincial governments could then retain autonomy in managing the details of the loans while securing more favourable terms through the central government.

17. Centrally co-ordinated loans amount to some kind of central support as the provinces may not be able to solicit and organize foreign loans independently, and the interest rates or repayment terms negotiated by the centre are often more favourable.

18. Shanghai has the highest extraction rate of all provincial-level jurisdictions in post-1949 China. In 1980, the extraction rate of local fiscal revenue to the central fiscal coffers was 91.4%, followed by Shandong's 90% and Zhejiang's 87%. See Tian Yinong *et al.* (1986: 88–9).

19. State Council Notice, 'On Approving the Temporary Regulation on Implementing the "Dividing Revenues and Expenditures, Contracting at Each Level" Fiscal System', 1 Feb. 1980, printed in State Planning Commission (1987b: 629–31).

20. See *Shanghai Economy Yearbook* (1984: 892). Shanghai failed to meet the

revenue target in 1976 by 5.3%, and planned expenditure was decreased by 85 million yuan. The fixed retention value remained unchanged at 0.15 billion yuan throughout 1976–81, and Shanghai obtained a cumulative additional retention of 0.93 billion yuan during 1977–81 by overachieving the revenue targets.

21. See Tu Jimo (1988: 47–52) and *Shanghai Industry Yearbook* 1989: 38.

22. For a discussion of the process see Chap. 6.

23. Mandatory sectoral control figures on fiscal expenditures were abolished formally in the State Council's Notice on the 1980 fiscal system, 1 Feb. 1980.

24. For a discussion on the process and considerations at that time, see Chap. 6.

25. Taking the average remittance rate of 88% as shown in Table 4.18, the average annual remittance between 1980 and 1984 amounted to 14.5 billion yuan. In the eyes of central government officials, the 1988 system had therefore already brought about a fairly significant improvement for Shanghai (interview, respondent no. 29, Beijing, Apr. 1994).

26. Shanghai officials often stressed during interviews the heavy burden on Shanghai and the lack of favourable central policy in explaining lacklustre economic development in the 1980s. When asked to mention some examples to illustrate what the municipal government leaders had previously done to advance the interests of Shanghai, the lowering of central extraction was amongst the popular answers. It was also revealed that because Shanghai traditionally had been the top contributor to the central coffers, the city was always the centre's first choice to turn to for 'additional contributions' in case of difficulties within central coffers. Such borrowing became almost a yearly routine in the late 1980s (interview, respondent no. 16, Shanghai, Jan. 1994).

27. See *Jiefang Ribao*, 22 Feb. 1994, 9.

28. The Shanghai government specifically asked for such autonomy in a report submitted to the central government in March 1983. In April, the State Council approved the report. Shanghai could thereafter decide the sectoral allocation of local fiscal investment expenditure, subject to other rules in the approval system for specific projects. Shanghai's autonomy in other areas such as the use of foreign investment and foreign trade was also enhanced via that report. See State Council Notice no. 55 (1983), 'On Approving the "Proposals on Developing Shanghai's External Business and Trade" by the Shanghai Government', 4 Apr. 1983, printed in State Commission for Economic System Reform (1983: 605–10).

29. In a report from the Shanghai Planning Commission released in early 1983, it was stated that the municipal Planning Commission would handle the investment application of between 30 million and 50 million yuan. There was no mention of the designation of industrial sectors; therefore the 50 million yuan jurisdiction was probably applicable to all projects in all sectors. See Shanghai Planning Commission (1987a: 28).

30. See *People's Daily*, 11 Mar. 1992, 1. Guangdong and Fujian were awarded the power when the centre extended the 'Special Policy' for the two provinces in 1985 (see Chap. 3.) During interviews in Beijing, Jan. 1994, respondent no. 31 mentioned that *all* provincial-level governments had in fact been approving investment projects under the 200 million yuan ceiling since the second half of 1992 as a result of the heightened 'atmosphere' for quicker economic development since the Southern Tour of Deng Xiaoping in January–February 1992. Such approval power, however, had not been formally conferred by the centre. The respondent revealed that the State Planning Commission had drafted a document with a view to recognizing the *de facto* enlarged power of the provinces in early 1993, but the document was held up in the Secretariat of the State Council, and had not since been approved. Therefore during this period only Shanghai received the formal power to approve projects under the 200 million yuan ceiling, although all provincial-level governments had in fact been doing likewise.
31. This was the result of a 'petition' from Shanghai. See State Council Notice, 'On Approving the "Proposals on Developing Shanghai's External Business and Trade" '.
32. See State Council Notice no. 138 (1984), 'Temporary Regulations on Improving the Planning System', 4 Oct. 1984, in State Planning Commission (1985: 1–12). It is stated that Guangzhou and Dailan could approve foreign investment projects of under US$ 10 million, while the remaining 10 open coastal cities could approve projects of up to US$ 5 million.
33. Interview, respondent no. 31, Beijing, Feb. 1994.
34. See for instance Wang Zhang (1991: pt. ii, pp. 14–15, 41). Wang was then a professor at Shanghai's Fuden University and later appointed the director of the Shanghai Economic Research Centre—a think tank of the municipal government. Despite complaints and some subsequent improvement, there is evidence that as late as 1994, foreign investors were still dissatisfied with the low efficiency and unco-ordinated policies among different departments of the Shanghai government regarding foreign investment. See *Jiefang Daily*, 21 Feb. 1994, 1.
35. See Jiang Zemin (1989: 94); *Shanghai Economic Yearbook* (1989: 85). Previously there had been modest measures towards decentralization, and bureau-level units were awarded the power to approve projects under 3 million yuan in 1984. See Shanghai Government Notice no. 99 (1984), 'Notice on Approving the Proposals of the Municipal Planning Commission on Improving the Planning System in Shanghai', printed in Shanghaishi Jingji Tizhi Gaige Lingdao Xiaozhu (1985: 91–9).
36. The relevance of this factor was confirmed during various interviews conducted in Shanghai in 1994. It should be noted that the central government never issued positive statements concerning the subdelegation of

authority by the provincial level to the subprovincials. Normally there would be a brief statement at the end of policy documents or regulations when the authority of the provincial level was adjusted, saying that the system at subprovincial levels was to be decided by the provincial level governments *accordingly*. Occasionally when the centre felt that sub-delegation had become too extensive it would issue directives voicing its disapproval. These were, however, vague and unspecific. At other times the centre would simply say nothing and acquiesce in whatever the provinces were doing. This reflected the 'stratified administration' approach of the Chinese government, whereby the central government set its eye mainly on the provincial level, which consequently had quite a free hand in its management of the subprovincial levels. Under such a system the power of the subprovincial levels of government varied substantially according to the choices and initiatives taken by the provincial leadership in different provinces.

37. *Wen Wei Po* (Hong Kong), 2 Oct. 1992, 1.
38. *Wen Wei Po* (Hong Kong), 3 Mar. 1993, 1. The Shanghai government included in their 1993 government work report a section on the subprovincial level. Because of the increased economic activities in the counties and districts subsequent to the decentralization in 1992, it was proposed that more powers should be delegated downwards to keep up the momentum. See *Shanghai Economy Yearbook* (1993: 34, 41).
39. Interview, respondent no. 14, Shanghai, Jan. 1994.
40. A standard entry in statistical publications, as well as in articles and books on the economic situation of Shanghai, is a list of contributions made by Shanghai to the centre and nationally. Examples are: Shanghai's GNP as a portion of the national GNP, the high remittance of local revenue to the national coffers, the percentage of Shanghai's internal and external trade in the national total, etc.
41. This is a comment made by several respondents in Shanghai during interviews in January and April 1994.

5 Discretion and Strategies in Guangdong

This chapter discusses the development of the discretion of the Guangdong government in the investment arena during the period 1979–93, using the typology of provincial discretion described in Chapter 1. The next chapter addresses the same issue for Shanghai. The purpose is to show, by explicating the details of provincial discretion and strategies, how provincial governments interacted with the centre and what strategies they undertook to gain more investment and faster economic development within the context of central policies. Discussions will follow the typology of discretion described in Fig. 1.2.

BARGAINING FOR MORE FAVOURABLE CENTRAL POLICIES

The first category of Guangdong's discretionary behaviour was targeted at obtaining the most favourable policies from the centre. Bargaining for the most favourable central policies that circumstances allowed was the major focus of the Guangdong government, particularly during the earlier years of the reform decade. This section outlines Guangdong's efforts in three areas which were pertinent to Guangdong's investment implementation, namely, the centre's 'Special Policy' on Guangdong, the fiscal system and the investment administration system. The importance of bargaining suggests that provincial governments relied on the goodwill of the centre to obtain favourable policies and were thus dependent on central support for any success. On the other hand, the prevalence of bargaining also confirms that provincial governments did have a substantial amount of influence on central policy making, and successes in bargaining produced a progressively more favourable environment in which to deploy other forms of discretion.

Special Policy

Reform in Guangdong took off with the announcement of the 'Special Policy' for Guangdong and Fujian in April 1979. The policy, embodied in State Council Document no. 50 in July 1979,[1] gave Guangdong and Fujian 'pioneer' status in the reform process, enlarged provincial autonomy in planning and fiscal aspects, and more power to attract foreign investment. Guangdong and Fujian officials had lobbied intensively for a preferential policy. After the Third Plenum of 1978, when the centre was eager about and receptive to new ideas on the economy, they succeeded. The Special Policy was important to Guangdong because it formally endorsed, as a matter of principle, the legitimacy of future provincial deviations from national practice. The only two preconditions were for Guangdong, first, to justify the merits of deviations in terms of economic performance and, secondly, to guarantee that the interests of the rest of the nation should not be too adversely affected. The wide umbrella of the Special Policy also facilitated Guangdong's pursuit of favourable treatment on more specific items.

The centre was receptive to Guangdong's bargaining, as the successful development of Guangdong and Fujian would fulfil an important political goal, as well as certain strategic concerns and tactical requirements.[2] Guangdong and Fujian are the neighbouring territories of Hong Kong/Macau and Taiwan respectively. The successful development of the economy of these two provinces could have a 'demonstration effect' on these neighbouring areas and this would encourage national unification, and integration, in the long run. Kinship ties between their residents could also be integral to the endeavour of Guangdong and Fujian to attract capital and management know-how from their richer neighbours, as well as to tap their connections to overseas markets. This tactical consideration was particularly relevant in 1979, as the financial situation of the country had been put under strain by negligent production during the Cultural Revolution decade of 1966–76 and by the 'Western-style Leap Forward' in 1977–9. Moreover, in revenue terms, Guangdong and Fujian are situated near the southern border of the country and had in times past been relatively insignificant contributors to total national revenue. Fujian had always been a deficit province requiring net inflow of central fiscal subsidy, and Guangdong's remittance to the centre in 1978 was 1.2 billion yuan, amounting to only 2.3 per cent of the total central fiscal expenditure of the year.[3] As seen in Chapter 3, historically the central government had not invested much in Guangdong. The low revenue baseline and marginal contribution of the border provinces to the national economy meant that little could be lost in the event of any failure in this experiment with reform and 'opening up'.

The various strategic considerations of the centre notwithstanding, it was officials from the Guangdong provincial government, not the centre, who first raised the idea of a preferential policy.[4] As neighbours of Hong Kong and Macau, Guangdong officials were able to move more quickly than their counterparts in other provinces in redirecting attention towards economic development after the downfall of the Gang of Four. The Third Plenum of the Eleventh Congress of the Party Central Committee gave Guangdong officials a clear signal that it would be politically safe to put forward new ideas regarding economic development. Serious consideration was promptly given within the provincial government to identifying specific measures through which an economic take-off could take place. A move was made in a central work conference held in April 1979, when 'there were strong calls for decentralization and reforms of the economic management system from the two provinces'.[5] The reward was the Special Policy, announced after the conference was concluded. In May a central working team headed by State Councillor Gu Mu was dispatched to Guangdong to devise concrete proposals together with Guangdong officials. By early June 1979, a proposal had taken shape. In the proposal the Guangdong provincial government made specific requests for a *dabaogan* fiscal system, as well as increased autonomy in investment planning.[6] The report was swiftly approved, thus establishing the fundamentals of the Special Policy for Guangdong.

This was only the beginning of a long process of continuous bargaining and consolidation, however. Apart from a few specific decisions such as those covering the new fiscal system, the Special Policy approved in 1979 included only general statements as regards the decentralization of authority to Guangdong.[7] This lack of specificity, together with the still conservative national environment at that time and the retrenchment campaign in 1980, posed difficulties for the implementation of the new powers, and as a result Guangdong officials often felt obliged to complain. For instance, during a meeting in Guangdong in March 1980, State Councillor Gu Mu was told that there was a lack of support and understanding among some central government ministries regarding the Special Policy.[8] A complaint was lodged again in September, when provincial officials in the Central Committee Secretariat reported on Guangdong's work before central leaders, including Hu Yaobang, Wan Li and Gu Mu.[9] Provincial Party Secretary Ren Zhongyi was recorded to have once remarked to Gu Mu that when the ministries do care and 'make some regulations [regarding the work of Guangdong], they are all negative in content and prohibit necessary action.'[10]

The lobbying for more clearly specified powers culminated in a meeting on the work of Guangdong, Fujian and the Special Economic Zones held in Beijing in May 1981. At the meeting officials from Guangdong, collaborating with their Fujian counterparts, requested specifically that the central government lay down a few major binding principles, such as avoiding the 'capitalistic road' and strictly following the four basic principles, and then leave the rest to them.[11] This request was granted. In the minutes of the meeting, as approved by the State Council in July, it was unambiguously written that,

Subject to the following major principles, the meeting agreed that the two provinces should be allowed the autonomy to go their own way, (1) abiding by the four basic principles, (2) following the major policy direction of the Party and fostering national unity, (3) obeying the guidance of the state plan, (4) completing the tasks handed down from above, and (5) maintaining a united front in external matters.[12]

It would appear that the central government effectively granted residual power to the two provinces. In addition, the content of the central government's Special Policy for the two provinces were laid down in still more specific terms:

(1) the two provinces should be more open to the outside world than other provinces, including the use of foreign investment, foreign technology and management, and the expansion of foreign trade; (2) the two provinces should practice more 'liberalized' domestic policies, such as the development of other modes of ownership and the expanded use of various economic levers; and (3) the two provinces should have enlarged authority, including the power to legislate on provincial matters, and more autonomy as regards economic, personnel and enterprise management.[13]

This was therefore a successful bid on the part of the Guangdong government to enrich and refine the vaguely worded Special Policy first announced in 1979. For the first time the two provinces were heralded explicitly as constituting the experimental base of economic reform. The coverage and policy dimensions theoretically applicable to the Special Policy were also explicitly laid down. It is true that the concept of residual power was somewhat alien to China's political culture, and announcements in an administrative document did not necessarily protect Guangdong from future encroachments on its delegated autonomy. The five major principles were undoubtedly still coined in general terms and were therefore open to interpretation. This was possibly why the central government saw no harm in approving them. However, despite such limitations, the significance of the overall success of this attempt should not be underestimated. That the two provinces could have obtained a pledge of 'non-intervention' from the centre was unprecedented. The Guangdong government had also made the centre specify, in a formal central document, the dimensions and coverage of the policy, and make explicit the 'taboo' areas. This in itself was a significant improvement on the previously nebulous concept of the 'Special Policy'. On this new footing the Guangdong government had improved its position for future bargaining with the central government, as well as enlarging its room for manoeuvre within and beyond existing central policies.

Fiscal system

As noted in Chapter 3, the *dabaogan* fiscal system was instrumental to economic development and investment growth in Guangdong. This was one of the few specific policies requested by Guangdong and obtained from the central government in July 1979, and which remained thereafter a focus for 'protection and enhancement' by the Guangdong provincial government.[14] The objective of this section is to discuss the process and the strategies whereby the Guangdong government sought to protect and enhance the fiscal system to its advantage.

The reduction of fiscal remittance

The amount of fiscal remittance was first set at 1.2 billion yuan in July 1979, and was supposed to be fixed for the two years 1980 and 1981. This was considered to be less than adequate by the provincial government. In the June 1979 report Guangdong did not specify the amount of fiscal remittance but requested that the amount be fixed for a period of five years.[15] Not entirely satisfied with what was offered, Guangdong officials began to 'rattle their tin' only three months after the passage of the report. At a meeting with Gu Mu in September 1979, they pointed out the need for additional expenditure as a result of price adjustments of agricultural products and salary rises, and asked that the remittance amount be lowered. The response from Gu Mu was very supportive, as can be seen from the following quote:

It does not really matter how much you remit to the centre next year, whether it is 1.2 billion or 1 billion yuan . . . The calculation of the remittance amount should not be a serious issue. The figure of 1.2 billion yuan is a little arbitrary. If it is not correct, simply redo the calculation.[16]

As a result, in May 1980 the amount of fiscal remittance was slashed by one-sixth to 1 billion yuan,[17] and after a further meeting with central leaders in September, the amount was fixed for a period of five years, just as Guangdong had originally requested.[18] At that time the centre was obviously more concerned with getting reforms off the ground in Guangdong than in extracting revenue. After all, the difference in remittance of 0.2 billion yuan represented only 0.18 per cent of the total national fiscal revenue for 1980. However, this was nevertheless of significant advantage to Guangdong, and it was noteworthy that in this case Guangdong succeeded in making the centre revise an earlier decision before it had even come into effect.

Defending the coverage of the contract

One area of frequent bargaining between the centre and Guangdong was the effect of reform measures on the revenue and expenditure of the province. Reforms brought about new sources of revenue as well as expenses. How should such revenue and expenditure be allocated? Should they go to the central or the provincial budgets? If they were assigned to the provincial budget, should the remittance amount be adjusted accordingly?

It was often emphasized by Guangdong provincial officials that the Guangdong government shouldered the 'burden' of reform on the centre's behalf. In one instance, officials from the Provincial Party Committee Secretariat calculated that, from 1980 to 1992, reform measures engineered by the centre had cost the provincial government over 13 billion yuan through increasing its expenditure and decreasing its revenue.[19] From the provincial standpoint the cost of these measures should have been shouldered by the central government budget. According to their account, the centre had increased *de facto* the annual remittance from Guangdong by an annual average of 1 billion yuan over the 13-year period since 1980, effectively doubling the remittance rate of the earlier years of that period.

Moreover, Guangdong had been made to give additional contributions to the centre exclusive of formal arrangements under the fiscal system. When the central government went into the red during the late

1980s, as was often the case, the 'extra-contract' remittances of Guangdong became increasingly hefty, often being several times that of the 'normal' remittances under the contract. Table 5.1 sets out the details.

TABLE 5.1. *Guangdong's Fiscal Remittances: 'Contract' and 'Extra-Contract'* (billion yuan)

Period	Total remittances	Contract	Extra-contract	
			Total	% of total remittances
1980–7	12.197	7.334	4.865	39.87
1987	2.319	0.778	1.541	66.45
1988–91	19.308	7.044	12.264	63.52
1991	6.985	1.995	4.990	71.44

Sources: Calculated from Dangdai Zhongguo Congshu Bianji Bu (1991: i. 686–7) and Guangdong Provincial Party Committee (1993: 59).

Available evidence shows that Guangdong resisted this imposed 'obligation', and at times won concessions from the centre. During a meeting in the Central Committee Secretariat in 1982, Guangdong officials together with Fujian officials complained about the additional burden imposed by central borrowing on local revenue.[20] They made remarks such as 'the centre gets the increases in revenue, the province shoulders all the increases in expenditure; we can hardly continue under this type of contractual system.' Some even said, 'Now we know how good the traditional system of "eating from the same pot" is.' In response to their complaints, central leaders agreed that the provinces could from then on retain all new sources of revenue arising from reform whilst, at the same time, the provinces would shoulder all additional expenditures. The meeting also pledged that the centre would not borrow from the two provinces again, and that revenue from the local sale of state bonds would go to the provincial coffers on the understanding that the provinces would also be responsible for their repayment. Revenue collected from the provinces in the form of the 'Energy and Transportation Fund' would subsequently be used to support investment projects in the provinces.[21]

It is noteworthy that the last item mentioned, the Energy and Transportation Construction Fund, had not yet been formally announced at the time of the meeting. Since the Fund was a tax on the extra-budgetary funds of local units, and most of the collected revenue was destined for the central coffers, it was regarded as a typical example of new measures cutting into the retained local revenue which so aggrieved the provinces. By obtaining a pledge that funds would be allocated back to the provinces, Guangdong officials sought to minimize the effect of the measure and to prepare the ground for future bargaining with regard to direct central support in the form of central investment projects.

The province again succeeded in reducing its remittances in 1985, when the *dabaogan* system was renewed for another five years. Annual remittances were reduced from 1 billion yuan to 778 million yuan on the premise that a number of local enterprises had been made central enterprises and the revenue base of the provincial government was thus adversely affected. This arrangement lasted for three years, from 1985 to 1987, and was terminated in 1988 when the fixed-sum contract system was changed to an incremental adjustment contract.[22]

Saving the contract

The most important discretionary behaviour in relation to the fiscal system following the establishment of the *dabaogan* system was that employed in the effort to save this system in 1987–8, and again in 1993, when there were growing signs that the central government intended replacing it with a 'tax-sharing' system. In 1988 Guangdong succeeded in its 'rescue attempt'. By proposing an annual incremental increase of 9 per cent to the original fixed lump-sum remittance, the Guangdong government alleviated the centre's concern that Guangdong might have retained too much for itself. When, in 1993, retaining the system was found to be impossible, the focus changed to that of safeguarding the local interests associated with the system.

1987–1988: Designing the incremental *dabaogan*   Guangdong's lump-sum *dabaogan* system, first established in 1980, was extended for another five years in 1985. In anticipation of its expiry at the end of 1989, the Guangdong government started lobbying again early in 1987. By this time Guangdong was under pressure from the central government to raise its remittances. Table 5.1 shows that in 1987, Guangdong remitted a total of 2.3 billion yuan, more than triple that of the originally contracted amount. Difficulties within the central budget and growing disparities in wealth between Guangdong and the inland provinces made Guangdong's position increasingly vulnerable, given the still very dominant belief in equalization of wealth. The idea of a tax-sharing system, whereby different levels of government have as their source of revenue different taxes and the discussion of which had first occurred in 1984–5, was picked up again in 1987–8. Guangdong did, therefore, have good grounds for concern over the fate of its *dabaogan* system.

In October 1987, around the time of the Thirteenth Party Congress, the Guangdong provincial leadership submitted a report to the Party Centre and the State Council lobbying for more autonomy.[23] With a forward-looking and progressive tone, the report described the surge in foreign investment which had occurred earlier that year and its international background, arguing that the surge signalled the beginning of a new era of development and a golden opportunity for Guangdong and China. Consequently, the centre should delegate further autonomy to Guangdong so that the province might better grasp this opportunity, and hence further advance the nation's quest for development and modernization. It was only at the end of the report that the demand for an extension of the fiscal contractual system was made. The message seemed to be: as more autonomy is needed to enable us better to serve our designated role for the nation, how could there be any question of doing away with existing autonomy (on the fiscal system)?

The lobbying worked. Fourteen days after the report was submitted, Zhao Ziyang, Li Peng and other central leaders received Guangdong's provincial leaders, who were at that time attending the Thirteenth Party Congress in Beijing. Zhao talked about making Guangdong an experimental site for comprehensive reforms, allowing, in principle, the provincial government to launch reform experiments on all fronts.[24] Noting Guangdong's worry about the tax-sharing system, Zhao also pledged that it would not be implemented in Guangdong.[25] Instead, Zhao indicated that the 'sharing-the-total' system could be considered for application to Guangdong.

At this point Guangdong's purpose was only half achieved. It had obtained Zhao's promise regarding the tax-sharing system, but the sharing-the-total system was not much better, given the experience of the three provincial-level municipalities, namely, Beijing, Tianjin and Shanghai, which operated under such a system until 1988. Therefore when the central government requested that Guangdong and the

Finance Ministry work together to produce a specific proposal on the fiscal system,[26] the Guangdong government immediately seized this golden opportunity to intensify its lobbying. A report was promptly submitted in January 1988. In the report, instead of proposing something along the lines of the sharing-the-total system, the Guangdong government proposed instead a modification of the original contractual system. To provide a sweetener, it also suggested that the expiry date of the original lump-sum system be moved forward for two years from the end of 1989 to the end of 1987. From 1988 onwards the annual remittance amount would no longer be a fixed lump sum, but rather increase by a fixed percentage over the remittance amount of the previous year. The incremental rate for 1988–91 was to be fixed at 9 per cent. The report also proposed setting the baseline figure for the calculation of the 1988 remittance figure at 1.414 billion yuan, which was the total fiscal remittance (including 'extra-contract borrowing') for 1987.[27] The incremental rate after 1991 could be subject to change.[28]

The strategy was to surrender part of the revenue voluntarily in order to retain more. The objective was to impress the centre that Guangdong had no intention of jealously hoarding local revenue at the expense of central revenue, thus pre-empting central moves which could prove more disadvantageous to Guangdong. In terms of action the Guangdong government undertook a three-pronged initiative: (1) to cut short the existing lump-sum arrangement for two years; (2) to voluntarily increase its future annual remittance amount by a fixed incremental rate; and (3) to raise the level of the baseline figure for the first year of the new system to include 'extra-contract' remittance, effectively increasing the level of its annual contractual remittance amount in future. The strategy worked, and in February 1988, Guangdong's report was approved by the State Council. As will be noted later in this chapter, many of the other areas of enhanced powers granted at this time were later recentralized in practice during the 1989–91 retrenchment. The agreement on the *dabaogan* fiscal system, however, remained intact.[29]

The flexibility of Guangdong's strategy notwithstanding, Guangdong's success in retaining the *dabaogan* system in 1987 was also due to developments on the national scene. At that time, the tax-sharing system had been little more than a talking point amongst academics and researchers. In view of the spectacular developments in Guangdong since 1979, it was in the interests of most provinces to adopt rather than to scrap the *dabaogan* system. Even among central think tanks, the formulation of the tax-sharing system was at that time still at a rudimentary stage. Consequently, in order to encourage the provinces to develop the economy, the central government was prepared in early 1988 to continue, and in fact to expand, the application of the *dabaogan* system. In 1987 Shanghai obtained approval to begin the new *dabaogan* system as from 1988. In July 1988, the contractual system was extended nationwide, allowing variations in different provinces.[30] In an environment such as this, it was no surprise that the Guangdong government succeeded in its lobbying effort.

1993: Guarding and maximizing vested interest   By the second half of 1993, the centre's intention to implement the tax-sharing system was clear and imminent.[31] Guangdong officials, however, were still inclined to keep the system, which had borne abundant fruit for the past fourteen years.[32] Even after the formal announcement of the new tax-sharing system in December 1993, a number of authoritative provincial government advisers still upheld the view that Guangdong should keep the *dabaogan* system at subprovincial level.[33] However, as the centre's determination to seek change was by then very clear, the focus of the provincial leadership became that of safeguarding Guangdong's vested interests under the new system. A provincial official revealed that the centre had originally intended to base calculations of revenue retentions under the new system on 1992 figures. However, as a result of intense lobbying by Guangdong officials in September 1993, at the time of Vice-Premier Zhu Rongji's visit to Guangdong, the centre agreed to use 1993 as the baseline year. Since the economy was growing rapidly during 1993, with government revenue swelling accordingly, the change of the baseline year from 1992 to 1993 enabled the provinces to retain more revenue under the new fiscal system.[34]

Fixing the base year at 1993 also brought another advantage by allowing the provinces to boost the base figures in the remaining three months of 1993. After Zhu's visit in September, fiscal revenue collected in Guangdong during the fourth quarter of 1993 increased spectacularly, accounting for 37 per cent of the total revenue of that year. Table 5.2 shows the spectacular surge in fiscal revenue collected after September 1993. The chase for more revenue in order to boost the baseline was, in fact, a nationwide phenomenon, but Guangdong was obviously among the more 'aggressive' provinces. Despite the issue of a notice by the central government in mid-November criticizing

TABLE 5.2. *Guangdong's Fiscal Revenue, 1993*
(100 million yuan)

Month	Revenue	% increase over same month in 1992
January	18.7	14.2
February	21.7	39.2
March	24.0	36.8
April	25.4	27.3
May	23.9	34.6
June	24.8	26.6
July	26.2	38.3
August	24.9	46.1
September	27.3	63.3
October	35.6	70.6
November	35.5	105.1
December	58.2	145.7

Source: Personal communication.

and banning such behaviour by provincial governments,[35] Guangdong's revenue nevertheless continued to surge and by an even larger percentage in December 1993.[36]

Guangdong officials could obviously see that this was their last chance to reduce, at relatively low risk, the potential damage to Guangdong's interests under the impending change of fiscal system. One major objective, among others, of the new fiscal system was to centralize more fiscal revenues at central level.[37] Guangdong as the largest benefactor under the *dabaogan* system therefore stood to lose the most. Enlarging the baseline was thus its last chance to cash in on benefits accrued from the old system. This was also why Guangdong officials had focused their lobbying of Zhu Rongji during his visit on the determination of the base year.

In addition to the benefits a higher baseline would bring, the risk of being penalized by the centre for being too aggressive in revenue collection was low. First, the design of the new system was to protect the vested interests of all provinces. Consequently, poor provinces also stood to gain from an inflated baseline. Guangdong was not, therefore, alone in this rush for a higher baseline, and as long as everyone was in the game, the risk of central repercussions on any particular province became much lower. Secondly, the risk was also low due to the unclear boundaries between 'irregular' and 'effective' revenue

collection. It was ironic that provincial governments should be criticized for collecting too much revenue in the fourth quarter of 1993,
when in the past they had been blamed for collecting too little. Since it
was not easy for the central government categorically to establish their
'hypothesis' (i.e., that the surge in fiscal revenue in the fourth quarter
was due to the provincial governments' deliberate effort to boost the
base-year revenue), provincial governments could justify the surge by
putting it down to faster economic growth and more effective and
efficient tax collection.[38]

This was thus a classic example of the interactive use of bargaining
and implementation deviation over a period of time in order further to
advance provincial interests. By first bargaining for a baseline which
was more susceptible to manoeuvre, and then making the best use of
such manoeuvrability, Guangdong was not only able to benefit from a
higher baseline of retained local revenue, but also improved its position
at the time of future bargaining under the new tax-sharing system.[39]

Investment administration

The development of Guangdong's investment authority has been described in Chapter 3. During each wave of national decentralization
Guangdong triumphed in gaining greater autonomy than other provinces nationwide. The focus of this section is on the process: through
what means and strategies the Guangdong leadership managed to
achieve such an advantage relative to other provinces.

Two areas formed the focus of bargaining between Guangdong and
the centre in this respect. First was provincial project approval authority. Given the importance of this authority as noted in previous chapters, the quest for a higher ceiling of provincial authority was ongoing
and relentless. The second area was the investment quotas prescribed
annually by the centre for the provinces. Guangdong's primary objective was always to raise the annual quotas, and abolish them if possible.
If a quota was necessary at all, Guangdong should be given the autonomy to plan its own.

The process whereby Guangdong won concessions in investment
authority from the centre could be boiled down to two tactics: (1) persistent lobbying, (2) trading in specific concessions for general authority. The latter tactic was used in 1979, when Guangdong's officials
traded in specific resource support for increased authority. First, the
centre was impressed about the urgent need for more investment in

Guangdong so that it might fulfil its new role as the forerunner of reform. In the concluding section of the June 1979 report, the centre was
therefore urged to support a number of investment projects in Guangdong. There was even a checklist of specific projects.[40] Strained already
by the huge financial commitments of the 'foreign leap' projects, the
centre was, as expected, not very forthcoming in providing direct
investment. The purpose was thus rather to acquire a higher level of
autonomy in investment administration as 'compensation' for the low
level of central investment funding. It should be noted however, that
the success of this strategy of 'trading in' specific support for greater
policy delegation depended as much on central preferences as on
Guangdong's skills in manoeuvring. Gu Mu, for instance, made it
clear that it would be more pragmatic to expect the centre to give leeway on policy rather than on the financial side. 'We [the centre] will
give neither money nor materials to Guangdong, but we will formu-
late specific policies [to let you develop on your own].'[41] This attitude
was formally adopted in the 24 December 1980 meeting between central, Guangdong and Fujian leaders, chaired by the Party Secretary
General Hu Yaobang, and attended by Zhao Ziyang, Yao Yilin, Gu
Mu and Yang Shangkun. The minutes of the meeting recorded that in
view of the central government being pressed for funds in the economic adjustment period (which lasted from 1980 to 1983), it would
be unable to give much financial support to Guangdong and Fujian.
The two provinces were, in fact, required to contribute still more to the
central coffers. In view of this lack of financial support from the centre,
however, the meeting agreed to simplify the approval procedures for investment and delegate more approval authority to the two provinces.[42]

  This tactic was used again in 1981, when Zhao Ziyang's concern for
the infrastructural sectors was exploited by the Guangdong government to obtain further investment authority. Since energy and transport were traditionally the responsibility of the central government,
Guangdong officials were able to gain some ground by agreeing to
fund a number of energy and transport projects.[43] This was the process leading to the one-step-ahead decentralization in 1982, whereby
Guangdong obtained an approval authority of 30 million yuan, and
50 million yuan for investment in infrastructural projects, two years
ahead of other provinces. Again, notwithstanding Guangdong's success in gaining additional power, the centre's decision brought benefits
for both sides. The central government saw benefits in delegating
authority, since this would help Guangdong to invest in projects

where, in any event, the centre had been unable to sustain the financial commitment single-handedly. It was thus the mutual perception by both parties of being able to benefit from a certain decision, in other words a positive-sum situation, that made changes possible.

Towards the late 1980s the ceiling of project approval authority became so high that the provincial government could plan and approve most, if not all, projects as it saw fit. At times when the value of an investment project exceeded the provincial jurisdiction and in theory should have required the approval of the State Council, a large project would be 'broken down' into several related projects whose separate funding fell well within the jurisdiction of the provincial government.[44] Under these circumstances, the means by which the centre could possibly exercise some control over provincial investment were stripped to only that of the annual central quotas on total investment.

The province was eager to get rid of this last means of central control, however. An attempt was made in 1988. Encouraged by Zhao's favourable response to its October 1987 report,[45] the provincial leadership in a follow-up report in January 1988 asked for further powers, and in particular, the autonomy to plan independently the amount of total investment to be made annually in the province.[46] This and many other requests, though originally approved, were not subsequently implemented, as the national economic situation quickly deteriorated during the second half of 1988 and the centre was keen on re-establishing control.[47] This aborted attempt nevertheless demonstrated that Guangdong's leaders were prepared to go a long way in order to obtain autonomy in investment administration.

BARGAINING FOR DIRECT CENTRAL SUPPORT

The second category of discretionary behaviour, with similar reliance on the centre's co-operation, was the struggle for direct central support to Guangdong's investment. This category differed from the first in that it was concerned with getting a direct injection of capital and resources, whilst preferential policies constituted a form of indirect central support. This had also been the traditional behaviour of provincial governments under the central planning system, when most investment resources came from the central government and the centre was responsible for the planning and approval of most investment projects. Although its significance receded greatly in the 1980s, this

type of behaviour often recurred, and was sometimes used interactively with other types of discretion to produce the desired results.

Direct central investments

The most obvious form of direct central support in the pursuit of
more provincial investment was, obviously, by means of central investment projects and central participation in central–provincial 'joint
venture' projects. The amount of central capital injection is, however,
difficult to ascertain, given the lack of statistical information on central investment by province.[48] In one calculation by Guangdong's
officials, cumulative central investment in Guangdong's electricity,
roads and bridges, and telecommunications sectors amounted to 580
million yuan, only 2.2 per cent of the total investment actually carried
out in these sectors in Guangdong.[49] However, this referred only to
central investment within the state plan. In addition there were those
central investments by various central ministries in Guangdong which
were *not* within the investment plan of the State Planning Commission, the so-called outside-plan projects. As the economy of Guangdong developed and the province became a still stronger magnet for
investment,[50] the number of outside-plan central projects increased.
An estimate by a Guangdong source put the share of central investment in total investment from 1980 to 1991 at 15 per cent.[51] How this
percentage was arrived at, however, was nowhere elaborated and so
remained unclear.[52]

Nevertheless, Table 3.8 has given the percentage of central and local
investment by administration subordination in Guangdong. This
could at least serve as a rough estimate of the amount of direct central
support Guangdong succeeded in attracting. The percentage of central investment by subordination from 1984 to 1992 was about 22 per
cent, and Table 3.10 shows that Guangdong has invested a not insignificant amount in central projects, probably as a result of bargaining with the central government to 'fish' for central investment.

'Mutual fishing' was the strategy taken by both the central and
provincial governments to attract the capital of the other party. In
order to succeed in 'fishing' others' resources, however, one was often
obliged to volunteer one's own resources in the first place. For provinces seeking to attract large-scale central investment projects, for instance, the willingness to shoulder part of the bill would enhance the
possibility of success, given the tight financial situation of the central

government. On the other hand, the centre had an interest in encouraging provincial governments to invest more in 'bottleneck' infrastructure facilities by itself providing part of the funds or other necessary resources for the projects. The expansion of Shantou Airport was one instance of central–provincial 'mutual fishing' in Guangdong. A quote from Zhao Ziyang speaking to Shantou's officials in 1986 reveals the dynamics of this practice:

I think the [Aviation Bureau] might be unable to allocate that much money for the project in a year, because they have made promises to many similar projects nationwide. If the costs of all these projects are added together, they simply do not have enough funds. Perhaps you should pay the bills first, or you can pay on behalf of the Bureau. . . . You promised to shoulder 20 million yuan, and now you say you also have difficulty in raising that amount all at once. How can you then expect the Bureau to raise the promised 40 million yuan all at once? You had better pay your part of the bill first, then I shall telephone Beijing to ask the Bureau to consider whether they can squeeze out any more.[53]

Despite the lack of clear and unambiguous data on the exact amount of direct central investment in Guangdong, the general impression in Beijing amongst planning and finance officials was that, contrary to the picture portrayed by Guangdong's officials, Guangdong had in fact fared quite well in attracting investment from central ministries. The remarks of a central planning official were revealing:

In some cases it is the richer localities who can do better in attracting funds and investments than the poorer guys, because those who have money to lend and invest expect a higher and quicker return.[54]

This remark reflects the changes in the rules of the game as a result of the progression of economic reform. Under the traditional system, when the concern of the central government ministries was less for economic benefits and more for social stability and resource equalization, a commonly used tactic for attracting central funding had been 'crying wolf', thus exaggerating crises within one's jurisdiction. Poorer areas might thus have had an edge over richer areas. Since reform the overall emphasis had shifted from one of even development to the pace of development. In this new context, central ministries when deciding on investment became more like profit/cost centres seeking to maximize returns. While the use of traditional tactics was not precluded, their use nevertheless had to be combined with new strategies.

One would have to be able to offer a prospect of high return, for instance, in order to be effective in attracting investment. Consequently, as the economy of Guangdong blossomed, the province became a strong magnet for investment capital as units nationwide were anxious to come to the province to make money.

This change in tactics in turn brought changes to the relationship between the investing central ministries and the receiving provinces. Under the traditional system resources were distributed via administrative channels, and this gave the central government a commanding position in the allocation of investment funding. Provinces seeking central investment resources were reduced to asking for favours from the relevant ministries. As the rules of the game changed under reform, fast-growing provinces like Guangdong consequently had a much improved position, as the previous 'central boss' had become more like a co-partner in economic development.

Such changes in the central–provincial relationship were also reflected in Guangdong's motives behind its attraction of central investment since reform.[55] The incentive had been, traditionally, one of economics: attracting external investment could help Guangdong to enlarge its investment capital and thus expand its economy. However, as capital supply improved substantially from the early 1980s, this economic motive became less significant and, therefore, much less dominant in the minds of Guangdong officials. Instead, investment from central ministries and other provinces was welcome as part of the effort to cultivate nationwide support for Guangdong. By sharing the prospect of economic growth with central ministries and other provinces, the Guangdong government sought to dispel misgivings and turn its competitors and potential 'enemies' into partners and supporters. This mentality is clearly expressed in the following comment by a Guangdong official:

some provinces, especially the inland provinces, are still endowed with the mentality of the central planning system, and regard central investment purely as an administrative appropriation of funds. They are therefore not prepared to accept that if they want central investment nowadays, they themselves need to offer something in return, either in the form of potential profits from the projects, or by the provinces sharing the investment capital and the cost of the project, or both. Guangdong has long recognized that the attraction of central investment is similar to the operation of a joint-venture business. Both parties [Guangdong and the central ministry] have to bear the costs, with both sharing the benefits.[56]

Bank finance

There are no clear sets of statistics on central financial support given to Guangdong's investment via the banking system. An account by Guangdong's planning officials put such financial support between 1980 and 1988 at some 26.6 billion yuan.[57] This was given in the form of central bank loans to cover the shortfall of deposit–loan balance in Guangdong's banks. After deducting the transfer to the centre of various bank funds, including deposit liquidity provision, and the 'involuntary' purchase of central bonds of about 13.4 billion yuan, the net injection of central money into Guangdong's banking system during 1980–8 amounted to 13.2 billion yuan. Since the interest rate on the central bank loans was very low, and much of the loans from Guangdong's banks was used for investment purposes, this amounted to a fairly substantial central subsidy to Guangdong's investment capital.[58]

Guangdong officials were keen to obtain central loans via the financial system. For instance, when Zhao Ziyang, Hu Qili and Tian Jiyun visited Shantou in February 1986, officials from Shantou lobbied the centre to increase the flow of central bank loans to Shantou's banks and to waive the 10 per cent remittance from Shantou's total bank deposits to the central bank. In response, Zhao revealed that the total value of cash circulation in Guangdong already amounted to one-third of the national total, and that money had already been diverted to Guangdong from inland provinces such as Xinjiang, Inner Mongolia and Gansu.[59] In other words, Guangdong had been using the deposit resources of the inland provinces to make up the shortfall of its own deposits in satisfying the demand for bank finance emanating from investment activities. Shantou's request was thus turned down by Zhao as utterly inappropriate. Guangdong's enthusiasm to obtain ever more central resources was, however, not dampened, and in fact persisted after there was no longer any shortfall in its deposit–loan balance after 1991. An informed source in Guangdong revealed that notwithstanding the abundance of deposits since 1991, the Guangdong government continued to bargain with the centre for fund injection, and succeeded in obtaining central bank loans amounting to some 1 billion yuan per year.[60] Apparently it was the view of Guangdong officials that so long as the centre required Guangdong's banks to give out 'policy loans' as prescribed in the annual bank finance plan, Guangdong should be entitled to some form of compensatory subsidy.[61]

Apart from direct central investment and subsidy through cheap bank loans, another form of direct central support in Guangdong was the injection of fiscal transfer funds to pay for specific social and economic needs. Some examples are the anti-poverty funds for poor counties and villages, subsidies for natural disasters and various types of price subsidies. The linkage of these central resources to provincial investment was more indirect, by making available the equivalent amount of local resources which could then be channelled into investment projects. Anti-poverty funds were, however, often found to have ended up in investment projects in the poor areas.

This kind of central fund injection in Guangdong was reportedly a very small amount. One estimate for the period 1980–8 was 2 billion yuan, about 3 per cent of the total provincial fiscal revenue for the period.[62] During interviews, Guangdong officials frequently stated that the province had shouldered most of the costs of reform which, according to the traditional division of responsibility, should have been met by the central government, and which was still the practice in the case of less well-off provinces.[63]

Sometimes the aim of winning central funds was attained the other way round: by remitting less to the centre. For instance, apart from the annual fiscal contractual remittance, part of the profits of those provincial departments which had traditionally been managed by the central ministries had to be remitted to the central ministries. Provincial officials would seek by any means to reduce such additional remittances outside the fiscal system. In 1983, for instance, Guangdong officials attempted to solicit the support of Gu Mu in abolishing the annual remittance of 2 million yuan to the Telecommunications Ministry during his visit to Guangdong.[64]

Asking for direct central support was a frequent occurrence in the interactions between Guangdong officials and central leaders, particularly in the earlier years of opening and reform. As previously noted, however, not all pledges of support Guangdong initially obtained from the centre materialized in practice.[65] Having won a pledge did, nevertheless, entitle Guangdong to bargain for other 'goodies' as 'compensation' and many favourable policies were subsequently obtained in this manner. Some examples of favourable policies won in this way are: the central endorsement for using foreign capital on infrastructural development, the introduction of tolls to finance the construction of highways and bridges, and the power to raise rail freight fares to finance railway developments, all of which had far-reaching significance for investment growth in Guangdong.[66] Another example was the expansion of Guangdong's project approval authority, which allowed Guangdong to invest more freely in energy and transport projects, which had traditionally been planned and financed by the centre. A popular statement often used by central leaders in the early 1980s was: 'Ask for money, no, sorry; ask for policies, take a few.'[67] This vividly reflects the situation whereby favourable policies were granted as compensation for aborted promises of direct support. The importance of this provincial discretionary behaviour of bargaining for central resources, therefore, lies beyond its immediate effect on the amount of resources it actually acquired.

FLEXIBLE IMPLEMENTATION OF CENTRAL POLICIES

A category of discretionary behaviour for which the Guangdong government became especially famous during the 1980s was flexible implementation of central policies. This section discusses Guangdong's flexible manoeuvres regarding two different kinds of central policies: (1) 'new' central policies which the province had bargained hard to obtain in the first place; (2) 'traditional' policies pre-dating the reforms, which the province still had to tolerate.

Shaping a new reform policy: the special economic zones

The idea of establishing special economic zones to speed up foreign investment and economic development was first suggested by the Guangdong provincial leadership to the centre at the Central Work Conference of April 1979,[68] and endorsed by the centre in July 1979. The primary purpose of the special economic zones, as then conceived, was to attract foreign investment. The influx of investment from inland provinces and the central ministries was to be strictly controlled. Prior approval also had to be obtained for domestic units outside Shenzhen, the first and largest special economic zone, seeking to set up companies within the zone.[69]

As soon as the construction of the zones took off, the detrimental effect of the tight restriction on the influx of domestic capital became apparent. Not only did the construction of the city's infrastructure desperately require investment from nationwide units, but the attraction of foreign investment also required the presence of a considerable number of domestic investors to act as partners in the joint ventures.

Subsequently domestic capital from all over the country flowed in and, by 1985, accounted for over 40 per cent of cumulative investment in Shenzhen, whilst foreign capital accounted for under 20 per cent.[70]

This development was clearly not in line with the original conception of the centre.[71] By 1989, 46 central ministries and 29 provinces had staked their claims in Shenzhen. A total of 3,900 enterprises were established with these central and provincial units, not including those foreign joint ventures of which these units were partners. Realized capital injection amounted to 3 billion yuan. This 'domestic' sector compared favourably with the foreign sector, which in 1989 consisted of just under 2,600 foreign-invested enterprises, with a total realized capital injection of US$2.7 billion.[72]

What had taken place was a transformation of the original policy of restricting domestic investment and participation to one of enthusiastic attraction. As early as 1982, the Guangdong leadership had pointed out that experience had proved the importance of soliciting the participation of the entire country in the construction and development of the special economic zones.[73] With some reluctance and after reflection, the centre also eventually acknowledged that the utilization of capital from all over the country and the participation of various domestic units nationwide was a major success factor in Shenzhen's development. In fact, the momentum of domestic investment in the zone was so strong during the 1980s that *ex post facto* central recognition was nearly mandatory.

This transformation was possible because from the beginning the original policy had been tentatively set and both the central and Guangdong governments had no definite idea regarding the development of special economic zones. Gu Mu's comments during a March 1980 meeting with Guangdong and Fujian officials substantiate this observation:

We have not specified in detail [in the July 1979 Central Committee Notice no. 50] the methods by which the special economic zones should be developed, nor how the zones should look in future. Comrades from Guangdong did write a few outlines, about one to two pages long, but we felt they were too abstract. We actually did not know how to get specific. Therefore we simply left the details unsaid.[74]

Neither the central government nor the Guangdong leadership had a firm or clear idea of how to proceed with the general concept of establishing special economic zones. Bearing this in mind, it is not surprising that the ostensibly clearly worded policy on restricting domestic investment in the special economic zones should have been so easily discarded in practice. As the provincial leadership, together with the leaders of the zones, were in the front line of policy implementation, they were able to realize at an earlier stage the folly of the earlier design to restrict the role of participation and investment of units nationwide, whilst central leaders were apparently stuck with the earlier preconception for a much longer period. Like all reform measures of the 1980s, the experimental nature of the policy allowed for, and necessitated, a substantial amount of flexibility at the implementation level.[75]

Discretion in the traditional system

China's economic reforms took place within the context of the traditional central planning system. This meant that at any one time, two systemic 'streams' were operating simultaneously. The first was the new reform systems, which were set up on a tentative basis. The other was the pre-existing systems operating under the central planning system of government and economic administration. The uneasy co-existence between the old and new systems demanded an innovative interpretation of traditional systems and policies. Discretion thus abounded.

Discretion regarding the traditional systems bore different characteristics, however. The old systems, as compared to those of the emerging reform policies, were relatively specific and had a clear purpose and rationale. There was, in other words, a more established and formidable body of vested interests. It was thus less easy simply to 'muddle through', and change the content of the policy through actual practice, than was the case in the new reform measures. Discretionary behaviour in this context was often applied within the confines of the policies, or failing that, more efforts would be required to justify the explicit violation of established policies. In this section these two varieties of discretionary behaviour are discussed in the context of the implementation of two specific policies.

Expanding the central quotas on annual investment

As previously discussed, the central quota, or the central control figure as it was known within China, on annual investment was one of the few major instruments through which the centre sought to control investment activities in the provinces. Guangdong's discretionary behaviour towards this central control instrument fell into three strategies: (1) seeking its abolition; (2) ignoring it; or (3) seeking to raise the ceiling.

An example of the first case occurred in February 1988, as discussed earlier in this chapter. The other two strategies were commonly used as a matter of routine. At times when the centre was more concerned about economic growth and was therefore more tolerant towards excess investment, the quotas would be more or less ignored by the provincial government. On the other hand, at times of economic retrenchment, when the centre became more serious about the scale of investment in the provinces, the provincial government had to act with more prudence. More efforts were made towards enlarging the quotas, instead of simply ignoring them.

Table 3.6 has shown that the central quotas were, as a rule, substantially exceeded in actual practice, normally by at least 100 per cent. In 1985 total investment reached 18.5 billion yuan, against a central quota of only 5.5 billion yuan, less than one-third the amount of investment. This exemplified the fact that the control figures were, for most of the time, not taken seriously. In early 1993, when the entire country was in a relaxed mood regarding central control, Guangdong Provincial Planning Commission, in a quite defiant move, even ceased its practice of assigning investment control figures to the subprovincial levels of government after it was assigned a lump-sum quota by the central government. The quota instruction was simply filed away. In the eyes of provincial officials, the task had become little more than a ritual surviving from the old system of central planning, and which, as such, had no place in the current drive towards a market economy.[76]

During retrenchment years, however, provinces were under much more pressure from the centre and the quotas could no longer be merely ignored. The added pressure usually came in two forms. First, the centre was likely to prescribe a smaller quota for annual investment than otherwise expected. If retrenchment came in the middle of the planning year, the quotas might even be reduced. Secondly, the centre would be more displeased if the quota was greatly exceeded than it would be in more 'normal' years. The usual response of provinces during such 'crisis' periods was to bargain for a larger quota from the outset, and when actual investment still exceeded the approved amount, to come up with various excuses by which to escape responsibility. Guangdong, with its active investment scene, was particularly sensitive to any tightening of central control.

A vivid example is found in Guangdong's bargaining for a higher investment quota for the 1981–5 period. In 1982 and 1983 the central government was eager to contain the investment drive set off by the earlier 'foreign Great Leap', and to restructure investment in preparation for further economic reforms. From the centre's point of view, outside-plan investment in Guangdong and Fujian was excessive and containment was necessary, as Yao Yilin made clear in February 1982:

Many economic activities in the two provinces took place outside the state plans. . . . The economic policy of the two provinces needs review . . . There are many outside-plan investment projects there. . . . The value of outside-plan investment in the two provinces is 44 per cent of the total of outside-plan investments nationally.[77]

In response the Guangdong government argued that the centre had failed to consider the requirements of Guangdong's assigned role in the economic opening up and reform of the country. The quota prescribed by the centre was, consequently, totally unrealistic.[78] First, economic development and reform would necessitate more investment. Secondly, the investment quota prescribed for 1981–5, which was only announced in February 1983 at 2.8 billion yuan, did not even allow for the investment already made in 1981 and 1982, amounting to 3.9 billion yuan. As briefly noted in Chapter 3, this was a *fait accompli* argument, despite the fact that much of the *fait accompli* actually consisted of outside-plan projects which, in theory, should not have existed in the first place.

The Guangdong government adopted a two-pronged strategy in order to overcome central pressure in this instance. First, repeated attempts were made during annual planning conferences to seek revisions of the quota. Secondly, central leaders were courted for their support whenever opportunities arose.[79] These two methods were used interactively. Lobbying central leaders was contingent on the cultivation of the 'right atmosphere', upon which success of bargaining at the operational level depended. On the other hand, nice words by central leaders had to be translated into specific concessions and resources through hard bargaining during annual planning conferences. Successful lobbying softened the centre's position, making way for the success in routine bargaining which actually delivered the results. Cumulatively, as a result of persistent bargaining during annual planning meetings, Guangdong's investment quota for the entire

1981–5 period was doubled to 6.3 billion yuan from the original figure of 2.8 billion yuan.

In the end local capital construction investment finally achieved in Guangdong during 1981–5 reached 12.5 billion yuan, exceeding the enlarged quota by nearly 100 per cent. By voicing protest at the outset, however, Guangdong had psychologically prepared central leaders for the later proven insufficiency of the quota. Bargaining served, therefore, a dual purpose. First, the frontier of central control was pushed back, thus enlarging room for legitimate investment. Secondly, the bargaining activity prepared the ground for central tolerance of the 'illegitimate' provincial implementation that might still have to take place.

One major tactic the Guangdong government used when bargaining with the centre was to focus on *specific* projects.[80] This tactic enabled Guangdong to enlarge its leeway even in 1989, which was the most severe retrenchment year in China in terms of contraction in investment since the commencement of economic reform.[81] In 1989 the centre initially applied a firm hand. The investment quota was 20.5 per cent and 57.8 per cent respectively less than the quota and provisional estimates of completed investment for 1988, as well as substantially below the expectation of the provincial government.[82] However, available data, as detailed in Table 3.6, show that the 1989 quota was eventually adjusted upwards to 14 billion yuan, a 42 per cent increase from the original level. Bearing in mind the original determination of the centre to reduce investment earlier in the year, this way by no means a small achievement of Guangdong. The method used to achieve this increase was, according to an informed source, by bringing the centre's attention to the practical difficulties the original quota had caused. The strategy was to focus on specific projects, arguing that severe reduction in the quota would delay valuable projects.[83] Rather than arguing with the centre on matters of principle, the Guangdong leadership brought up 'mundane' concerns and put forward specific calculations of costs and benefits. In this way Guangdong managed to loosen the tight reins imposed by the centre, even at a time of 'crisis'.

The Guangdong government was thus able to enlarge its room for manoeuvre, even under more difficult circumstances, by playing around the confines of central policies and asking for 'minor' adjustments. In order to deliver the greatest results, the Guangdong government tailored its strategies to the calculated responses of the centre. Notwithstanding its ineffectiveness most of the time, the investment quota had a special place in the minds of central officials, not least because it was almost the last means with which the centre could ostensibly exercise some control over provincial investment. Consequently, with the exception of the 1988 attempt as discussed earlier in this chapter, Guangdong avoided openly challenging the central policy of investment scale control, choosing instead to bargain for special consideration on a more mundane level. The purpose was to avoid unnecessarily provoking the centre and inviting backlash. However, in areas where central determination was more ambiguous, as the following section shows, Guangdong's discretionary behaviour was more straightforward.

Justifying the breaking of 'traditional' rules on bank finance management

The central policy on bank loans required state banks from 1979 to distinguish two kinds of loans made to enterprises. One kind of loans supplied the working capital, while the other financed investment. Separate quotas were assigned for each. The purpose was to allow the central government to control the amount of funding used for investment, and thus indirectly control the amount of investment made by enterprises. In practice, this policy was extensively circumvented as a substantial portion of loans originally assigned for working capital was actually spent on investment projects.[84] The precise extent of the diffusion of funds is difficult to ascertain, however. The State Audit Commission has also recently started auditing the work of banks. In the case of Guangdong, only one bank has been inspected each year due to limitations of manpower and other resources.[85] In an audit inspection of the Construction Bank conducted in 1993, it was discovered that in some Guangdong branches up to 3 per cent of the loans ostensibly used for financing working capital was actually spent on investment. On average the proportion in Guangdong in 1992 was about 1 to 2 per cent.[86] In 1992 the value of bank loans directed towards working capital, in accordance with official statistics, was 141.36 billion yuan, and the value of investment loans was 23.58 billion yuan.[87] A diversion of 2 per cent of the former kind of loan means that, apparently, investment loans had been increased by more than 10 per cent.

The scale on which central rules had been violated was, however, not the most significant feature of this discretionary behaviour. The significance lay in the almost overt advocacy of the abolition of the central rules. Local bank officials wrote openly for the diversion of loans for investment purposes. The 'flexible' approach to the management of the two quotas was, for instance, heralded by a Shenzhen bank official as one major 'reform measure' that had helped solve the capital problems of Shenzhen.[88] This view was echoed by an audit official in the provincial government.

There are both positive and negative reasons for this [extensive occurrence of loan diversion]. The negative reason is corruption. Some bank staff have been able to obtain 'benefits' from enterprises in return for their 'support' to investment projects. This works in such a way that when quotas for investment have been used up, or if the projects concerned do not meet the criteria for investment loans, bank staff may lend the money in the form of working capital loans. . . . As regards the positive reasons, the system of separate quotas for working capital and investment loans was in fact a product of the central planning system. When the system was first set up, there was the concern that loans for investment would, in practice, be little more than grants by another name [traditionally most investment projects were financed by state fiscal grants]. Control on the scale of loans was therefore necessary. However, nowadays as the market economy gradually develops in Guangdong, the capacity for cost control by enterprises has been increasing substantially. Under such circumstances the banks in Guangdong feel that they should be able to use the capital available to them more flexibly.[89]

Among Guangdong officials there was thus a feeling that the system of separate quotas for working capital loans and investment loans had become outdated. The above comment suggests that provincial auditing officials appeared to take a similar view towards the legitimacy of what was, strictly speaking, 'unlawful' behaviour from an auditing perspective.

The 'flexibility' with which the Guangdong government implemented central policies attracted much attention both inside and outside China. It raised eyebrows the most because, unlike the first two types of discretionary behaviour, implementation discretion required more calculation and strategic analysis on the part of provincial officials. Provincial officials first had to assess the suitability of central policies for local application, and subsequently undertake the course of action which would bring the most benefit and incur the least cost, in terms of 'penalties'. Whether in theory or in practice, implementation discretion reflected a higher degree of provincial independence than did the scramble for preferential policies and direct central support.

Relative to the other two categories of discretionary behaviour, i.e. the development of the non-state sector and the embracing of internationalization, which will be discussed below, implementation discretion was also more directly targeted at central policies. Such close relations with and yet independence from the centre made the controversies which consequently resulted come as no surprise.

The controversy reached a climax during the 1989 retrenchment, when Guangdong came under great pressure to conform to central requirements and, therefore, to cut investment. The flexibility with which the province had implemented central policies in the past came under severe attack. Despite the harsh approach adopted by the centre towards the Guangdong government at that time, the latter nevertheless still published in a provincial paper an up-front counter-attack on the criticisms. This article defended Guangdong's flexible implementation of central policies, and argued that, rather than blindly following the vagaries of central policies, 'unsuitable policies' should be either ignored or at least revised. The following self-explanatory quotes fully explicate the conflict and are indicative of the degree of independence which had developed within the provincial leadership. On the inevitability of flexible implementation, in the generic sense:

the directives and policies of the Party are formulated in accordance with the objective and practical situations of a certain time; they themselves are not constant and are subject to change. . . . Some policies and directives no longer suit the changed objective situation. We should take the initiative to discard these, rather than try to retain the unretainable.

In the particularistic sense:

the directives and policies of the Party were formulated to reflect the long-term interests of the community as a whole. But there are huge differences between various sectors and regions. . . . When these policies do not suit the particular circumstances of the local situation, there is no need to apply them strictly and without adaptation.

For an example of this case:

the commodity economy has become quite well developed in the coastal region. The prices of many commodities in this region have already been deregulated. There is thus no need and no sense in going back to the old ways of administrative control of prices and the use of rationing in the effort to contain inflation.

And for the case of Guangdong:

The Party Centre and the State Council previously instructed Guangdong and Fujian to go one step ahead of the rest of the country . . . and allowed the two provinces to act according to the Special Policy, and 'flexible measures'. This means that the centre does not require the two provinces to follow strictly the policy documents which are meant for the use of the rest of the country, but rather to follow the Special Policy documents tailored specifically for these regions.

On the need to implement reform policies flexibly:

as reform is a totally new task and there is no precedent in this area, mistakes are inevitable. It is therefore inevitable that some reform policies are later found to be unsuitable when applied to the actual situation. With this under-standing, . . . we should then move quickly to adjust and revise policies which are found to be inappropriate to the practical situations.

And, on the ultimate criterion of whether or not one has followed the (centre's) policy:

The four modernizations are the major tasks of the entire party, and product-ivity is the criterion by which to judge whether our work is good or not . . .

Finally, the counter-attack on the critics:

Now that the centre has flashed a 'special green light' to the two provinces, and we [in going in the direction of this special green light] are merely going around the 'ordinary' red light [meant for the rest of the country], what is there to be criticized? On the contrary, if somebody does not implement the Special Policy formulated by the centre or if somebody tries to put their own limita-tions on it, then this should amount to the flouting of [Party] discipline. . . . Isn't this going against economic opening up and reform, the highest-order policy directive of the Party?[90]

As seen in this counter-attack launched by the Guangdong govern-ment, Guangdong was not only defending its flexible measures in specific circumstances, but also challenging the orthodoxy of specific central policies on retrenchment at a general level. The implication of this shift in emphasis from operational applicability under specific cir-cumstances to the general 'correctness' of central policies will be dis-cussed in Chapter 7.

DEVELOPING THE NEW HORIZON: BEYOND THE BUDGET

The three types of discretionary behaviour discussed so far share a char-acteristic. These were responses calculated by the provincial leadership to achieve the greatest benefit in a centrally dominated environment. In comparison this fourth type of discretion had a strong flavour of 'self-reliance'. Efforts were oriented to developing the strength of the province in investment, and in so doing the provincial government moved beyond the traditional domain of governmental action in China: the state sector and, within this, the budgetary sector. Discretionary actions taken in this respect can be summed up in three major categories. First, more funds were allowed to be retained at the enterprise level to facilitate investment by enterprises. As long as Guangdong had enough revenue to pay the contracted remittance amount to the centre, there was no point in raising too much revenue as this would result in too large a surplus in the provincial budget, which would, in turn, invite 'borrowing' requests from the centre, or worse still, an upward adjustment of the contracted amount. Revenue left at the level of enterprises could, on the other hand, increase investment further within the province. Secondly, policies and practices were devised to encourage the development of the collective and individual/private sector, and new state enterprises beyond the domain of the budget. These enterprises had the advantage of falling outside, or at the periphery of, the ambit of the central planning system. The various control instruments of the central government did not usually touch these sectors, and when they did, they were ineffective. Expanding these sectors would therefore enlarge the part of the provincial economy which was less subject to central control, both in terms of investment plans and revenue extraction. The next, and third, category of discretion aimed at recentralizing those funds which had been diffused to enterprises back to the provincial coffers. In the 1980s social and economic development in China was still at a stage whereby the government had a major and direct role both as investor and financier. Therefore while the provincial government was reducing the taxes of enterprises in order not to swell its fiscal coffers and thereby attract the unwelcome attention of the centre, the province had to re-collect at least part of that revenue in order to be able to finance its investment and other economic activities. Unlike fiscal revenue, which was collected primarily by the finance department, which then allocated the funds to various user departments as fiscal expenditure, this income was usually collected in the form of fees separately by different user departments. Such revenue was often placed outside the budget as part of the extra-budgetary revenue of the collecting departments. As a result of these manoeuvres, extrabudgetary revenue grew rapidly during the 1980s.

TABLE 5.3. *Budgetary and Extrabudgetary Revenues in Guangdong* (billion yuan)

Year	Budgetary		Extrabudgetary	
	Total	Growth (%)	Total	Growth (%)
1982	3.83	—	2.90	—
1983	3.63	–5.2	3.17	9.3
1984	4.96	36.2	3.70	16.7
1985	6.97	40.5	4.56	23.2
1986	n/a	n/a	5.20	14.0
1987	9.59	n/a	6.72	29.2
1988	10.76	12.2	8.41	25.2
1989	13.69	27.2	9.08	8.0
1990	13.10	–4.3	9.84	8.4

n/a = not available

Source: Ministry of finance (1986*a*: 54 and 144; 1992: 59, 204).

Cutting back the budgetary sector

The provincial governments could achieve their aim of retaining more funds outside the budget, and thus artificially keeping the provincial fiscal coffers 'slim', in three major ways. These were: (1) applying the policy of tax exemption and reduction extensively and generously; (2) manoeuvring the method of calculation and tolerating tax evasion; and (3) diverting part of the fiscal revenue collected by finance departments to the extrabudgetary sector through, for instance, setting up 'private accounts'. Tax revenue was thus sieved during various stages of tax evaluation, collection and accounting, swelling the extrabudgetary revenue as a result.

Exempting and reducing tax payments

Reducing the tax burden of enterprises via various tax exemption and reduction policies was in fact an approach adopted by the central government after reform in order to develop the economy and attract foreign investment. In 1977, the State Council approved a notice drafted by the Finance Ministry on the tax administration system. This notice recognized the necessity sometimes to reduce and exempt taxes payable by state enterprises whose difficulty was traceable to government policies. Different levels of government were assigned different jurisdictions regarding the approval of tax exemption/reduction applications.[91] In theory, only the State Council had the power of promulgating new taxes and changing the tax rates. In practice, however, since provincial governments were explicitly allowed a wide range of discretion in the implementation of the tax policies, they in effect decided the effective tax rates. The trend of offering ever more favourable tax policies by provincial governments nationwide to encourage domestic and foreign investment was, therefore, arguably only an extended version of the original central policy.

The notice also stated that authority should, in principle, not be delegated further to subprovincial levels. Presumably, therefore, the subprovincial levels did not have authority over tax exemption and reduction.[92] However, in practice the delegation of authority to subprovincials was a widespread and accepted practice throughout the provinces, to the extent that even central officials appear at one time to have endorsed such a supposedly illegal practice. In a book on tax exemption/reduction policies written by officials from the Finance Ministry, the State Taxation Bureau and the State Audit Commission in 1993, the division of jurisdiction amongst the provincial, district and county levels was described as part of the country's tax exemption/reduction policy.[93] The tax/finance department at the county level, it was written, had the jurisdiction to exempt or reduce taxes of up to 30,000 yuan in a single application. The district level had a jurisdiction of up to 100,000 yuan, above which the provincial tax bureau would be responsible. The contradiction between such practices and the provision of the 1977 notice, which was still officially in force, was obvious. These practices were the result of provincial discretion beyond the general provision of central regulations.[94] However, such 'native' policies were described by central officials in a neutral manner as 'the' policy on tax exemption, reflecting the ambiguity of lawfulness regarding provincial discretion.

There is evidence that the above description of subdelegation is still an understatement of the practice in Guangdong. In a provincial government notice in 1992, a county-level city, Shunde, was given the authority to approve applications for tax exemption and reduction of amounts under 600,000 yuan.[95] This level of authority was six times that of the 100,000 yuan jurisdiction of district-level governments in the country, according to the account by the central officials. This 'enhanced' jurisdiction was indicative of the substantial amount of tax alleviation in Guangdong. One estimate from the Guangdong government put the total value of tax exemption and reduction from

1979 to 1987 at 3.54 billion yuan, which was equivalent to over 8 per cent of the total revenue from industrial and commercial taxes, the major source of fiscal income in China.[96] Due to the sensitivity of the issue and the consequent difficulty in calculating the total amount of tax revenue forgone as a result of tax exemption and reduction, the above estimates are likely to be a gross understatement of the total picture.[97]

The 'unenthusiastic collectors'

Apart from generously reducing the tax burden of enterprises, provincial and lower-level governments could reduce revenue inflow to the state budget by manipulating tax assessment, and by being lax in collection. This tactic was particularly common in the case of new taxes imposed by the centre. One example was the implementation of the Energy and Transport Strategic Construction Fund.[98] In theory, payments into the Fund would increase in line with the extrabudgetary funds of a unit. This, however, was not the case as regards the public roads department in Guangdong. In order to retain more funds within the department with which to finance the province's road construction programme, the Guangdong Government froze the payments of the department into the Fund at the level of 1984. As a result the department was able to retain several hundred thousand yuan in the 1980s.[99]

The Construction Tax was another example. Imposed by the centre from 1983 to 1989, 10 per cent of the value of investment using funds outside the state budget, and including local budgetary funds used in outside-plan projects, was required to be paid as this tax. However, in practice, whilst investment in Guangdong continued to grow spectacularly during the 1980s, the amount of Construction Tax collected remained more or less static, and at an extraordinarily low level. Total investment in 1985, 1986 and 1987 was 18.46 billion yuan, 21.65 billion yuan and 25.1 billion yuan respectively,[100] whereas Construction Tax collected in these three years amounted to only 90 million yuan, 107 million yuan, and 115 million yuan, accounting for 0.5 per cent, 0.49 per cent and 0.48 per cent of total investment.[101] In some periods the tax revenue even dropped in relation to a rising investment total. The amount collected in 1987 and 1988, for instance, amounted to only 40 to 50 per cent of the amount payable, according to one official estimate.[102]

A major method through which to retain more revenue outside the state budget was that of manoeuvring the baseline of the remittance contracts with enterprises. The contracting system regarding enterprises' payable tax/profit was endorsed and its application extended to nearly all state enterprises by the centre in 1987. The system was intended to cultivate a greater potential for growth among the traditionally weak state enterprises. As the calculation of the baseline was based on the average tax level of enterprises over the previous few years, this method of tax assessment resulted in more revenue being retained by the enterprises, an advantage similar to that gained by the provincial government in the fiscal system. Moreover, in the event of straitened times when profits fell below average, enterprises would still be able to apply for temporary tax reduction or exemption.[103]

The contracting system counted on the superordinate departments and provincial governments negotiating an adequate 'contract' through which to find a balance between the competing needs to encourage the incentives of enterprises on the one hand and to ensure an adequate level of fiscal income on the other. However, bearing in mind the possible adverse impact of a large provincial revenue on its fiscal negotiations with the centre, the provincial government was careful not to let the local coffers swell too much, and as a result opted for retaining more within the enterprises. Pushing down the baseline of contracts with enterprises was therefore commonplace amongst local finance departments in Guangdong.[104] Moreover, when first conceived the contracting system was supposed to cover the remittance of profit and profit tax only. However, in the course of implementation the provincial and lower-level governments often also included industrial and commercial taxes, thus further aggravating the drain on fiscal revenue.[105]

In an annual finance inspection in 1989, nearly 60 per cent of the inspected enterprises in Guangdong's state and collective sectors, and 80 per cent of the inspected central enterprises in Guangdong, had experienced such problems.[106] It was nearly impossible, however, to know exactly how much revenue had been kept from the state budget in this way.[107] Apart from the expected difficulty regarding access to such information, an added difficulty was the murky boundary of revenue haemorrhage. For instance, as long as the rules of accounting had been duly observed, the manipulation of the remittance contracts of enterprises was not easily disclosed by ordinary audit scrutiny. Grey areas abounded so that it was difficult to differentiate legal and illegal practices. As an informed source described it, practical situations in the country had changed so much and so rapidly that many accounting and financial rules had become inapplicable and obsolete. When inspecting the accounts of the various units, the audit personnel could not follow the straightforward approach and focus on just the books and rules, but needed to look at the actual situations in order to arrive at a sensible judgement of whether or not a certain act was 'against the rule'. There was, therefore, an inevitable element of subjectivity, adding to the difficulty in ascertaining the extent of revenue haemorrhage in an objective sense.[108]

Diverting budgetary revenue to extrabudgetary funds and
'private accounts'

After initially reducing the tax burden, then manipulating the calculation of tax payments, local finance departments could ultimately reduce the size of fiscal revenue by appropriating part of the collected fiscal revenue to the extrabudgetary funds of the departments. Alternatively, they might divert part of the collected budgetary revenue to 'hidden' or 'private' accounts beyond the coverage of both the budgetary and extrabudgetary fiscal finance.

Budgetary revenue of an *ad hoc* nature was more susceptible to such diversion efforts. One example was income arising from various administrative penalty fees. In 1986, it was discovered that less than 30 per cent of the penalty income entered the budget, as compared to the 70 per cent prescribed by central finance regulations.[109] The relationship between such diversion of funds and investment expansion was apparent as, in this instance, at least 13 per cent of the total revenue arising from such penalty fees and retained outside the state budget had been used for capital construction. Moreover, many such investment projects had not obtained the necessary approval and were thus 'hidden' projects.

Sometimes funds diverted from the state budget did not enter the extrabudgetary funds of the provincial government, but rather entered some obscure accounts kept beyond both the budget and extrabudgetary accounts. The purpose of doing so was to give the diverted funds a greater possibility of escaping central control. In theory the central government knew the amount of funds kept in the extrabudgetary sector, as reflected in the statistics on extrabudgetary funds. Extrabudgetary funds were, therefore, still potentially susceptible to central control.[110] The 'private accounts', on the other hand, were supposedly non-existent and there was, consequently, no control mechanism in force for them at all. This absence of control made the setting up of 'private accounts' even more attractive to provincial and lower-level governments, as they were able to have an even larger degree of autonomy over this part of revenue. 'Private accounts' were thus a widespread phenomenon, existing in all kinds of units at various levels.[111] Even the finance bureaux at provincial and subprovincial levels, which should have acted as guardians of the local budget, had their own private accounts. The finance departments in some Guangdong cities, for instance, opened separate bank accounts to keep their 'private money', diverted from taxes paid by extrabudgetary state enterprises and income from anti-smuggling activities.[112]

Developing the extrabudgetary and non-state sector

The state sector was traditionally the focus of concern within the central planning system. As Guangdong progressed in its economic development, the constraints on the state sector of the economy emanating from the traditional system were increasingly felt. Therefore, moving beyond the traditional model of state enterprises became increasingly the consensus of the Guangdong leadership as regards the direction of Guangdong's economic development. Lin Ruo, Guangdong's former Party Secretary (1986–90), and subsequently Chairman of the Provincial People's Congress Standing Committee, made explicit this strategy and approach of the Guangdong leadership in an article which said:

As state enterprises would not be able to get rid of the centralized control of the state for some time to come, Guangdong has taken the approach of circumventing this obstacle by focusing on the development of collective enterprises of various types. We have not placed these enterprises under the control of the budget. This has worked well and these enterprises have succeeded. That is why the proportion of our state enterprises within the budget has been constantly declining whilst the proportion of collective enterprises of various types is constantly increasing.[113]

In encouraging the development of the collective and private sectors, the Guangdong government not only granted generous tax reduction policies and reduced the taboo areas of private sector activities, it also provided the organizational cover for the new and emerging private sector. In 1989 there were an estimated 800,000 to 900,000 private enterprises in Guangdong. However, the number of private enterprises in the formal register of the Industry and Commerce Bureau was under 6,000, a registration rate of only 0.7 per cent. The vast majority of these private enterprises had been registered as collectives with governmental connivance.[114]

Having been all too aware of 'exploitation' within private enterprises, the central government was slow to recognize the legitimacy of private enterprises. Prior to 1988, private enterprises were deprived of legal existence.[115] Many had existed as individual businesses, although the number of employees had far exceeded the permitted ceiling of eight persons. Many more had operated as collectives due to the convenience resulting from the legitimacy accorded to collective enterprises in an economic management system which was still seriously biased towards the public sector. One major advantage of collective enterprises was their ability to obtain bank finance. Under the constraints of traditional rules, very limited banking services were available to private enterprises. In Foshan, loan policies in the late 1980s prescribed that private individuals and enterprises could normally borrow only 3,000 to 5,000 yuan at one time, and could under no circumstances borrow more than 10,000 yuan. There was, however, no ceiling for collectives. The interest rate for private enterprise loans was also substantially higher than that of loans for collectives.[116] By loosely enforcing the registration of private and collective enterprises, the Guangdong government sought to facilitate the development of an emerging sector outside the auspices of the traditional control systems within a still restrictive macro-environment.

Another category of enterprises promoted by the Guangdong government in order to circumvent the traditional state sector was the so-called 'extrabudgetary state enterprises'. In terms of modes of ownership these enterprises were still owned by the state. Their major difference from the traditional sector was that they were not placed within the state budget, thus the description 'extrabudgetary state enterprises'.

The existence of extrabudgetary state enterprises was not new, but as a major phenomenon it came into being only in the 1980s when investors and funding channels proliferated. Most state enterprises were, traditionally, established by budgetary grants from the state. However, even during the pre-reform period, there were a small number of enterprises which were set up by various departments using their own extrabudgetary funds. These enterprises were usually small in scale and performed only a subsidiary role in the economy. As their

capital came from the extrabudgetary funds of the relevant departments, these enterprises were consequently placed outside of the budget and, after paying indirect taxes (the industrial and commercial
taxes, for instance) to the state coffers, their profits would be shared
entirely between these enterprises and their 'mother units'.[117]

These extrabudgetary state enterprises had obvious utility in provinces' efforts to increase discretionary revenue. All after-tax profits
were shared between the enterprises and the local 'mother units', and
taxes, as discussed previously, could be subject to multiple manipulations by the provincial finance authority. Specifically, Guangdong
finance officials cited three reasons for their placing new state enterprises in the extrabudgetary sector.[118] The first was to help enterprises
to repay bank loans with which most extrabudgetary enterprises were
established. Placing enterprises outside of the budgetary system made
tax reduction and exemption easier. The enterprises could then have
more retained resources with which to repay the loans. Secondly,
placing enterprises outside the budget helped to contain the budgetary revenue baseline of the province, thus reducing the exposure of the
province to extraction pressure from the centre. Thirdly, it was felt that
the province was often left to shoulder additional expenditure arising
from reform or central initiatives. Under the *dabaogan* system, however, it was not easy for the province to bargain for a smaller remittance subsequent to its increased expenditure obligation. Under such
circumstances, the availability of a second source of fiscal revenue to
make up for the new expenditures could help the provincial treasury to
stay afloat.

Moreover, contrary to the central policy that extrabudgetary state
enterprises had to pay taxes into the state budget, all revenues derived
from these enterprises in Guangdong were often placed outside the
budget. A provincial government notice in 1985 openly prescribed
that profit tax revenues from extrabudgetary enterprises be managed
outside the budget even though central policy was that extrabudgetary
enterprises should pay both profit and indirect taxes.[119] This violation
of central policy was only rectified in 1992, after pressure from the
central government following an audit inspection from Beijing, when
another provincial government notice rescinded the 1985 rule, and
proclaimed that taxes paid by the extrabudgetary enterprises would
thereafter be included in the budget.[120]

In a sense the concept of extrabudgetary enterprises was a marginal
and transient one. Before the 1980s these enterprises had been

relatively few in number, small in scale, and therefore largely neglected by the central government. Some regarded the concept as a contradiction in terms, since state enterprises should, by definition, be governed by the state budget.[121] As their numbers grew phenomenally during the 1980s, it was argued that the concept, which had from the beginning been a product of the centrally planned economy, would become increasingly irrelevant in the age of the market economy.[122]

Echoing the confusion in the concept, there were no official statistics on their total number. An account from the State Planning Commission in 1990 estimated the total number nationwide at the end of the 1980s as over 10,000, and the production value of these enterprises as tens of billions of yuan.[123] No similar estimates were available for Guangdong, but officials in Guangdong admitted to an increasing number of extrabudgetary enterprises in the province from 1980. The number of extrabudgetary enterprises in one city, for instance, nearly tripled from 51 to 138 between 1985 and 1991, so that by the end of 1991 the turnover revenue of extrabudgetary enterprises amounted to 60 per cent of the total of the budgetary sector.[124] It was therefore not surprising that many new state enterprises established in the 1980s were said to have been placed outside the budget.[125]

One example was the Guangdong Development Bank, established in 1988, whose shareholders included Guangdong's Finance Department, several specialized state banks, several major provincial enterprises and the China Bank Group based in Hong Kong. Being 'extrabudgetary' the bank was said to be wholly supported by the 'own funds' of the shareholders, and no fiscal funds were used in its establishment.[126] On the other hand, the Finance Department, as one of the shareholders, had reportedly provided at least several hundred million yuan from the provincial budget as the initial capital of the bank.[127] The bank was still exempt from profit taxes in 1993.[128]

Through developing the non-state sector and placing new state enterprises beyond the budget, the Guangdong leadership sought to speed up economic development by ignoring the relatively stagnant traditional state sector and focusing on the more flexible non-state and extrabudgetary sectors. Not only did these enterprises operate more flexibly, and with less red tape, they were also more susceptible to manoeuvring by the provincial and lower-level governments. As local enterprises they were under the sole management of Guangdong's authorities. This made it easier to manoeuvre their tax payments, and, when the need arose, to extract their funds.

Recentralization of societal resources

Additional resources retained at enterprises and grassroots units through tax reduction and exemption could be recentralized by the imposition of various fees. These revenues were usually placed outside the budget in order to reserve the revenue exclusively for local use. Through first reducing taxes and then levying local charges, the provincial and lower-level governments were able to retain more resources within Guangdong and to minimize the possibility of extraction by the centre, whilst still being able to gain access to local resources for their own disposal and allocation.

There were two major ways in which the provincial government recentralized societal resources. One was through various types of capitalization exercise, including the sale of local public bonds, the assignment of capitalization quotas, and high-interest loans. In one report, for instance, it was stated that Dongguan city, a hub of export-processing activity in the Pearl River Delta Region, planned to raise 600 million yuan of capital between 1989 and 1991 with which to finance infrastructure investments, despite the fact that the national economy was at that time in the throes of an austerity programme.[129] The other means was via levying various fees and charges, or by adjusting the prices of commodities.

The Electricity Fund established in Guangdong in 1987 was an example of those extrabudgetary funds which were derived from the budget. In March 1987, the Guangdong provincial government approved a proposal from the provincial electricity bureau that taxes formerly paid by the bureau be waived. Meanwhile an equivalent amount of funds would be paid into a newly formed Electricity Fund to be placed outside the budget for the bureau's discretionary use. In return the bureau would take up the responsibility, including the provision of capital, for the construction of an agreed list of electricity projects. In addition, the electricity bureau was allowed to charge an electricity construction fee to users.[130] A total of more than 8 billion yuan had been raised by this extrabudgetary fund by the end of 1990.[131]

Apart from the Electricity Fund, it was found that Guangdong had also collected more than 20 billion yuan since 1980 via road tolls, additional charges on freight transport, installation fees for new telephones, etc. These funds were used to finance the construction of roads, bridges and ports, and the development of the telecommunications service within the province.[132] Part of this sum came from new charges, for example adjusted freight prices and telephone installation fees. Part was derived from what had originally been the revenue of the budget. For instance, the port authorities were exempted from paying into the Energy and Transport Strategic Construction Fund and the Budget Adjustment Fund by the provincial government in order that the resources could be used to develop the port facilities locally.[133] This, in effect, amounted to a transfer of budgetary resources to extra-budgetary funds.

According to one report, in some provinces there were more than 100 different channels whereby extrabudgetary funds were obtained and used by various units for investment purpose.[134] Eighty per cent of these funds were kept in state enterprises and their superordinate departments-in-charge. Government departments and various administrative (*shiye*) units kept about 18 per cent, with the remaining 2 per cent being kept in the local finance departments. In Guangdong, the share was 64 per cent, 32 per cent and 4 per cent respectively for the period 1986 to 1990.[135] The share kept in the government departments, *shiye* units and local finance departments was considerably larger in Guangdong than the national average, suggesting a higher than average degree of centralization of extrabudgetary funds in Guangdong. This appears to tally with the aggressive involvement of the Guangdong government in investment, through, for instance, the establishment of utility funds.

There are, however, no comprehensive statistics on the total number of extrabudgetary fees and charges levied by various government and administrative units, either nationwide or in Guangdong. The possible scale of the practice might nevertheless be gauged by means of information made available during campaigns to stamp out excessive levies. In late 1991 it was reported that, in total, 70,378 categories of fees and charges involving a total sum of 3.3 billion yuan were screened during the 1990–1 inspection campaign concerning excessive fees in Guangdong. In the end about 7,200 categories were either abolished or revised, thus lowering the level of fees by about 800 million yuan.[136]

One major use of extrabudgetary funds in Guangdong was to finance investment in the 'bottleneck' sectors of energy, transport and telecommunications. The flexibility and added autonomy of this resource enabled Guangdong to overcome, to an extent, traditional bias against investment allocation to these sectors. For this reason the experience of Guangdong was made the subject of intensive examination and was evaluated positively by the central government in a high-level study in the early 1990s.[137] This also helped the province to escape the brunt of central censure during later national campaigns on excessive fees.[138] In November and December 1993, a total of 143 administrative charges by various departments were abolished in two batches.[139] Nevertheless, given the good performance of Guangdong's extra-budgetary funds in terms of their effect on investments in bottleneck sectors, and the fact that Guangdong had sought the approval of the State Council for at least some of its major initiatives, the brunt of the ban fell mostly on the other provinces.[140]

INTERNATIONALIZATION

'Internationalization' refers to the opening of the domestic economy to the international community. As a general description it includes the increasing use of foreign capital, the adoption of international practices, and the establishment of transnational linkages not directly related to the injection of foreign capital. One question is this: is 'internationalization' a *provincial* strategy, or is the practice in Guangdong only a loyal implementation of the national policy of opening China's 'door' to the world? In this respect one is reminded of the fact that one of the earliest national reform measures involved the promulgation of laws regarding foreign investment. In July 1979, a mere seven months after the close of the landmark Third Plenum of the Eleventh Party Congress, the Law of the People's Republic of China on Chinese–Foreign Joint Ventures was promulgated, allowing the inflow of foreign capital as equity capital for Chinese–foreign joint venture enterprises. Getting foreign investors in has thus been a national policy from the very early days of economic reform, stemming from important practical concerns. The national economy as of 1978 was under serious strain after decades of political mobilization and neglect of economic efficiency. Under these circumstances external capital was regarded as crucial for setting the modernization process in motion, and for turning the vision of change into reality.

The fact that opening China's 'door' to the international market has been a national policy from the initial stage of China's reform also explains why Guangdong's suggestion of special economic zones in 1979, an idea regarded as very radical at that time, was quickly endorsed by central leaders. In any event, prior to Deng Xiaoping's resumption of the leadership role, Hua Guofeng during his brief reign had launched in 1978 and 1979 a massive importation of foreign capital and technology.[141] There was thus a recurring continuity within the central government regarding the importance of foreign capital.

'Internationalization' as practised in Guangdong was not merely the implementation of national policy, however. Successive Guangdong governments have used the 'foreign factor' in the provincial economy to bargain for various kinds of favourable treatment from the centre. What occurred is that the implementation of the national policy of 'open doors' in Guangdong went well beyond the additional resources which foreign capital brought to Guangdong's investment plans. Although the use of foreign capital is the stated policy of the centre, the way in which the Guangdong government implemented this general policy has had a significant effect on its relations with the centre.

The use of foreign capital, in Guangdong and nationally, started in the early 1980s with the initial aim of supplementing domestic investment capital and bringing in foreign technology and management techniques to speed up modernization. At that time it was largely a demand-driven exercise, particularly as the onset of economic adjustment between 1980 and 1983 tightened the supply of domestic capital when additional input was badly needed for the take-off of economic experiments in Guangdong. From 1979 to 1995, a total of US$53 billion of realized foreign capital was used in Guangdong, of which 8.4 per cent, or US$4.4 billion, was invested in infrastructure projects such as roads, ports, electricity stations and telecommunications equipment.[142] The use of foreign capital in infrastructure projects, an area of investment traditionally the domain of central planning and their finance borne by budgetary, and often central, resources, was initially a practical response by the Guangdong leadership to the shortage of central investment input.[143] As central leaders in the early 1980s repeatedly warned against any expectation of substantial central capital injection, provincial leaders had no choice but to turn to external sources.

In September 1979 Guangdong leaders suggested to central leaders the idea of using foreign capital in infrastructural investment for the first time, and received a favourable response.[144] Central approval was formally given in Central Committee Notice no. 41 in May 1980, which authorized Guangdong and Fujian to utilize foreign capital in infrastructural projects in view of the shortage of state funds.[145] In 1981, it was further announced that infrastructural projects using foreign capital could be exempt from taxes and profit remittance for a certain period in order to facilitate loan repayment.[146] This means that within the first two years of the commencement of the Special Policy, the door to extensive use of foreign capital in nearly all corners of the provincial economy was already opened for Guangdong.[147]

Circumventing central control

The extensive use of foreign capital in Guangdong not only brought in a massive amount of external resources from abroad,[148] but, no less importantly, it enabled the Guangdong government to circumvent some of the control measures imposed by the centre on provincial investment. The Guangdong leadership has, over time, learnt to make use of the 'foreign factor' in the provincial economy as a means of obtaining favourable treatment from the centre. Foreign investment was, for instance, instrumental to the upward adjustment of central control figures prescribed for Guangdong during times of economic retrenchment in 1986 and 1989. The argument the Guangdong officials made in their bargaining with central authorities was simple: more domestic capital had to be made available to Guangdong to enable it to make use of the hard-won foreign capital.

The rationale of the argument needs to be understood in the context of the regime of investment control in China. Foreign investment is excluded from the coverage of central quotas on total investment, which are designed as a control instrument on the use of *domestic* investment resources only. However, since most foreign investment projects are joint venture projects with the Chinese side often accounting for half of the equity, the use of a certain amount of foreign capital involves the use of a more or less equivalent amount of domestic capital, which, being domestically derived, falls under the coverage of the central control figure on total investment. Because of this linkage of foreign and domestic capital, the contraction of investment quotas during retrenchment can seriously affect foreign investment projects. On the ground that Guangdong absorbs the largest amount of foreign capital in the country, the Guangdong government has been quite successful in exacting concessions from the centre and having the quotas increased. In 1986, for instance, in the middle of a retrenchment exercise, a State Council notice stated that

for those foreign investment projects which are already registered or under construction, provincial governments and various ministries should ensure

the provision of the capital required by the Chinese partners in foreign investment projects within the central control figure. If that is genuinely impossible,
this year's control ceiling on scale of investment and total bank finance could
be raised. . . . From 1987 onwards, the investment and bank finance required
by the Chinese partners in foreign investment projects will be covered in separate quotas in the central and provincial plans.[149]

It was likely that, in that instance as well as others, provincial
governments had deliberately held back capital for foreign enterprises
in order to press for a higher investment ceiling.[150] From the perspective of the provincial officials, when foreign investors complain about
the tightening capital supply, the centre, being anxious to maintain
foreign confidence, is likely to yield to pressure and loosen its grip. In
this way, both control over the total investment ceiling and the supply
of domestic capital to the province may be eased.

Bargaining in this respect sometimes involved the highest level of
central leadership. In October 1986, for instance, Guangdong's leaders
took up their case with Zhao Ziyang during Zhao's visit to Zhuhai and
complained about the shortfall of bank finance. Guangdong's leaders
told Zhao that there had been a mismatch between investment plans
and the centrally authorized supply of investment capital, and that
there was often no capital provided for projects within the approved
plan. Zhao replied:

Nationwide there are now about 6,000 foreign joint ventures . . . involving a
total foreign investment of US$20 billion, and requiring 'partner capital' from
our side of over 10 billion yuan. . . . We do not have the capacity to provide that
much. . . . There is probably not enough money.[151]

Despite Zhao's lukewarm response, getting the attention of top
leaders did help Guangdong to gain additional resources from the
centre. Within a year, in October 1987, the centre agreed an additional
100 million yuan of special 'circulating' loans to Guangdong to solve
the shortage of domestic 'partner capital' arising from the increase in
foreign capital investment since 1986.[152] A petition was filed with central leaders reporting a good inflow of foreign capital in 1986 and the
promising prospect of having even more foreign investment in the
coming years. Corresponding 'adjustments' in policy and domestic
capital supply, according to the report, were thus necessary so as not
to waste the 'golden opportunity'.[153] Guangdong thereby 'fished' for
domestic capital using its success in attracting foreign investment, and
it succeeded.

The foreign factor was put to use again in 1989, when the centre ordered a severe cut in investment nationwide. The ceiling then prescribed for Guangdong was substantially less than the provincial government had contemplated. The strategy of the provincial leadership was to shift the emphasis of the provincial investment plan to the foreign sector. Efforts to attract foreign investment intensified. As a result, more, not less, foreign capital was used in Guangdong in the three years of nationwide retrenchment between 1989 and 1991. The total value of realized foreign capital from 1989 to 1991 was US$6.8 billion, 13 per cent more than the total value realized in the four years preceding 1988.[154]

Putting the effort into the foreign sector in 1989 served two purposes for the Guangdong government. First, the foreign sector enabled the provincial government to bargain for preferential treatment for Guangdong, which included exempting the province from some central control measures imposed nationwide from late 1988. Consequently Guangdong managed to raise its investment quota,[155] relax central control over bank finance, and remove customs duties on imported raw materials and semi-finished parts for export processing.[156] In other words, the foreign sector was 'held hostage' by the Guangdong leadership in its bargaining with the centre for preferential treatment, and the domestic sector benefited as a 'free rider'.[157] Secondly, the increased use of foreign capital enabled Guangdong's economy to continue to develop at a time when most other provinces were badly affected by the straitened financial situation caused by retrenchment.[158] Since the use of foreign capital effectively brought additional resources into the domestic economy, in theory it could only improve the supply and demand situation within the economy. In the event that the use of foreign capital had an adverse effect in terms of continuing to 'heat up' the economy, it would nonetheless be difficult for the centre to dampen Guangdong's enthusiasm for attracting foreign investment, due to the negative repercussions this might have within the international community and on Guangdong's future prospects of attracting foreign investment.

In order to make the most from the 'exemptional policies' awarded to the foreign sector, the Guangdong government also moved beyond the traditional approach of attracting *new* foreign investment projects. More emphasis was placed instead on linking the domestic sector to a foreign element, thereby expanding the benefits originally intended only for the foreign sector to the domestic sector. A mixed sector would maximize flexibility as it would be able to enjoy benefits derived from its foreign as well as domestic linkages. Yu Fei, then Guangdong's Vice-Governor, made this intention explicit in a speech to a provincial planning and economic meeting:

We must make every use of the favourable conditions provided by the 'exemptional policy'. Those capital construction projects which have a linkage with foreign-invested enterprises should be supported by every means. We should try to convert some domestic investment projects and find a foreign linkage for them so that they can enjoy the 'exemptional policies'. (Yu Fei 1989: 4–5)

Consequently, the number of co-operative joint ventures formed between existing state enterprises and a foreign partner rose conspicuously in 1989. For Guangzhou alone, the number of such contracts from January to April 1989 was 3.5 times as great as those of the same period the previous year, with the value of realized foreign capital leaping by more than 20 times.[159] This tactic was repeated in the second half of 1993 when the centre once more tightened its supply of funds and clamped down on investment projects. In July 1993, at the onset of the centre's tightening of bank credit, the Mayor of Guangzhou, Lai Ziliu, said that his government would expand the use of foreign capital in the city, thereby enabling local enterprises to withstand the capital shortage problems resulting from the centre's move.[160] Foreign investors were offered, as an incentive, the prospect of a larger share in the domestic market, more profits, and shares in the existing state enterprises.

One strategy effectively used by the Guangdong leadership in loosening the centre's grip was bargaining at the margins. When seeking to expand the investment quotas, increase the supply of domestic capital, or abolish customs duties, Guangdong's officials seldom argued squarely with central officials, but would stress the utility and value of *specific* investment projects, in terms of, for instance, the value of foreign investment involved, or the gap the projects would fill in the existing industrial structure.[161] This was especially true during periods of retrenchment, when the economic situation nationwide made the centre more strongly in favour of control. During such instances, for example during 1989–91, the strategy of the Guangdong leadership was to express openly support for the retrenchment policy, but at the same time to keep raising 'practical difficulties' with central leaders. Hints of this approach may be recognized from the remarks of Yu Fei, Vice-Governor in 1989, at the same provincial planning meeting noted above:

The adjustment and retrenchment policy of the centre not only suits the needs of our country, the policy is also good for the situation in Guangdong . . . We should take the initiative of adjusting our economy, based on Guangdong's local conditions, and should not regard retrenchment as a matter of obeying orders [from the centre]. Moreover, we have to start early and be progressive in our specific actions. (Yu Fei 1989: 4–5)

One specific progressive action Yu Fei had in mind is, obviously, the establishment of linkages between the domestic sector and the new foreign sector. The tactic of Guangdong was not to argue with the centre on matters of principle, especially during periods of retrench-ment when the centre tended to be less flexible in terms of policy, but to focus its bargaining on 'mundane' issues. Using a language shared with the centre, Guangdong officials then put forward specific calcu-lations of costs and benefits and convinced the centre that it was in the interest of the country, and thus of the centre, to allow Guangdong to launch more investment. The tactic paid off, and the central quota prescribed for Guangdong in 1989 was adjusted upwards by 42 per cent, to 14 billion yuan, as a result of Guangdong's persistent bar-gaining 'at the margins'.[162]

Building international centres

As more foreign capital was absorbed and the provincial economy became more externally oriented,[163] there arose, inside and outside Guangdong, the call to develop Guangzhou and Shenzhen, the two major economic centres of Guangdong, into 'international cities', with an economic influence eventually comparable to cities like Hong Kong, Tokyo and New York. The purposes of such a call, from a provincial perspective, are twofold. First, it would justify Guang-dong's plans for more and higher-quality investment projects in order to make the infrastructure and industrial structure of the two cities commensurate with the standards of international cities. Secondly, it would strengthen Guangdong's bargaining position for more auto-nomy from the central government, as a high degree of autonomy in the domestic setting was often both a symbol and characteristic of international cities.

Bearing in mind the utility of the call for provincial purposes, the origin of the idea might be attributed to Deng Xiaoping as early as 1987. When receiving a foreign delegation, Deng stated that a few more 'Hong Kongs' would be built in Mainland China, and the idea was raised again during Deng's Southern Tour in February 1992 (Lin Zhuji 1993: 4). As Hong Kong is an international city, the call for the building of several more international cities was regarded as obvious. With the end of the retrenchment policy and the change towards a more optimistic economic atmosphere after the Southern Tour, the call for building international cities was taken quite literally in the more developed coastal regions, and particularly in Guangdong and Shanghai.

For the Guangdong leadership, the opening of Pudong in Shanghai in 1990 posed new challenges to the status and prospects of Guangdong, and to its special economic zones in particular. There is increasing concern among the Guangdong leadership that other open areas and cities are enjoying preferential policies similar to, if not more favourable than, those once exclusively found in the special economic zones, and that the special economic zones are no longer that 'special'. There is therefore a need to find new goals in order to keep up the momentum of development, and to sustain the image of the province as the pioneer of economic reform. For Guangdong as a whole, the new aim is to reach and surpass the economic and social development of the 'four little dragons' in two decades.[164] For Guangzhou and Shenzhen, their sights are set on becoming the first two international cities in Mainland China.[165]

International cities require good infrastructure as well as a correspondingly high standard of economic development. Thus the quest for investment has obtained a legitimate and clear-cut focus. The prospect of being an international city provides an objective yardstick against which the investment and development plans of Guangdong, and Guangzhou and Shenzhen in particular, may be evaluated. Since it is obvious that the standards of the two cities still lag substantially behind most international cities, the city governments have found a plausible pretext to justify their ambitious investment plans and, in the event of pressure from the centre to cut investments, a legitimate position from which to defend their investment activity and to bargain for exemptional and preferential treatment.

To make way for the realization of this goal, for instance, the Guangzhou city government has planned to build a new airport with the capacity to handle 63 million passengers per year—more than twice the capacity of Hong Kong's Kai Tak Airport. Ten billion yuan is to be spent on building a mass transit rail system in the city area, and a long list of road and railway projects are also in the pipeline.[166] In Shenzhen, investment projects for the 1990s would require more than 100 billion yuan of capital (Lin Zhuji 1993: 6). To finance development plans on such an immense scale, however, more foreign capital would need to be used. Increasing internationalization of the economy of the two cities is, therefore, an inevitable consequence. More importantly, making internationalization the goal of the two cities increases the chance of the city governments obtaining the necessary clearance from the central government for their ambitious investment plans.

Another interesting implication of the new goal of international cities is the legitimization of provincial calls for less central control and more provincial autonomy generally. Ever since the conception of the Special Policy for Guangdong and Fujian in 1979, the prospect of more autonomy for Guangdong has been discussed as the necessary *expedient* whereby the province would act as a spearhead in economic development and reform. The goal has been national economic development, to be achieved through local autonomy for Guangdong. The delegation of additional authority to Guangdong in the 1980s was necessitated by the difficulty in bringing changes to the country as a whole all at once. With the progress of reform and the subsequent changes in other parts of the country, Guangdong was, however, becoming less 'exceptional' in terms of the application of central policy, and during recent retrenchment drives its economy had more often been placed within the same jurisdiction of central control as other provinces. There was concern among the Guangdong leadership that the Special Policy no longer existed in practice, and that the autonomy of the Guangdong government to manage its own economy would gradually be reduced.[167]

By setting itself the new goal of building international cities, under these circumstances, the Guangdong government is striving to transcend the crisis arising from the end of the experimental role of Guangdong during the initial stage of China's reforms. Not only does the idea of international cities represent a new and higher-order goal in the development of China's reforms, and thus extend Guangdong's pioneer position among other provinces, this new goal also requires an essential level of autonomy for the provincial government. The Guangdong government can easily refer to the achievements of other international cities outside China when arguing for a higher degree of local autonomy for Guangzhou and Shenzhen, and by extension, for the provincial government itself. Power and autonomy are no longer merely the expedient; they constitute an integral part of the goal of internationalization.

The discussion in this chapter has shown that through skilful manipulation of national policies the Guangdong provincial leaders have sought and achieved, to a significant extent, the bypassing of central controls and the creation of new room for discretion. Given the constitutional and political arrangements in the political system, the central government is no doubt the stronger party in an asymmetrical relationship. Yet power is not solely determined by a comparison of resources, and as this chapter illustrates, political strategies do help a weaker party to wield its influence and gain favourable results.

NOTES

1. The document is printed in full in Guangdong Provincial Party Committee (1986–8: iii. 18–40).
2. Ezra F. Vogel (1989: 82–3) briefly discusses these political and strategic concerns.
3. The contracted remittance sum of Guangdong originally agreed in Central Document no. 50 (1979) at 1.2 billion yuan was based on the actual performance in 1978. Fujian had the centre agree in the same document to give it an annual subsidy of 100 million yuan.
4. Interview, respondent no. 9, Guangzhou, Dec. 1993. This is also supported by documentary evidence. The idea of setting up special economic zones first appeared in a Guangdong Party Committee meeting in January 1979. See Liu Zhongxiu (1991: 162). Vogel (1989: 84) states that Guangdong's leaders and those in the central government concerned with Guangdong had been forewarned of the new policy of economic opening and development prior to the Third Plenum of the Eleventh Party Congress in late 1978 and as a result Guangdong's leaders had had more time to contemplate how the new turn in the centre's attitude might be applied. In the end they came up with the idea of the Special Policy for Guangdong.
5. See 'Ye Jianying's Speech in Meeting with Guangdong's Party Secretaries at the District, City and County Levels, June 1979', Guangdong Provincial Party Committee (1986–8: iv. 446). Ye, one of the first-generation leaders of the Chinese Communist Party and a Guangdong native (of Mui County), served as the first First Party Secretary and Governor of Guangdong after 1949. His son, Ye Xuanping, subsequently served as Governor of Guangdong from 1985 to 1991.
6. See 'Report by the Guangdong Provincial Party Committee on Utilizing Guangdong's Favourable Conditions, Expanding External Trade, and Speeding Up Economic Development', 6 June 1979. This was approved

by the centre via State Council Notice no. 50 (1979), 15 July 1979. See Guangdong Provincial Party Committee (1986–8: i. 18–40).

7. For a description of the general powers Guangdong acquired as a result of the approval of the Special Policy in 1979, see Cheung (1994: 25–8).

8. This is inferred from Gu Mu's speech on the meeting and from the minutes of the meeting. Guangdong's officials at the meeting included the First Party Secretary Xi Zhongxun and Vice-Governors Lau Tianfu and Wu Nansang. See Guangdong Provincial Party Committee (1986–8: i. 57, 60–71).

9. See Guangdong Provincial Party Committee (1986–8: i. 94–108).

10. Guangdong Provincial Party Committee (1986–8: i. 122). This remark was made in a meeting between the two in Guangdong in December 1980, when Gu Mu urged Guangdong to take the initiative and to propose bills for approval rather than waiting for the central ministries to take action.

11. See Guangdong Provincial Party Committee (1986–8: i. 153).

12. See Central Committee Document no. 27 (1981), 'On Approving the Notes of Meeting on the Work of Guangdong, Fujian and the Special Economic Zones', 19 July 1981, printed in State Commission for Economic System Reform (1983: 558–66).

13. Central Committee, 'On Approving the Notes of Meeting on the Work of Guangdong, Fujian and the Special Economic Zones'. For the specific policy benefits Guangdong extracted from the centre in this document, see Cheung (1994: 28).

14. The other specific preferential policy obtained by Guangdong concerned more favourable foreign exchange retention. Other preferential policies such as the delegation of planning authority and the enhancement of investment approval authority had been coined in loose and general phrases in the 1979 report.

15. See Guangdong Party Committee's Report, 6 June 1979, in Guangdong Provincial Party Committee (1986–8: i. 18–40).

16. Gu Mu speaking to Guangdong provincial officials on 22 Sept. 1979. See Guangdong Provincial Party Committee (1986–8: i. 42, 48).

17. See Central Committee Notice no. 41 (1980), 'On Approving the Notes of the Meeting on Guangdong and Fujian', 16 May 1980, in State Commission for Economic System Reform (1983: 500–4). The meeting was held on 30 March.

18. See 'Notes of Dialogue of Central Committee Members when Hearing Briefing by Guangdong Officials', 24–5 Sept. 1980, and 'Notes of Meeting of the Central Committee Meeting', 28 Sept. 1980, in Guangdong Provincial Party Committee (1979–88: i. 94–112).

19. See Guangdong Provincial Party Committee (1993: 59).

20. See 'Report for the Central Committee Meeting: The Implementation of Special Policy in Guangdong and Fujian and the Trial Operation of the

Special Economic Zones', 15 Nov. 1982, in Guangdong Provincial Party Committee (1986–8: i. 405–6). In Central Committee Notice no. 41 (1980), it was stated that the remittance amount was to be adjusted according to changes in the local revenue base and at times when the financial situation of the provinces was affected substantially by major economic measures taken by the centre. A major grievance of provinces was that while extra revenue went to the centre, the provinces were often left to shoulder additional expenditure alone. The pledge that the two provinces could retain extra revenues generated from new revenue sources was therefore an improvement.

21. The Energy and Transportation Construction Fund was a new tax announced in December 1982. The fund, with a tax rate of 10%, was imposed on the extrabudgetary funds of all units and local governments. All revenue collected within the prescribed quota was to go to central coffers. The provincial and lower-level governments could keep all revenues collected above the quotas for local use (70% as from 1985). See 'Collection Rules For the State Energy and Transportation Construction Fund', announced by the State Council on 15 December 1982, printed in State Planning Commission (1987b: 664–6).

22. See Dangdai Zhongguo Congshu Bianji Bu (1991: i. 687).

23. Guangdong Provincial Party Committee and Provincial Government, 'Proposals on Fully Utilizing the Current Opportunities to Speed Up Economic Development', 12 Oct. 1987, in Guangdong Provincial Party Committee (1979–88: iv. 370–5).

24. 'Zhao Ziyang Discusses Guangdong Becoming the Experimental Zone for Comprehensive Reform', 26 Oct. 1987, in Guangdong Provincial Party Committee (1986–8: iv. 384–6).

25. At that time the centre had not yet arrived at a mature view of the tax-sharing system. But when the system was finally implemented in 1994, the *target* of the centre was to funnel 60% of total national fiscal revenue into the central budget, before some portion of the revenue was redirected to the provincial level as transfer payments. See State Council Notice no. 85 (1993), 'State Council's Decision on Implementing the Tax-Sharing Fiscal Management System', 15 Dec. 1993, printed in *Caizheng* 2 (1994): 18–20.

26. 'Central Finance and Economy Leading Group on Guangdong's October 12 Report', 27 Oct. 1987, in Guangdong Provincial Party Committee (1986–8: iv. 387–91).

27. The contracted remittance in 1987 was 778 million yuan, and the centre 'borrowed' an extra amount of 635 million yuan that year. The two sums together, 1.414 billion yuan, became the new baseline figure for the calculation of the new contracted remittance for 1988, which was 1.54 billion yuan. See Huang Haichao *et al.* (1993: 31).

28. Guangdong Provincial Government, 'Proposals on Deepening Guang-
    dong's Reforms, Expanding the Opening to the World, and Speeding Up
    Economic Development', 7 Jan. 1988, in Guangdong Provincial Party
    Committee (1986–8: iv. 427–41). According to respondent no. 6, (inter-
    view, Guangzhou, Sept. 1993), eventually the 9% rate was retained for
    1992 and 1993 in later negotiations.

29. For the State Council Notice, 2 Feb. 1988, approving Guangdong's Janu-
    ary 1988 report in principle, see Guangdong Provincial Party Committee
    (1986–8: iv. 426). See Yang Xiaohui (1990: 43–5) for a discussion of the
    Guangdong January report and the subsequent lapse of many of the ap-
    proved powers, in investment, bank finance, pricing, etc.

30. From 1988 all provinces were therefore practising some kind of *dabaogan*
    system, in six major variations. See Xu Yi and Xiang Jingquan (1993: 74–7).

31. According to a report by the Finance Ministry, it was at the conclusion of
    the Fourteenth Party Congress in late 1992 that the tax-sharing system
    progressed from being only a discussion topic amongst the academics and
    government think tanks to a formidable policy proposal. The Finance
    Ministry started to work out the specifics of a tax-sharing system in May
    1993. In July, the new system was presented for discussion at the National
    Finance Work Conference for the first time. After further revisions in
    August, the reform plan was presented to and approved by the State
    Council and the Politburo of the Party in late August/early September.
    Another meeting with provincial finance officials was held in late
    October/early November to solicit opinions and to check the budgetary
    figures of the provinces for the preliminary calculation of the central
    transfers in 1994. See 'Guanyu Fenshuizhi Caizheng Tizhi Ruogan Wenti
    de Shuoming', by the assistant of the Finance Minister, compiled from
    working papers of the National Finance Work Conferences, printed in
    State Audit Commission (1994: 99–109).

32. Interviews with respondents no. 6 and 9, Guangzhou, May and Sept. 1993.

33. Opinions of this sort appeared in several articles on the tax-sharing sys-
    tem in *Guangdong Finance* 1 (1994), which is a publication of the Guang-
    dong Finance Bureau. The articles include: Zeng Zhiwen, 'A Collection of
    Views on the Tax-Sharing System' (pp. 8–9), which is a summary of views
    emanating from a seminar in Guangdong; Wang Guanjiu, 'An Alternat-
    ive View on the Tax-Sharing System' (10–13), which is an explicit defence
    of the advantages of the *dabaogan* system; and Zeng Xiaohong, 'Thinking
    and Worrying about the Tax-Sharing System' (18–19). For suggestions
    regarding the continuation of the practice of the old system at subprovin-
    cial levels, see p. 9 of Zeng Zhiwen's article.

34. Interview respondent no. 9, Guangzhou, Dec. 1993. The lobbying took
    place during Zhu Rongji's tour to the coastal provinces in September
    1993. The purpose of Zhu's tour, which included Guangdong, Shanghai,

Zhejiang, Jiangsu and Hainan, was to discuss the centre's plan to implement the new system with the provincial leadership and get their support. According to the respondent, Guangdong provincial officials told Zhu that given Guangdong's rapid economic development in 1993, the enthusiasm of the grassroots officials to develop the economy would be seriously dampened if the lower figure of 1992 was used as the baseline to calculate Guangdong's retained revenue in 1994.

35. In mid-November 1993 the State Council issued a severely worded notice warning against provincial government moves to boost the revenue baseline via irregular means. Three types of irregular moves were identified: (1) collecting 'prepayments': revenues not yet realized being taxed in advance, advancing the payment dates of taxes accrued, etc.; (2) collecting bad debt taxes by requiring the enterprises concerned to take out bank loans or borrow fiscal funds from the finance department in order to pay the taxes (the provincial governments allegedly volunteered to lend the money and also instructed the local banks to do so); (3) delaying the normal refund of taxes to exporting enterprises, or reducing the amount refunded, thereby increasing the total fiscal revenue for the year. See 'State Council's Notice on Issues relating to the Implementation of the Tax-Sharing System', 15 Nov. 1993, printed in State Audit Commission (1994: 20–2).

36. An interview with respondent no. 11 (Guangzhou, Dec. 1993) confirmed that there was revenue-scrambling behaviour in Guangdong in the fourth quarter of 1993.

37. In an article explicating the tax-sharing system the Deputy Minister of Finance made it clear that increasing the proportion of fiscal revenue in the central government was one of the four major reasons for the new system. The other three purposes were: (1) to stabilize the revenue sources of the central and provincial governments, minimizing the 'haemorrhage' of fiscal revenue; (2) to reduce the arbitrariness of the distribution of fiscal revenue amongst different levels of government, and enhance the role of the fiscal system in the allocation of resources across the country; (3) to facilitate the conversion of government functions and powers, contributing to a unified national market and optimizing on resource allocation. See Xiang Huaizheng (1994: 32–6).

38. Guangdong officials confirmed that as long as the provincial government acted discreetly, it was difficult for the centre to prove that they had done wrong. Revenue collection was after all the duty of the government (interview, respondent no. 11, Guangzhou, Dec. 1993). In the official report on Guangdong's 1993 budget implementation and the 1994 budget, issued on 19 February 1994, the Director of Guangdong's Finance Bureau cited both 'objective' and 'subjective' reasons in accounting for the overachievement of fiscal revenue. These included: robust economic performance,

206   Discretion and Strategies in Guangdong

policy factors (the rise of business tax for retail transactions by two percentage points, inflationary effects, etc.), improved implementation of central orders to stop new tax exemption and reduction in the second half of the year, and the adherence to central regulations on plugging the 'holes' in tax collection, etc. For the report see *Guangdong Caizheng* 4 (1994): 4–10.

39. The announced intention of the centre was that the fiscal system would gradually be changed to a more uniform system whereby a larger share of the national revenue would go to the central coffers. Further rounds of bargaining were, therefore, inevitable. See State Council Notice no. 85 (1993), 'State Councell's Decision on Implementing the Tax-Sharing Fiscal Management System', as printed in *Caizheng* 2 (1994): 18–20.

40. See Guangdong Provincial Party Committee (1986–8: i. 29).

41. See 'Gu Mu Speaking when Inspecting Work in Zhuhai', 10 Dec. 1980, in Guangdong Provincial Party Committee (1986–8: i. 114).

42. See 'Central Party Secretariat Approving the Notes of Meeting of the Guangdong and Fujian Seminar', 21 Jan. 1981, in Guangdong Provincial Party Committee (1986–8: i. 128–31). Following this, Guangdong and Fujian were allowed in July 1981 to approve medium-sized and large projects, whereas other provinces would still require approval at State Planning Commission level.

43. In a meeting between Zhao and Guangdong officials, Zhao asked Guangdong to place priority on transport and energy when planning local investment projects. Vice-Governor Liu Tianfu immediately requested that the centre raise the limit on the scale of investment. Zhao agreed to this request. See 'Zhao Ziyang Speaking when Receiving the Briefing of the Guangdong Party Committee', 18 Aug. 1981, in Guangdong Provincial Party Committee (1986–8: i. 213–14).

44. In the situation where a provincial government could approve projects of up to 30 million yuan, an industrial project with a total scale of investment of, for instance, 40 million yuan could be broken down into two projects each of 20 million yuan, so that the provincial government could approve the project(s) independently without submitting the project(s) to the State Planning Commission for approval. This has been the most extensively used, and successful, method of provincial governments to expand their *de facto* authority on investments *vis-à-vis* their superiors (interviews, respondents no. 31 and 35, Beijing, Nov. 1993 and Aug. 1994 respectively).

45. See 'Zhao Ziyang Approving Guangdong's Two Petition Reports', 6 Oct. 1987, in Guangdong Provincial Party Committee (1986–8: iv. 374).

46. See 'State Council Approving Guangdong's Petition on Further Opening and Speeding Up Economic Development', 10 Feb. 1988, in Guangdong Provincial Party Committee (1986–8: iv. 374).

47. One important provision did survive the economic retrenchment, namely,

the incremental *dabaogan* fiscal arrangement, as noted in an earlier section of this chapter.

48. There is no readily available information on this aspect, as statistical data on central investment projects or central–local joint ventures, normally large-scale projects listed under the State Planning Commission annual investment plan, do not contain a breakdown by province. As these are usually infrastructure projects stretching over several provinces, it would not be easy to disaggregate the total central investment by province (interview, respondent no. 36, Beijing, Apr. 1994). It should be noted that 'central investment' here refers to the amount of capital the centre put into investment projects in Guangdong, and not only to centrally subordinated investment projects.

49. See Guangdong Provincial Party Committee (1993: 57).

50. Officials in both Guangdong and Beijing commented that Guangdong had been a strong magnet attracting investment from central ministries and other provinces, including poor provinces short of capital. This 'magnetic power' became stronger each year (interviews, respondent no. 9, Guangzhou Dec. 1993, respondents No. 36 and 38, Beijing, Apr. 1994).

51. See *People's Daily*, 8 Aug. 1992, 1. Another figure, 16%, appeared in an article by the Guangdong Provincial Planning Commission, 'The Plan and the Market in the Investment Scene of Guangdong', in State Planning Commission (1992: 70).

52. How the Figure of 15% was calculated was unclear even to an informed source in Guangdong (interview, respondent no. 9, Guangzhou, Apr. 1994).

53. See 'Zhao Ziyang Speaking when Hearing the Briefing on Shantou's Work' 2–5 Feb. 1986, in Guangdong Provincial Party Committee (1986–8: iii. 28). Another example of centre–Guangdong joint investment is the project to build hydroelectric power stations in south-west China to supply electricity to Guangdong. The project involved the co-operation of four provinces, namely, Guangdong, Guangxi, Yunnan and Guizhou, and the central government. Total investment up to the year 2000 was projected to exceed 20 billion yuan. In some parts of the project Guangdong's contribution in terms of investment capital reached a level of 50%–70%, an exceptionally high percentage to be shouldered by a province in a central–provincial joint project. See *Nanfang Ribao*, 29 Dec. 1993, 2.

54. Interview, respondent no. 35, Beijing, 1994.

55. This paragraph is based on the views of respondent no. 9 (interview, Guangzhou, Dec. 1993).

56. Interview, respondent no. 9, Guangzhou, Dec. 1993.

57. See Yao Dinghai and Zeng Shunming (1989).

58. This interpretation was confirmed by respondent no. 9 (interview

Guangzhou Dec. 1993). He commented that it was difficult to ascertain the full extent of central support as it was supplied in an obscure fashion.

59. See 'Zhao Ziyang, Hu Qili and Tian Jiyun Speaking when Receiving Officials of Shantou', 5 Feb. 1986, in Guangdong Provincial Party Committee (1986–8: iv. 44). The centre finally agreed to Guangdong's requests and exempted banks in Shantou, Zhuhai and Xiamen from remitting the 10% deposit contingency allowance to the centre. This portion of resources was instead retained by the local branch of the People's Bank of China for local use. See 'Notes of Meeting of the 1987 Work Conference of the Special Economic Zones', 10 Feb. 1987, in Guangdong Provincial Party Committee (1986–8: iv. 297).

60. Interview, respondent no. 8, Guangzhou, Dec. 1993.

61. Interview, respondent no. 8, Guangzhou, Dec. 1993.

62. See Leung Kwaichuen *et al.* (1992: 42). The 2 billion yuan figure was reportedly given by Guangdong Finance Bureau.

63. See the discussion earlier in this chapter. The cost of reform that Guangdong was said to have shouldered during 1980–92 amounted to 13 billion yuan.

64. See 'Gu Mu Speaking when Inspecting the Shenzhen Special Economic Zone', 7–18 Apr. 1983, in Guangdong Provincial Party Committee (1986–8: iv. 540).

65. The 'softness', or unreliability, of central pledges of support was revealed in this comment of Zhao Ziyang made in August 1981, the midpoint of the 1980–2 economic adjustment: 'the several power stations already mentioned [in the July 1979 Central Committee Document approving Guangdong's June 1979 report on the Special Policy) could be undertaken by the centre, but given the current national economic situation, we can only discuss the extent to which the centre will be responsible for these projects.' See Guangdong Provincial Party Committee (1986–8: i. 214).

66. See Guangdong Provincial Party Committee (1986–8: i. 47, 51, 64 and 214).

67. Gu Mu uttered this phrase frequently in his conversations and meetings with Guangdong officials. See for instance Guangdong Provincial Party Committee (1986–8: i. 114 (Dec. 1980), i. 385 (Sept. 1982)).

68. See Liu Zhongxiu (1991: 162).

69. See Central Committee Document no. 41 (1980), 'Approving the Notes of Meeting on Guangdong and Fujian, 30 March 1980', 16 May 1980. A Central Committee Document (no. 17) issued on 1 March 1983 instructed that *all* unauthorized temporary or permanent offices/companies set up by central ministries and other provinces in Guangdong and Fujian, including those in the special economic zones, be withdrawn. See Guangdong Provincial Party Committee (1986–8: i. 310). The context of the directive was ostensibly to curb smuggling and speculative trading activities

in Guangdong, but it actually reflected the lack of concern of the central
leaders about the possible role of domestic investment in the special economic zones.

70. See Pei Guanzhong (1990: 3), quoting a source from the *Shenzhen Special
    Economic Zone Daily*, Dec. 1985.

71. The declining share of foreign capital in investment activities in Shenzhen
    caused displeasure to as supportive a central leader as Gu Mu. The con-
    cern came in the context of a nationwide economic retrenchment which
    started in 1985, whilst investment in Shenzhen continued to grow by 141%
    in 1985. See 'Gu Mu's Speech in the Special Economic Zones Meeting',
    5 Jan. 1986, in Guangdong Provincial Party Committee (1986–8: iii. 16).

72. See Huang Haichao *et al.* (1993: 127).

73. See 'Guangdong Party Committee and Guangdong People's Govern-
    ment on the Preliminary Appraisal of the Experiment of the Special Eco-
    nomic Zones', 22 Oct. 1982, in Guangdong Provincial Party Committee
    (1986–8: i. 380, 382).

74. See 'Gu Mu Speaking in the Meeting on the Work of Guangdong and
    Fujian', 24 Mar. 1980, in Guangdong Provincial Party Committee
    (1986–8: i. 57).

75. Implementation discretion and the interactive relations between policy
    formulation and implementation are generic phenomena of the policy
    process. The magnitude of implementation discretion in China is related
    to two factors. One is the experimental approach of China's reforms, which
    made many policies necessarily vague and tentative. The other is the
    slackness of law/ policy enforcement in China. Consequently provincial
    governments could often openly violate the confines of a stated policy
    without feeling compelled to amend the policy first, no matter how vague
    and general the amended policy might still be.

76. Interview, respondent no. 9, Guangzhou, Sept. 1993.

77. See 'Yao Yilin's Speech in a Meeting on Guangdong and Fujian', 13 Feb.
    1982, in Guangdong Provincial Party Committee (1986–8: i. 287).

78. See Wang Zhongliang, 'The Capital Investment and Macro-Management
    of Guangdong in the Sixth and Seventh Five-Year Plan Periods', in Wang
    Kunwei (1989: 82).

79. For instance, when Gu Mu came to Guangdong to inspect work in
    December 1983, the Guangdong leadership presented Gu Mu with a de-
    velopment plan for the Pearl River Delta region. After winning his admir-
    ation for their achievements and initiatives, they then asked Gu Mu to
    help to solve a few 'specific problems'. All these 'specific problems' were
    concerned with obtaining more favourable treatment of Guangdong's in-
    vestment. See Gu Mu, 'On the Planning of the Pearl River Delta Region
    and the Work of the Special Economic Zones', 12 Dec. 1983, in Guang-
    dong Provincial Party Committee (1986–8: ii. 87–90).

80. Interview, respondent no. 9, Guangzhou, Dec. 1993.

81. Table 3.5 shows that during that year, the value of total investment nationwide dropped by 8%. In Guangdong, where investment had grown by 40% in 1988, there was a negative growth of –1.8% in 1989.

82. See Wong Guiying, 'Report on the Preparation of the 1989 National Economic and Social Development Plans of Guangdong Province' (summary), *Jihua Yu Fazhan* 1 (1989): 6–12. In the report it was revealed that the centre had made the central control figure on scale of investment a mandatory order. Lending more than the planned total of bank loans was strictly prohibited.

83. *Zhongguo Jinbao*, 7 Oct. 1989: 1, contains a report which shows precisely the practical approach through which the Guangdong government managed to enlarge the approved scale of investment. The report was about a glass factory whose construction was prohibited in February 1989 as a result of the retrenchment exercise. It was argued that stopping the construction would do more harm than good because a total of US$2 million of imported equipment would stand idle, and compensation would have to be made for previously signed sale contracts. As nearly 5 million yuan in bank loans had already been used, interest therefore still had to be paid even though the project would be halted with no prospect of realized income.

84. For instance, during the retrenchment of 1985, State Councillor Chen Muhua, visiting Zhuhai as head of the People's Bank of China, criticized the use for investment projects of bank finance originally intended for working capital. See 'Chen Muhua Speaking when Visiting Zhuhai Special Economic Zone', 12 Dec. 1985, in Guangdong Provincial Party Committee (1986–8: ii. 428).

85. Interview, respondent no. 10, Guangzhou, Dec. 1993.

86. Interview, respondent no. 10, Guangzhou, Dec. 1993. The percentage tallies with the percentage quoted in an article from the Shaoxing city Audit Bureau in *Guangdong Audit* 2 (1991): 14–15. In the article, it is stated that inspection of the two kinds of bank loans in local banks in 1988 found that 2.2% of working capital loans were spent on investment projects.

87. See *Statistical Yearbook of Guangdong* (1993), 385.

88. See Li Zhaoyong (1990: 59).

89. Interview, respondent no. 10, Guangzhou, Dec. 1993.

90. See Wang Hao (1989). The author was alerted to the article by Yang Xiaofei, 'Discretionary Behaviour of the Provincial-Level Government'. According to Yang, Wang was the propaganda chief of the Guangdong Provincial Party Committee.

91. Interview, respondent no. 34, Beijing, Mar. 1994. For the 1977 notice, 'The Regulation by the Ministry of Finance on the Tax Management System', 13 Nov. 1977, see State Planning Commission (1987*b*: 877–8).

92. This interpretation was confirmed by respondent no. 34, (interview, Beijing, Mar. 1994).
93. See Han Shaochu (1993: 293).
94. According to respondent no. 34, such local policies were tolerated by the central government before 1990. However, in 1990 the State Council issued a notice which explicitly prohibited the delegation of tax exemption and reduction authority to the subprovincial levels (interview, Beijing, Mar. 1994).
95. The notice (no. 337, 1992) was published in *Guangdong Zhengbao*, no. 9 (1992): 50.
96. See Yang Ming (1989: 29). Revenue from the industrial and commercial taxes often approached, and sometimes exceeded, the level of total fiscal revenue because revenue from state enterprises (in terms of profit and profit tax) was either very small or negative due to huge losses in the state sector.
97. Respondent no. 12 (interview, Guangzhou, Dec. 1993) admitted that the issue of tax exemption and reduction was a sensitive one in the context of central–provincial relations.
98. This was a new tax imposed by the centre in December 1982 to tap the growing extrabudgetary funds in the provinces. The tax amounted to 10%, rising to 15% from August 1983, of the extrabudgetary funds in various units.
99. See Lou Jingfen and Guo Shuqing (1993: 234). This is a book by officials from the State Planning Commission.
100. See *Statistical Yearbook of Guangdong* (1993), 236.
101. See Yang Ming (1989: 29). Total investment is used here as the comparison base. Because the proportion of investment using budgetary funds was getting increasingly smaller in the 1980s, this does not greatly affect the accuracy of the whole picture.
102. See Yang Ming (1989: 29). During the first 9 months of 1988, the value of investment in the state sector increased by 37.4% over the same period last year. Meanwhile the amount of construction tax revenue for the period dropped by 13.3%.
103. For discussion of the practice of collecting tax via 'tax contracts', and criticisms of the practice by some local tax officials in Guangdong, see Zhu Jiangchou (1992: 8–9).
104. In an article from the Audit Bureau, Jiangmen city, Guangdong, it was stated that some local finance departments, in order to retain more discretionary revenue in the locality, would undertake various tactics through which to reduce the recorded fiscal revenue for the year, whilst exaggerating the level of fiscal expenses. These tactics included transferring part of the revenue for the current year to the following year, and of the following year to the next; and treating the unspent cash in hand as spent expenditure. See Ngan Shaoping (1990).

105. Such extension of the coverage of enterprise remittance contracts received explicit criticisms from the Director of the State Taxation Bureau, Jin Xin. See *Guangdong Taxation* 10 (1992): 24.
106. See *Zhongguo Jinbao*, 16 June 1989, 1.
107. Annual inspections in 1988 and 1993 recovered, respectively, 400 million yuan and over 700 million yuan lost in this manner, but these amounts were likely to be tiny tips of the iceberg. See *Zhongguo Jinbao*, 16 June 1989, 1; *Nanfang Ribao*, 8 Jan. 1994, 1.
108. Interview, respondent no. 10, Guangzhou, Dec. 1993. The respondent regarded the inevitability of a subjective element as one of the peculiar difficulties of audit work in China. Because of the experimental nature of China's reforms in the 1980s and the fact that laws and regulations lagged substantially behind the actual situation, audit officials in their work often had to 'cross the river by touching the stones'.
109. See 'The Guangdong People's Government Notice no. 125 (1986) Approving the Provincial Audit Bureau's Report on the Auditing of the Penalty Income of Guangdong', 26 July 1986, in Guangdong People's Government and Provincial Commission for Economic System Reform (1988: 450–1). The remaining 30% could be retained by the units to cover administration and related expenses.
110. The Energy and Transport Strategic Construction Fund, started in 1983, and the Budgetary Adjustment Fund, started in 1989, were two such examples. Both had the extrabudgetary funds as the tax base. The two together could take away 25% of total extrabudgetary funds.
111. The scale may be glimpsed in a nationwide clampdown in 1989, when 1 billion yuan of funds was recovered from 'private accounts' (State Council Notice no. 77 (1989), 'Notice on the Inspection and Wiping Out of "Private Treasuries" ', 14 Nov. 1989, printed in *State Council Gazette* 24 (1989): 867–8).
112. See Lin Zhengbo (1990: 9–10).
113. See Lin Ruo, 'Looking Back and Rethinking: The Track of Reform and Opening of Guangdong', in Zhang Hanqing (1992: 18).
114. See an article by Guangdong's Industry and Commerce Bureau, 'The Present Status and Future Development Strategies of Private Enterprises in Guangdong', in Lok Chaopei and Zheng Yanchao (1989: 257–8).
115. Guangdong Industry and Commerce Bureau, 'The Present Status and Future Development Strategies of Private Enterprises in Guangdong'. It was only in 1987 that the centre first endorsed the existence of private enterprises, and only in 1988 that the constitution was amended to give legitimacy to the private sector. The rights of private enterprises started to get some form of legal protection with the passage of the first administrative regulation on the private sector in 1988.
116. See Fong Jishun (from the Industry and Commerce Bureau of Foshan),

'A Study into the "Pseudo"-Collectives in Foshan', in Lok Chaopei and Zheng Yanchao (1989: 164–9).

117. For a succinct discussion of the distinguishing characteristics, state of development and existing problems of extrabudgetary state enterprises, see Wang Weijian (1990: 59–62). Wang was from the General Planning Department of the Finance Ministry.

118. Interview, respondent no. 7, Guangzhou, Dec. 1993. For an explicit advocacy of the establishment of extrabudgetary enterprises by the local financial department, see Zhong Qijun (1993: 55–6).

119. This is revealed in Guangdong Provincial Government Notice no. 3 (1992), 'On the Inclusion in Budgetary Management of Profit Taxes and Adjustment Taxes Paid by Extrabudgetary Enterprises', printed in *Guangdong Zhengbao* 1 (1992): 34, which states that the 1985 notice would hereafter be superseded.

120. Interview, respondent no. 7, Guangzhou, Dec. 1993. For the 1992 notice, see *Guangdong Zhengbao 1* (1992): 34.

121. *Guangdong Zhengbao* 1 (1992): 59. The experience of the author during field trips to Beijing gave the same impression that the concept of extrabudgetary enterprises was not commonly known. Several respondents from the economic and planning stream appeared never to have heard of the concept.

122. See Lou Shangxi *et al.* (1993: 13).

123. Wang Weijian (1990: 59).

124. See Zeng Xianyou (1993: 46).

125. Interview, respondent no. 7, Guangzhou, Dec. 1993.

126. Respondent no. 7 admitted that the bank was within the extrabudgetary enterprise category (interview, Guangzhou, Dec. 1993). See also a report in *Nanfang Ribao*, 6 Feb. 1990.

127. Interview, respondent no. 6, Guangzhou, Sept. 1993.

128. Interview, respondent no. 7, Guangzhou, Dec. 1993.

129. See *Nanfang Ribao*, 27 Feb. 1989, 1.

130. See Guangdong Provincial Government Notice no. 20 (1987), 'Guangdong People's Government's Notice of Approval of the Proposal by the Provincial Electricity Bureau on Contracting the Electricity Development Targets of the Seventh Five-Year Plan Period', 20 Mar. 1987, in Guangdong People's Government and Provincial Commission for Economic System Reform (1988: 225–9).

131. See Guangdong Planning Commission Research Institute, 'The Plan and the Market in the Investment Scene of Guangdong', in State Planning Commission (1992: 72).

132. See State Planning Commission (1992: 73).

133. See Luo Jingfen and Guo Shuqing (1993: 235).

134. See Gui Shiyong (1991: 79).

135. Calculated from Ministry of Finance (1992: 294).
136. See *Nanfang Ribao*, 11 Dec. 1991, 1.
137. The experience of Guangdong was evaluated in a positive light in a study by the State Planning Commission, the State Council, the Construction Bank and the Ministry of Finance in 1991–2. The findings of the study were published in Luo Jingfen and Guo Shuqing (1993). For more discussion see Ch. 7.
138. In October 1993, as part of an effort to rein in the runaway financial activities, the central government announced that all administrative charges and fees, which had previously been placed outside the budget, should thereafter be subsumed under the budget and remitted to the state treasury. See 'Central Committee Secretariat and State Council Secretariat Approving Ministry of Finance's "Regulation on Implementing the Budgetary Management on Administrative Fees and Penalty Revenues" ', released in *Beijing Daily*, 24 Oct. 1993, and reprinted in State Audit Commission (1994: 75–9).
139. State Audit Commission (1994: 84–94).
140. The two lists of banned charges included exemptions of those already approved by the centre. For instance, it was explicitly stated in the announcement that surcharges levied on freight transport, an item banned in the second list, would not include those surcharges already approved by previous State Council documents. Since Guangdong had already obtained approval for freight transport surcharges in the mid-1980s, these surcharges would not be affected. Respondent no. 9 confirmed that Guangdong had obtained the approval of the centre to raise charges for freight transport as early as 1984 or 1985 (interview, Guangzhou, Feb. 1994). A report by the State Planning Commission also stated that it was the preferential policy of the centre to allow Guangdong to levy higher charges for newly built railroads financed with locally raised funds. See Luo Jingfen and Guo Shuqing (1993: 235).
141. The value of foreign capital and technology imported during 1978–9 amounted to nearly US$8 billion, over 55% of the total between 1950 and 1979. See Fan Yongming (1992: 4).
142. *Guangdong Yearbook* and *Statistical Yearbook of Guangdong*, various years.
143. The share of infrastructure projects in total realized foreign capital amounted to 18% before 1992, when realized foreign capital increased by 88% over 1991. See Lou Jingfen and Guo Shuqing (1993: 120–1). Realized foreign capital in Guangdong continued to increase significantly thereafter, reaching US$9.65 billion in 1993, US$11.45 billion in 1994, and US$12.1 billion in 1995.
144. Guangdong's Vice-Governor, Wu Nansang, raised the idea of using foreign capital in electricity and highway projects whilst Gu Mu was

visiting Guangdong in September 1979. See Guangdong Provincial Party Committee (1986–8: i. 47). Gu Mu immediately agreed to the suggestion, and added that since both the central government and the Guangdong government were short of funds, foreign capital should also be used to finance roads and power stations.

145. Central Committee Notice, 'On Approving the Notes of Meeting on Guangdong and Fujian'.

146. Central Committee Notice, 'On Approving the Notes of Meeting on the Work of Guangdong, Fujian and the Special Economic Zones'.

147. This is not to say that all obstacles to the use of foreign capital in investment were removed in these two central documents. The approval given in 1980 and 1981 focused on roads, ports and railroad projects. In 1983, Guangdong approached the centre for approval to use foreign capital on telecommunications investments. The response from the relevant ministry initially was not positive. But later Guangdong's idea was supported by Hu Yaobang. See 'Hu Yaobang Speaking when Inspecting Guangdong', 6–14 Feb. 1983, in Guangdong Provincial Party Commitee (1986–8: ii. 23). The importance of the developments in 1980–1 is that they laid the ground for later specific bargaining with the centre.

148. The total value of foreign capital used from 1979 to 1991 accounted for more than 25% of total investment in the province. See Zhang Hanqing (1992: 120).

149. State Council Notice no. 6 (1986), 'On Further Improving the Production and Operation Conditions of Foreign-Funded Enterprises', in Guangdong Provincial Party Committee (1986–8: iv. 137–8).

150. Author's interviews in Guangzhou, Dec. 1993.

151. See 'Zhao Ziyang Speaking when Inspecting the Zhuhai Special - Economic Zone', 18 Oct. 1986, in Guangdong Provincial Party Committee (1986–8: iii. 195).

152. See 'The Central Leading Group on Guangdong's Report', 27 Oct. 1987, in Guangdong Provincial Party Committee (1986–8: iv. 389).

153. Guangdong Party Committee and Guangdong People's Government, 'A Petition on Fully Utilizing the Current Opportunity to Speed Up Economic Development', 12 Oct. 1987, in Guangdong Provincial Party Committee (1986–8: iv. 370–5). Realized foreign capital in Guangdong rose by 55% from 1985 to 1986.

154. See *People's Daily*, 23 Jan. 1992, 2.

155. See Sun Jian (1989: 18). Sun Jian was a central government official who was then inspecting Guangdong's retrenchment efforts. After the inspection, however, he suggested that consideration be given to the special needs of the foreign-funded enterprises in Guangdong, apparently having been convinced by Guangdong's presentation of its special circumstances.

Respondent no. 9 also admitted to the author that Guangdong had played the 'foreign investment card' in fighting for a more relaxed environment in the retrenchment years (interview, Guangzhou, Dec. 1993).

156. *Zhongguo Jinbao*, 21 Apr. 1989, 8, and 10 Mar. 1989, 1.

157. This is confirmed by respondent no. 9 (interview, Guangzhou, Dec. 1993).

158. The growth rates of GDP in Guangdong during 1989–91 were consistently higher than the national average. GDP grew by 16.2%, 10.9% and 17.3% in 1989, 1990, and 1991 in Guangdong, against the national rates of 11.7%, 8.8% and 14.2% (*Statistical Yearbook of China* and *Statistical Yearbook of Guangdong*, various years).

159. *Zhongguo Jinbao*, 21 July 1989, 1.

160. *Ming Pao Daily* (Hong Kong), 8 July 1993.

161. This did not preclude the occurrence of more direct criticisms of central policy, however, or articulations for policy change of a comprehensive nature. During 'more normal' periods when the economy was developing well and the reformers at the centre were more secure in their positions, Guangdong leaders occasionally lobbied for more fundamental changes in central policy. One example is the suggestion of special economic zones in 1979, as mentioned earlier, when central leaders had decided to embark on reform and were receptive to suggestions of specific policies. Guangdong was less successful in 1988, however, when it requested comprehensive reform status and a host of aggressive policies, including the abolition of the central control figures on provincial investment. The Guangdong leadership also attempted, in early 1989, to challenge the retrenchment policy imposed in late 1988, as noted earlier in this chapter.

162. Interview, respondent no. 9, Guangzhou, Sept. 1993. The original quota prescribed for 1989 was 20.5% less than the quota and 57.8% less than the provisional estimates of completed investment for 1988 in Guangdong, and was substantially below the original expectation of the Guangdong government. See Wong Guiying (1989).

163. Shenzhen took over Shanghai's long-held position as the number one city in export trade in 1993. The total export value in Shenzhen in 1993 reached US$8.33 billion, 15% of the national total, surpassing Shanghai's US$7 billion. Foreign-funded enterprises, together with enterprises engaging in export processing, accounted for 87% of the total export trade of Shenzhen (*Shenzhen Special Economic Zone Daily*, 8 Mar. 1994, 1). If compared on a provincial level, Guangdong has, since 1986, surpassed Shanghai as the number one exporter in the country.

164. In a speech at a provincial government meeting in July 1992, Guangdong's Governor, Zhu Senlin, stated that Guangdong aimed to reach the standards of the 'four little dragons' in 20 years. The provincial government had already completed a preliminary plan for the attainment of

this goal (*Nanfang Ribao*, 25 July 1992, 1). The description 'four little dragons' refers to four newly industrialized countries/territories in East Asia whose rapid economic development since the 1960s has startled the international community: South Korea, Singapore, Taiwan and Hong Kong.

165. The Vice-Mayor of Guangzhou, Dai Zhiguo, stated unambiguously that the target of Guangzhou was to develop into an international city. He revealed in a press interview that Guangzhou had applied for membership of the Association of International Cities in May 1993, and was accepted in September, the first city in China to become a member of the worldwide association. See *Economic Daily* (Hong Kong), 15 Feb. 1994, 2. This demonstrates the determination of the Guangzhou government to elevate the status of Guangzhou internationally, and to acquire the recognition of international associations ahead of other competitors such as Shenzhen and Shanghai. In the case of Shenzhen, the Shenzhen government spearheaded a seminar in February 1993 on strategies to realize the goal of becoming an international city. The seminar essays were published in Lin Zhuji (1993).

166. *Economic Daily* (Hong Kong), 15 Feb. 1994, 2.

167. Reduced, of course, more in a relative sense than an absolute sense. As a result of the economic reforms, the degree of planning and administration from the centre had already been substantially reduced. In other words the centre had been issuing fewer detailed prescriptions to the provincial government. However, as decentralization of authority extended nationwide, the Guangdong government had a feeling that its autonomy *vis-à-vis* the centre as compared with other provinces was less than before.

6 Discretion and Strategies in Shanghai

As the largest economic centre and the number one contributor to total national revenue until 1991,[1] Shanghai was in a policy and economic environment very different from that of Guangdong. Notwithstanding the fact that the same five categories of discretionary behaviour were apparent in both Guangdong and Shanghai, such behaviour had entirely different emphases. The details of these differences, as well as the context, are discussed comparatively in terms of Guangdong in the next chapter. This chapter discusses the development of Shanghai's discretion in detail, following the typology of discretion outlined in Fig. 1.2.

BARGAINING FOR MORE FAVOURABLE CENTRAL POLICIES

Shanghai's capacity to bargain for favourable changes to its macro-policy environment has been seriously jeopardized due to its special position amongst other provincial-level units. As the 'eldest son' of the centre and the 'elder brother' of other provinces, Shanghai was expected to shoulder more responsibilities for the 'father', and act as rear guard whilst younger brothers were left to make their way through the reform experiment. As a result of this greater responsibility, it took the Shanghai government relatively longer to achieve a favourable macro-policy environment comparable to that of Guangdong. Whilst Guangdong was awarded the Special Policy early in 1979, and was able to focus its subsequent efforts on a fuller implementation of that Special Policy, Shanghai spent the entire 1980s in pursuit of a more favourable policy environment. It was no surprise, therefore, that this special responsibility was considered by Shanghai's officials, in *post facto* analysis, as the major 'stumbling block' inhibiting rapid economic development in Shanghai in the 1980s.

1979–83: Early manoeuvres

As soon as Guangdong and Fujian were granted a preferential investment and revenue policy in July 1979, Shanghai and the other two provincial-level municipalities also pressed for preferential treatment. A meeting between the three municipalities and the centre was held between July and September 1979, in which Beijing, Shanghai and Tianjin asked for half of the new powers of Guangdong and Fujian.[2] In a work conference held in November 1981, it was agreed that the coastal provinces should lead the inland provinces in the modernization of the economy, the so-called principle of 'trickle-down economics'. In order to fulfil this role the coastal provinces were urged to promote foreign trade and the use of foreign capital.[3]

These concessions bore only a pale resemblance to those perquisites given to Guangdong and Fujian two years previously. Discussions were largely restricted to the allocation of foreign exchange and the attraction of foreign investment. Other issues of major importance to greater provincial autonomy concerning which generous powers had been delegated to Guangdong—the fiscal system, the planning system and price controls, for instance—were simply not touched on. The central government also made clear that any reforms in the approved areas should be implemented in a cautious and case-by-case manner. The cautious attitude of the central government is apparent in the notice approving the minutes of the 1981 meeting:

Situations vary between the coastal provinces and municipalities. We should therefore start from the actual situation of each locality, and develop our external economic work in a gradual but progressive manner. You should not blindly emulate one another . . . In order to adjust to the need for the development of foreign trade, it is necessary to expand the authority and autonomy of coastal provinces and municipalities as regards the conduct of foreign trade. . . . But we would consider this issue on a case-by-case basis, and approve each case-as-and when the situation is ripe for change.[4]

The centre was obviously anxious to contain the aspirations of coastal provinces and to pre-empt any further demands for policies as favourable as those granted to Guangdong and Fujian. Therefore, whilst recognizing the leading role of the better-endowed coastal provinces relative to the inland region in economic development, the central government emphasized that there were also significant differences *between* coastal provinces which necessitated their being dealt with on an individual basis. Consequently, Shanghai did not gain much. Apart from the general recognition of the need to use more foreign capital, the only specific authority of significance won by Shanghai from the 1981 meeting was that of having its project approval authority on foreign investment raised to US$ 5 million.[5]

In order to obtain more benefits, the Shanghai government submitted a report to the centre in March 1983 putting forward its own case. The report, entitled 'A Petition on Several Issues concerning the External Economic and Trade of Shanghai', urged the central government to delegate more investment authority to Shanghai. Specifically, it called for greater approval authority regarding foreign investment, and the authority to borrow foreign loans independently. It also demanded more favourable tax policies for enterprises using foreign capital for technical renovation, the abolition of central sectoral figures on the allocation of budgetary investment funding, and more direct central support in the form of investment funding and foreign exchange supply.[6]

As a result of this petition, the ceiling of Shanghai's approval authority for foreign investment projects was raised from US$5 million to US$10 million. Central sectoral control over the allocation of budgetary investment was also cancelled, thereby enabling the Shanghai government to distribute budgetary investment funds amongst different sectors and industries as it saw fit. Shanghai also gained more autonomy in the management of bank investment finance. By 1983 Shanghai had thus obtained its slice of favourable policies, albeit four years after the announcement of the Special Policy for Guangdong and Fujian. It was, however, a very small slice. The central government was very cautious in its policy towards Shanghai. During a visit to Guangdong shortly after Shanghai's petition had been approved, State Councillor Zhang Jingfu made clear to Guangdong officials that Shanghai's favourable policies were very limited and its enhanced autonomy not comparable to that of Guangdong's:

this autonomy [of Shanghai] has a special meaning. The centre has given Shanghai the task of developing a group of industrial projects to an internationally advanced level. . . . Under this condition, the centre has allowed Shanghai 300 new industrial projects, at a total value of US$300 million. This is the 'cage' [scope of manoeuvre] the centre has allowed Shanghai. Within this 'cage', we might loosen the 'strings'. However, this 'cage' has its defined limits. We are not loosening the 'strings' in an abstract [general] way, but only under specific preconditions. . . . As special economic zones you definitely have more power than Shanghai. . . .[7]

The concessions Shanghai achieved in 1983 were, therefore, highly circumscribed. Enlarged autonomy on foreign investment approval was not accompanied by any loosening in other areas of central planning. There was no general endorsement of the enhanced autonomy

of Shanghai to decide on municipal affairs, as was the case in Guangdong. The fiscal system, in particular, was left totally untouched.
Shanghai was then still practising the 'sharing the total' system in
place since 1976, whilst other provinces had had a more favourable
fiscal system since 1980. In fact, as seen in Chapter 4, instead of having
a swelling local coffer as was the case in most other provinces, the local
fiscal revenue of Shanghai *decreased* in absolute terms from 1981 to
1983. The macro-fiscal policy environment in Shanghai had not,
therefore, seen any improvement since the start of the reform decade,
and could even be described as having deteriorated from the pre-1980
conditions.

1984: Grand development plans

The quest for a better policy environment therefore continued. A year
later, in August 1984, the Shanghai leadership met Zhao Ziyang and
other central leaders of the State Council and the (Party) Central
Finance and Economy Leading Group. During the meeting the
Shanghai leaders sounded out the centre's views on a more aggressive
development plan in Shanghai. Subsequent to this meeting, the State
Council sent a research team to Shanghai for further investigation.
After rounds of discussions, a report on the future development
strategies of the Shanghai economy was produced in December 1984,
and approved by the State Council in February 1985.[8]

The report confirmed the pioneer status of Shanghai in the modernization and development of the national economy, and accordingly
called for more delegation of power and resources from the centre to
facilitate the realization of this role. The most important change was
in the fiscal system. As noted in Chapter 4, the original 'sharing the
total' system was ditched and replaced by a system whereby the local
retention rate was fixed at 23.5 per cent for six years. The intention
was, first, to instil a degree of financial security in the Shanghai government, and secondly, to improve Shanghai's financial situation by
allowing an additional 1.5 billion yuan in the calculation of the retention rate. Notwithstanding this and despite the positive tone of the report, not many policy concessions were granted, and the macro-policy
environment of Shanghai remained largely unchanged. In the absence
of substantial concessions in the form of preferential policies, the
affirmation of Shanghai's position as the pioneer of modernization
sounded hollow. The changes in the fiscal system were, in any event,

too insignificant to offset the negative impact of rising costs of production. Shanghai's fiscal revenue subsequently fell again from 1986
to 1988.

There is evidence that the 1985 fiscal arrangement was not what
Shanghai had originally asked for, and was the result of a compromise
made during negotiations with the centre. This hypothesis is based on
two observations. First, the preference of Shanghai's officials as early
as 1984 had been for some form of tax-sharing system through which
the municipal and central governments would retain their respective
taxes as sources of revenue. Secondly, as soon as the deal with the
centre had been struck, some Shanghai officials started to complain
that the 1985 system was inadequate for the needs of Shanghai, and
could serve only as a transient arrangement pending the anticipated
full establishment of the tax-sharing system.[9]

Another shortcoming of the 1984 report lay in its underlying as-
sumptions. As a petition for more powers, the report was heavily
imbued with Shanghai's traditional thoughts about its role. As the
'eldest son' of the centre, it was unthinkable to Shanghai's leaders that
Shanghai should have no major role to play in reform. However, given
its greater responsibility to the national economy, it was accepted
that its development strategy had to differ from that of the southern
provinces. The following quotes from the report fully reflect this
attitude:

Shanghai should become the pioneer of the 'four modernizations' of the
country. This is preconditioned by its status in the country and in the whole
world. . . . As the largest industrial and economic centre in the country, Shanghai should make the largest contribution to the national goal of 'quadrupling
production output' by the end of this century. . . . As for the production plan
of Shanghai during the Seventh Five-Year Plan period [1986–90], we should
be pragmatic . . ., and should not blindly pursue projects with the sole aim of
doubling the production output by 1990 . . .[10]

In other words, whilst the Shanghai leadership were eager to jump
on the economic development bandwagon and sustain the leading
position of Shanghai, their views had been so conditioned by Shanghai's traditional role as the leading municipality in China that they
effectively temporized their own demands. The situation was similar
to that of one party at the negotiating table willingly agreeing to all
the major arguments of its opponent. In such a situation Shanghai's
'defeat' in the negotiations with the centre was, to an extent, self-
inflicted.

1987: Saving the 'dragon head' position

The limitations of the 1984 attempt were fully reflected in the second, and more serious, slide in fiscal revenue during 1986–7.[11] As a result of this slide, Shanghai's local fiscal revenue in 1987, at 16.5 billion yuan, was only 7.3 per cent of the national total, a substantial fall from its 16 per cent share in 1981.[12] The average annual economic growth rate also fell well behind the national average. The national annual average for national income growth from 1981 to 1987, for instance, was 9.73 per cent, as compared to 7.85 per cent in Shanghai. The national annual average growth rate of total production output was 11.44 per cent, as compared to Shanghai's 10.16 per cent.[13] In sharp contrast to Shanghai's lacklustre performance, Guangdong's economy was booming, with the annual average growth rates for the two indices at 11.7 per cent and 15.3 per cent.[14] Among Shanghai officials and Shanghai watchers abroad, there developed at the time a sense of crisis, a sense that Shanghai's leading position might be taken by the southern provinces.[15]

The repeated falls in fiscal revenues soon caused concern for the centre. In late 1987 central leaders Zhao Ziyang and Yao Yilin went to Shanghai to investigate the difficulties faced by the city. The Shanghai government took this opportunity to submit a petition report asking for more powers, which was approved in February 1988.[16] The Shanghai government demanded a version of the *dabaogan* responsibility system whereby local fiscal remittance would be fixed at 10.5 billion yuan for a period of five years. From the fourth year, that is 1991, onwards, if total local fiscal revenue exceeded 16.5 billion yuan, half of the excess would be forwarded to the central coffers on top of the 10.5 billion yuan remittance. In addition, the Shanghai government asked for more autonomy in export trade and in price management. It demanded the power to determine independently the level of local wages and incomes. Moreover, it wanted the development of financial institutions accelerated, in order to re-establish Shanghai's pre-1949 financial centre status. It asked for investment quotas to be increased, and local state enterprises to be allowed to issue more bonds to raise capital, as well as more direct central support in the form of funds and capital.[17]

These demands spanned the most important policy areas and, if fully realized, would signal a substantial change in Shanghai's macro-policy environment. Implementation was not smooth, however, and most of the powers and additional resources requested by Shanghai, and initially granted in principle by the centre, did not materialize in practice. With the onset of nationwide retrenchment as from the fourth quarter of 1988, most of the new powers were either rapidly re-centralized or simply not implemented. For instance, the power to manage the prices of seventy-six more categories of industrial goods was undermined by the centre's determination to stamp out inflation-ary pressures, and the price management authority of eight products was formally recentralized. Shanghai's efforts to obtain larger quotas for investment and bank finance simply failed to bear fruit. The 100 million yuan additional quotas for investment and bank finance, and the additional bank capital for infrastructural investments, were either cancelled or substantially reduced.[18]

The *dabaogan* system was relatively secure, but this was considered far from satisfactory by itself. First, the change in the economic macro-environment caused by the centre's retrenchment policies resulted in increases in local expenditures which had not been taken into account at the time the 10.5 billion yuan contract sum was calcu-lated. This meant that the municipal government had to shoulder additional burdens, estimated in 1989 at about 1.6 billion yuan, which would have been shared with, if not entirely borne by, the centre under the pre-existing 'sharing the total' fiscal system. Secondly, there was the feeling that the centre had not given Shanghai a fair deal. Due to Shanghai's historical legacy before 1949, the bulk of Shanghai's pre-1949 fixed assets had been substantially underestimated when private enterprises were converted into private–public joint enterprises, in order that less interest be paid to the former owners. The implication was that the cost of renovating this part of the city's fixed assets could be two to three times that of the official estimates as stated in the ac-count books.[19] Under the contractual *dabaogan* system the municipal government would be responsible for footing the entirety of the bill. Since the account books had substantially undervalued the costs and thus inflated the profits of many old local enterprises inherited from the pre-1949 industrial infrastructure, the 10.5 billion yuan figure, cal-culated on the basis of existing accounts, was similarly inflated. In other words, while the contractual system was intended to delineate the respective responsibilities and resources of the centre and the provinces, Shanghai had, from the perspective of municipal officials, entered a deal which gave it heavy responsibilities but a less than fair share of resources.[20]

It is worth recalling here that Shanghai was not alone in having its reforms cut back. Guangdong's attempt to expand its autonomy further in early 1988 was likewise curtailed later that year. The main difference between the two, however, was that Guangdong fell back to a much higher base, whilst the 1987 deal had been the first occasion on which the Shanghai government had obtained favourable measures on a more substantial scale. With many new powers cancelled or severely watered down, and more expenditure burdens placed on local fiscal shoulders, it was no surprise that Shanghai officials should feel that its *dabaogan* system had not in practice been very favourable to Shanghai. This was apparent in the fact that the macro-environment of Shanghai's economy had not seen any significant improvement.[21]

1990: Favourable policies on Pudong

In April 1990, Premier Li Peng announced in Shanghai the centre's decision to 'open' the Pudong area in east Shanghai. Ten favourable policies along the lines of those in the existing five special economic zones (including Hainan) were granted to Pudong to boost its development.[22] The announcement ended the situation whereby the policy environment and power of the Shanghai government was substantially less favourable than that of the southern provinces, a change long sought by the Shanghai leadership.

This change in policy was in part a result of active and persistent lobbying by Shanghai leaders. When Yang Shangkun, then the President, visited Shanghai during the Spring Festival of 1990, Shanghai's leaders complained to him about the plight of their city, asking Yang whether it was the centre's policy to see the decline of Shanghai. Yang reassured the Shanghai leadership that the centre was determined to assist Shanghai.[23] Deng Xiaoping, who was also visiting Shanghai at that time, also indicated that the centre would give Shanghai additional support.[24] Having sounded out the views of the centre,[25] the Shanghai government promptly submitted a petition in February with detailed policy proposals for the development of Pudong.[26] The petition included requests for eighteen favourable policies, of which ten were finally approved.[27]

The April 1990 announcement ended the decade of 'policy discrimination' which, in the eyes of Shanghai's officials, had been the major cause of the decline in Shanghai's economic status in the 1980s.[28] How was this turnaround possible? The Shanghai economy had been facing grave difficulties for quite a considerable period, and the Shanghai leadership had time and again lobbied for changes throughout the 1980s. Why did the Shanghai leadership finally succeed at that particular point in time?

When seeking an explanation for this change of central policy it is important to take note of the national and international situation at that time. A number of Shanghai officials admitted that, despite the persistent lobbying of Shanghai leaders for a change of policy, national political considerations at that time was possibly the critical factor at work, and that the specific circumstances of Shanghai might not have been directly relevant.[29] One possible explanation goes as follows. Less than a year before the announcement, many foreign investors fled the country in the aftermath of the Tiananmen incident. China's international image was seriously damaged and some major trading partners announced economic sanctions against China. This was an undesirable situation both in terms of China's international relations and its unfinished task of modernization. It was felt necessary to divert the attention of international investors and foreign governments from the events of 1989 back to the economic development programme of the country. Guangdong and its special economic zones had made an impression on the international community, but developments there were no longer a 'fresh' phenomenon. Shanghai, with its historical fame within the international community, its dominant position in the national economy, and its strong association with the planned economy, was the ideal candidate. According to this theory, the opening of Pudong in Shanghai would send a clear message to the international community that the Chinese government was, despite the 'setback' of 1989 and continued economic retrenchment, serious about economic reform.[30]

Alternatively, the reason could be that, in 1990, the centre considered the time ripe for a shift in the focus of economic reform from the southern provinces to more centrally situated and, traditionally, more important economic centres such as Shanghai.[31] In any event this extension of the reform was a logical development in the progress of China's reform. As the largest city and economic centre of the country, Shanghai's historical status made it the ideal medium through which to consolidate the reform experience of the southern provinces and to extend them inland.

The national environment of 1990 lends more credibility to the first explanation. It must be remembered that in 1990 China was in the middle of an economic retrenchment which had begun in late 1988. When the Special Policy for Guangdong and the establishment of special economic zones were announced in 1979 and 1980, the national economic situation was relatively normal. The decision on Guangdong was, it may be noted, made well in advance of the announcement for economic adjustment in 1980. In Shanghai's case, retrenchment had already been in operation for a year and a half with no sign of ending at the time the Pudong policies were announced in April 1990.[32] Consequently, economic development in Shanghai and Pudong in the immediate aftermath of the 1990 announcements remained lacklustre. Under severely straitened circumstances it was also difficult for the centre to live up to its promised extra funding support, amounting to 1.3 billion yuan per year for a total of five years.[33] There was talk as late as December 1991 that the time was not yet ripe for the opening of Pudong.[34] The development of Pudong and Shanghai only entered the 'fast lane' after Deng Xiaoping's Southern Tour in January–February 1992. In March 1992 Huang Ju, Shanghai's Mayor at the time, announced that the centre had approved additional powers and extra capital support for Shanghai. Thus it was only after the national economic situation changed to one of promoting rapid growth that Shanghai's favourable policies gradually had some impact, and Shanghai's economic environment saw its first substantial improvement.[35] These developments indicated that whilst the centre had announced the opening of the Pudong Development Zone early in April 1990, the priority of the centre at that time was nonetheless the implementation of economic retrenchment. Pudong and Shanghai thus had to wait until the end of the retrenchment policy before their development could gather momentum. This fact supports the suggestion that the announcement made in April 1990 was of a more symbolic than material nature, political considerations having been amongst the major motivations behind the centre's decision on Pudong at that particular juncture in 1990.[36]

1993: Protecting the Pudong policies

The Pudong policies of 1990 and 1992 marked the change in central policy towards Shanghai. Subsequent to these announcements, the next important task of the Shanghai government was to eliminate the doubts abounding in 1990–1 regarding the viability and prospects of the development of Pudong. The Shanghai government was anxious to convince potential investors that Pudong's policies were the most favourable in the country, and that Shanghai, with its new initiatives in Pudong, was about to become the most important growth area in China. Consequently, comparisons between favourable policies in special economic zones in the south and those in Pudong became, at that time, hot topics of discussion in official and semi-official publications.[37]

Moreover, as a late beneficiary Shanghai's officials were particularly weary of any hint of erosion of their hard-won favourable policies, and of being left once more outside the fast lane of economic development. When Zhu Rongji came to Shanghai in October 1993 to solicit Shanghai's support for the imminent tax and fiscal reforms, therefore, the overwhelming concern of the Shanghai leadership was to protect Pudong's favourable policies from any possible threat. Shanghai officials were worried that the central policy to control tax exemption, announced in July 1993 as part of the macro-economic adjustment measures, and likely also to form part of the pending tax and fiscal reforms, would in effect mean the withdrawal of the Pudong policies. The preferential policies were, after all, largely built around favourable tax rates and generous tax exemptions. Thus when Zhu Rongji finally gave his pledge that Pudong's policies would not be touched under the 1994 tax and fiscal reforms, the Shanghai leadership was immediately contented. As a gesture of support, and as a 'trade-off' for the centre's pledge, the Shanghai leadership agreed to remit an additional sum of 600 million yuan in 1993 over and above the originally agreed sum of 11.5 billion yuan.[38] In the end Shanghai's support proved critical to Zhu in pushing through the fiscal and taxation reforms at the Third Plenum in November 1993.

The priority and emphasis of the Shanghai leadership was, therefore, very different from that of Guangdong. The Guangdong leadership was more concerned with the effect of the tax-sharing reform on its retained fiscal revenue, and consequently focused its lobbying on the determination of the baseline year during Zhu's visit. Since this concession would be universally applied, the Shanghai leadership stood to gain in any event. Consequently, Shanghai sought to expand its benefits further by focusing its own bargaining on preserving its hard-won favourable policies.

THE FIGHT FOR DIRECT CENTRAL SUPPORT

Due to the slow pace of change in the macro-policy environment, and because Shanghai was traditionally a major base of central planning, securing central support in the form of direct investment projects, capital finance and enlarged investment quotas represented one important and frequently employed means by which the Shanghai government sought to increase investment and boost the local economy.

Central investment projects

In Chapter 4 it was noted that the share of central investment in Shanghai's state sector investment during the 1980s was larger than that of the pre-1980 years. From 1950 to 1980, the share was around 30 per cent, surging to 36 per cent during the 1981–93 period. Counting only capital construction projects, central investment projects reached their zenith at 66 per cent during 1981–5, declining only slightly to 59 per cent between 1986 and 1990, and to 36 per cent during 1991–3.[39] These high proportions reflected the substantial amount of central investment in Shanghai. Amongst the more notable and larger projects were the expansion of the Shanghai Petrochemical Plant, the first phase of which was completed in 1978, the formation of Shanghai Baoshan Iron and Steel Corporation, Hongqiao Airport, and an electricity power plant in Pudong. As noted in Chapter 4, despite the proliferation of funding channels in the 1980s, there are solid indications of quite a substantial inflow of central fiscal investment funds to Shanghai in particular years of the 1980s.[40]

The tendency among Shanghai's officials was, however, to play down the contribution of central investment projects to the local economy and to the local fiscal coffers.[41] This was partly a bargaining tactic and partly a result of subjective evaluation. There were frequent complaints about the extra burdens posed by central enterprises on Shanghai's capital supply,[42] about food subsidies,[43] and about other demands on the city infrastructure and community facilities. The fact that central investment could have a multiplier effect on the local economy and was itself a major source of local fiscal revenue in terms of turnover taxes was apparently ignored. There was a feeling within Shanghai, for instance, that the profit tax revenue of central enterprises entered the central government coffers directly, and that other taxes, including the turnover taxes, paid by central enterprises to local coffers were relatively minor and insignificant. The fact was, on the contrary, that turnover taxes were the largest revenue item in the state budget, and that central enterprises in Shanghai were a major contributor to these taxes. For instance, local revenue from turnover taxes in the first nine months of 1993 was 800 million yuan more than that for the same period the previous year, of which 500 million yuan, or 63 per cent of the increase, came solely from the Baoshan Iron and Steel Corporation alone.[44]

Interestingly, therefore, although the Shanghai government was eager to obtain direct central support in investment (and statistical information does suggest a strong presence of the central government in investment activities during the 1980s), the general perception amongst Shanghai officials was that Shanghai had not benefited much from central investment in Shanghai, and that the amount of investment made during the decade had not been that substantial.[45] Whatever benefits central investment brought to Shanghai, in terms of increased tax revenue and job opportunities, were regarded as neither substantial nor material in terms of the benefits Shanghai should, in theory, have obtained. Part of the benefits were cancelled out, it was felt, by the additional financial burdens Shanghai had to bear for accommodating these central enterprises. More importantly, Shanghai officials generally expected a higher level of central support in return for their previous contribution to the national coffers. The feeling was that Shanghai deserved more.

This feeling of discontent amongst Shanghai officals reflected their failure to adapt to changes in the rules of the game since reform. As discussed in Chapter 5, the progress of economic reforms in the 1980s had significantly altered the nature of what had once been largely an administrative exercise in the allocation of investment resources. In order to attract central investment one would now have to offer good prospects for profits. At a time of tight capital supply and keen competition for capital, one also needed to be willing to shoulder part of the investment. In other words, one needed attractive bait in hand to succeed in 'catching' central investment, and one had to be prepared to give away something before any return could possibly be obtained. Shanghai's complaints about the 'burdens' imposed by central projects thus reflected the fact that the Shanghai government had yet to adapt to the requirements of its new operating environment.

Capital supply

Another way to increase investment in Shanghai was by getting more capital supply from the centre, either in the form of fiscal grants or bank finance. This was an even better method than having central direct investments, as the municipal government could then have more autonomy in the use of capital, and the profits generated from new local projects would enter local fiscal coffers instead of central coffers as was the case for central direct investments.

There were various types of capital supply. There were, first, grants and loans designated for specific investment purposes. For instance, from 1984 to 1991 Shanghai obtained 2.9 billion yuan of additional capital from the centre for renovating the city's infrastructure,[46] and a total of US$1.3 billion of additional central bank loans to finance the technical renovation of its ageing state enterprises.[47] In 1987, the Shanghai government, together with Beijing and Tianjin, solicited the support of the State Council in providing new money for the development of export-oriented industries in the three municipalities. Additional funds were thus put aside for the competitive bidding for enterprises by the three cities.[48] Although such capital usually came with strings attached, in practice it was not difficult for the municipal government to circumvent control and divert the funds to other uses. The 2.9 billion yuan targeted for city infrastructure renovation was, for instance, appropriated to other uses.[49]

Central fiscal grants for purposes other than investment could be a support to local investment, because under the *dabaogan* system the municipal government would be able to deploy more resources for investment if other expenditure items were borne by the central government. Central fiscal grants in 1992 amounted to about 1.4 billion yuan,[50] accounting for some 16 per cent of the disposable local revenue of Shanghai.[51] In the absence of more comprehensive data, this suggests, tentatively, that central fiscal grants had much more weight in Shanghai's fiscal budget relative to Guangdong's.[52]

Loans from the central bank were also a form of central financial subsidy because of the low borrowing rates. From 1986 to 1990 Shanghai's cumulative deposit–loan deficit reached 17.5 billion yuan,[53] which was largely covered by loans from the central bank.[54] However, information on the transfer of various bank funds to the centre—13.4 billion yuan in the case of Guangdong from 1980–8—is not available for Shanghai. Nevertheless, information on Guangdong indicates the possible proportion of the net central fund injection into the local bank system in the case of Shanghai.[55] As in the case of direct central investment, the Shanghai government often felt that the amount of cheap central loans which were given to Shanghai was not commensurate with its role in and contribution to the national economy. For instance, it was stated on one occasion that the direct supply of bank funds from the central bank had declined substantially, from 4.8 billion yuan in 1986 to 1.6 billion yuan in 1987.[56] This was considered totally inadequate for the development of Shanghai's economy.

The largest inflow of extra investment capital came as a corollary of the favourable policies for Pudong, announced in 1990 and reinforced in 1992. Extra capital totalling 6.5 billion yuan, to be provided during 1991–5, was promised to the Shanghai government in April 1990. The 6.5 billion yuan was in four parts: (1) US$100 million per annum of foreign capital with favourable interest rates, equivalent to 2 billion yuan over five years; (2) central fiscal grants of 200 million yuan per year, totalling 1 billion yuan over five years; (3) additional bank loans amounting to 1.5 billion yuan over five years; and (4) loans from the central Ministry of Finance with negative interest rates of 3 to 4.32 per cent, totalling 2 billion yuan in five years.[57] Then, in March 1992, the centre pledged to give additional capital of up to 4 billion yuan more each year, or 16 billion yuan in total from 1992 to 1995. This included (1) allowing the Shanghai government to issue 500 million yuan of bonds each year; (2) twice as many foreign loans as those of 1990 to be arranged with favourable interest rates, making a total of US$300 million per annum; (3) an additional 100 million yuan in annual quotas of enterprise share issue; (4) the authority to issue B shares amounting to US$100 million per annum; and (5) an additional annual central fiscal grant of 100 million yuan, totalling 400 million yuan over four years.[58] Adding these to the 1990 promises, the centre pledged to supply a total of 22.5 billion yuan of capital to Shanghai.

It should be noted, however, that of the total 22.5 billion yuan, only a fraction would be directly supplied through traditional channels. Money directly from the central government, consisting of fiscal grants and negative-rate fiscal loans, totalled 3.4 billion yuan. This sort of capital incurred the least cost from the viewpoint of the municipal government, and was traditionally the most welcome. Next came the 1.5 billion yuan of domestic bank loans and the US$1.7 billion of foreign loans. These loans would be arranged by the central government, and although the municipal government had to repay them in due course, the favourable interest rates amounted to some kind of subsidy. Most of the new capital promised in 1992 belonged to the third type, whereby what the Shanghai government obtained from the centre was not the actual supply of capital, whether as grants or loans, but the *power* to raise capital from the market. This included the power to issue 2 billion yuan in bonds, 400 million yuan in enterprise shares and US$400 million in B shares. In such cases whether or not the capital could be realized would depend on the management ability of the Shanghai government, and on market situations.[59]

Expanding the 'cages'

The central control figures on the scale of total bank finance and total investment have been described by Chinese officials as 'cages'. This term conveys the message that provincial governments were, in theory, to confine their discretionary investment decisions and planning within the limits of investment and bank finance totals prescribed by the centre. Although the control figures were actually only an index, itself not denoting any inflow of central resources to the provinces, expanding the size of the 'cages' was synonymous with attracting more investment capital from the centre. This was particularly the case as regards bank finance quotas. As the centre expanded the quotas for bank finance, Shanghai would be able to obtain more central bank loans to make up for its shortfall of deposit.

The Shanghai government was most concerned about the constraints imposed by the central control figures as, on the whole, it took the quotas more seriously than did Guangdong. This was especially the case regarding investment quotas, which, as previously noted, were not very seriously observed in Guangdong. In Shanghai, data in Table 6.1 suggest that the quotas were more or less followed.

The extent of excess investment was modest compared to that of Guangdong.[60] Taking into account that some categories of investment were, as a matter of central policy, excluded from the coverage of the quota, such modest excess investment meant that the centrally imposed quota was largely followed.[61] Consequently, very substantial effort was spent every year with a view to securing as large a 'cage' as possible. In a work report by Shanghai's Vice-Mayor and head of the Planning Commission, having raised the investment quotas and secured the associated supply of investment capital from the centre was hailed as a major accomplishment.[62] A major objective of

TABLE 6.1. *Differentials BetweenPlans and Performance[a] in Shanghai (billion yuan)*

Year	Quotas	Actual investment[b]	Excess investment (%)
1987	11.2[c]	12.6	12.5
1988	13.0[d]	17.3	33.1
1991	14.2[e]	18.5	30.3
1992	22.0[f]	28.7	30.5

[a] Performance means total local investment made in the year, as in Table 3.7.
[b] From *Statistical Yearbook of Shanghai* (1988, 1989, 1992, 1993).
[c] From *Shanghai Economy* (1988): 558.
[d] From *China Capital Construction* 5 (1989): 4.
[e] Calculated from *Shanghai Statistics* 5 (1992): 2–5.
[f] From *Shanghai Jihua Jingji Tansuo* 1 (1992): 2.

Shanghai's bargaining with the centre had always been a higher investment quota.

This concern for investment quotas was fully revealed in Shanghai's reactions to the announcement of the Pudong policies in 1990. Under the new policy more investments were destined to be allocated to Pudong. The Shanghai government, in response, was keen to have a separate investment quota for the Pudong area in order to prevent any negative displacement effect on the old city area.[63] This was eventually achieved in 1992.[64] In 1993, the quota for annual investment in the old city area was 30 billion yuan, and the quota for Pudong 10.4 billion yuan. Having a separate quota for Pudong, therefore, amounted to an increase of the total investment quotas for Shanghai by one-third.[65]

The meaning of the central quotas to the Shanghai government was considered by some Shanghai officials as analogous to the significance of rice coupons to Chinese city residents living in a system of central planning. To be able to buy rice one first had to obtain rice coupons, regardless of whether or not there was, in fact, sufficient rice in supply in the government reserves.[66] However, the central quotas had more utility than rice coupons for coupon-holders. The supply of rice was ultimately determined by the actual quantity of the rice harvest, a factor which was not susceptible to manipulation, or certainly not on a substantial scale, at any particular point in time. On the other hand, the supply of capital in China, at least until the early 1990s, was very much a matter of the will of the central government, and developments suggested that it was possible to 'push' the central government, via the central bank, to increase the supply of money. In other words, as far as investment was concerned, the primary concern of provincial governments was that of expanding their investment and bank finance quotas. Having achieved a larger quota, they would then be in a position to ask for the 'associated' supply of capital with which to finance the investment.

Some other provincial governments might simply ignore the quotas and implement their own investment plans. In this way their behaviour might be compared to offenders in the case of rice control who either hoarded up rice privately for their own consumption, or simply broke into the official godowns to take the rice. Bargaining with the authorities for more rice coupons was no longer their major means of access to an increased rice intake. This had been largely the case in Guangdong, where there had been substantial excess investment over and above the central quotas which were being increasingly ignored. In the case of Shanghai, the modest excess of investment suggested that, on the whole, obtaining more rice coupons was still considered to be the major and most appropriate route to a full stomach.

IMPLEMENTATION MANOEUVRES

That the Shanghai government was more rule-abiding than Guangdong did not imply that there was no occurrence at all of deviant behaviour. A municipal finance official admitted that the Shanghai government had been adapting generally worded central policies and laws so that they were 'tailored' to the local circumstances.[67] For instance, there was ample evidence of multiple manipulations regarding the investment quotas, subsequent to efforts in obtaining an enlarged quota as outlined previously. However, as we shall see below, the cautious mentality of Shanghai officials had exercised an obvious influence upon the scale and content of these manoeuvres.

Manipulating the central investment quotas

As discussed in Chapter 3, some categories of investment were excluded from the central control figures on annual investment as part of the central policy to encourage socially desirable and non-profit-making projects such as schools and staff hostels. One way of beating the centre's investment control was, therefore, through manipulating these legitimate exemption categories. The Shanghai government was apparently an active exponent of this practice. Data available show that as much as 36 per cent of Shanghai's local capital construction investment in 1987 belonged to these exempted categories.[68] Total local investment in 1987 surpassed the original plan by 12.5 per cent (Table 6.1). If the exempted categories are excluded (as they should be), the total investment was even less than the value prescribed by the centre.

It thus appears that the exempted categories became a convenient vehicle through which the Shanghai government could legitimately increase investment beyond the approved ceiling. Some investments were simply placed in the exempted categories so that more investment could be made without exceeding the investment quotas too much.[69] The Shanghai government was eager to expand investment, and to remain righteous. There was a limit, however, to which one could be both rule-abiding and self-cultivating. The concern to appear to be abiding by the rules imposed a strong self-restraint on the investment behaviour of the Shanghai government, and explained its relative modesty in terms of excess investment over the centrally prescribed quotas, as shown in Table 6.1.

Another method through which to achieve a bigger 'cage' was by excluding projects regarded as important by the centre from those investments covered by the central quota. A difficult situation was thus deliberately created by giving desirable projects a low priority within the centrally approved scale of investment. This tactic was used particularly during periods of retrenchment when the centre was more stringent on excess investment. For instance, during the retrenchment in 1989 when the investment quota of Shanghai was cut by 40 per cent, the strategy employed by the Shanghai government was that of excluding a number of profitable industrial projects from the plan, and using this as a bargaining chip when negotiating a larger quota from the centre.[70] The centre was thus confronted with a 'problem' which could only be solved by enlarging the quota.

Increasing the revenue base of 1993

Another instance of 'flexible implementation' by the Shanghai government was the effort to increase the revenue base on the eve of the implementation of the tax-sharing system in late 1993. Table 6.2 shows month-by-month local fiscal revenue in 1993.

TABLE 6.2. *Shanghai's Local Fiscal Revenue, 1993*
(100 million yuan)

Month	Revenue	% increase over same month in 1992
January	11.8	23.1
February	10.6	−2.3
March	15.9	26.9
April	24.6	25.0
May	21.1	36.2
June	13.7	2.0
July	19.6	20.4
August	18.8	32.5
September	25.2	105.6
October	31.6	65.1
November	20.4	32.4
December	29.0	8.5

Source: Personal communication.

It can be seen that from September to October, Shanghai's local fiscal revenue increased at a substantially higher rate in comparison with the same period the previous year. This suggests the possibility that deliberate action was taken to collect more revenue before the end of the year.[71] The pattern of development from September to December was, however, interesting. Contrary to the 'upward trend' in Guangdong, where the rate of increase accelerated towards the end of the year (see Table 5.2), the trend in Shanghai was quite the opposite. The rate of increase was at its highest in September, and fell substantially each subsequent month.

As mentioned in Chapter 5, the central government, noting the sudden rise in fiscal revenue in September and October, issued a notice in November 1993 warning against the premature and improper collection of revenue. In a national finance meeting in early December, the Finance Minister Liu Zhongli reiterated this warning.[72] Apparently this had its desired effect on the Shanghai government, as in early December many enterprises in Shanghai received 'refunds' of a substantial part of the tax payments they had paid earlier.[73] Many enterprises were reportedly caught off guard when they received these tax refunds, for which no reason was given, suggesting the abruptness with which the decision on refunding the taxes was made.

The motive behind this swift turnabout concurred with that behind the original revenue-grasping behaviour. Since the central government had made clear its position on the issue, to continue such behaviour was likely to invite penalties. More importantly, there was strong concern within the Shanghai government that collecting too much revenue might be detrimental to the city in the long run, since it would raise the expectations of the centre regarding the financial strength of Shanghai, and thus invite more 'requests' for additional 'contributions'.[74] Abiding by the central instructions thus served a dual purpose: it projected a positive image for Shanghai as 'loyal follower' of the centre, and shielded local revenue from future central encroachments.

REACHING OUT FOR THE NEW HORIZON

Until the late 1980s, the attention of the Shanghai leadership was largely preoccupied with relieving its heavy financial commitments. Much time was spent on bargaining with the centre for a lower fiscal remittance level and more central resources. Various tactics were employed to ensure that more could be achieved under a veil of compliance. In these circumstances, manoeuvres were largely built around the established area of the central plan system and squarely within the bounds of the traditional state sector.

It is, however, incorrect to conclude that the Shanghai government did not use, or failed to notice the importance of, manoeuvring tactics beyond the traditional boundaries of state control which had been widely used in Guangdong. The issue was more often a matter of affordability than of willingness. When the Shanghai government finally secured a more relaxed macro-environment towards the end of the 1980s, such tactics increasingly characterized its discretionary behaviour. By focusing on the non-state and extrabudgetary sectors, as opposed to the state and budgetary sectors, these more recent forms of discretion became the major factors underlying the surge of local investment activity from the late 1980s.

There is evidence that, from at least as early as 1984, some officials in the Finance Bureau explicitly advocated the use of, as well as actually adopted, tax alleviation to promote local economic development.[75] From 1980 to 1983, whilst Shanghai was still operating the 'sharing the total' fiscal system of 1976, the total value of tax revenue forgone as a result of exemption and reduction by the municipal government amounted to nearly 600 million yuan. This was about 1 per cent of the total local fiscal revenue of the period.[76] A finance official aptly described the early thinking of some Shanghai officials on this issue:

We have to drop the old way . . . the attitude of being satisfied simply with increasing the amount of revenue collected, containing expenditure, and balancing revenue and expenditure bills. We should instead emphasize the promotion of production. . . . We have to learn a new approach to the management of our finance. In order to take more, we first have to give; to give a small piece in return for a larger piece.[77]

Notwithstanding this early call for a more aggressive attitude, it remained the fact that as of the mid-1980s, many officials in Shanghai were not very receptive to the idea of tax alleviation being incorporated as a major part of Shanghai's development strategy. In fact the above quote points out precisely that the dominant approach amongst Shanghai finance officials in the mid-1980s was still very much focused on the due collection of revenue. Nonetheless, if it had not been for the stringent financial situation during the 1980s, i.e. the existence of formidable objective obstacles, the change in attitudes might have been achieved sooner.

A report completed in 1991 by the Shanghai Institute for System Reform includes a frank reference to the implications of the objective circumstances for the municipal government's room for manoeuvre:

The contradiction arising from the excessively heavy fiscal remittance, itself a leftover from the old centralized system, has yet to be solved. This has placed a limit on the capacity of the local finance [bureau] to adjust and regulate the economy. Some fiscal measures which would have made a substantial impact on the development of the economy could not, as a result, be implemented. For instance the municipal government has been unable, whether in terms of its authorized powers or in terms of the limits posed by the actual circumstances, to implement measures on depreciation, which would have a major effect on our industrial and investment structure, or to devise favourable policies on profit taxes.[78]

The background to this report was the two slides in local fiscal revenue of 1981–3 and 1986–8, as described in Chapter 4. In 1988 the size of Shanghai's local fiscal revenue had fallen to *less* than that of the previous decade.[79] The high base of fiscal remittance meant there was little room for the government to relieve the burden on its local state enterprises, which had been paying taxes at a rate generally higher than that of the national average.[80] The weight of these pressures was such that, even when the macro-environment finally improved in Shanghai's favour in the early 1990s, the *initial* reactions of the Shanghai government were stubbornly anachronistic.

The initial response of the Shanghai government to the announcement of the Pudong policies was indicative of the prolonged effect of austerity. In the aftermath of the excitment after the 1990 announcement, there was widespread and strongly felt anxiety within the Shanghai government that the centre's high-profile plan for Pudong would have a negative impact on Shanghai's old city area. As noted earlier in this chapter, the Shanghai government at the time bargained for a separate investment quota for Pudong. The following quote shows clearly that the worry over displacement was the major concern behind the fight for a separate quota.

To build a modernized new area in Pudong will require the injection of a huge amount of capital. . . . Under the existing investment administration system, the central government has a tight control on the scale of investment activities. This would engender competition between Pudong and Puxi [the old Shanghai city] for the supply of capital and the planned quotas on investment. Three types of situation can thus result as a consequence: (a) investment will flow to Pudong on a substantial scale, and Puxi as a result declines rapidly; (b) investment will flow to Puxi instead; Puxi is revitalized but the development of Pudong is delayed and slowed down as a result; (c) investment will flow to both Pudong and Puxi without any emphasis; but since the supply of capital is limited, the amount of investment will be insufficient to achieve a breakthrough in either area. . . . the third situation is the most probable.[81]

Instead of considering how to make use of the new policies so as to benefit Shanghai as a whole, the Shanghai government was preoccupied with the restrictions of the pre-existing system. It worried that the preferential treatment given to Pudong would make the fulfilment of pre-existing duties more difficult still. For instance, nearly one-third of the chapter on Pudong development in the above report was devoted to a section titled 'The System Frictions between Pudong and Puxi'.[82] The subsequent long list of 'system frictions' spanned the enterprise, investment, material supply, finance and banking, fiscal, foreign trade, price, employment, social security and management systems. The worries of the Shanghai government were apparent in the following quote from the discussion of fiscal system frictions:

the 10.5 billion yuan remittance task has become an increasingly heavy burden [since 1988]. . . . This fixed remittance target will inevitably come into sharp conflict with the tax alleviation policies in Pudong. The conflict could give rise to three scenarios. (1) Existing enterprises in Pudong are currently supposed to remit 2 billion yuan to the municipal coffers. If we allow these enterprises to enjoy policies similar to those existing in the special economic zones, fiscal revenues from these enterprises will drop by a significant margin. (2) If we allow those Puxi enterprises resiting to Pudong to enjoy the same favourable policies, there will be another shortfall. (3) Enterprises in Puxi will have to bear an increasing [fiscal] burden [in order to make up for the reduced revenue from Pudong], or we will not be able to fulfil our remittance obligation to the centre. All scenarios will similarly incur a decrease in local fiscal revenue. The effect is that over a relatively long period of time, there would be a dilemma between the needs of the Pudong area and the [requirements of the] local fiscal finance [to increase local fiscal revenue and to fulfil central remittance targets].[83]

The stringent fiscal and other operating conditions of the 1980s thus had a decisive effect on the behaviour of the Shanghai government. Not only did manoeuvres of a more substantive scale outside the traditional state and planning sector come much later, the configuration of the manoeuvres also bore witness to a preoccupation with old concerns. This is more obvious in the following section.

Cutting back the budgetary sector

As noted above, the utility of tax alleviation in economic development was recognized by at least one group of Shanghai finance officials in the early 1980s. Its use was, however, very limited until the early 1990s due to the constraints of Shanghai's tight fiscal situation throughout the 1980s.

Tax alleviation

Tax alleviation in Shanghai, or generously applying the policies on tax exemption and reduction, according to an official account, underwent three major developments from the 1980s.[84] The first, in 1985, was the alleviation of the profit adjustment tax of state enterprises, first imposed in 1984. This incurred reductions in local fiscal revenue of several thousand million yuan. The second was in 1988, when the Shanghai government basically transferred the additional resources retained from the new fiscal *dabaogan* system to the state enterprises. A total of 1.2 billion yuan of taxes was exempted at this time.[85] The third major development occurred in 1991, when the central government announced a series of measures to alleviate the burden of the medium-sized and large state enterprises which had accumulated amid the recession of the 1989–91 retrenchment. The amount of tax exempted or reduced as a result of these measures was estimated to reach 1.3 billion yuan.

It should be noted that apart from these three major instances of tax alleviation, there was also the 'regular' tax alleviation granted to enterprises either upon application or as a result of case-by-case bargaining with enterprises through their departments-in-charge. The objective of such tax alleviation was generally to help with the development of the enterprises. The growth of this category of tax alleviation was restrained by the tight financial situation of the 1980s, but towards the late 1980s its scale had grown to a substantial level.[86]

No comprehensive statistics are, however, available for the total volume of fiscal revenue forgone as a result of tax alleviation measures. Earlier it was noted that the amount forgone between 1980 and 1983 was about 1 per cent of the total local fiscal revenue for the period. During a tax inspection in 1989, a total of 153 million yuan of improper tax reductions/exemptions was detected in Shanghai, which was also just under 1 per cent of the total local fiscal revenue for the year.[87] The amount detected from inspections was inevitably a small part of the whole picture, suggesting, therefore, that the value of tax alleviations had grown substantially from its original level in the early 1980s. Changes in the macro-environment after 1988 had thus finally released Shanghai's long-suppressed urge to relieve the burden of its local enterprises. In 1991, there were even proposals to relax the requirements for regular tax alleviation from the existing ceiling of 250 yuan profit per worker to a higher level, although they were not subsequently adopted.[88] In 1992, the generous use of tax alleviation was finally adopted as a major strategy, if not a 'policy', of the Shanghai government to promote the economy,[89] after lagging behind Guangdong for almost a decade.

The stringent financial situation of the 1980s continued, however, to have delayed effects. The cautious attitude towards fiscal revenue, inevitable after decades of tight central control and the pressure to fulfil a high remittance task, could not be done away with in a couple of years. An illustrative example is the implementation of the centre's measures to revitalize state enterprises announced in 1991. There is evidence to suggest that some measures approved by the centre were not adopted, at least not as swiftly as would expected, by Shanghai's local-level authorities.[90] An investigation report by Shanghai Audit

Bureau discovered that local authorities were slow and unenthusiastic in the promotion and implementation of the centrally approved policies. A major factor was the concern over the possible loss of local fiscal revenue as a result of the policies. Locally devised application and implementation rules were bureaucratic and cumbersome, it was found, and often conflicted with the actual circumstances. The enterprises themselves were also sceptical, suspicious that any benefits gained from the new policies might be re-collected on an even larger scale in later inspections, as had previously occurred.[91]

Another facet of the delayed effect occurred when existing favourable policies were seemingly under threat. In these circumstances the motive for making full use of such policies would become very strong. On the eve of the implementation of the new tax and fiscal system in 1994, for instance, the Shanghai leadership was adamant in retaining Pudong's favourable policies, despite their earlier doubts about the benefits of the policies. There was a 'last-minute rush' of tax alleviation applications by Pudong enterprises in 1993, when the prospect of the continuation of the policies was beset by uncertainties.[92] The message is clear: while the Shanghai government might still have been constrained, to an extent, by the hangovers of past financial difficulties in carrying through the tax alleviation policies at enterprise level, it was unwilling to be stripped of the *power* to do so as a result of changes in central policies. This was especially so when other provinces, and in particular Guangdong, had been able to tap the benefits of tax policies a decade earlier.

Ineffective revenue collection

The Shanghai government was not quite the same 'unenthusiastic tax collector' as Guangdong. This difference was due, on the part of Shanghai, to pressure to collect enough revenue to cover both the central remittance and necessary fiscal expenditures. Revenue manipulation was, however, far from non-existent. Tax revenue which had been collected was occasionally refunded in order to pre-empt possible central borrowing. In one instance, a tax department at the district level was found to have returned, without due approval of the district government, over 10 million yuan in taxes.[93] As noted previously, such manipulations reached another high level in late 1993 on the eve of the implementation of the tax-sharing system. This meant that despite the pressure for revenue collection, the Shanghai government also had a tendency to conceal part of its revenue from the centre. When circumstances permitted, this tendency would be translated into action. In fact, Shanghai ranked second, after Guangdong, in the list of provincial levels having the highest number of 'improper' accounts in the early 1990s.[94] From 1985 to 1991, about 3.7 billion yuan of lost fiscal revenue was discovered during annual inspection exercises.[95] Lost revenue in 1990 and 1991 amounted to 600 million yuan and 340 million yuan respectively.

As in Guangdong, new revenue items were often the major source of revenue haemorrhage. According to data available for 1991, the Energy and Transport Strategic Development Fund and the Budget Adjustment Fund accounted for a substantial 13.5 per cent share of the rediscovered fiscal revenue for the year. This suggested a difficulty in collecting new revenue items similar to that in Guangdong. Deliberate accounting manoeuvres by state enterprises to exaggerate expenditures and conceal revenues accounted for 35 per cent, while the rest was primarily due to evasion of various industrial and commercial taxes.[96] Notwithstanding Shanghai's image as a diligent and sometimes overdiligent revenue collector, therefore, the city still had the second largest sum of 'improper' accounts, and a substantial amount of revenue was simply not collected. It is difficult, though, to ascertain the extent to which the lost revenue was a result of action by the municipal government.

Diverting budgetary revenue to extrabudgetary investment

A third means provincial governments might use to undercut the budget and thus retain more resources locally was to divert collected budgetary revenue to extrabudgetary and other 'hidden' accounts. Given the rule-abiding image of the Shanghai government, it would be expected that the extrabudgetary part of Shanghai's revenue would be relatively small. Evidence available suggests the contrary, as shown in Table 6.3.

Table 6.3 demonstrates that the average growth rate of extrabudgetary revenue was conspicuously higher than that of budgetary revenue, which had an average annual negative growth rate of minus 0.3 per cent during the 1980s. In fact, the total value of extrabudgetary revenue was nearly one-third more than that of Guangdong (Table 5.3). Shanghai's total budgetary revenue, at 128.38 billion yuan (discounting the year 1986 for the sake of comparison with Guangdong,

TABLE 6.3. *Budgetary and Extrabudgetary Revenues in Shanghai* (billion yuan)

Year	Budgetary		Extrabudgetary	
	Total	Growth (%)	Total	Growth (%)
1982	16.51	—	4.10	—
1983	15.37	–6.9	4.52	10.2
1984	16.11	4.8	5.30	17.3
1985	18.16	12.7	6.75	27.4
1986	17.61	–3.0	8.43	25.0
1987	16.51	–6.2	9.68	14.8
1988	14.68	–11.1	10.94	13.2
1989	15.27	4.0	10.52	–3.8
1990	15.77	3.3	10.34	–1.7
Total	145.99		70.58	
Average growth (%)		–0.3		12.8

Note: The budgetary revenue figures shown for the period 1988–90 are less than those in the *Statistical Yearbook of Shanghai* (1993: 55). For purpose of consistency the latter set of figures has been ignored. The 1986 figure is taken from the *Statistical Yearbook of Shanghai* (1993: 55).

Source: Ministry of Finance (1992: 68, 199; 1986a: 54, 144).

for which the 1986 figure was not available), was also much larger than Guangdong's, at 66.53 billion yuan. However, this latter differential was attributable to Shanghai having started from a high base in the first place. Moreover, a large portion of Shanghai's budgetary revenue, over two-thirds for 1990, was remitted to the central coffers, whilst a much smaller proportion of Guangdong's revenue was sent to the centre.[97] Therefore although Shanghai had, at face value, a higher level of revenue both inside and outside the budget *vis-à-vis* Guangdong, it was only extrabudgetary revenue that could be material in terms of Shanghai achieving a higher level of retained revenue for local discretionary use than Guangdong.

Since extrabudgetary revenue was completely under local control and deployment, this provided a strong motive for provincial governments to increase this kind of revenue. On not infrequent occasions, budgetary revenue was diverted to the extrabudgetary stream of the local coffers. The heavy remittance task of Shanghai did, however, limit the extent of such diversionary behaviour. Nevertheless, if sufficient budgetary revenue had been collected and the remittance target had been met, it was always in the local interest to expand the extrabudgetary part of revenue. In this way more resources could be deployed and allocated locally with minimal oversight from the centre. More importantly, this could pre-empt possible 'requests' from the centre for additional contributions, and sustain Shanghai's image of being in need of support from the centre.

The apparently contradictory interest of the Shanghai government in collecting a sufficiently high level of fiscal revenue, whilst retaining the surplus in the extrabudgetary part so as to forestall central encroachment upon its resources, resulted in the composition of Shanghai's extrabudgetary revenue being quite different from that of the national average, and particularly of Guangdong. Table 6.4 shows that the extrabudgetary revenue kept by state enterprises and their departments-in-charge, primarily in the form of profit retentions and technical renovation funds, grew at a much lower rate in Shanghai.

TABLE 6.4. *Growth of Extrabudgetary Revenue by Institution, 1986–1990*

Institution	Growth of extrabudgetary revenue, 1986–90 (%)		
	National	Shanghai	Guangdong
Local finance bureau	40.3	34.2	26.4
Administrative/*Shiye* units	96.1	106.4	103.4
State enterprises and departments-in-charge	48.4	10.9	89.1
Total	55.9	23.2	89.2

Source: Ministry of finance (1992: 189, 199, 204).

On the other hand, revenue kept by the local finance bureau grew at a substantially faster rate than it did in Guangdong. The funds kept by various administrative and non-profit-making institutions (the *shiye* units) grew at the fastest rate, exemplifying the fast growth of various investment funds which had been kept in the units since the late 1980s. Table 6.5 shows the trend of the composition percentages over the years: Shanghai's extrabudgetary revenue in state enterprises and their departments-in-charge declined steadily from a very high share in 1986. The original high share was probably attributable to the large number of relatively old state enterprises in Shanghai. Technical renovation funds, the major form of investment of these enterprises, were

TABLE 6.5. *Composition of Extrabudgetary Revenue: A Comparison* (%)

	Shanghai	Guangdong	National
1986			
Local Finance bureau (L)	4.4	6.5	2.5
Administrative/ *Shine* units (A)	11.8	29.1	16.3
State enterprises and	83.9	64.4	80.6
department-in-charge	(5)		
1987			
L	4.6	5.0	2.2
A	13.3	28.4	17.7
S	82.1	66.6	80.1
1988			
L	4.4	4.4	2.1
A	13.8	30.2	18.6
S	81.7	65.4	79.3
1989			
L	4.7	3.5	2.0
A	17.1	28.9	18.8
S	78.3	67.6	79.1
1990			
L	4.8	4.3	2.2
A	19.7	31.3	21.3
S	75.5	64.4	76.5
1991			
L	5.3	n/a	2.1
A	19.8	n/a	21.5
S	74.9	n/a	76.4
1992			
L	9.9	n/a	n/a
A	37.2	n/a	n/a
S	52.9	n/a	n/a

n/a + not available

Sources: For 1986–91, Ministry of Finance (1992: 191, 199, 204). For Shanghai Figures for 1991 and 1992, personal communication.

a form of extrabudgetary revenue. This part of extrabudgetary funds grew very slowly, however, as shown in Table 6.4. By 1992, it accounted for just over half of total extrabudgetary funds in Shanghai. The main growth points were those handled by the local finance departments and by the administrative units, the latter to be discussed later in this chapter. As regards the portion held by local finance departments, this share increased steadily, becoming higher than that of Guangdong towards the end of the 1980s. It was also much higher than the national average, despite a higher growth in absolute value in the latter, as shown in Table 6.4.

The picture emerging from the data is one of the Shanghai government balancing the need to contain the amount of revenue exposed to possible manipulation by the central government, whilst centralizing as much resources as possible for its own flexible deployment. The slow growth of extrabudgetary funds as handled by enterprises demonstrates the reluctance and consequently slow pace of the Shanghai government in dispersing newly gained resources amongst enterprises, as discussed in the section on tax alleviation. This is particularly clear when contrasted with the strong and rapid surge of extrabudgetary funds in state enterprises in Guangdong. On the other hand, increasingly more extrabudgetary funds were held by the local finance departments. The proportional share was consistently about double that of the national average, and the share in 1992 was more than double the share of 1986. Provisional figures for 1993 projected a doubling of this part of revenue in terms of absolute value.[98] The implication is clear. The pressure of a high remittance target, and the heavy burden of fiscal subsidies, resulted in a strong inclination within the Shanghai government to seek some form of financial security. Funds dispersed amongst state enterprises, even though these would be local resources and would benefit the development of enterprises and thus the local economy, would still be beyond the direct control of the municipal government and would thus not ease the concern over security. Extrabudgetary funds of the local financial departments, on the other hand, fulfilled the dual requirements of keeping the resources at a distance from the central government and allowing close and direct control by the municipal government.

Developing the extrabudgetary and non-state sectors

Encouraging the development of enterprises outside the traditional state sector was, as noted in Chapter 5, one major strategy used by the Guangdong government to circumvent central control and develop the provincial economy. The attitude of the Shanghai government towards the non-state sector until the early 1990s was, however, characterized by control. Instead of finding a way to create a favourable environment out of an otherwise hostile national policy context, as in the case of Guangdong, the emphasis in Shanghai was squarely on 'proper management' in accordance with prevailing rules. In the late 1980s, when the success experience of the southern provinces became loud and clear, the Shanghai government started to reorient its emphasis and pay more attention to the extrabudgetary and non-state sectors.[99] However, as a result of its preoccupation with financial security, the Shanghai government was still more interested in developing the extrabudgetary part of the state sector than the more socially oriented, independence-prone non-state enterprises. In fact, until 1992 over 60 per cent of industrial output value and over 80 per cent of total investment in Shanghai was accounted for by the state sector.[100] One new area of emphasis was fiscal credits, as reflected in the words of a Shanghai finance official in 1993:

Strengthening the credit function of the local finance department is necessary for the development of the local economy. The support of local finance is a vital part of the development of the local economy... It is the duty of the local finance department to utilize fully local fiscal funds [through fiscal credits] to support the local economy...[101]

'Fiscal credits' refers to the management by the local finance and tax departments of funds originally derived from budgetary fiscal funds for investment and other purposes *outside* the purview of the budget. In a sense it was the local finance departments acting as banks providing loans to enterprises for investment or production,[102] or sometimes acting as investors themselves via investment companies formed under their auspices. This use of fiscal funds was a relatively recent phenomenon, although it had existed in embryonic form since the 1960s. In 1988, the Shanghai government specifically set up an investment company, under the auspices of the municipal finance bureau, to engage in lending and investment activities, using capital from the municipal budget.[103]

The funds originally diverted from the municipal budget and subsequently placed beyond the budget should, in theory, form part of the total extrabudgetary funds, and in particular, part of the extrabudgetary fiscal revenue held by the local finance departments. However, as this practice had begun only relatively recently, and as it was in the vested interests of the provincial governments to conceal the size of local resources from central scrutiny, this part of funds was not, in practice, included in the compilation of the statistics as shown in Tables 6.3–6.5.[104] The value of these funds is estimated to have increased by 1 to 2 billion yuan per annum in the early 1990s,[105] which was nearly double that of the 'official' extrabudgetary fiscal revenue of 1992, and up to nearly a quarter of the total 'official' extrabudgetary funds for 1992. Whilst the budget was the 'first finance', and the 'official' extrabudgetary funds formed the 'second finance', this new commercialized use of budgetary funds constituted the 'third finance' of the Shanghai government.

Probably due to its large scale, and its potential to shake off central control, the status of this 'third finance' within the central government had been highly controversial. The central bank had expressed reservations regarding the development of banklike business by the finance department. The Ministry of Finance, on the other hand, seeing its functions under the old central planning system on the decline, was happy at the prospect of an enlarged scope of activity, and thus influence, in the economy. The provincial governments therefore had a powerful ally in this respect.[106] Finally a notice was issued by the Ministry of Finance in late 1993 regulating the management of funds in the 'third finance', implying that the Ministry of Finance, together with the provinces, had tentatively won the battle for the legitimate status of fiscal credits.[107]

Recentralization of societal resources

At this point it is worth recalling that fiscal credits were a major phenomenon only from the late 1980s. For most of the 1980s, the majority of extrabudgetary resources were in the hands of state enterprises and their departments-in-charge. At that time, in order that these resources could be utilized more efficiently, specialized funds were set up under the auspices of the departments-in-charge to centralize extrabudgetary funds dispersed amongst state enterprises.[108] By 1988, it was estimated that not less than twenty-two specialized funds had been set up in Shanghai, of which at least seven were geared towards investment and economic development. The rest were of a more 'social and welfare' nature.[109] As of 1989, investment-oriented funds had accumulated a total value of 1 to 2 billion yuan.[110] As in the case of fiscal credits, these specialized funds had not been included in the official statistics of extrabudgetary funds.[111]

As in the case of Guangdong, these funds mostly originated from three sources: (1) diversion from budgetary revenue; (2) imposition of administrative fees and price adjustments; and (3) capitalization exercises targeted at enterprises and private individuals. For instance, more than 1 billion yuan per annum of fiscal budgetary funds was reportedly allocated to the investment arm of the municipal government, the Shanghai Jiu Shi Corporation. In another case, on the establishment of the new electricity development company in 1987, some 200 million yuan of budgetary funds was granted.[112] The Electricity Fund derived part of its capital from an increase in the price of electricity. In some cases, administrative fees were even collected and imposed directly by the fund managers, instead of by government departments.[113] Where the purpose of a fund was to finance the construction of specific projects, capitalization exercises might be the major means to acquire capital.[114]

Specialized funds, therefore, were a major source of investment capital in Shanghai towards the late 1980s. The upper estimate of their value as of 1989, at 2 billion yuan, is equivalent to 18 per cent of the investment in Shanghai's local state sector for the same year, or more than seven times that of local budgetary investment.[115] Dispersed in various departments and agencies, this part of local investment capital could easily escape central scrutiny. There are indications that, in some cases, there was a management problem even within the municipal government.[116]

A major reason for the loss of central control was that the establishment of specialised investment funds was largely a local initiative, although some individual funds were established on the basis of centrally approved policies.[117] There were no central regulations or policies requiring the funds to obtain central approval. Consequently, all specialized investment funds were basically approved independently by the Shanghai municipal government, and the centre did not have any means to scrutinize these funds, not even in theory.[118]

The attitude of the centre to the specialized funds was ambivalent. The centre had not conferred any authority over these funds on the provinces. However, neither was there any explicit condemnation of the 'initiatives' provinces had taken. From the viewpoint of the centre, the funds were one of those 'new phenomena' of reform, and its attitude was one of 'wait and see'. In fact, in 1991 the centre contemplated either centralizing this approval authority in the Ministry of Finance or explicitly delegating the authority to the provinces.[119] In the end no action was taken. Provincial governments have since continued their adventure in this 'no-man's land' with the unspoken tolerance and acquiescence of the centre.[120]

INTERNATIONALIZATION

Notwithstanding Shanghai's history as a hub of foreign economic activities, internationalization came slowly onto the agenda of the Shanghai government. The recency of internationalism as a development strategy was especially ironic, given Shanghai's success in winning preferential policies in foreign trade and investment, as noted earlier in this chapter. Unlike other policy areas, where the Shanghai government could attribute their failure in development to a stringent central policy, the 'opening up' of Shanghai since the early 1980s had been a development encouraged by central leaders. The authority of the Shanghai government in foreign investment, for instance, was even larger than its Guangdong counterpart during the early 1980s. Moreover, given its tight financial situation, turning overseas for investment capital would appear a natural recourse. However, foreign investment in Shanghai as of 1993 was only a tiny fraction of that in Guangdong. By 1993 Shanghai had attracted a total cumulative value of direct foreign investment contracts of US$13.71 billion, of which US$5.13 billion had been realized,[121] whilst Guangdong had a cumulative realized direct foreign investment five times greater, amounting to US$26 billion.[122] As a result of the much smaller size of total foreign investment in Shanghai, the economy of Shanghai was, at the end of the 1980s, still largely inward-oriented.[123]

It is not easy to give a straightforward explanation of the slow pace of foreign investment in Shanghai. It was very likely only one facet of the general performance of Shanghai's economy in the 1980s, and a product of the centre's reform strategy and its specific policies on Shanghai. The geographical position of Shanghai, and the attitude and management style of the Shanghai government, are also likely to have had a bearing on the matter. These issues will be the subject of discussion in Chapter 7.

Nevertheless the change finally came. The announcement of the opening of Pudong in 1990 was a prelude; and this was affirmed and elevated to an even higher profile in 1992. At the Fourteenth Party Congress convened in October 1992, Shanghai was hailed as the 'dragon head' of the development of the entire River Yangzi region. The centre also unambiguously stated, for the first time, that Shanghai should be developed into an international economic, financial and commercial centre. Direct foreign investment contracted in 1992 alone, at the value of US$3.36 billion, was consequently US$30 million more than the total cumulative value of the previous twelve years.[124] In 1993, another peak was reached with the contracted value of projects reaching US$7 billion, more than double the level achieved in 1992. The value of realized foreign investment, at US$2.3 billion, was about the equivalent of the total realized between 1980 and 1992.[125] Momentum had finally been gained.

Internationalization as a development strategy was, however, not simply about foreign investment. Attracting more foreign investment was only a necessary component of, and a *means* to, becoming international. The objective was to make Shanghai a modernized international economic, financial and commercial centre. Foreign investment was the means by which the Shanghai leadership sought to raise the standards of Shanghai's economic and management make-up to an internationally advanced level. Wu Bangguo, then Shanghai's Party Secretary, made this intention explicit in his report to the Shanghai Sixth Party Congress in December 1992:

To open and develop Pudong would inevitably break ground for the all-round opening of Shanghai. We have to utilize fully the high degree of openness of Pudong . . . to bridge Shanghai with the international economy in the areas of finance, commerce, industry and management. We have to expand the areas in which foreign capital may be used. . . [We need] to establish multinational corporations of our own, so as to enhance the capability of Shanghai in international economic participation.[126]

As in the case of Guangzhou and Shenzhen, having set such a goal was instrumental to Shanghai's bargaining for more resources and autonomy. In comparison Shanghai had the added advantage that this goal had also been endorsed by the centre and included in documents of the Fourteenth Party Congress, as mentioned earlier. The Shanghai government thus had a stronger position than Guangdong from which to argue legitimately, in terms of the requirements of progressing towards its international position, for more central concessions.[127]

The importance of this strategy of internationalization has to be understood in the context of the reform development process. The decentralization of authority in the 1980s was originally conceived with the purpose of facilitating a greater role for provincial governments in experimentation with reforms. Reform experiments and economic developments in the 1980s, however, necessarily started from a low base. Whilst the general direction was clearly to develop the economy, there was a lack of specific and clearly envisaged objectives.

Under these circumstances the formulation of detailed reform measures was largely a result of the 'push effect' of the inadequacies of the pre-existing system, and reforms in the 1980s were thus largely incremental. They also tended to be piecemeal and relatively limited. The devolution of authority to provincial governments was correspondingly and primarily a series of piecemeal adjustments to the pre-existing management systems. With Shanghai specifically setting a goal of reaching an advanced international standard, the inadequacy of the previous approach became all too obvious.[128] Whether in terms of the amount of resources available to the Shanghai government to attain the goal, or in terms of its power effectively to steer the economy, there was a substantial gap between the *status quo* and the projected requirements for building an international city on a par with those of advanced industrialized countries. This gap thereby became the fertile grounds on which the Shanghai leadership could bargain with the centre.

NOTES

1. Shanghai's number one position in terms of total fiscal revenue was assumed by Guangdong in 1991, when Shanghai's fiscal revenue was 19.19 billion yuan and Guangdong's 19.21 billion yuan. It should be noted that the concept of fiscal revenue being compared here is the total value of fiscal revenue collected by the local collectors, and *not* the retained local fiscal revenue after remittance to the centre. For the figures see Ministry of Finance (1992: 59).

2. This was revealed by Gu Mu while he was visiting Guangdong on 22 September 1979. He urged Guangdong's officials to move faster in implementing the Special Policy because other provinces were very envious of their position. He said, 'Since the release of the central documents on these two provinces, the three municipalities, Beijing, Tianjin and Shanghai, have become very envious of you. They demand to enjoy one-half of your new powers ... After we satisfied their demands, several other coastal provinces, Jiangsu, Zhejiang, Shandong and Liaoning, expressed their desire to join in the opening drive as well'. See Guangdong Provincial Party Committee (1986–8: i. 41).

3. See State Council Notice no. 6 (1982), 'On Approving the Notes of Meeting of the External Economic and Trade Work Conference of the Nine Coastal Provinces and Municipalities (29 November 1981)', 15 Jan. 1982, in State Commission for Economic System Reform (1983: 574–81).

4. See State Commission for Economic System Reform (1983: 574).

5. See State Commission for Economic System Reform (1983: 577). The authority of Shanghai, Beijing and Tianjin to approve foreign investment projects was raised to US$5 million, while the other coastal provinces got the US$3 million ceiling.
6. See State Council Notice no. 55 (1983), 'On Approving the "Proposals on Developing Shanghai's External Business and Trade" by the Shanghai Government', 4 Apr. 1983, in State Commission for Economic System Reform (1983: 605–10).
7. See 'Zhang Jingfu Speaking when Hearing the Briefing of the Shenzhen City Party Committee', 26 May 1983, in Guangdong Provincial Party Committee (1986–8: iv. 559).
8. See the opening paragraphs of the 'Report on the Development Strategy of the Shanghai Economy', printed in *Shanghai Economy* (1983–5), 25.
9. See Xu Riqing *et al.* (1985); Xu Riqing (1985: 247–8); Tu Jimo (1985: 11). Respondents no. 23 and 27 also confirmed that the ultimate goal of the Shanghai government since the 1980s regarding the fiscal system had been the tax-sharing system, which was considered fairer to Shanghai (interviews, Shanghai, May 1994).
10. See 'Report on the Development Strategy of the Shanghai Economy', 26–7.
11. The average annual rate of decrease was 3.8% for 1981–3 and 4.2% for 1986–7.
12. Calculated from Ministry of Finance (1992: 59, 102); *Statistical Yearbook of China* (1993: 229); *Statistical Yearbook of Shanghai* (1993: 55).
13. Calculated from *Statistical Yearbook of China* (1993: 35, 52); *Statistical Yearbook of Shanghai* (1993: 40, 44).
14. Calculated from Guangdong Statistical Bureau (1989*b*: 69).
15. A number of foreign experts from the United States and Europe reportedly made the observation when visiting China in 1987 that the economic centre of China was moving southwards to Guangzhou, and Shanghai was on the decline. Such comments raised alarm amongst the Shanghai leadership, and reminded them of the danger of having moved too slowly in economic reforms. See Yu Xiangnian (1988: 10). Yu was the Vice-Director of the Shanghai Economic Research Centre, a high-profile think tank of the Shanghai leadership.
16. The report was Shanghai Government Notice no. 123 (1987), entitled 'A Report on Deepening the Reform, Expanding the Opening, and Speeding Up the Development of the Externally-Oriented Economy in Shanghai'. See *Shanghai Industry Yearbook* (1988): 10–11 for an extract of the report.
17. More details of the 1987 report may be found in a report reviewing the implementation of the 1987 report conducted by Shanghai planning officials one year later. See Cai Laixing *et al.* (1989).
18. See Cai Laixing *et al.* (1989: 8).

19. In 1984 the Shanghai government openly expressed its concern over the historical undervaluation of fixed assets in Shanghai, with the implication that the depreciation provision made for the state enterprises was inadequate. See Lin Qiushi (1984: 10–12).

20. See Cai Laixing *et al.* (1989: 6–7). The politics of asset valuation has subsequently entered a new phase with new and shifting issues in the 1990s, as the new trend of liquidization of state assets in the burgeoning state assets market triggers new conflicts of interest between local and central governments as to how the proceeds of sales should be shared. Respondent no. 19 remarked that as a result of the low depreciation provisions since 1949, the net worth of state assets in state enterprises in Shanghai as of the 1990s was grossly *overvalued* (interview, Hong Kong, Nov. 1993). Given that an estimated 80% of investment in Shanghai state enterprises was made in or before the 1970s, thus coming from the central investment, the 'ownership shares' of the centre in the assets were correspondingly inflated. Respondent no. 27 admitted that it was difficult to divide properly the return from the sale of state assets between the centre and Shanghai (interview, Shanghai, May 1994).

21. Respondents No. 23 and 27 stressed that 10.5 billion yuan was a large sum, and Shanghai had to give half of the local revenue in excess of 16.5 billion to the centre after 1991. They agreed that the tax-sharing system should be a fairer system, as the allocation of resources between the centre and provinces would be based on responsibilities and actual needs rather than historical precedents which were less than fair (interviews, Shanghai, May 1994).

22. See *Shanghai Economy* (1990): 20–1 for the ten favourable policies announced in April 1990.

23. Information from respondent no. 23 (interview, Shanghai, May 1994).

24. See *Wen Wei Po* (Hong Kong), 23 Apr. 1990. See also Yu Xiguang *et al.* (1992: 177).

25. Another elderly leader, Chen Yun, did not make public his views on Pudong until May 1992, when he visited Shanghai on the eve of May Day and expressed unambiguous support. That he had not clarified his views in public is evident from his conversation with Shanghai's Mayor Huang Ju. Chen Yun reportedly said to Huang Ju, 'Aren't there some journalists asking you about my views on the opening of Pudong? Your answer to them is appropriate. I very much support the opening and development of Pudong . . . and you have done a great job here.' See *People's Daily*, 2 May 1992.

26. See 'The Two Reports by Huang Ju on the Opening and Development of Pudong', *Shanghai Economy* (1991): 22. The petition report submitted to the centre was entitled 'A Petition on Opening Up and Developing the Pudong Area'.

27. Eight proposals were turned down by the centre. Among the rejected proposals were some radical ones such as allowing foreign joint ventures in the communications and publication industry (Interview, respondent no. 25, Shanghai, May 1994). According to the respondent, the inclusion of more policy proposals, some of which are more radical, was a bargaining tactic of the Shanghai government.

28. One usual comment of Shanghai's government/Party officials and enterprise officials after 'study tours' to Guangdong in the 1980s was: 'If we were given the same policies by the centre as those of Guangdong, we could certainly have done better than they did.' Jiang Zemin also made similar comments while he was the Party Secretary of Shanghai (interviews, respondents no. 23 and 25, Shanghai, May 1994).

29. Interviews, respondents no. 23 and 25, Shanghai, May 1994.

30. This was described to the author by respondents no. 23 and 25 (interviews, Shanghai, May 1994).

31. This is the reason cited by a number of Shanghai officials for the change of central policy regarding Shanghai in the 1990s and the fast economic development in Shanghai since then (interviews, respondents no. 14 and 22, Shanghai, Jan. 1994).

32. That the decision on Guangdong was made prior to the 1980 adjustment decision was clearly demonstrated in Gu Mu's talks with the Guangdong leadership in December 1980. Gu Mu reassured Guangdong's leaders in a provincial Party committee meeting that the decision on special economic zones had been made more than a year before the announcement of the economic adjustment measures. 'Therefore Guangdong could not retreat from what had just been started.' See Guangdong Provincial Party Committee (1986–8: i. 125).

33. In April 1990 the centre promised a total of 6.5 billion yuan of additional capital within 5 years in the form of loans and grants. See *Shanghai Economy* (1991): 27. For a breakdown of the 6.5 billion yuan, see Shenzhen City Study Group (1990).

34. Some scholars and experts, in a seminar on Pudong and the Yangzi River Delta, commented that the immediate prospects for Pudong were dim. Major reasons included the unfavourable international environment, the burden of the Shanghai municipality in the planned economy, and the lack of competitiveness of Pudong's favourable policies as compared to the established special economic zones. See *Ming Pao* (Hong Kong), 5 Dec. 1991. The occurrence of such negative comments reflected the fact that developments in Pudong and Shanghai since the April 1990 central government announcement had been less than impressive.

35. Substantive improvement in Shanghai's economic performance in 1992 is obvious in terms of various economic indicators, including national

income growth, fiscal revenue growth, the increase in foreign investment, and the development of commodity markets. See *Shanghai Caishui* 11 (1992): 4.

36. According to respondent no. 25, the Shanghai government had submitted a development proposal to the centre in 1987, outlining the development plans of Pudong in detail along with some policy requests. Zhao Ziyang was supportive whilst other central leaders were more critical. As a result the report was not approved. However, in 1990 this same group of leaders was very enthusiastic as regards the opening up of Pudong area. Their political motive was self-evident (interview, Shanghai, May 1994).

37. See for instance two articles from the Pudong Administration office: Huang Qifan (1992) and Gu Xingquan (1992).

38. Information from respondents no. 19, 20 and 21 (interviews, Shanghai, Jan. 1994). Shanghai's contracted remittance sum was originally only 10.5 billion yuan, but since 1992 400 million yuan of 'additional contribution' had been added. 500 million yuan was added in 1993 as Shanghai's additional remittance for local fiscal revenue in excess of 16.5 billion yuan under the contractual scheme. This constituted substantially less than half of the excess prescribed by the original agreement, which would amount to some 3.7 billion yuan, given that Shanghai's local fiscal revenue for 1993 was 24 billion yuan. This represented the success of the Shanghai leadership in bargaining with the centre. On the other hand, the Shanghai leadership agreed to remit an additional 600 million yuan as Shanghai's contribution to the pending tax reforms and in return for the centre's assurance that Shanghai's favourable policies would continue to be implemented.

39. See Tables 4.5 and 4.6.

40. See Table 4.10.

41. Respondent no. 19 admitted that this was a bargaining tactic of Shanghai in its dealings with the centre. By 'crying wolf' and playing down the positive side, Shanghai sought to attract the attention of the centre and succeed in winning more resources (interview, Shanghai, Jan. 1994). This of course did not mean that the complaints were entirely unfounded.

42. The Shanghai government had originally obtained the consent of central leaders, around 1983–4, to guarantee additional funds to finance the working capital for central enterprises in Shanghai, in order that the capital needs of these enterprises would not crowd out the limited amount of capital which was to be used solely by local enterprises. However, the policy had not been implemented by the relevant central ministries. The Shanghai government eventually lodged a formal but coded complaint in their December 1987 report, which stated that central projects had used up a substantial portion of Shanghai's finance capital. See Cui Laifu (1989: 49).

43. Price subsidies accounted for an increasing proportion of Shanghai's total local fiscal expenditure during the 1980s, rising from under 700 million yuan in 1985, or 16% of total fiscal expenditure, to 3.8 billion yuan in 1990, or 53% of the total. A substantial amount of this was spent on food subsidies (interviews, respondents no. 20 and 21, Shanghai, Jan. 1994). This increase was because the retail price level was artificially suppressed for socio-political reasons, and this pressure was particularly high in Shanghai, as historically Shanghai's retail price level had risen more slowly than the national average. From the point of view of the Shanghai government, Shanghai was thus subsidizing a portion of the costs of the central enterprises.

44. Interview, respondent no. 21, Shanghai, Jan. 1994. Prior to the tax reforms in 1994, all revenue from the turnover taxes went into the local fiscal coffers.

45. Interview, respondent no. 27, Shanghai, May 1994. The respondent remarked that while central investment projects to inland provinces involved 'real' injection of capital, central investment projects in Shanghai usually involved substantial capital contribution by the local government, whether in the form of infrastructure investments such as roads and other community facilities or working capital finance. Some existing central enterprises were even originally local investment projects and were made central enterprises upon their completion.

46. See Jin Wen (1992: 6).

47. See *Guangming Daily*, 24 Feb. 1993, 1. The sum was reportedly used as from 1987. See also *Shanghai Statistics* 8 (1993): 3 for a reference to additional loans by the centre to renovate Shanghai's industrial infrastructure, the quota of 1992 being 1.3 billion yuan, which had, however, not yet been realized.

48. See Lou Rucheng (1987: 16–17).

49. See Jin Wen (1992: 6).

50. See Zhou Youdao (1993: 4).

51. Disposable local fiscal revenue is total local fiscal revenue (including the central grants) minus the remittance to the centre. For the figures see Zhou Youdao (1993: 4).

52. Data available for Guangdong show that central fiscal fund injections during 1980–8 amounted to 2 billion yuan and accounted for 3% of Guangdong's local fiscal revenue. See Chap. 5.

53. See *Almanac of Chinese Finance and Banking* (1992: 229).

54. This was generally the normal mode of operation (interview, respondent no. 8, Guangzhou, Dec. 1993).

55. As stated in Chap. 5, the net injection of central money into Guangdong's banking system from 1980–8 amounted to 13.2 billion yuan, which was about 50% of the value of central bank loans to Guangdong in the same period.

56. See Cui Laifu (1989: 48).
57. See Shenzhen City Study Group (1990: 11).
58. See *People's Daily*, 11 Mar. 1992, 1.
59. Respondent no. 28 confirmed that the pledges of additional capital were, basically, realized in full. The buoyancy in the securities market ensured full utilization of the quotas of share issues allowed by the centre (interview, Shanghai, May 1994).
60. Excess investment in Guangdong for 1988, 1991 and 1992 amounted to 139.8%, 75.4% and 139.2% of the central quotas respectively (see Table 3.7).
61. Some categories of investment were excluded from the coverage of the scale control so as to encourage investment in specified sectors. Some others were considered too trivial to merit control. For more discussion see Chap. 4.
62. See Xu Hangdi (1992: 1).
63. Ensuring that no extra burdens would be imposed on the old city area was a major consideration of the Shanghai government in the immediate aftermath of the announcement of the Pudong policies. See Cai Laixing (1990: 1–6).
64. See Jin Wen (1992: 4).
65. For the figures on the quotas, see Shanghai Audit Bureau (1993: 16–17).
66. This analogy was suggested by respondent no. 28 (interview, Shanghai, May 1994).
67. Interview, respondent no. 20, Shanghai, Jan. 1994.
68. See *Shanghai Economy* (1988): 558–9.
69. This was admitted by respondent no. 15 (interview, Shanghai, Jan. 1994). There was, however, a limit to the amount of investment one could safely place beyond the coverage of the quotas without inviting queries and disapproval from the centre.
70. See Chan Xianglin (1989: 4–5).
71. According to respondent no. 21 (interview, Shanghai, Jan. 1994), the Director of Shanghai's Finance Bureau issued an internal directive in early October 1993 to finance departments at the district and county levels to order them to collect 'all revenues which should have been collected'.
72. See a report on the meeting in *Shanghai Caishui* 12 (1993): 5.
73. Interview, respondent no. 21, Shanghai, Jan. 1994.
74. Shanghai's local fiscal revenue in 1993 amounted to 24.2 billion yuan, an increase of 30% over 1992. This was a huge jump when compared to the sluggish performance and the slides of the 1980s. The increase would have been greater if not for the substantial refunds in December 1993. As the provincial government did not have legislative power over taxes and other fiscal revenue, there was concern that, under the tax-sharing system, more local fiscal revenue would be transferred to the central coffers through the

shared taxes. The desire to retain more resources in the locality, by collecting *less* tax, was therefore still quite urgent, as had been the case under the *dabaogan* system (interviews, respondents no. 19 and 21, Shanghai, Jan. 1994).

75. See Tao Changyuan and Lin Weiting (1984: 28–30).

76. Tao Changyuan and Lin Weiting (1984: 28–30). Of the total of 600 million yuan, 58% was directed to support state enterprises which were operating either in the red or on the verge of a loss, 12% to support export-oriented production, 25% to collective enterprises and 4.5% to support the production of new products.

77. See Xiong Ruixiang (1985: 4).

78. See Shanghai Institute for Economic System Reform (1991: 238).

79. Shanghai's local fiscal revenue for 1988 was 15.75 billion yuan at current prices, which was 94.4% of the revenue level of 1978. See *Statistical Yearbook of Shanghai* (1993: 55). Please note that 'fiscal revenue' here refers to the budgetary revenue of the local government. The figures in the statistical table of the yearbook include both the budgetary and extrabudgetary revenues of the local finance bureau.

80. The practical tax burden of Shanghai's state enterprises was about 40.8%, which was substantially higher than the national average. See Lou Jiwei (1992: 11). Lou was then a senior official of Shanghai's Commission for Structural System Reform.

81. See Shanghai Institute for Economic System Reform (1991: 283).

82. The chapter on Pudong spans 23 pages (276–98), of which 7 pages are on the system frictions between Pudong and Puxi.

83. Shanghai Institute for Economic System Reform (1991: 285–6). The 10.5 billion yuan target of contracted remittance negotiated in 1988 was later felt amongst Shanghai officials to be too heavy a burden and an unfair deal for Shanghai generally.

84. See Zhou Youdao (1992: 7). Zhou was the Director of Shanghai Finance Bureau.

85. The Shanghai government retained an additional 1.4 billion yuan of local fiscal revenue in 1988 relative to the 1987 level as a result of the *dabaogan* system. See Chap. 4 for more discussion.

86. The Director of the Shanghai Finance Bureau stated in a speech during a tax and fiscal reform seminar in November 1992 that regular tax reductions and exemptions during the past several years accounted for a substantial portion of Shanghai's local fiscal revenue. See Zhou Youdao (1992: 4).

87. See Wu Jinglian (1988: 53).

88. A major type of regular tax alleviation was granted to state enterprises operating at, or on the verge of, a loss, in the hope that the enterprises could thereby improve their financial position and continue production. The

proposal was made by the Research Office of the Shanghai Party Committee. See 'Proposals to End the Difficulties Faced by Shanghai's Industries', *Shanghai Reform* 3 (1991): 20–2. Respondent no. 21 (interview, Shanghai, May 1994) confirmed that the ceiling was still 250 yuan as of 1994.

89. See a speech by a Shanghai vice-mayor, Xu Hongdi, in the city finance meeting in early 1993, printed in *Shangha Caishui* 1 (1993): 6, in which Xu stated that the Shanghai government in 1992 had focused on 'letting in water to feed the fishes', a description long used to describe the use of tax alleviation to vitalize enterprises in Guangdong.

90. See *Shanghai Caishui* 1 (1992): 12, and 4 (1992): 1, for inferences that the Shanghai government should make more effort to implement the central government measures. This suggests that the central measures had yet to be implemented in Shanghai.

91. See Shanghai Audit Bureau, Changling District, 'An Audit Investigation on the Implementation of State Enterprise Policies', *Shanghai Audit* 6 (Dec. 1992): 15–18. Similar problems existed in collective enterprises. See Zeng Niansi and Sui Liang (1992: 8).

92. Between January and November 1993, more than 800 applications from Pudong enterprises for the alleviation of circulation taxes were approved. This rush was in order to take advantage of the favourable policy of reducing/exempting circulation taxes during the first year of operation of any Pudong enterprise. The tax revenue forgone as a result of the rush amounted to more than 70 million yuan (interview, respondent no. 21, Shanghai, Jan. 1994).

93. This occurred around November–December 1992. See Zheng Rujuan (1993: 17).

94. Interview, respondent no. 10, Guangzhou, Dec. 1993. According to the respondent, the 'improper' accounts discovered in annual inspection exercises during recent years in Guangdong amounted to over 2 billion yuan. Shanghai was second to Guangdong, though there was a considerable gap between the two.

95. Calculated from *Shanghai Jingji* 5 (1989): 23; *Shanghai Caishui* 2 (1991): 14; *Shanghai Caishui* 3 (1992): 31.

96. See Qin Li and Qian Zhiping (1992: 6–7).

97. For the later years from 1988 to 1990, a total of 12.32 billion yuan was remitted to the centre, accounting for 32.8% of the total fiscal revenue of the three-year period. See Table 5.1.

98. See 'An Analysis of the Local Fiscal Revenue and Expenditure of Shanghai in 1993 and a Forecast for 1994', in Shanghai Institute of Economic Development (1994: 75). This article was reportedly written by informed sources in the municipal finance bureau. The value of extrabudgetary local fiscal revenue in 1993 was estimated at 2 billion yuan, which was over 8% of the total fiscal revenue for the year.

99. This was reflected in an article from the Municipal Planning Commission in 1987 calling for a broadening of the scope of planning work beyond the budgetary sector and the plans. See Shanghai Planning Commission (1987*b*: 36).

100. See *Statistical Yearbook of Shanghai* (1993: 99, 244). The more rapid development of the non-state sector from the late 1980s was partly a result of the devolution of fiscal and investment authority to the subprovincial levels. See Zeng Niansi and Sui Liang (1992: 7).

101. See Yang Sheng (1993: 29).

102. One major business of fiscal credit was to serve as the agent of loan finance between two groups of enterprises (interview, respondent no. 27, Shanghai, May 1994).

103. See *Shanghai Economy* (1989): 482.

104. Interviews with respondents no. 22 (Shanghai, Jan. 1994), no. 27 (Shanghai, May 1994) and no. 34 (Beijing, Mar. 1994) confirmed that the official statistics on extrabudgetary funds *nationwide* and in Shanghai in particular, did not encompass the funds diverted, generated and kept outside the budget. Respondent no. 38 (interview, Beijing, May 1994) remarked that it was very difficult to require the local governments and units to provide information on *new* types of locally retained resources beyond the traditional coverage dating back to the pre-reform period. A classic example was the data regarding the part of extrabudgetary funds held by state enterprises and their departments-in-charge. This entire area of information was simply not available when the statistics on extrabudgetary funds were compiled for 1993, since the accounting books of state enterprises were completely revamped with the implementation of international accounting rules with effect from July 1993. According to respondent no. 38, there was a real possibility that data on this part of extrabudgetary funds would not be reported in future. It was simply that a convenient pretext had been found to enable localities and enterprises to escape central scrutiny.

105. Estimate from respondent no. 34 (interview, Beijing, Mar. 1994).

106. Interview, respondent no. 34, Beijing, Mar. 1994. According to the respondent, Vice-Premier Zhu Rongji, once concurrently head of the People's Bank of China after the dismissal of the former head Li Guixian in July 1993, was inclined to support the position of the banks. A report from the Ministry of Finance stated that the development of fiscal credits was 'an inevitable requirement of the marketization process.' See Ministry of Finance (1993: 22).

107. Ministry of Finance Notice no. 189 (1993), 'A Notice on Promulgating the "Management Rules of Fiscal Credits (Provisional)" ', 19 Nov. 1993, printed in State Audit Commission (1994: 71–4).

108. Yu Daxiang (1984: 5–7). It was suggested that funds should be set up to

centralize extrabudgetary funds dispersed among individual state enterprises to ensure better utilization and to minimize wastage.

109. See Bao Youde (1988: 7). Bao was then the director of Shanghai Finance Bureau. See also Tu Jimo (1990: 27).

110. Tu Jimo (1990: 28).

111. This was confirmed by respondent no. 27 (interview, Shanghai, May 1994). The respondent argued that since the specialized funds all have their uses specified and the local finance departments could not freely deploy these resources, there was no need to include the funds in the statistics on extrabudgetary funds.

112. Interview, respondent no. 26, Shanghai, May 1994. Shanghai Jiu Shi Corporation was set up in 1987, initially to manage and co-ordinate the use of the newly approved US$3.2 billion of foreign capital. It subsequently developed into a major investment arm of the local government with an expanded scope of business spanning real estate development and foreign trade.

113. See Tu Jimo (1990: 29).

114. This was the case of the fund for the construction of the television tower at Pudong, completed in 1994. Capital came primarily from enterprises and individuals (interview, respondent no. 27, Shanghai, May 1994). According to the respondent, the municipal government would normally impose stricter rules on funds soliciting 'share capital' from individuals, who were more vulnerable than enterprises to unscrupulous capitalization practices.

115. Total investment in Shanghai's local state sector in 1989 was 11 billion yuan, of which 277 million yuan came from the state budget. See *Statistical Yearbook of Shanghai* (1990: 240).

116. It has been stated that there was inadequate oversight and management of the funds at the government level, with management left largely to the fund managers. See Tu Jimo (1990: 28–9). This is also the view of respondent no. 34 (interview, Beijing, Mar. 1994).

117. An example was the Shanghai Jiu Shi Corporation. In 1986 the central government authorized Shanghai to borrow foreign capital to finance infrastructural projects. Part of the capital could be used to start profitable industrial products in order to provide the necessary returns to pay back the loans. The corporation was set up in Shanghai to take charge of the raising of foreign capital and management of the investment projects. See Ni Wen (1987: 48–51). Strictly speaking, the establishment of the corporation itself was a discretionary action of the Shanghai government in the implementation of the centrally approved policy.

118. Interview, respondent no. 27, Shanghai, May 1994.

119. In 1991 there was a big surge in various kinds of specialized funds in many provinces and particularly at the subprovincial levels. There was

therefore a heightened worry in the centre that the situation might develop out of control. Several documents were subsequently drafted to tighten control of the funds (interviews, respondents no. 34 and 38, Beijing, May 1994).

120. The centre's attitude was one of 'passive tolerance' because, according to respondent no. 38, the reason why the drafted documents were not adopted was the concern that the establishment of a formal approval and control system by the centre would amount to giving a legitimate and formal status to the funds, at a time when the centre had yet to arrive at a firm view of the future of the funds. This might create difficulties for future plans to replace these funds with more proper means of financing local investments (interview, Beijing, May 1994).

121. *Statistical Yearbook of Shanghai* (1994: 102).

122. See Zhang Hanqing (1992: 125); *Statistical Yearbook of Guangdong* (1994: 318).

123. See Rui Mingjie and Yu Wenyi (1992: 12–13). It was reported that the share of export value in total GNP in Shanghai in 1989 was only 7%, while Guangdong's was 13%. Part of the reason was the much lower level of foreign investment in Shanghai, since most of the output in foreign enterprises was exported.

124. See *Statistical Yearbook of Shanghai* (1993: 306).

125. Interview, respondent no. 24, Shanghai, May 1994. See also *Statistical Yearbook of Shanghai* (1994: 102).

126. See *Statistical Yearbook of Shanghai* (1993: 306).

127. For instance the Shanghai government contemplated asking for more favourable policies for Pudong when the original favourable policies, such as the bonded area policy, were subsequently also practised in other centrally approved development areas. The new policies included allowing foreign investment in trading companies and enlarging the use of foreign capital in the tertiary sector. See Huang Qifan (1993: 35). Huang was the Vice-Director of Pudong Management Committee.

128. An official of the State Council Development Research Centre admitted that the task of establishing Shanghai as an international city had encouraged the municipal government to ask for new powers from the centre. See Zhu Ronglin (1993: 44).

7   Centre and Provinces: Interactive Processes

This chapter focuses on the linkage between the institutional context posed by the centre and the resultant discretionary behaviour of the Guangdong and Shanghai governments. Specifically, this chapter seeks to examine the mediating process whereby central policies influenced and constrained the choices and behaviour of Guangdong and Shanghai, as well as the process whereby provincial discretion influenced central policies. Fig. 7.1 depicts the interactive relationship between the centre and the provinces.

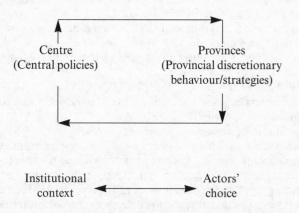

FIG. 7.1.   Centre and provinces: interactive relationship

There are two important points to note in Fig. 7.1. First, both the centre and the provinces act as institutional constraints on one another. Secondly, both exercise choice within and despite the constraints they impose on one another. The upper loop of Fig. 7.1 depicts the influence of central policies on provinces and the exercise of provincial discretion within such influence. The centre, via its policies, provides the institutional context for the choices of provincial actors. The lower loop, on the other hand, indicates the flow of influence of provincial discretionary behaviour upon the choice of policies at the centre. The discretion available to the provinces now constitutes the institutional context in which the centre formulates its policies.

IMPACT OF CENTRAL POLICIES ON
PROVINCIAL CHOICE

The obvious differences between the discretionary behaviour adopted by the Guangdong and Shanghai leaderships since 1978, as described in the previous two chapters, reflect the impact of central policies on provincial discretion. Fig. 7.2 gives a clear visual picture of the differences.

The four lines in Fig. 7.2 represent the four quadrants of provincial discretion in Fig. 1.2. Their characteristics in terms of degree of provincial independence are depicted in Fig. 7.3.

The order of provincial independence of these different categories of discretionary behaviour is, from highest to lowest, C, A, D, B. Both Guangdong and Shanghai started off in 1978 with a high level of occurrence of discretionary behaviour which was highly dependent on the centre, as reflected by line b in Fig. 7.2. In the case of Guangdong, discretionary behaviour showed an obvious trend of increasing provincial independence and decreasing central dependence. This is most markedly indicated by the crossing of lines b and c, each representing the more extreme cases of central dependence and provincial independence respectively. Meanwhile, the intermediate cases of A and D start at a fairly high level in 1978, and show a gradual increase over the reform period. However, into the 1980s, the line (b) declines substantially in the case of Guangdong, while other lines which denote a higher order of provincial independence, (c) and (a), increased steadily over the decade.

On the other hand, the discretionary behaviour of Shanghai in the 1980s was far more centre-oriented than that of Guangdong. Throughout the entire decade of the 1980s the most important single objective of the Shanghai government was to bargain for more favourable central policies in order to improve its macro-economic environment. Since it took Shanghai so long to achieve this end, bargaining for more central investment and reducing annual local fiscal remittance accounted for a very large part of the day-to-day dealing between Shanghai and the centre during the 1980s. The lines b and d for Shanghai thus remained at a high level throughout the decade. Room for discretion in implementation was limited, thus the relatively low level of the line a in Fig. 7.2b. When the economic situation of Shanghai improved towards the beginning of the 1990s, however, the Shanghai government increasingly adopted discretion of a kind which

(a) Trends of Guangdong's discretionary behaviour, 1978–1993

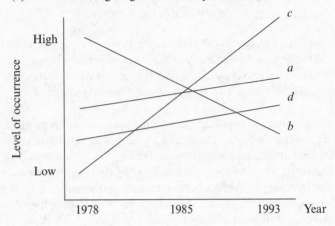

(b) Trends of Shanghai's discretionary behaviour, 1978–1993

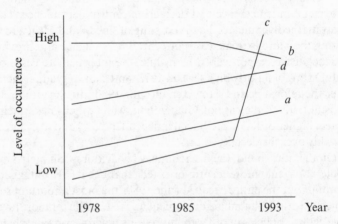

FIG. 7.2. A comparison of provincial discretionary behaviour:

Guangdong and Shanghai

Categories of discretionary behaviour:
a Flexible implementation of central policies
b Bargaining for more favourable central policies and more direct central
   support (in the form of planned resources)
c Developing the 'new horizon' beyond the budget; internationalization
d Bargaining for more direct central support (in the form of extrabudgetary resources)

	Provincial autarchy	Central dependence
Central plans/policies	(A): High	(B): Lowest
Local plans/markets	(C): Highest	(D): Low

FIG. 7.3. Provincial discretionary behaviour: degree of provincial 'independence'

was less focused on the centre and, like that of Guangdong, more 'independence-oriented'. This is represented in Figure 7.2*b* by the sharp rise of line *c* from a fairly low base during the 1980s. In other words, until the early 1990s, the discretionary behaviour of the Shanghai government exhibited a heavy reliance on the centre, while that of Guangdong saw a steady progression towards a higher level of independence during the 1980s.

The provincial leaders of Guangdong and Shanghai thus chose different tactics in their efforts to increase investment under different circumstances. Chapters 3 and 4 described the different institutional contexts, as imposed by different central policies, of investment implementation in Guangdong and Shanghai. Chapters 5 and 6 then discussed the choice of provincial discretion in such contexts, as well as the dynamic process in which different choices were made as the contexts (of which central policies formed a major part) changed over time. The substantial differences between discretion in Shanghai and Guangdong indicated the impact of different central policies on the provinces, the upper loop of Fig. 7.1. Such influence was, however, more on the choice by provincial leaders of what specific discretion to pursue than on the presence or absence of discretion. Notwithstanding differences in their choices, both Shanghai and Guangdong were capable of, and undertook, very substantial manoeuvres. It would thus appear that there was a limit to central power over the provinces.

THE POWER OF THE PROVINCES

There was a limit to the centre's influence on the provinces because influence also flowed from the provinces to the centre. This influence is expressed in the lower loop of Fig. 7.1. Instead of asking how provincial discretionary behaviour was influenced by central policies, this section asks how the Guangdong and Shanghai leaderships sought, and managed, to influence central policies through their discretionary behaviour.[1] As this discussion shows, the role of provinces was not confined to one of responding to central policies. It was also one of competing with the centre in defining the contents of the central policies. Provinces thus formulated policies as well as creatively implementing them.

Guangdong

The Guangdong government frequently challenged the legitimacy and appropriateness of existing central policies and rules when implementing central policies. Towards the end of the 1980s, as Guangdong's economy continued its growth and the province became more affluent, the provincial leadership had a feeling that its local policies had been vindicated. In the meantime, as the progress of reforms brought about more difficulties and tensions within the nation, conflicts between the centre and Guangdong became intense. A more confident Guangdong government, in these circumstances, felt it necessary to 'persuade' the centre to formally approve of its local practice. The result was a proliferation of local publications from the late 1980s summarizing and publicizing the 'Guangdong experience'.[2]

The most explicit instance of Guangdong's competition with the centre for orthodoxy was the 'Three "Sayings", Three Defences' article published by the Guangdong leadership in January 1989 (Wang Hao 1989). As noted in Chapter 5, this article amounted to an open protest by the Guangdong government against the effect of the centrally imposed austerity programme, started in late 1988, upon its reform efforts. Discouraged by the twists and turns of central policies and the withdrawal of many of its special powers since late 1988, the Guangdong government launched one of the most explicit and outright attacks ever made by a provincial government on central policies. The thrust of this articulation, through a series of three articles by the provincial Party propaganda chief in a provincial Party paper, went far beyond the usual lobbying for exceptional treatment based on local conditions. It was instead a general and fundamental challenge to the orthodoxy of central policies.

The argument went as follows. The fundamental central policy since the 1978 Third Plenum had been that of economic reform, 'opening up' and modernization. Thus, productivity was the only criterion against which the work of Guangdong should be judged. Moreover,

Guangdong had been assigned the task of pioneering the means to modernization and reform. Consequently, it should not be governed by any of the pre-existing central rules and regulations created before the new central policy of economic reform and development came into being. Nor, it was argued, should the province be bound by national rules formulated thereafter for nationwide application. Its role as a pioneer should preclude such a 'blanket' treatment. Whatever the justification of these national regulations for the rest of the nation, they should be subordinated to the fundamental policy of reform and development as regards Guangdong. Constraining Guangdong's ability to pioneer reform, it was further argued, was tantamount to sabotaging crucial central policy through pedantic regulations. Therefore, unless the centre changed its fundamental policy and abandoned reform and modernization, or unless Guangdong's methods of fulfilling this goal failed to bear fruit, those national rules and policies which obstructed Guangdong's experiments should give way.

Chapter 5 also described other, more specific examples of Guangdong officials seeking to redefine central policies. For instance, Guangdong's officials called for the abolition of central rules regarding the management of bank loans. They argued openly that the rules had become outdated, grounded in rationales of an earlier period. Such rules were therefore obstructing the needs of economic development and reform. It was pointed out, for instance, that the segregation of bank loans into investment loans and working capital loans arose from an earlier concern to contain the former, which the central government had not expected to have repaid. But as market reforms progressed, enterprises were, at least in theory, required to repay both kinds of loans. While some enterprises might be unable to repay their loans in practice, it was argued, this was not the reason to arbitrarily impose administrative quotas. The quotas had the effect of displacing the independent professional judgement of local banks, thus inhibiting the spirit of the bank reform. By ignoring the central rules, the Guangdong officials argued, they were in fact helping to advance economic reform, a role they were assigned to perform. After all, they argued, the amount of loans by a local bank should be restricted by the total amount of deposits, and banks should not be forbidden to lend out their available resources to viable projects.

There are indications that Guangdong's arguments had impact an national policies. A report by the State Planning Commission, published in 1993, acknowledged the wisdom of Guangdong's flexible implementation of these bank rules as well as its flexible attitude to rules regarding the central quotas of annual investment. The report noted that by 'flexibly handling' these rules, Guangdong's authorities had successfully developed the infrastructural facilities of the province. Since the centre and other provinces had generally found it difficult to divert enough investment to the low-profit infrastructural sectors, Guangdong's success by *not* strictly following central prescriptions could not but give the centre a disturbing and yet illuminating message. The report of the State Planning Commission was generally supportive of Guangdong's argument, noting that 'taking into account Guangdong's success, the centre should perhaps change the rules to accommodate, rather than merely tolerating, such so-called "illegal manoeuvres" of the existing system' (Luo Jinfen and Guo Shuqing 1993: 239). The report also noted that Guangdong's extensive use of extrabudgetary funds in investment had played a material role in enabling the province to finance an ambitious infrastructural and energy investment plan (Luo Jinfen and Guo Shuqing 1993: 232–41). Financing capital was raised directly from the immediate users of the facilities, while in other provinces investment in infrastructure had always depended heavily on the state budget. Investment had thus been limited, given the declining share of budgetary revenue in national income generally and competition from other spending priorities. Guangdong's success in overcoming these difficulties had an impact on the centre's consideration of the most appropriate way of financing investment. It paved the way for the new central policy regarding the capital market and the issuing of stocks and shares in the 1990s.

Shanghai

If the influence of the Guangdong government on central policies derived in part from its pioneering role and experience in reform, the power of Shanghai was rooted in its established status as the 'eldest son' of the centre. As the 'eldest son', the Shanghai leadership historically had a close relationship with the centre. As Chapter 6 has noted, the Shanghai leadership was eager to maintain a veil of feigned compliance, even with those central policies with which they did not agree, in order that their status as the 'right-hand man' of the centre could be maintained. Observing central rules was, in this way, seen as the best strategy through which to sustain Shanghai's influence on their making.

One fairly obvious indicator of Shanghai's influence at the centre was the career mobility of its leaders. From 1949 a considerable number of Shanghai leaders led both provincial and central government careers. To mention the more recent developments, both the current Secretary General of the Party and a prominent vice-premier, Jiang Zemin and Zhu Rongji, served in Shanghai immediately before their promotion to the central leadership. In September 1994, as previously noted, the then Shanghai Party boss, Wu Bangguo, after being made a Politburo member in 1992, was elevated to an important position at the Central Party Secretariat, while its Mayor, Huang Ju, was made a Politburo member. Wu subsequently became a vice-premier in March 1995.

Nevertheless, a clear statement of provincial power requires us to explore the processes whereby Shanghai's leaders exerted their influence. This examination has, however, proved to be plagued by immense difficulties. Not only is there the problem of ascertaining articulations of interests from within a closed political system, but the relationship between the centre and its 'lieutenant' was also, by its nature, an 'internal' matter. Opinions and advice were, as a rule, discussed and delivered in private. Wherever possible, the centre and its lieutenant maintained a 'united front' in public. As in the relationship between the political master and the senior civil servant in the West, this veil of homogeneity and harmony is necessary for the public image of effective governance. The veil only drops to reveal the underlying dissension on rare occasions where fundamental and material disagreements are involved.[3]

Notwithstanding such difficulty in detection, fragments of the arguments which were put forward by the Shanghai government to influence central policies in the 1980s have come to light. One major case is the fiscal system. Shanghai's finance officials had advocated a tax-sharing fiscal system since the early 1980s.[4] During the early to mid-1980s, at a time when the recently installed contractual fiscal system was bringing in sustained benefits to the centre as its share of national fiscal revenue rose,[5] Shanghai's officials were nevertheless adamant that this was not the proper fiscal system. They argued for a system whereby fiscal authority and responsibility between the centre and the provinces should be clearly delineated through separate taxes. In other words, revenue would no longer be divided according to the subordination relations of enterprises as it was under the existing system. Instead, some taxes would form the revenue of the centre, and others that of the province. These principles in fact formed the backbone of the new tax-sharing fiscal system of 1994, although many of the more radical changes to the pre-existing system have been subsequently watered down. In the 1980s, however, Shanghai's preference for a tax-sharing system was motivated by local interests. A tax-sharing system was regarded as the best option for defining the powers and responsibilities of the centre and Shanghai. The contractual system was considered unsatisfactory and of only transient utility not merely because Shanghai had not obtained much benefit under such a system, but also because provinces generally had remained dependent on the centre for a good contract. Without a clear-cut division of central and local taxes, it was felt, provinces would remain vulnerable to arbitrary central intervention and unable to exercise their independent authority.

This is not to say, however, that Shanghai officials sought deliberately to influence adversely the interests of the centre. There was no simple dichotomy of municipal interests versus central government's interests. As Peter Ferdinand (1984: 18–19) has pointed out, it is often immaterial to try to discern motives behind behaviour in terms of private or altruistic interests. Very often motives have both private and altruistic facets. In the search for a 'proper' central–provincial fiscal system, it was in the interests of the Shanghai government to have a system which guaranteed a higher and more stable fiscal revenue over which the municipal government might exercise autonomous control. The national interest lay in having a system which would proportionately assign authority and responsibility to each level of government, whilst maintaining the overarching authority of the centre. These two motives did not necessarily contradict one another. From the point of view of Shanghai officials, tax-sharing was the best design because it could more specifically delineate the power and responsibilities of both the centre and the provinces. Both the centre and Shanghai might thereby benefit from a stable and secure fiscal relationship. In the opinion of Shanghai officials, in the long run a system that enabled both sides to benefit and feel secure was the only kind likely to survive. The interests of the centre and of Shanghai, in other words, did not constitute a zero-sum game.

There was a strong affinity between these early opinions in Shanghai and the rationale behind the institution of the new tax-sharing system in 1994. This similarity suggests the extent of Shanghai's influence on the central decision to implement the tax-sharing system in 1994.

In fact, there is evidence that Shanghai's officials and scholars participated extensively with central government officials in the search for a long-term central–provincial fiscal system. One example was the research on fiscal system reform during the latter half of the Seventh Five-Year Plan (1986–90) organized and co-ordinated by the Research Institute for Fiscal Science of the Ministry of Finance (Song Xinzhong 1992). Amongst the participants were a number of scholars from the Shanghai Academy of Social Sciences. The major thrust of the findings of the project was a critique of the continued operation of the contractual fiscal system of the 1980s. This research also suggested fiscal reform along the lines of a tax-sharing system. The continuity with Shanghai's earlier position was thus obvious.

Shanghai's participation in the formulation of the new tax-sharing policy continued as the system entered its early phase of implementation in 1994. The early months of 1994 saw numerous detailed expositions from Shanghai on how the new system should and could operate.[6] As new policies in China were often only half-implemented initially, partly due to a lack of detailed implementation rules and partly to the ponderousness of the pre-existing system, Shanghai's pro-active suggestions constituted a *de facto* draft of new central regulations.

Thus, both the Guangdong and Shanghai governments, in their own characteristic ways, played a considerable role in the formulation of central policies. Guangdong's approach was led by implementation. It was only after the successful implementation of its own 'native' policies that the Guangdong government ever challenged the legitimacy of central policies whilst simultaneously pushing for amendments. In the case of Shanghai, participation in central policy formulation followed a more conventional sequence. First, there would be advocacy of policy options, followed by participation in policy deliberations within the centre. When the centre adopted a new policy, the municipal government would continue its participation through recommendations on implementation details. Fig. 7.4 summarizes the approaches of Guangdong and Shanghai in exercising their influence on central policies.

THE INTERVENING VARIABLE: PERCEPTIONS OF THE PROVINCES' ROLES

Discussion so far has elaborated on the mutual influences of the centre

Guangdong

Flexible provincial implementation of central policies → *de facto* amendments to central policies (at provincial level) → official amendments to central policies

Shanghai

Advocacy at municipal level → participation in policy deliberations with central officials → [central policy adopted] → recommending details for smooth implementation of the policy

FIG. 7.4. Processes of provincial participation in the formualtion of central policy

and provinces upon one another, as expressed in the upper and lower loops of Fig. 7.1. There is still the need to explain the differences between the cases of Guangdong and Shanghai. In other words, what has this comparison between Guangdong and Shanghai told us regarding the interactions between centre and provinces?

In this respect, case data from Guangdong and Shanghai suggest a major intervening variable permeating the choice by both central and provincial actors of their behaviour towards the other: the perceptions by the provincial as well as the central leaderships regarding the national roles of the two provinces. Thus the historical importance of Shanghai in the nation and its role as the 'eldest son' and the 'right-hand man' of the 'father' centre both constrained Shanghai's choice of discretion and gave it a stronger voice and earlier participation in national policy making. Conversely, Guangdong's historical marginality in the national economy until the 1980s became its greatest advantage in the 1980s, as the province was allowed more freedom to pioneer and to deviate from national rules. This, however, also explained the anxiety of successive Guangdong leaderships to sustain a high economic growth rate and to maintain Guangdong's image of being at the cutting edge of reform, since these were essential to Guangdong's retaining if not enhancing its status nationally. Guangdong's participation in national policy making was accordingly largely *post hoc* and founded on its successful 'flexible implementation'. Without an established record like that of Shanghai to influence the process of policy deliberation *a priori*, Guangdong in the 1980s and early 1990s had focused its effort on building one.

Table 7.1 provides some basic data regarding the different status and roles of Guangdong and Shanghai in the national economy on the eve of economic reform.

The substantial gap in 1978 between Guangdong and Shanghai in

TABLE 7.1. *Guangdong and Shanghai: Major Economic Indicators*, 1978

	Guangdong			Shanghai		
	Total (billion yuan)	% of national total	Rank[a]	Total (billion yuan)	% of national total	Rank[a]
GNP	18.5	5.1	6	27.3	7.6	1
Societal output	35.0	5.1	7	59.2	8.7	1
Export[b]	1.4	14.2	n/a	2.9	29.7	n/a
Total local fiscal revenue	3.9	3.5	n/a	16.7	14.9	1

n/a = not available

[a] Position among all provincial-level administrations.

[b] Export values in billion US dollars.

Sources: Guangdong Statistical Bureau (1989a: 74, 162, 175); *Statistical Yearbook of Shanghai* (1993: 54, 300); *Statistical Yearbook of Guangdong* (1993: 350); *Statistical Yearbook of China* (1993: 215, 633).

terms of their importance to the national economy suggested their different status in the family of provinces. Two different sets of policies were consequently conferred on them. In 1978 Guangdong was weak and relatively unimportant to the centre. The centre could, therefore, afford to allow it to be 'special'—meaning preferentially treated. Guangdong was thus awarded the 'Special Policy' early in 1979, which enabled the province to retain more resources, as well as a larger scope of authority in the administration of investment policies. Shanghai, on the other hand, was asked to 'integrate horizontally' with the poorer inland provinces—in other words, to play the fraternal role of 'elder brother' and share its wealth with its weaker brothers. Being relatively better off, Shanghai was required to support the development of other provinces in the form of both direct provision of technical and financial assistance, and indirect fiscal transfers via the centre.

These different central policies, themselves a result of different perceptions of the national roles of Guangdong and Shanghai, further led to the development of different attitudes among the Guangdong and Shanghai leaderships regarding their choice of discretion. In Guangdong the Special Policy conferred on the provincial leadership a clear role in achieving the targets of economic development and reform. The Guangdong government thus enjoyed a greater latitude of

manoeuvre than other provinces, and exceptions were made in its case
to central policies and rules in order to facilitate its experiments. The
task entrusted to the province of the pioneer and experimenter in economic reform required in fact a new outlook and attitude amongst
provincial officials. In the early years of reform, therefore, Guangdong's leaders were encouraged by central leaders themselves not to
be too concerned with the loyal implementation of central rules. They
were instead urged to be bolder, less conventional and more aggressive
in pushing forward new initiatives.

In contrast to Guangdong's clear role, the role of Shanghai at the
start of the reform decade was confused and ambivalent. Shanghai
was required to perform the role of a 'rearguard', supporting experiments in the southern provinces. However, the Shanghai leadership
expected to do more than simply provide resources for other provinces. Similarly, the central leaders were eager to tap the strengths of
Shanghai, such as its edge in technology and its educated workforce,
as well as to ensure a high level of fiscal remittance. Consequently, the
role of Shanghai as perceived by both Shanghai and central leaders
was less than clear-cut. While the Guangdong leaders were able to progress through the 1980s deepening their understanding and fulfilment
of their defined role within the reform, leaders of Shanghai underwent
a decade of confusion. From the beginning the message from the
centre was that Shanghai could best serve reform by sustaining its
traditional roles. Disruptions in the macro-operating environment
caused by the reform, however, placed the Shanghai government, acting in a traditional manner, in a difficult position. As noted in previous
chapters, the Shanghai leaders gradually discovered that things were
not working in the same way as before. However, central policies were
slow to change, as were their own attitudes and accustomed behaviour. Both contributed to the reactions of the Shanghai leaders to their
new-found difficulties during the first decade of reform, which have
been detailed in Chapter 6.

Understanding the attitude of Shanghai officials regarding Shanghai's role in the nation is pertinent to comprehending their choice of
discretionary behaviour. In this respect, their perception of being the
'eldest son' of the centre was the key. First, as the eldest son, the
Shanghai government was also the right-hand man of the father
centre. This required the Shanghai government to offer its advice and
comments on central policy options, as well as on the implementation
of existing policies. Secondly, the eldest son had to share the burden of

responsibility of the father for the younger brothers. This required the Shanghai government to follow in the footsteps of the centre and be the model for emulation by other provinces. Shanghai's leaders, therefore, were constantly under the self-imposed pressure to act in accordance with the rules, or, at least, to appear to have acted within the rules. As the eldest son, Shanghai also occasionally acted as 'surrogate father' in helping the centre rein in other provinces.[7]

What was required would appear to be contradictory behaviour patterns. The Shanghai government was to take the lead in strictly following central rules and policies, as well as promoting the rationale of policies which had not been well received by other provinces. On the other hand, as the right-hand man, the Shanghai government also had to act as the critical adviser of the centre, pointing out the inadequacies of existing and provisional central policies, as well as offering constructive suggestions. This would apparently require Shanghai's officials to criticize rather than obey central policies. In reality the contradiction was superficial. The Shanghai government had an interest in assisting the centre to maintain its authority among other provinces, since the central policies were often, to an extent, a product of Shanghai's advice and therefore worked towards its own interests. Critical advice and articulations of interest to the centre were largely an 'internal' matter between the centre and its major assistant, and were kept as far as possible from public view.[8] The remarks of Shanghai's Party Secretary, Wu Bangguo, during the Second Session of the Eighth Party Congress in March 1994 reflected this aspect in the relationship between Shanghai and the centre:

Regarding the distribution of interests between the centre and the provinces, our position is: once the centre has made its decisions, Shanghai unambiguously follows and loyally implements them. Shanghai does not seek exceptions as all issues must be uniformly handled.[9]

The relationship between public statements of support and loyalty and private communications of criticisms and opinions, in the case of Shanghai, is interestingly analogous to the relationship between senior civil servants and their political masters in Western countries within a Weberian bureaucracy. The main contrast with Western countries is, perhaps, the circumstances under which articulations of interest and internal communications were revealed to the public. In the West, procedural rules have been established to regulate disclosure in most circumstances. In China, disclosure was often a result of power conflicts in the system. When conflicts of interest between the centre and its main lieutenant became serious and intense, and when their differential power narrowed to the extent that neither could be coerced into silence, differences might then emerge.

The role perception among Shanghai's leaders explained many of Shanghai's apparently peculiar reactions and its remarkable self-restraint in view of the centre's discriminatory policies. One example was that, despite their discontent, Shanghai's officials nevertheless re-signed themselves to the inevitability of their misfortune. While Deng Xiaoping himself finally expressed regret in having neglected the development of Shanghai during his 1992 Southern Tour, the general feeling amongst Shanghai officials was, rather peculiarly, that what had occurred had been, by and large, inevitable. In their opinion, Shanghai's importance to the national economy destined it for its rearguard role in the early stage of reform. In the words of a municipal planning official, 'it would have been too risky for the centre to "open" Shanghai and try out experiments there in the early 1980s.'[10] Shanghai was not comparable to the remote village of Shenzhen and the humble towns of Zhuhai and Shantou, the beneficiaries of the early stage of reform. The pride of Shanghai officials over Shanghai's 'eldest son' status and national role therefore resulted in a strangely mixed feeling of righteous deprivation and stoic acceptance.

The above discussion indicates that the process whereby central policies had an impact on provincial behaviour, and vice versa, was not straightforward. Provincial and central leaders did not merely re-spond and react to the behaviour of one another, but their responses were mediated by their perceptions regarding the national roles of the two provinces. At times of radical change, there might be a time-lag between changes in the macro-environment in the wider context and changes in such perceptions and associated attitudes. The resultant behaviour was thus often coloured by yesterday's policies or an object-ive situation which had subsequently changed. This characteristic of the mediating factor explains some of the ostensibly peculiar choices of discretion by provincial leaders and the responses of central leaders.

For instance, Guangdong's perception of its role in the nation was, in the early 1990s, largely unchanged despite its emergence as a major economic power. In 1993, Guangdong became the top exporter in the nation for the eighth consecutive year.[11] Its gross national product sur-passed that of Shanghai in 1981,[12] and since 1989 has topped the national ranking.[13] Economically, therefore, the province had become

a formidable national force. However, the role of the province as perceived by the Guangdong leadership and by the centre apparently
remained that of the favoured younger child. As pioneer, the Guangdong leadership had, since 1979, been aggressive in asking for central
concessions. The centre had, for its part, tolerated and sometimes encouraged such 'aggressiveness' by Guangdong. After a decade of reform, this pioneer was no longer the weak and unimportant
peripheral province whose possible failure in the reform experiment
would not cost the nation too dearly. Nevertheless, since the early
1990s the Guangdong government had, as before, displayed little hes-
itation in pushing for concessions from the centre at times when it felt
that its interests were under threat.[14] The aggressiveness and openness
of its lobbying for concessions and support, and its success in getting
them, demonstrated that old attitudes still held amongst both the central and Guangdong leaders regarding the role, and thus the responsibility, of Guangdong for the nation.

A similar logic applied in the case of Shanghai, where a different
perception regarding its national role resulted in substantially different behaviour on the part of Shanghai and central leaders. As discussed in Chapter 6, the Shanghai government, in a manner similar to
other provinces, sought to expand the revenue base of 1993 in order to
increase its retained local revenue under the new fiscal system. However, after the centre detected such manoeuvring behaviour and issued
a stern warning, which applied to all provinces and not specifically to
Shanghai, the Shanghai government immediately obliged. Some collected revenue was even refunded to enterprises. The Shanghai leadership might have felt obliged to follow the centre's instructions as a
result of its traditional role of 'setting a good example' to other provinces. They might also have acted out of calculated interest, believing
that this approach would best serve Shanghai's interest in the long
run.[15] It was strongly felt among Shanghai's officials that the centre
would not tolerate explicit deviations from central instructions by
Shanghai. In the words of a Shanghai official, it was 'totally unacceptable to the centre if leaders of Shanghai do not see things from
the national viewpoint'.[16] The Shanghai leadership might thus have
considered such a temporary retreat as a necessary means of maintaining its status in the country, thus enabling it to sustain its influence
on the centre and obtain more favourable policies over the long run.[17]

Thus, as Guangdong had become economically strong but still
clung to the role of a younger child, Shanghai had chosen to continue

to perform its 'eldest son' role. The Shanghai leadership apparently came to the conclusion that its interests might be better served through strengthening its position as the right-hand man of the centre, and that added responsibility was the inevitable price to be paid. This was notwithstanding the fact that, as of the late 1980s, Shanghai had already been surpassed by Guangdong and other provinces in terms of important economic indicators. In fact, the more vulnerable the Shanghai leadership felt in the face of the threat to its traditionally dominant position, the more anxious it was to maintain its status by acting even more like a 'good son' than it otherwise would.

CONCLUSION: AN INTERACTIVE CENTRAL–PROVINCIAL RELATIONSHIP

This chapter has sought to demonstrate one point: that political influence has many manifestations. The centre obviously had leverage over the behaviour of provincial governments: its policies defined the scope of provincial manoeuvre. Through their circumscribing effect on the attitudes and role perceptions of the provincial leaders, specific central policies often had an impact on provincial behaviour outlasting their very existence. However, the existence of central influence did not necessarily mean that provincial leaders were merely the agents of the centre, or that they would respond and react to stimuli from the centre in accordance with a preconceived formula determined at the centre. On the contrary, provincial leaders had ample choice within the contextual constraints of central policies, and the resultant provincial behaviour was the product of *both* central policies and provincial choices. The institutional context posed by central policies and the actors' choice of the provincial leaderships interacted with each other to produce the manifest behaviour and strategies described in detail in Chapters 5 and 6.

The interactive relationship also applied from the other direction: the influence of provincial discretion on central policies. For instance, the success of Guangdong's flexible implementation of central policies in delivering positive results enabled the Guangdong leadership to vie with the centre in defining the content of its policies. Shanghai's historical importance in the nation permitted its sustained participation in the formulation of central policies from the initial stages. For both provincial governments, their leverage on the centre was, however, dependent on their success in achieving their national roles, which were partly a result of central policies. The concern for maintaining a favourable perception of their roles and thus enhancing their leverage consequently affected the choice of discretion by provincial officials. The Guangdong leadership took great care to sustain its momentum of economic growth and, therefore, its image as the successful pioneer of reforms. The Shanghai leadership was highly aware of the importance of maintaining its image of trustworthiness in its capacity as 'eldest son', whilst also sustaining its economic strength in the nation.

Fig. 7.5 modifies Fig. 7.1 to depict the interactive relationship between central policies and provincial discretion, taking into account the mediating factor of national roles.

These findings about central–provincial relations, based on the case data for Guangdong and Shanghai, have important implications for the understanding of central–provincial relations in general. First, on a theoretical level, the interactive processes as exposed in these case studies firmly refute the centrist, top-down perspective which has dominated previous studies of spatial politics inside and outside China studies. The power relationship between centre and provinces is mutual and interactive, rather than unilinear. This study has thus provided a new theoretical perspective with which we may proceed to explore questions which have been left unanswered. One important question which can be more fruitfully addressed by this interactive model, as suggested in Chapter 1, is the question of the possibility and process of change. Chapter 8 will discuss this issue further.

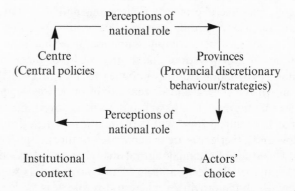

FIG. 7.5. Centre–provincial relations: an interactive process

Secondly, despite the 'atypical' situations of Guangdong and Shanghai among the family of provinces, these findings about the interactive nature of central–provincial relations do have nationwide relevance. It is true that most other provinces, without Guangdong's special status as the reform pioneer, or Shanghai's status as the centre's right-hand man, may find themselves with fewer bargaining chips in their dealing with the centre. However, the difference is likely one of degree rather than one of kind. The resources and the perceived national roles of each individual province may differ, and thus the centre's treatment of that province and its choice of discretion will differ accordingly. Such differences in resources and specific behaviour choices mean that the power relationship with the centre in some provinces may be more asymmetrical than in the case of others. These differences will not, however, change the fundamental nature of the power relationship between the centre and each of these other provinces, which is likely to be characterized by the same kind of dialectical interactions and mutual power as in the cases of Guangdong and Shanghai.

The details of the relationship in other provinces must await future projects. In this study of Guangdong and Shanghai, however, it has been firmly established that provinces were capable of exerting, and have successfully exerted, influence over the centre. Provinces were not only the flexible implementers and half-hearted agents of the centre, and orthodoxy was not the monopoly of the central government. As in the case of Guangdong, previously 'orthodox' central policies could be displaced and amended by flexible implementation from below. Alternatively, as in the case of Shanghai, central policies could literally be written by provincial officials in conjunction with central officials. As resourceful provinces Guangdong and Shanghai provide clear-cut test cases regarding provincial behaviour by ruling out the possibility that provinces comply simply because they have to as a result of absolute deprivation. The relative wealth of these two provinces allows us to enquire directly into the variables affecting the exercise of provincial power, and of central power. It was suggested in Chapter 1 that the provinces, as well as the central government, may be a locus of the 'central zone' within the political system, from which ideas flow and experiences are disseminated to the 'periphery' of the system. This study of Guangdong and Shanghai provides evidence of the possibility of this 'central' role of the provinces, as well as the means by which the provinces achieved this role. It is likely that this demonstrated provincial power to influence the centre will also be found in the case of other provinces, albeit possibly of a different magnitude and using different means.

NOTES

1. As noted in Chap. 1, the influence of the provinces on central policies has been one major theme of Susan Shirk's work. See Shirk (1990, 1993: chap. 9). Shirk's focus of analysis is, by and large, on the centre, and her discussion elaborates how central officials feel about being constrained by the provinces. The influence of the provinces is deduced from articulations by central officials about their difficulties in imposing their will. In the present volume, on the other hand, the power of provinces is discussed via explicit description of the behaviour of provincial leaders.
2. This is a point raised by respondent no. 9 (interview, Guangzhou, Dec. 1993).
3. One recent case in which dissensions between political masters and civil servants in the West were brought into the open was the provision of overseas development aid by the British government in the early 1990s to the Pergau Dam Project of the Malaysian government. The senior civil servant involved held opposing views to those of the ministers and provided evidence to parliamentary hearings and judicial review proceedings on the propriety of the aid decision. Eventually the court ruled that the government had acted illegally. See *The Guardian* 11 Nov. 1994. A similar and more dramatic case, again in Britain, occurred over the Falklands War when a senior civil servant was sued by the government as a result of his making his dissensions public. See Ponting (1985).
4. This is reflected in a report by Shanghai officials during the discussion over Shanghai's development strategy in 1984, in which it is written that 'the current [1985] changes to Shanghai's fiscal system are . . . largely of a transitional nature, and cannot solve many fundamental problems. To improve fundamentally the local fiscal system, the obvious situation has to be a system whereby the centre and the local governments obtain their share of total revenue according to the types of taxes . . . This should be the basic direction of future fiscal system reform.' See Xu Riqing *et al.* (1985: 247). For a later, even more specific advocacy of a tax-sharing system, see for instance Xu Yunren (1990: 17–20) (Xu was then the Vice-Director of the Institute of Fiscal Science, Shanghai Fiscal and Tax Bureau) and Yan Bin (1991: 3–10).
5. The share of centrally collected fiscal revenue had been rising since the institution of the contractual system in 1980, only beginning to drop in 1987. See Ministry of Finance (1992: 102).
6. See for instance Ke Tizuo (1994: 8–14), Gu Xingquan (1994: 10–11, 31), and Wu Jianguo (1994: 12–14).

7. The idea of the role of 'surrogate father' was brought to the author's attention by respondent no. 23 (interview, Shanghai, May 1994).

8. This explains why what is publicly available in documentary evidence regarding Shanghai's articulation of interest and criticisms directed at central policies is generally very mild and lightly worded.

9. See *Jiefang Daily*, 11 Mar. 1994, 5. Wu was speaking with reference to growing central–provincial tensions at the time regarding the introduction of the tax-sharing system in 1994.

10. Interview, respondent no. 27, Shanghai, May 1994. Similar comments were made by respondent no. 23 (interview Shanghai, May 1994).

11. See *Jiefang Daily*, 22 Feb. 1994, 9.

12. Calculated from Guangdong Statistical Bureau (1989*b*: 69); *Statistical Yearbook of Guangdong* (1993: 27); *Statistical Yearbook of Shanghai* (1993: 35).

13. See Guangdong Statistical Bureau (1989*b*: 176) and State Statistical Bureau (1992: 8).

14. One revealing example was Guandong's response to the centre's plan to replace the *dabaogan* fiscal system of 1980 with a tax-sharing system as from 1994. Another instance was its bargaining with the centre in 1991 to obtain cheap central bank loans amounting to some one billion yuan annually, even though local bank deposits at that time exceeded the local demand for loans. See Ch. 5.

15. According to respondent no. 21 (interview, Shanghai, Jan. 1994), underlying the decision to refund taxes in December 1993 was the worry that the rapid surge of fiscal revenue in Shanghai might raise the future expectations of the centre regarding the financial strength of Shanghai, and therefore invite further extraction from the centre.

16. Interview, respondent no. 23, Shanghai, May 1994. The respondent remarked that given the difference in the historical and strategic roles of Guangdong and Shanghai, the centre was generally more tolerant of deviations in Guangdong than in Shanghai. While the centre generally required an expression of 'loyalty' from all provincial leaderships, localist tendencies in some provinces were more tolerable than in others. The expectation of the centre for Shanghai in terms of loyalty was especially high.

17. The fact that Shanghai's Party Secretary, Wu Bangguo, was promoted to the Party Central Committee Secretariat, and Mayor Huang Ju concurrently to the Politburo in the Fourth Plenum of the Fourteenth Party Congress in September 1994, might indicate that this strategy of Shanghai had paid off in enhancing its influence on the centre. See *Wen Wei Po* (Hong Kong), 1 Oct. 1994.

8 Shifting Central–Provincial Relations: Emerging Trends

An interactive relationship emphasizes the interdependence of and mutual influences between the centre and the provinces. This concluding chapter highlights the dynamic aspects of this interactive relationship, and demonstrates that the central and provincial actors, by influencing each other, themselves constitute the forces of change for their relationship. This chapter also identifies the emerging trends of change in central–provincial relations in the post-Mao period. It explains their emergence and draws preliminary conclusions as to the significance of these trends regarding political processes in the Chinese system generally.

Before proceeding further it may be helpful to go back to a question first raised in Chapter 1: why did the centre not simply obliterate the unwelcome discretion of the provinces by utilizing its superior organizational position and command of coercive forces? The centre possessed at least two forms of coercive resources which could have been used against the provinces. The first was the use of sheer physical force through the centre's superior command of the military. The second was the dismissal of provincial leaders through the centre's *nomenklatura* control of personnel. The answer lies in the unreliability of these coercive resources. First, coercive power is a blunt instrument of control and, given its limited supply, can only be used intermittently and sparingly. Secondly, provincial governments are an indispensable ally of the centre in its task of governance. The utility of the provinces as an intermediate level of government imposes a structural constraint on the extent to which they can be crushed. Consequently, although the centre sometimes used its superior power to stamp out excessive provincial discretion, such use of coercion was tempered by the indispensability of provincial discretion, at least to some degree, to any kind of effective governance. Due to this fundamental mutual interdependence of the centre and the provinces, it was simply not feasible for the centre to crush its provincial opponent as a means to resolving central– provincial conflicts. This was not because the centre was loath to do so, as some analysts have argued, but that it was patently unable to.[1]

Co-existence has thus obliged the centre and the provinces to find a means of resolving their conflicts. As reform policies accentuated old conflicts and created new ones, the pressure for a solution also built up. New trends in central–provincial relations thus emerged from the intense conflicts, manoeuvres and counter-manoeuvres during the reform years. Such emerging trends embodied the attempts by both the centre and the provinces to adjust their relationship to the new circumstances of the reform period so as better to advance their respective interests within their respective constraints.

The traditional means of ameliorating conflict before reform was for the centre and provinces to 'paper over' conflicts and feign a state of harmony. The rhetoric was that the interests of the centre as representative of the nation, and the particularistic interests of the provinces, were fundamentally reconcilable. Consequently, any manifest sign of central–provincial conflict was regarded as having only minor significance. Such an approach had its rationality. There were, historically, few regularized means to reconcile conflicts within the political system, and thus it was politically necessary to restrain the manifest occurrence of conflicts by downplaying if not ignoring their existence. Conflicts, when they occurred and could no longer be evaded, often required the direct intervention of the centre. What often happened was that a high-ranking central official would preside over the arbitration of conflicts between a province and a central government ministry. This method allowed the centre to contain conflicts and pressurize both sides to co-operate. This also enabled the provinces to benefit, as more often than not the centre would make concessions to the provinces as a result of the aforementioned bargaining and arbitration process.[2]

The problem was that the ability of central leaders to arbitrate and resolve conflicts between provincial and central agencies depended on the resources at their command. In order that compliance could be exacted from provinces without the explicit use of direct coercive power, the centre needed to possess other resources through which to solve conflicts in an equitable manner. Conflicts could thus be more easily 'papered over' at a time when the political system was more centralized, and the centre commanded more vital resources with which to 'buy off' provinces and 'resolve' conflicts. In the 1950s the success of the Socialist Revolution brought immense political capital to the central leadership and helped to keep the level of central–provincial conflict at a relatively low level. However, as more and more resources were, over time, siphoned off to the provinces, partly as a result of this 'buying off' process, the provinces became more and more assertive. Possessing fewer resources after the 1970s, the centre found it increasingly difficult to arbitrate conflicts amongst its own assistants and intermediaries. Coercion had to be employed more frequently in these circumstances in the form of retrenchment campaigns and reshuffles of provincial leaderships. Ironically, however, more coercion brought diminishing returns, as provinces became increasingly adept at dodging the consequences of any 'crisis', 'sitting it out' until the return to 'normality'. With fewer 'carrots' to hand out and 'sticks' becoming more costly to administer, the traditional means of conflict resolution became increasingly ineffective after the onset of reform.

THE EMERGING TREND: INSTITUTIONALIZATION

The major trend emerging from the intense conflicts and interactions between the centre and the provinces in the reform period, as illustrated in the case studies on Guangdong and Shanghai, was that of a gradual move towards institutionalization. This move was characterized by shifts in two aspects. First, the emphasis shifted from an unscrupulous scramble for resources to a clearer definition of jurisdiction. Whilst resources were still the ultimate concern in central–provincial relations, jurisdiction was gradually regarded as the best means for securing new resources, as well as retaining existing ones. Secondly, the centre and the provinces found that in order to protect their respective interests they would need a clearer specification and a closer observance of the rules. Clarity had to replace ambiguity in the definition of their relationship and in the conduct of their interactions.

From resources to jurisdiction

The intense bargaining between provincial governments and the centre over resources during the 1980s has been described in detail in previous chapters. This focus on resources has resulted in provincial governments appearing 'Machiavellian' and incredibly 'flexible' over policy matters. Although the Guangdong and Shanghai leaderships also bargained for better central policies, their major concern was nevertheless for the increased amount of resources these new policies might bring. Additional authority was welcome because and only when it could gain more resources. Conversely, on the part of the centre, the adjustment of central policies also revolved around the allocation of resources and the authority to deploy resources, and resources and authority on various occasions were devolved to, and taken back from, the provinces. Policies were always subject to change, as was the delegated authority of the provinces.

Against this background, it is interesting to note that towards the late 1980s bargaining between the centre and the provinces was increasingly preoccupied with a better demarcation of jurisdiction.[3] Not only should the specific assignment of authority and responsibility be fair and consistent, it was argued, but, more importantly, the demarcation of jurisdiction should be laid down in law, and even included in the constitution, to ensure its relative stability and its security from encroachment on both sides.[4] These calls for a clearer demarcation of the jurisdiction of the central and provincial governments were unprecedented and went beyond mere requests for an adjustment to the existing distribution of power and resources. In calling for the institution of a regularized avenue through which to resolve disagreements in future, they embodied a new recognition of the need for a higher level of institutionalization within central–provincial relations.

The question is: what was it that caused the centre and the two provinces, from the late 1980s, to move away from their previous focus on resources, requiring instead a clearer institutionalization of their respective authorities? Did this shift of focus from resources to jurisdiction as the objective of central–provincial interactions signify the failure of previous manoeuvres on both sides to deliver on their respective interests? What were their grievances as regards the *status quo*, and why did they believe that institutionalizing their relationship would be the solution?

Both the centre and the provinces had their grievances. On the one hand, the centre grew increasingly weary of its sustained failure to contain the 'deviant behaviour' of provincial governments. The decentralization reforms of the 1980s further accentuated the trend of dispersion of resources and authority in place since 1958 and especially since the Cultural Revolution. As the power of provincial governments increased, the centre felt itself to be losing control, and blamed provinces for failing to fulfil their proper share of national responsibilities. This perception was reinforced by the fact that, despite the frequent extra-contractual 'borrowing' from the provincial coffers throughout the 1980s, the share of central fiscal revenue in total national fiscal revenue, relative to provincial fiscal revenue, continued to decline conspicuously and successively. The centre, therefore, yearned for a clearer demarcation of jurisdiction in order to contain the unwelcome discretion of the provinces, as well as to enhance its power.

On the other hand, provinces also had serious complaints, especially over the insecurity of their decentralized powers and the arbitrariness of central intervention. They were particularly tired of the annual central 'borrowing' and the pressure of having to provide additional 'contributions' to central fiscal revenue. They also resented the arbitrary withdrawal of policies by the centre. The low level of institutionalization in the political system gave provincial governments little protection should the centre change its mind and opt, once more, for recentralization. Under the system provinces might abort the centre's moves or cushion their impact, but they could not stop the centre from embarking on a clampdown. Provincial governments, once having tasted the benefits of enhanced power, were thus naturally all the more resentful of such threats to their authority. Consequently, provinces also yearned for a more specifically defined jurisdiction through which to protect their hard-won resources and authority.

A revealing example of this common interest in increased institutionalization was the institution of the tax-sharing system in 1994, replacing the fiscal contractual system in place since 1980. The significance of the tax-sharing system reform, as opposed to previous reforms to the fiscal system, lay in the emphasis given to the uniformity and legality of the distribution of fiscal authority between the centre and the provinces. The system would be uniform and standardized, by and large, for all provinces. Moreover, and most importantly, the delineation of the authority and responsibility of the centre and the provinces under this system would have to be legally codified, and both the centre and the provinces would have to abide by it. Given the magnitude of vested interests involved in the pre-existing fiscal contractual system, such a change would have been inconceivable unless both the centre and the provinces stood to gain from the move.

From ambivalence to clarity

A corollary development was the gradual move from ambiguity to clarity in central–provincial interactions. Central–provincial relations in China were traditionally characterized by a high degree of ambiguity regarding what constituted provincial 'deviations'. Under the pre-reform political system, when the power of the centre was much stronger, provincial governments often sought to blur the clarity of central policies. Vague policies increased the latitude for provincial discretion during implementation. This preference for ambiguity did not change with the commencement of economic reform. At a time when the situation was changing rapidly and uncertainties abounded, clarity and precision in policies and rules could only restrict provincial discretion when it was most necessary. There was, therefore, a consistent tendency on the part of the provincial leaderships to blur the instructions of central documents, no matter how precise they might originally have been. The ambivalence of central policies and the inconsistencies within different central policies also allowed provincial governments to play off one central prescription against another, as well as to escape responsibility for their discretion.

'Manipulating ambiguity' was thus cherished as an important success factor for provincial manoeuvres in the 1980s. The famous 'red light theory', based on Guangdong's experience, was a summary of the strategies a provincial government could deploy to manipulate the ambiguity of central rules and policies. The resultant 'flexible implementation' of central policies contributed to the rapid economic growth of Guangdong during the 1980s. Conversely, the lacklustre performance of Shanghai's economy in the 1980s, it was widely felt, was partly attributable to the 'loyal' implementation by Shanghai's officials of central rules and policies.

The benefits of this ambiguity cut both ways, moreover, extending beyond that of the provinces alone. The centre also required a degree of ambiguity and ambivalence in its policies and rules in order to conduct experiments and to minimize the political risk of failures. The centre would, therefore, tolerate provincial discretion when either the resultant impact tallied with its objective, or when it had yet to decide on an alternative. Normally the ambiguity would be ended when the positive impact of the move proved undeniable, at which time local experiments became national policy. Alternatively, it was ended when the negative impact of ambiguity became too much to tolerate.

Ambiguity and ambivalence, therefore, were engineered and reinforced by both the provinces and the centre. The provinces sought ambivalence because of the latitiude it gave them. By watering down central documents and creating a *fait accompli*, provinces could circumscribe the range of actions which the centre might take in future, and thereby restrict the power of the centre. Meanwhile ambivalence enabled the centre to turn a blind eye to supposedly illegal activities without being branded as politically impotent. In the event of things going badly, the superior organizational power of the centre would enable it to intervene at will, if at a cost. Both the centre and the provinces thus had interests in maintaining a degree of ambiguity over the boundaries of legitimate discretion and improper deviations. Rather than being a reflection of the loss of power by either of them, as normally suggested in a unilinear, zero-sum power framework, the tolerance of ambiguity in policy implementation reflected a compromise struck by both the centre and the provinces, each seeing their interests served by having some ambiguity in the system.

A typical example of the politics of ambivalence is found in the 'automatic' enhancement of the investment project approval authority of provincial governments nationwide subsequent to Deng Xiaoping's Southern Tour in early 1992, and in the subsequent reaction of the centre regarding this obvious violation of central rules. As noted in Chapter 4, the call from Deng Xiaoping for faster economic development and reform was interpreted by provinces as signalling a further round of decentralization. As a result, provincial governments nationwide coincidentally seized the initiative to 'simplify approval procedures and speed up economic development' by approving, independently, domestic investment projects of under 200 million yuan. By doing so the provinces were acting against formal central rules regarding their approval jurisdiction of investment projects.[5] Interestingly, even though the provinces clearly acted beyond the prescription of central rules, the centre did not utter a word, thereby tacitly acquiescing in this 'illegal' behaviour. Even more interestingly, when the centre later became concerned about excess investment and the prospect of 'overheating' in the economy in 1993, its disapproval was still starkly ambivalent.[6] A central government official's comments are revealing in this respect:

We have recently been studying the meaning and implications of the [State Council] Notice on provincial governments' investment approval authority . . . Regarding the reference to subdelegation of authority, our judgement is that the notice definitely means that local governments at various levels should not further delegate their existing authorities to lower levels, but nothing is said about the propriety of the *status quo*, that is, the discretionary, or deviational, expansion of provincial government authority to under 200 million yuan, and the subsequent subdelegation to city and lower levels. Therefore the *status quo* can probably continue. In other words, provincial-level governments can continue to approve projects under 200 million yuan. What is the implication of the notice for the legitimacy of the approval decisions made earlier by local governments beyond their formal limit of jurisdiction? This is absolutely not an issue here. The notice has left them untouched.[7]

It is worth noting that the centre initially moved in 1992 to recognize formally the legality of the provincial practice regarding approval authority, but subsequently chose to do nothing.[8] By 1994 the economic situation had changed and the centre, whilst determined to have a fast economic growth rate, was increasingly worried about the 'overheating' of the economy as a result of the investment boom since 1992. In acting to stamp out excessive investment, the centre failed, however, to specify exactly what kind of behaviour was really problematic and needed correction. The above remarks by a central official illustrate the ambivalence even of an ostensibly sternly worded order. It was thus difficult to distinguish what was legal and legitimate from what was otherwise.

Notwithstanding the dominance of ambiguity in central–provincial interactions, a new trend was nevertheless emerging. As long as central–provincial politics revolved around resources, ambivalence could serve both the provinces and the centre well. The indeterminancy of one's rights and privileges did not matter as long as one got the desired resources. However, as the objective of both the centre and the provinces gradually shifted away from resources to the demarcation of authority, this change of objective called for a different tactic in interactions. There would still be bargaining, but the context and content of bargaining would change substantially. Success and failure in the power game no longer depended as much as before upon one's ability to manipulate ambivalence. Of increasing importance was one's ability to define and clarify the boundaries of jurisdiction to one's advantage, and make it binding on the other parties. This task necessitated a greater regard for laws and regulations and for a more institutionalized manner of interacting.[9] In other words, despite the initial effectiveness of the manipulation of ambiguity in winning resources, both the centre and the two provincial governments of Guangdong and Shanghai finally felt the need for the law in order to protect the hard-won results of their bargaining efforts from the encroachment of the other party.

TOWARD A POLITCS OF COMPROMISE

The move towards institutionalization in central–provincial relations during the 1990s was a result of intense conflicts between the centre and the provinces originating in the 1980s. The centre saw itself as losing out to the provinces as a result of its earlier decentralization programme, and was desperate to regain control. The provinces regarded themselves as unfairly treated by the centre, who penalized them for doing what had previously been encouraged and, indeed, assigned to them. The forces behind the trend towards institutionalization were therefore the centre and the provincial governments themselves. Both being dissatisfied with the *status quo*, they each looked for change in order to improve their situations.

There was, therefore, no single winner or loser in the conflicts between the centre and the provinces. It was not a case of the centre losing out to the provinces, or of the provinces losing out to the centre. On the one hand, there was undoubtedly a clear trend of diffusion of resources from the central level to the provincial and lower levels of government. Attempts by the centre to rein in excessive provincial discretion were increasingly ineffective. In this respect it would appear that the centre lost and the provinces gained. However, it was also true that the provinces were operating under the constant threat of central interference in their delegated jurisdictions. From the provincial perspective, their new tasks in the changed environment of reform had not been balanced by appropriate changes to their authority and resources. In practice, both the centre and the provinces saw themselves as the 'loser' in the relationship. The centre complained of its weakening capacity to preside over the increasingly assertive and, from its point of view, irresponsible provinces. The provinces wondered how they were to fulfil the assigned task of reform and development with so little authority and support from the centre.

A situation of a 'negative-sum' game is necessary to produce the impetus for change. Changes occur when both parties locked in conflict simultaneously perceive a gain on their own part by achieving such changes, at which time the relationship becomes one of 'positive sum'. Fig. 8.1 depicts the process of change in the relationship from a situation of 'negative sum' to one of 'positive sum'. This is a dynamic process of change, resulting from changing perceptions of one's fortunes in the interaction with the other party over time. Changes in perceptions may be a result of changes in the external environment, or

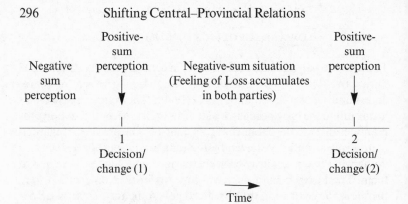

FIG. 8.1. The process of change

due to the differential ability of actors in manoeuvres, which together constitute the unintended consequences of decisions made at an earlier point in time. As a consequence of such changes, the *status quo* arising from previous decisions becomes increasingly unacceptable, and eventually a new deal is struck between the actors. This new decision enables both parties to improve their situation.

Such dynamic changes are inconceivable in the framework of a zero-sum relationship. A zero-sum situation means that one party gains to the extent that the other party loses. In so far as the party who gains is thus satisfied with its situation, it will not force change, other than in a direction that increases its gains. The loser, being dissatisfied with its situation, constitutes a potential force for change. However, as the loser it has diminishing power within the system, so that it is less likely to be able to change the course of events and become an actual force of change. Changes in a zero-sum situation can thus run only in a unilinear direction, as cumulative additions to the gains of the winning party. More radical or 'qualitative' changes rely on *ad hoc* factors beyond the zero-sum framework, for instance a change of heart by the winner.

Using an implicit zero-sum framework, some analysts have discussed the possibility of a trend towards national disintegration in China.[10] While their conclusions vary as regards the prospects of disintegration, such differences are more a matter of judgement regarding the extent to which the forces of fragmentation in the provinces might overwhelm the integrating forces of the centre. Central–provincial relations in China are, therefore, seen as being trapped in a paradox of highly centralized control *vis-à-vis* fragmentation and dis-integration. Either the system will continue on its path towards increasing fragmentation, to the point of dissolving the Chinese nation, or the centre will choose to use its superior coercive power to crush the centrifugal forces once and for all. The system might then relapse into a situation involving a high degree of centralized control, as in the past. Changes beyond these two static poles are inconceivable in a zero-sum framework of central–provincial relations.

Against these analyses this study has provided evidence that relationships between the centre and the provinces do not constitute a zero-sum game. It is not zero-sum because, contrary to the assumption of a zero-sum framework, power does not flow in a single direction. As this study has shown, both the centre and the provinces were actors exerting influence over each other, and their relationship was interactive rather than simply top-down or bottom-up. This mutual influence provided the necessary context for compromise. Despite the concern of the dissatisfied centre for enhancing its control, it was nevertheless obliged to use its superior organizational power with restraint. It had to be highly selective in flexing its muscles at the provinces, since excessive use of coercion would bring a diminishing return of desirable results, and could be counterproductive in its effects on the political legitimacy of the regime in the long run. Similarly, there was a broad gap between dissatisfaction amongst the provinces over authority and resources and any move towards secessionist disintegration. Provinces could be both 'loyal' to the existence of a central authority and enthusiastic in pursuing deviations and expanding their autonomous jurisdiction.

What has occurred in China since reform, therefore, indicates the emergence of a politics of compromise between the centre and the provinces. As a result of the intense conflicts they experienced, which have led some analysts to contemplate the possibility of China disintegrating, the centre and the provinces have been forced, albeit gradually, to acknowledge that the best way to advance their respective interests is through institutionalizing their new relationship. Institutionalization would provide a regularized avenue through which to arbitrate conflicts, and require, as well as result in, a clearer delineation of jurisdiction and better observance of rules and regulations. This rezoning of authority would assuage the centre by preventing unruly provinces from chasing resources whilst shirking responsibilities. Specifically, the burden of the senior central leadership, which has

become overloaded by the necessity of presiding over increasingly intense conflicts between provincial and central units, might thereby be
ameliorated. For the provinces, institutionalization of their authority
would ward off unwelcome central intervention, as well as enable
them to keep safe the resources and authority they have already obtained. By reaching a compromise, the centre and the provinces both
stand to gain in a 'positive-sum' relationship.

WIDER RAMIFICATIONS: TENTATIVE THOUGHTS

It is likely that the central–provincial interface will become the breakthrough point for a qualitative change in the political processes within
the Chinese system. The core characteristic of the Chinese political
system, placed in the context of the modern era, is its low level of institutionalization of power. The Socialist Revolution of 1949 substantially expanded the scope and the depth of state power, which Tang
Tsou describes as 'totalism',[11] but the problem of low institutionalization has remained. To an extent this problem has been accentuated by
the radicalism of the revolution, which saw institutionalization as an
enemy to its continuing progress. The expansion of state activity also
made the deficiency in institutionalization more important in terms of
its repercussions. During imperial times, any negative effects of
insufficient institutionalization were tempered by the ethos of the
mandarinate in favour of a limited government, which ordained that
the monarch should simply reign, but not rule, for the best governance
of his people. This ethos was completely reversed after 1949, if not before, as the 'modernizing' government had to lead the entire nation,
down to the grassroots level, towards a new way of life. The confusion
over power and responsibilities amongst the constituent parts of the
state—a noted feature of low-level institutionalization—has since resulted in numerous conflicts between the different state actors embarking on their new duties. Whilst the level of conflict was low during
the imperial period, due to the low level of state activity, conflicts
snowballed as the socialist state took over all the major activities
within society.

A number of analysts have elaborated on the linkage between the
low level of institutionalization of the political system and the difficulties of governance of the socialist government.[12] They have rightly
pointed out that in order for such difficulties in policy implementation

and interest reconciliation to be resolved, a change towards a higher level of institutionalization is required. To move towards institutionalization requires all actors in the political system simultaneously to abandon the perception of political conflicts as necessarily constituting a 'total victory, total failure' situation, and to adopt a new politics of compromise.[13] The unanswered question is one of *how* this change, this 'historic compromise' between the 'warring' parties, may be effected.

It is towards answering this previously unanswered question that this study makes its contribution, by showing that such a change is likely to occur first of all at the central–provincial interface. A breakthrough is possible because the centre and the provinces, though engaging in perpetual conflict, are ultimately interdependent. The intensity of central–provincial conflicts forces both the central and provincial actors to search for new ways to handle their relationship, and thus further to enhance their respective interests. Their mutual indispensability and long-term co-existence require each to recognize the interests of the other and to seek compromise. This interdependency, and in particular the indispensability of the provincial governments to the centre as its intermediary, gives the central–provincial interface an obvious advantage relative to state–society confrontation in the control of the arbitrary exercise of power.

Changes do not come, therefore, because some central leaders are wise enough to design a new relationship with the provinces. Rules and regulations, as the centre and the provinces have gradually come to recognize, can protect one party whilst constraining the other, as long as both parties observe the rules. One's power is first to be delineated, and thus limited, in order that it can be protected from encroachment. As a result of their experience in the 1980s, both sides have seen themselves as the loser and therefore vulnerable to the encroachment of the other. The centre and the provinces are therefore well placed in the political system to see the dialectical utility of restricting their own power in order to restrict the power of the other, thus enhancing their own power as a result.

NOTES

1. Barry Naughton (1987: 78) argued that the centre had been acting with one hand tied behind its back as a result of its reform intentions, which required devolution of power to the provinces and enterprises. See Chap. 1 for more discussion on the problem of such an interpretation.

2. This ability of the lower levels to extract concessions from superiors has been noted by Lucian Pye (1981*a*: 20) in his discussion of 'the comfort of dependency'.

3. This is reflected in open articulations by central and provincial officials. For articulations by central government officials, see Gu Guoxin (1989: 4–7). Gu was an official from the State Planning Commission. For articulations by Shanghai officials, see Mou Shide and Wu Guoqing (1989); Dong Dingrong and Zhou Xiaoyun (1992). For articulations by Guangdong officials, see Li Chunhong and Wu Yixin (1991); The Project Group, 'The Adjustment of Industrial Structure and Deepening Economic System Reforms in Guangdong', in Xiao Ruchuan (1991). For articulations by officials from other provinces, see Xu Fengchao and Zhang Tianping (1989).

4. See Mou Shide and Wu Guoqing (1989: 13); The Project Group, 'The Adjustment of Industrial Structure', 259. Both articles, from Shanghai and Guangdong respectively, stressed the need for legal protection of the demarcation of jurisdiction of the central and local governments. In a work adopting a centralist theme, there is a similar call for the demarcation arrangements to be written into the constitution. See Wang Shaoguang and Wu Angang (1993: 168).

5. According to the rules, provinces are allowed to approve projects of up to 30 million yuan only, and in the case of 'bottleneck' projects, i.e., those infrastructural and energy projects specified by the centre, up to 50 million yuan. Projects above these ceilings up to 200 million yuan require the approval of the State Planning Commission and projects of over 200 million yuan have to go to the State Council.

6. The State Council issued a notice on 29 January 1994 ordering the strengthening of the macro-adjustment of investment in the country. The notice denounced the excessive growth of investment in 1993 and called for a halt to discretionary subdelegation of project approval authority beyond what had been approved by the centre. It did not, however, categorically announce the 'new' power which many provincial governments had been exercising since 1992 to be illegal. See *Guangming Daily*, 30 Jan. 1994, 1.

7. Interview, respondent no. 31, Beijing, Feb. 1994.

8. Interview, respondent no. 31 Beijing, Jan. 1994. This change of mind suggested that the central government had been uncertain about the proper approval jurisdiction of the provinces, and insecure about its ability to recentralize power formally awarded to the provinces. The news regarding a proposal being formulated during the national economic conference of early 1993, to recognize the *de facto* power of provinces by the State Planning Commission, was also reported in *Shanghai Guanli Kexue* 2 (1993): 10.

9. The importance of institutionalization has become the theme of an increasing number of articles since the late 1980s. See for instance Zhu

Xiaoming (1990); Zhang Linghan (1989); Xuan Zhuxi (1992); Mou Shide and Wu Guoqing (1989).

10. See, for instance, Segal (1994), Chang (1992), Joffe (1994), and Goodman (1994).

11. Tang Tsou uses the concept of 'totalism' to describe the high degree of state penetration into society in a political system. Unlike the concept of 'totalitarianism', which assumes that a government which penetrates deeply into society is also 'undemocratic', thus the usual term 'totalitarian dictatorship', Tsou's concept of 'totalism' refers only to the state–society relationship. In other words, it is theoretically possible to have a totalist and yet democratic government, as well as a totalist and dictatorial government. Similarly, 'liberalism', the opposite of 'totalism', can theoretically come with a dictatorial as well as a democratic political institution. For the most recent and comprehensive exposition of this concept of totalism and its use in the analysis of political systems, see Tang Tsou (1994).

12. See Zhao Suisheng (1990); Oksenberg (1993); Jia Hao and Lin Zhimin (1994); Fewsmith (1994).

13. See Tang Tsou (1991: 319).

Appendix: Data Collection

DOCUMENTARY MATERIALS

The documentary materials used in this study can be classified into five general types:

1. national and provincial newspapers;
2. monographs and edited volumes;
3. national and provincial periodicals;
4. statistical information;
5. policy documents, rules and regulations, as well as records of central–provincial communications.

The utility of the different types of materials varies, as each sheds light from a different angle.

In general, information drawn from newspapers serves both to sensitize the researcher to the pertinent issues involved in the subject at an early stage of the research and to provide data on a specific aspect of the subject. At times the information can be very important and revealing. In 1989, for instance, Guangdong's ardent articulation of its views against central retrenchment policies appeared in an article in a provincial newspaper.

Monographs and edited volumes, meanwhile, provide detailed information on pertinent topics. It is not unusual to find important reports written by officials in the provincial and central governments published in the form of monographs or edited books, providing valuable information on the investment administration system as well as on the implementation problems of investment policies and reforms. There has also been an increasing flow of books written from the provincialist perspective. These books, sometimes written and published by senior official sources in the provinces, themselves represent *par excellence* the efforts by the provinces to influence the agenda of national discussion of their work.

Periodicals published by relevant national and provincial units have provided probably the most important source of documentary information in terms of scope and depth. Since nearly all major government units in China publish their own periodicals, this source provides invaluable information regarding the most up-to-date situation in the relevant areas. For instance, the periodicals published by the provincial finance bureaux of the Guangdong and Shanghai governments, as well as by the Ministry of Finance in Beijing, give detailed and revealing information regarding the fiscal system and its operation nationally and in the two provinces. The authors of articles in these periodicals are usually officials of the units publishing the periodicals, so that the articles provide an insightful peek into aspects of their work. A careful combing of these sources can surprise the researcher as to the richness of information available for public scrutiny within an ostensibly 'closed' political system.

Statistical information on investment and fiscal finance provides the necessary context for the interpretative discussion of central and provincial manoeuvres and counter-manoeuvres. In general, statistical information on investment, and to a lesser extent on fiscal finance, abounds, but more specific information, for instance that on the flows of central investment funds to provinces and vice versa, is less readily available. However, specific information of the latter type is pertinent to this study of central–provincial relations. More information of this type has been found in the field for Guangdong than for Shanghai.

The last, but not the least important, type of documentary information is information on relevant national and provincial rules and regulations, as well as on central–provincial communications. There a number of published compendia of national and provincial rules which provide the basic framework of formal policies regarding the operational environment of the two provincial governments. In general information of this kind is quite adequate. Information on central–provincial communications, on the other hand, is scantier. Such information is, however, very important since it points directly at the interface of central policies and provincial discretion. A detailed record of central–provincial communications also illuminates the process of central–provincial bargaining and how deals have been struck. The utility of this kind of source is illustrated by the four volumes of records of central–Guangdong communications between 1979 and 1987, compiled by the Guangdong authorities, and available in the Universities Services Centre, Chinese University of Hong Kong. The availability of this important source on Guangdong enables this study to break through much of the 'black box' in the process of interactions between the central and Guangdong leaders. No similar information on Shanghai is available, however.

INTERVIEWS

Apart from documentary materials, interviews conducted in the field with central officials and with provincial officials in Guangdong and Shanghai have provided important and revealing information. These interviews have been important in four respects. First, some important documentary materials which were otherwise unavailable were obtained only through these interviews. Secondly, the interviews enabled the author to clarify, confirm or elucidate information contained in documentary materials. Thirdly, discussions in interviews alerted the author to pertinent documentary information which would otherwise have remained 'buried' in the vast quantity of materials.

Fourthly, interviews produced new information which was not available in the documentary materials. An important area of information for which the author has relied heavily on interviews is the process of central–provincial bargaining and interactions. Another important area concerns the considerations and strategies used by the provincial governments in handling their relationship with the Centre. Interviews were also pertinent to understanding the 'grey areas' of legitimacy regarding provincial discretionary behaviour—for instance, by getting information from central government respondents regarding the 'informal' interpretation of formal central rules and policies.

I made three trips to Guangzhou, the provincial capital of Guangdong, in 1993, and two to Shanghai in 1994. From October 1993 to August 1994 I lived in Beijing and was able to conduct quite a few interviews with the relevant authorities. Altogether there have been about fifty face-to-face interviews with over forty different individuals, supplemented by follow-up telephone conversations. On the whole, the officials I contacted were very helpful. The level of contact was mostly at the middle level of the hierarchy in a government department. Officials I interviewed generally had a very good knowledge of how policies were worked out and implemented. As the ones who were actually responsible for the 'implementation' of policies, they provided details of how the system actually worked. Nevertheless, the subject of central–provincial bargaining is a very sensitive one, and getting information on the bargaining process is extremely difficult. Provincial leaders were loath to reveal their bargaining details since these might embarrass and annoy the centre, thus jeopardizing their future relations with the centre. They also might not have wanted to reveal details because if the province had been the loser in its past bargaining with the centre, revelations would only put the province in a poor light.[1]

In Guangdong I was able to conduct interviews with officials involved in planning, finance, statistics, auditing, taxation, land administration and banking, as well as with members of the local academic community. The ranks of officials interviewed ranged from the division-chief level to section level of a provincial department. Impressions gathered from these interviews suggest the development of a fairly open attitude within the provincial bureaucracy. In general Guangdong's officials displayed good sense and independent judgement, and appeared to feel quite comfortable and confident in using discretion as to whether a particular piece of information could be released.

In Shanghai, interviews were conducted with officials from streams spanning finance, planning, Pudong administration, banking and policy research, as well as with members of universities and independent researchers in the burgeoning 'private sector' of research consultancy. The range of rank of the officials was similar to that of Guangdong. Shanghai's officials were, however, generally more cautious than their Guangdong counterparts. They showed less willingness to use discretion over the dissemination of information. Their analytical capacity was impressive, however. As long as one could break the ice, they were willing to talk and could be very helpful. Shanghai's officials often had rather strong feelings concerning their relationship with the centre. They were also inclined to compare their situation with that of Guangdong, pointing to the preferential treatment Guangdong had received ahead of them and to the prospect of Shanghai overtaking Guangdong in the near future. In some respects, the latter was regarded as already accomplished.

Interviews in Beijing focused on more or less the same group of institutions. These included finance, planning, auditing, policy research, law and the universities. The range of the rank of officials was similar to those in Guangdong and Shanghai. Most were of the division-chief rank, with some higher and some lower. The purpose of the interviews was to obtain information on the centre's side of the story. The focus of the interviews was threefold. First, questions were asked regarding information on relevant central policies, especially those 'informal' policies which existed beyond the letter of the formal rules and regulations. These usually involved interpretations of the formal rules which were adopted by the central officials in their interactions with the provinces, and were material in defining which specific discretionary actions by provinces were tolerated or considered deviant by the centre. Secondly, questions were directed to obtain the centre's assessment regarding the implementation of relevant central policies by the Shanghai and Guangdong governments, and by other provinces in general, and the difficulties which the centre had experienced in imposing its will. Thirdly, questions were asked regarding the centre's previous actions, as well as plans of action, in view of the above difficulties caused by the provinces. Questions were also asked on the process of bargaining between the centre and the provinces.

In general the interviews in Beijing were very useful in shedding light on the difficulties experienced by the centre in imposing its will on the provinces. But officials at the centre generally did not know much about the workings of the provinces. Except for those who had previous experience of working in the provinces, most respondents elaborated on the difficulties of the centre and the contradictions of the existing system. Moreover, most respondents from Beijing appeared to have adopted an implicitly centrist perspective. Some were adamant that the provinces should be reined in for their 'unscrupulous' behaviour. Others were more resigned to provincial power and unruliness. Officials at the centre were obviously, and understandably, more concerned with maintaining the predominance of the centre than were officials in Shanghai and Guangdong. Some even expressed a conspicuous sense of cultural or intellectual superiority over the provinces. As a result they expressed a predisposition to exerting control in a traditional way, although they also recognized that any such attempt would probably be futile. On the occasions when such attempts have failed, they have had no option but to work out alternative measures together with the provinces. The *affective inclination* of central officials is therefore for centralization and control, but this has become an increasingly difficult task, now that the provinces have accumulated power as a result of the successive decentralization programmes of the centre. The overall impression that arises from the interviews is this: the forces of 'qualitative' change in the relations between centre and provinces, from fragmentation to legitimate autonomy, reside more within the provinces than within the centre. The centre is, more and more, being forced to seek compromises with the provinces.

NOTES

1. An example of such sensitive central–provincial bargaining is negotiations over the annual control figures for investment. The centre wanted to keep the information confidential not because of national security considerations, but because the centre did not like provinces to know how others had fared, so as to prevent provinces from exerting pressure on the centre based on what the centre had or had not done to other provinces (respondent no. 29, interview, Beijing, May 1994). Similarly, provinces normally kept a low profile concerning their success in gaining concessions from the central government so as not to embarrass the centre and reveal their strategies to other provinces (respondent no. 9, interview, Guangzhou, Dec. 1993).

Bibliography

MAJOR CHINESE MATERIALS

Almanac of Chinese Finance and Banking (various years), ed. Zhongguo Jinrong Xuehui, Beijing: Zhongguo Jinrong Nianjian Bianjibu.

Bai Yang, Wu Zhihui, and Lin Tinglie (1992), *Jihua Yu Shichang* (The Plan and the Market: Thoughts on the Socialist Market Economy), Guangzhou: Guangdong Higher Education Press.

Bao Youde (1988), 'Shenhua Caizheng Gaige, Zhenxing Shanghai Jingji' (Deepening the Fiscal and Tax Reform, Vitalize Shanghai's Economy), *Shanghai Jingji* 2 (Mar.): 5–8.

—— (1989), 'Dangqian Caizheng de Kunnan Yu Chulu' (The Current Fiscal Situation: Difficulties and the Way Out), *Shanghai Jihua Jingji Tansuo* 7 (Dec.): 1–6.

Bo Guili (1988), *Jinxiandai Difang Zhengfu Bijiao* (A Comparative Study of Contemporary and Modern Local Governments), Beijing: Guangming chubanshe.

—— (1991), *Zhongyang Yu Difang Guanxi Yanjiu* (A Study of Central–Local Relations), Changchun: Jilin University Press.

Bo Yibo (1993), *Ruogan Zhongda Juece yu Shijian de Huigu* (Looking Back at some Important Decisions and Events), 2 parts, Beijing: CCP Central Party Academy Press.

Cai Laixing (1990), 'Kaifang Pudong, Kaifa Pudong, Zhenxing Shanghai' (Open Pudong, Develop Pudong, Revitalize Shanghai), *Shanghai Jihua Jingji Tansuo* 3 (June): 1–6.

—— *et al.* (1989), '123 Hao Wen Guanche Qingkuang Pouxi' (An Anatomy of the Implementation Status of the Report No. 123), *Shanghai Jihua Jingji Tansuo* 2 (Mar. Special Issue): 2–14.

CCP [Chinese Communist Party] (Central Committee) (1993), *Zhonggong Zhongyang Guanyu Jianli Shenhuizhuyi Shichang Jingji Tizhi Ruogan Wenti de Jueding* (Decision of the Chinese Communist Party Central Committee on Issues concerning the Establishment of a Socialist Market Economic Structure), Beijing: Renmin chubanshe.

Chan Menzhi (1985), 'Shanghai Jingji Fazhan Zhanlue Cuoyi' (A Preliminary Deliberation on the Development Strategy of Shanghai's Economy), in Zhongguo Gongye he Diqu Jingji Fazhan Zhanlue Yanjiu Lunwenji Editorial Group, *Zhongguo Gongye he Diqu Jingji Fazhan Zhanlue Yanjiu Lunwenji* (A Collection of Essays on the Development Strategies of China's Industries and Regional Economy), Beijing: Jingji Guanli chubanshe, 324–41.

Chan Menzhi (ed.) (1985), *Shanghai Jingji Fazhan Zhanlue Yanjiu* (A Study of Shanghai's Economic Development Strategy), Shanghai: Shanghai Renmin chubanshe.

Chan Xiangli (1989), 'Tiaozheng Yiding Yao Cong Shiji Chufa' (Adjustment Must be Based on the Actual Circumstances), *China Capital Construction* 5 (May): 4–5.

Chen Dongqi *et al.* (1988), 'Local Government Behaviour and its Mechanism Reform', *China's Industrial Economics Research*, 3 (June): 16–24.

Cui Laifu (1989), 'Shanghai Zijin de Xianzhuang, Wenti Yu Duice' (Shanghai's Capital Supply: Present Situation, Issues and Solutions), *Shanghai Economic Review* 4 (July): 46–52.

Dangdai Zhongguo Congshu Bianji Bu (1985), *Dangdai Zhongguo de Jingji Guanli* (The Economic Management of Contemporary China), Beijing: Zhongguo Shehui Kexue chanbanshe.

—— (1988), *Dangdai Zhongguo Caizheng* (The Fiscal Finance of Contemporary China), 2 vols., Beijing: Zhongguo Shehui Kexue chunanshe.

—— (1989*a*), *Dangdai Zhongguo de Guding Zichan Touzi Guanli* (The Administration of Fixed Asset Investment in Contemporary China), Beijing: Zhongguo Shehui Kexue chubanshe.

—— (1989*b*), *Dangdai Zhongguo de Jiben Jianshe* (Capital Construction in Contemporary China), 2 vols., Beijing: Zhongguo Shehui Kexue chubanshe.

—— (1989*c*), *Dangdai Zhongguo de Tongji Shiye* (Statistical Work in Contemporary China), Beijing: Zhongguo Shehui Kexue chubanshe.

—— (1991), *Dangdai Zhongguo de Guangdong* (Guangdong in Contemporary China), 2 vols., Beijing: Dangdai Zhongguo chubanshe.

—— (1993), *Dangdai Zhongguo de Shanghai* (Shanghai in Contemporary China), 2 vols., Beijing: Dangdai Zhongguo chubanshe.

Deng Xiaoping (1993), *Deng Xiaoping Wenxuan* (Selected Works of Deng Xiaoping), vol. 3, Beijing: Renmin chubanshe.

Deng Yingtao *et al.* (1990), *Zhongguo Yusuanwai Zijin Fenxi* (An Analysis of the Extrabudgetary Funds), Beijing: People's University of China Press.

Deng Zhijiang (1989), 'Guangdongsheng Guding Zichan Touzi Qingli de Qingkuang, Wenti ji Duice' (The Review of Fixed Asset Investment in Guangdong: The Situation, Problems and Solutions), *Jihua Yu Fazhan* 5 (Oct.): 40–1, 45.

Difang Zhengquan Yanjiu Editorial Group (1986), *Difang Zhengquan Yanjiu* (A Study of Political Authority at the Local Level), Chongqing: Junzhong chubanshe.

Dong Dingrong and Zhou Xiaoyun (1992), 'Gaige Zhongyang Yu Difang Shuishou Guanli Quanxian de Jidian Sikao' (Several Thoughts on Reforming the Tax Management Jurisdiction of the Central and Local Governments), *Shanghai Caishui* 11 (Nov.): 14–17.

Fan Gang (1993), *Jianjin Zi Lu* (The Incremental Path: An Economic Analysis of Economic Reforms), Beijing: Zhongguo Shehui Kexue chubanshe.
—— et al. (1990), *Gongyouzhi Hongguan Jingji Lilun Dagang* (A Sketch of Macro-Economic Theories under a Public Ownership System), Shanghai: Shanghai United Bookstore Press.
Fan Yongming (1992), *Zhongguo de Gongyehua Yu Waiguo Zhijie Touzi* (Industrialization and Foreign Direct Investment in China), Shanghai: Shanghai Academy of Social Sciences Press.
Fang Weizhong (ed.) (1984), *Zhonghua Renmin Gongheguo Jingji Dashiji, 1949–1980* (The Major Economic Events in the Peoples' Republic of China, 1949–1980), Beijing: Zhongguo Shehui Kexue chubanshe.
Gao Shanquan *et al.* (1984), *Dangdai Zhongguo de Jingji Tizhi Gaige* (Current Reforms in the Economic Structure in China), Beijing: Zhongguo Shehui Kexui chubanshe.
Gong Xiangrui (ed.) (1993), *Fazhi de Lixiang Yu Xianshi* (Ideal and Practice of the Rule of Law), Beijing: Zhengfa Daxue chubanshe.
Gu Guoxin (1989), 'Zhongyang Yu Difang Zhengfu Jingji Shiquan Huafen Zhi Wojian' (My View on the Demarcation of Economic Management Authority of Central and Local Government), *China Administration* 8 (Aug.): 4–7.
Gu Xingquan (1992), 'Pudong Xinqu Caizheng Zhengce de Xinyi Ji Tezheng' (The Characteristics and New Aspects of Pudong's Fiscal and Tax Policies), *Pudong Development* 3 (Mar.): 12-13.
—— (1994a), 'Dahao Zhengti Gaige de Guanjian Zhanyi' (Fight the Key Battle of Comprehensive Reform Well: A Preliminary Discussion of the Fiscal and Tax Reforms), *Shanghai Reform* 3 (Mar.): 7–9, 31.
—— (1994b), 'Fenshuizhi de Tansuo Yu Xuanze' (Probes and Choices concerning the Tax-Sharing System), *Shanghai Caishui* 3 (Mar.): 10–11, 31.
Guangdong Commission for Economic System Reform (1989), 'Guanyu Guangdongsheng Zijin "Tiwai Xunhuan" de Fenxi' (An Analysis of 'Underground Capital Circulation' in Guangdong), *Jihua Yu Fazhan* 4 (Aug.): 12–19.
Guangdong Jingji Xuehui (1986), *Guangdong Jingji Tizhi Gaige Yanjiu* (A Study of the Economic System Reform in Guangdong), Guangdong: Zhongshan University Press.
Guangdong People's Government and Provincial Commission for Economic System Reform (1988), *Jingji Tizhi Gaige Wenjian Huibian, 1986–1988* (A Compendium of Economic System Reform Documents, 1986–1988), Guangdong: Neibu.
Guangdong Provincial Party Committee (Secretariat) (1986–8), *Zhongyang Dui Guangdong Gongzuo Zhishi Huibian* (A Collection of Central Government's Instructions for the Work of the Guangdong Provincial Government), 4 vols., Guangdong: Neibu.

310 Bibliography

Guangdong Provincial Party Committee (Secretariat) (1993), *Guangdong Gaige Kaifang Qishi Lu* (A Record of Insights into Opening and Reforms in Guangdong), Beijing: Renmin chubanshe.

Guandong Statistical Bureau (1985–93), *Guangdongsheng Guding Zichan Touzi Tongji Ziliao* (Guangdong's Fixed Asset Investment Statistical Information), annual (vols.) Guangdong: not openly published.

—— (1989*a*), *Guangdongsheng Guomin Jingji he Shehui Fazhan Tongji Ziliao, 1949–1988: Guding Zichan Touzi Bufen* (Statistical Information on Guangdong's National Economic and Social Development, 1949–1988: Part on Fixed Asset Investment), Guangdong: Neibu.

—— (1989*b*), *Guangdongsheng Guomin Jingji he Shehui Fazhan Tongji Ziliao, 1949–1988: Pingheng Tongji Bufen* (Statistical Information on Guangdong's National Economic and Social Development, 1949–1988: Part on General Statistics), Guangdong: Neibu.

Gui Shiyong (ed.) (1987), *Lun Zhongguo Hongguan Jingji Guanli* (On the Macro-Management of China's Economy), Beijing: Zhongguo Jingji chubanshe.

—— (1991), *Xianshi Yu Jueze: Lai Zi Guojia Jiwei Jingji Yanjiu Zhongxin de Baogao* (The Reality and the Choice: A Report from the State Planning Commission), Shanghai: Shanghai Renmin chubanshe.

—— (ed.) (1993), *Hongguan Jingji Yu Juece: Lai Zi Guojia Jiwei Jingji Yanjiu Zhongxin de Baogao* (The Macro-Economy and Policy Making: A Report from the State Planning Commission, Shanghai: Shanghai Renmin chubanshe.

Han Shaochu (ed.) (1993), *Shuishou Jianmian Zhengce Yu Guanli* (The Policy and Administration of Tax Reduction and Exemption), Beijing: Zhongguo Wuzi chubanshe.

He Gaosheng *et al.* (1984), 'Shanghai Jingji Tizhi de Lishi Yange' (Shanghai's Economic System Reforms: a Historical Chronology), 3 parts, *Shanghai Jingji Kexue* 5 (May): 19–26; 6 (June): 21–4; 7 (July): 23-33.

Huang Guanjiu (1994), 'Fenshuizhi Bieyi' (An Alternative View on the Tax-Sharing System), *Guangdong Caizheng* 1 (Jan.): 10–13.

Huang Haichao *et al.* (1993), *Mengxiang Chengzhen* (The Realization of Dreams: Guangdong Advancing to the Market Economy), Guangzhou: South China University of Technology Press.

Huang Kuanwei *et al.* (1988), 'A Review of the Reforms of Guangdong's Planning Systems', *Jihua Yu Fazhan* 1 (Feb.): 8–12.

Huang Qifan (1992), 'Shanghai Pudong Xinqu Touzi Kaifa de Zhengce Tedian' (The Specialities of Pudong's Investment Policies), *Pudong Development* 4 (Apr.): 15–17.

—— (1993), 'Pudong Kafa: Shanghai Jiancheng Gujihua Dadushi de Xiwangdian' (Pudong Development: The Hope of Building Shanghai into an International Metropolis), *Economic Forecasting* 4 (Dec.): 35.

Huang Weijian (1990), 'Dui Yusuanwai Qiye Ruogan Wenti de Sikao' (Thoughts on some Issues concerning the Extrabudgetary Enterprises), *Jihua Jingji Yanjiu* 7 (July): 59–62.

Jiang Jian and Lin Yaoping (1992), 'On the Implementation Deviations of Tax Policies in China', *Guangdong Taxation* 5 (May): 6–10.

Jiang Weiguo *et al.* (1994), 'Fenshuizhi Tiaojianxia Qu Caizheng Tizhi Yanjiu' (A Study of Fiscal System at the District Level under the Tax-Sharing System), *Shanghai Reform* 3 (Mar.): 10–13.

Jiang Yiwei (1985), *Jingji Tizhi Gaige He Qiye Guanli Ruogan Wenti de Tantao* (Probing into some Issues of the Economic System Reform and Enterprise Management), Shanghai: Shanghai Renmin chubanshe.

Jiang Zemin (ed.) (1989), *Shanghai Jingji Tizhi Gaige Shinian* (Ten Years of Economic Reform in Shanghai), Shanghai: Shanghai Renmin chubanshe.

—— (1992), 'Speeding up Reform and Opening and the Pace of Modernization Construction: Grasping a Bigger Victory in Building Socialism with Chinese Characteristics', *Qiushi* 21: 2–21.

Jin Wen (1988), 'Qieshi Jiajiang Shanghai Fazhan Waixiangxing Jingji de Yanjiu' (Strengthening Research Efforts on How to Develop Shanghai's Externally Oriented Economy), *Shanghai Jihua Jingji Tansuo* 2 (Apr.): 1–13.

—— (1992), 'Yao Qieshi Jiajiang Shiji Jianshe Zijin de Hongguan Guanli' (To Strengthen Substantially the Macro-Management of Shanghai's Investment Capital), *Shanghai Jihua Jingji Tansuo* 1 (Feb.): 4–6.

Ke Tizuo (1994), 'Fenshuizhi de Tansuo Yu Xuanze' (Probes and Choices concerning the Tax-Sharing System), *Shanghai Caishui* 2 (Feb.): 8–14.

Ke Xiaoxing (1989), 'Difang Zhengfu Touzi Pingjia' (An Assessment of Local Government Investment), *Touzi Lilun Yu Shijian* 1 (Jan.): 25–7.

Labour and Personnel Ministry (1985), *Zhonghua Renmin Gongheguo Zuzhi Fagui Xuanbian* (A Compendium of the Organization Laws and Regulations of the People's Republic of China), Beijing: Jingji Kexue chubanshe.

Lei Pushi and Wu Jinglian (eds.) (1988), *Lun Zhongguo Jingji Tizhi Gaige de Jincheng* (Debating the Progress of China's Economic System Reform), Beijing: Jingji Kexue chubanshe.

Leung Kwaichuen *et al.* (1992), *Qifei de Guiji: Guangdong Jingji Fazhan Shizheng Fenxi* (The Track of Rising Economy: A Sample Analysis of Guangdong's Economic Development), Guangzhou: Guangdong Renmin chubanshe.

Li Chunhong and Wu Yixin (1991), 'Guanyu Jianli Fencengci Hongguan Tiaokong Tixi de Gouxiang' (Thoughts on Establishing a Multi-Layered Macro-Management System), *Social Sciences in Guangdong* 3: 101–7.

Li Fan and Zheng Xiaohe (1991), *Zhongguo Touzi Zhuti Ji Qi Touzi Xingwei Yanjiu* (A Study of Investment Actors and their Investment Behaviour in China), Beijing: not openly published.

Li Huan (1990), 'Guangdong Touzi Guimo Jiegouxing Pengzhang Fenxi' (An

Analysis of the Structural Expansion of Investment in Guangdong), *Jihua Yu Fazhan* 4 (Aug.): 54–8.

Li Weiwu (1994), 'Tairan Renshi Fenshuizhi' (Understanding the Tax-Sharing System Calmly), *Guangdong Caizheng* 2 (Feb.): 20–1.

Li Zhaoyong (1990), 'The Capital Problem in the Development of the Externally Oriented Economy of the Special Economic Zones', *Theory and Practice of the Special Economic Zone* 4 (Aug.): 58–61.

Lin Qiushi (1984), 'Dui Guding Zichan Buchang Gengxin de Yixie Kanfa' (Some Opinions on the Replacement and Renovation of Fixed Asset Investment), *Shanghai Caizheng Yanjiu* 1 (Jan.): 10–12.

Lin Senmu and Jiang Guangxin (eds.) (1992), *Zhongguo Jiben Jianshe Gongzuo Shouce* (Handbook of Capital Construction Investment in China), Beijing: Fazhan chubanshe.

Lin Zhengbo (1990), 'A Preliminary Analysis of the Rule-Abating Behaviour of Local Finance Departments and some Possible Solutions', *Guangdong Audit* 5 (Oct.): 9–10.

Lin Zhuji (ed.) (1993), *Shenzhen Guojixing Chengshi Lunwenji* (A Collection of Essays on Shenzhen Becoming an International City), Beijing: Zhongguuo Jingji chubanshe.

Liu Guoguang *et al.* (ed.) (1988), *Zhongguo Jingji Tizhi Gaige Moshi Yanjiu* (Analysing the Models of China's Economic System Reform), Beijing: Zhongguo Shehui Kexue chubanshe.

Liu Shangxi *et al.* (1993a), 'Caizheng Lilun Chuangxin de Lishi Fenxi' (An Appraisal of the History of the Creativity of Fiscal Theories), *Caizheng Yanjiu* 7 (July): 9–18.

—— (1993b), 'Woguo Caizheng Lilun Gengxin de Lishi Sikao' (Thoughts on the History of the Evolution of China's Fiscal Theories), *Caizheng Yanjiu* 9 (Sept.): 19–26.

Liu Wei *et al.* (1989), *Ziyuan Peizhi Yu Jingji Tizhi Gaige* (Resource Allocation and Economic System Reform), Beijing: Zhongguo Caizheng Jingji chubanshe.

Liu Weiyung *et al.* (1988), *Lun Woguo Touzi Tiji Gaige* (On the Reforms of China's Fixed Asset Investment System), Beijing: Zhongguo Jingji chubanshe.

Liu Zhenghe (1987), 'Preliminary Analysis of the Management of Extra-budgetary Funds', *Jihua Yu Fazhan* 6 (Dec.): 40–2.

Liu Zhongxiu, (ed.) (1991), *Baiwei Xuezhe Dui Shenzhen de Sikao* (Thoughts on Shenzhen by 100 Scholars), Shenzhen: Haitian chubanshe.

Lok Chaopei and Zheng Yanchao (eds.) (1989), *Guangdong Siying Jingji Yanjiu* (A Study of the Private Sector Economy in Guangdong), Beijing: Zhongguo Jingji chubanshe.

Lou Jiwei (1988), 'Ying Bimian Jixu Zou Difang Fenquan de Daolu' (Continuing the Road of Administrative Decentralization should be Avoided), in Wu Jinglian and Zhou Xiaochuan *et al.* (1988), 204–13.

—— (1992), 'Shanghai Jingji Fazhan Zhanlui Xuanze he Gaige Celue' (Reform Strategies and Choices Available for Shanghai's Economic Development Strategy), *Comparative Economic and Social Systems* 1: 10–13.

Lou Rucheng (1987), 'Tantan Ruohe Jiakuai Shanghai "116 Jijian Xianmu" Jianshe Bufa' (On How to Speed Up the Pace of Shanghai's No. 166 Capital Construction Project), *Shanghai Investment* 5 (May): 16–17.

Lou Shengxi *et al.* (1993), 'An Appraisal of the History of Creativity of Fiscal Theories', *Caizheng Yanjin* 7 (July).

Lu Wei (1994), '1994 Nian Caishui Gaige Bingfei Yilu Tantu' (The 1994 Fiscal and Tax Reforms are not a Straight and Trouble-Free Route), *Guangdong Caizheng* 5 (May): 4–6.

Luo Jingfen and Guo Shuqing (eds.) (1993), *Jichu Chanye Jianshe Zijin Chouji* (Capital Mobilization for Infrastructural Construction), Beijing: Jingji Guanli chubanshe.

Ma Hong and Sun Shangqing (eds.) (1992), *Zhongguo de Jingji Xingshi Yu Zhanwang, 1991–1992* (The Economic Situation and Prospects of China, 1991–1992), Beijing: Zhongguo Fazhan chubanshe.

—— (eds.) (1993), *Zhongguo de Jingji Xingshi Yu Zhangwang, 1992–1993* (The Economic Situation and Prospects of China, 1992–1993), Beijing: Zhongguo Fazhan chubanshe.

Ma Qibing *et al.* (1989), *Zhongguo Gongchandang Zhizheng Sishi Nian* (The Chinese Communist Party: Forty Years in Power), Beijing: Zhonggong Dangshi Ziliao chubanshe.

Mao Zedong (1977), *Selected Works of Mao Zedong*, vol. 5, Beijing: Renmin chubanshe.

Ministry of Finance (General Planning Department) (1982), *Zhonghua Renmin Gongheguo Caizheng Shiliao* (Historical Materials on the Fiscal System in the People's Republic of China), vol.1, Beijing: Zhongguo Caizheng chubanshe.

—— (General Planning Department) (1986*a*), *China Finance Statistics (1950–85)*, Beijing: Science Press.

—— (Jiao Yu Shi) (1986*b*), *Zhongguo de Caizheng Gaige* (The Fiscal Reform of China), Beijing: Beijing Daxue chubanshe.

—— (Tiao Fa Shi) (1989), *Zhonghua Renmin Gongheguo Caizheng Fagui Huibian, 1988* (A Compendium of Financial Rules and Regulations of the People's Republic of China, 1988), Beijing: Zhongguo Caizheng Jingji chubanshe.

—— (General Planning Department) (1992), *China Finance Statistics 1950–1991*, Beijing: Science Press.

—— (Research Institute for Fiscal Science) (1993), 'Woguo Zhongchangqi Caizheng Zhengce Quxiang de Yanjiu' (A Study of the Policy Orientations of Medium- to-Long-Term Fiscal Policy), *Caizheng Yanjiu* 3 (Mar.): 14–24, 57.

Mou Shide and Wu Guoqing (1989), 'Cong Shanghai Shijian Kan
Zhongyang Yu Difang Shiquan Huafen' (The Demarcation of Jurisdiction
of the Central and Local Governments: A Perspective from Shanghai's
Practice), *China Administration* 8 (Aug.): 11–13.

National People's Congress (Standing Committee Secretariat, Research
Office) (1992), *Difang Renda Shi Zenyang Xingshi Zhiquan de* (How the
Local People's Congresses Exercise their Authority), Beijing: Zhongguo
Minzhu Fazhi chubanshe.

Ngan Shaoping (1990),' A Preliminary Discussion of the Auditing Work of
Local Fiscal Budgets under the *Dabaogan* Fiscal System', *Guangdong Audit*
4 (Aug.): 16.

Ni Wen (1987), 'New Attempts in the Changes in the Functions of the
Government', *Shanghai Jihua Jingji Tansuo* 2 (Apr.): 48–51.

Pei Guanzhong (1990), *Caizheng Yu Jinrong* (Finance and Banking), Beijing:
Haiyang chubanshe.

Quan Zhiping and Jiang Zuozhong (1992), *Lun Difang Jingji Liyi* (An Analysis
of the Local Economic Interests), Guangzhou: Guangdong Renmin chubanshe.

Ren Zhongping (1994), 'Various Levels Unite in the Reform Breakthroughs
this Year', *People's Daily*, 10 Mar.: 1.

Rong Jingben (1992), 'Zhidu Bianqian he Jingji Fazhan' (Institutional
Changes and Economic Development: A Comparative Perspective on Economic Reforms in China, the Soviet Union and Eastern European Countries', *Comparative Economic and Social Systems* 2: 1–8.

Rui Mingjie and Yu Wenyi (1992), 'Huyue Liangdi Waishang Touzi de Bijiao
Fenxi' (A Comparative Analysis of Foreign Investments in Shanghai and
Guangdong), *Shanghai Investment* 7 (July): 12–13.

Shanghai Applied Statistical Science Institute (1989), 'Shanghai Caizheng
Wenti Tanyuan' (Probing the Roots of the Fiscal Problems of Shanghai),
Shanghai Jihua Jingji Tansuo 5 (Aug.): 52–61.

Shanghai Economic Commission (various years), *Shanghai Gongye Nianjian*
(Shanghai Industry Yearbook) (various years), ed. Shanghai Academy of
Social Sciences, Shanghai: Shanghai Ci shu chubanshe.

Shanghai Economy Yearbook (various years), ed. Shanghai Academy of
Social Sciences, Shanghai: Shanghai Renmin chubanshe.

Shanghai Institute of Economic Development (1994), *Shanghai Jingji Fazhan,
1993* (Shanghai Economic Development, 1993), Shanghai: China Business
Weekly Press.

Shanghai Institute for Economic System Reform (1991), *Jiushi Niandai
Shanghai Gaige de Zhanlue Gouxiang* (Thoughts on the Strategies of
Shanghai's Reforms in the 1990s), Shanghai: not openly published.

Shanghai Planning Commission (1987*a*), 'Zhilingxing Jihua he Zhidaoxing
Jihua Gaige de Huigu Yu Tansuo' (A Review of the Reform of Mandatory
and Indicative Plans), *Shanghai Jihua Jingji Tansuo* 2 (Apr.): 25–34.

—— (1987*b*), 'Zonghe Yunyong Jingji Gangan de Shijian Yu Tansuo' (The Use of Economic Leverage: Probes and Practice), *Shanghai Jihua Jingji Tansuo* 2 (Apr.): 34–43.

Shanghai Statistical Bureau (1989), *Xin Shanghai Sishi Nian* (Forty Years of New Shanghai), Beijing: Zhongguo Tongji chubanshe.

Shanghaishi Jingji Tizhi Gaige Lingdao Xiaozhu [Shanghai Economic System Reform Leading Group] (1985), *Shanghaishi Jingji Tizhi Gaige Wenjian Huibian* (A Compendium of Economic System Reform in Shanghai), part 2, Shanghai: Qiye Guanli Xuehui.

—— (1986), *Shanghaishi Jingji Tizhi Gaige Wenjian Huibian* (A compendium of Economic System Reform in Shanghai), part 4, Shanghai: Qiye Guanli Xuehui.

Shanghaishi Renshi Bu and Shanghaishi Keji Ganbu Ju (1987–8), *Shanghai Renshi Gongzuo Wenjian Xuanbian* (A Compendium of Personnel Documents in Shanghai), 2 vols., Shanghai: Neibu.

Shenzhen City Study Group (1990), 'Pudong de Kaifa Jidui Shenzhen de Qishi' (Pudong's Opening and Development and its Message to Shenzhen), *Theory and Practice of the Special Economic Zone*, 5 (Oct.): 11.

Song Xinzhong (ed.) (1992), *Zhongguo Caizheng Tizhi Gaige Yanjiu* (A Study of Fiscal System Reform in China), Beijing: Zhongguo Caizheng Jingji chubanshe.

State Audit Commission (Finance Audit Bureau) (1994), *Caishui Tizhi Gaige Xueshi Ziliao* (Study Materials on Taxation and Fiscal Reforms), Beijing: Neibu.

State Commission for Economic System Reform (Secretariat) (1983), *Jingji Tizhi Gaige Wenjian Huibian, 1978–1983* (A Collection of Documents on Economic System Reforms, 1978–1983), Beijing: Zhongguo Caizheng Jingji chubanshe.

State Economic Commission (Economic Structure Reform Bureau) (1985), *Zhongguo Jingji Guangli Zhengce Faling Xuanbian, July 1983–June 1984* (A Collection of Policies and Regulations on China's Economic Management, July 1983–June 1984), Beijing: Jingji Kexue chubanshe.

State Planning Commission (Capital Construction (General) Bureau) (1985), *Jiben Jianshe Guanli Tizhi Gaige Wenjian Huibian* (A Collection of Documents on the Capital Construction System Reform), Beijing: Hongqi chubanshe.

—— (Fixed Asset Investments (General) Bureau) (1987*a*), *Jiben Jianshe Fagui Dadian* (A Comprehensive Collection of Rules and Regulations on Capital Construction), 2 vols., Beijing: Hongqi chubanshe.

—— (Regulations Office) (1987*b*), *Zhongyao Jingji Fagui Ziliao Xuanbian, 1977–1986* (A Selected Collection of the Major Economic Regulations 1977–1986), Beijing: Zhongguo Tongji chubanshe.

—— (Economic Research Centre) (1992), *Zhongguo: Jingji Tiaojie de Lilun he Shijian* (The Theory and Practice of Economic Adjustment in China), Beijing: People's University of China Press.

—— (Investment Research Institute) (1993), *Touzi Tizhi Gaige Yanjiu* (A Study on the Reform of the Investment System), Beijing: not openly published.

—— (Investment Research Institute) and State Statistical Bureau (1991), *Zhongguo Touzi Baogao, 1991* (China Investment Report, 1991), Beijing: Zhongguo Jihua chubanshe.

—— (Investment Research Institute) ——(1992), *Zhongguo Touzi Baogao, 1992* (China Investment Report, 1992), Beijing: Zhongguo Jihua chubanshe.

State Statistical Bureau (1982), *Jiben Jianshe Tongji Guanli Xuexi Ziliao* (Study Materials of Capital Construction Statistics and Management), Beijing: Zhongguo Tongji chubanshe.

—— (1986), *Statistics on Investment in Fixed Assets of China*, (1950–85), Beijing: Zhongguo Tongji chubanshe.

—— (1989), *Statistics on Investment in Fixed Assets of China, (1986–7)*, Beijing: Zhongguo Tongji chubanshe.

—— (1991), *Statistics on Investment in Fixed Assets of China (1988–9)*, Beijing: Zhongguo Tongji chubanshe.

—— (1992*a*), *Guding Zichan Touzi he Jianzhuye Wenjian Huibian* (A Compendium of Documents on Fixed Asset Investment and the Construction Industry), Beijing: Zhongguo Tongji chubanshe.

—— (1992*b*), *Quanguo Zhuyao Shehui Jingji Zhibiao Paixu Nianjian, 1992* (The 1992 Yearbook of the Ranking of Provinces in Major Social and Economic Indicators), Beijing: Zhongguo Tongji chubanshe.

—— (1993), *Statistics on Investment in Fixed Assets of China (1990–1991)*, Beijing: Zhongguo Tongji chubanshe.

Statistical Yearbook of China (various years), ed. State Statistical Bureau, Beijing: Zhongguo Tongji chubanshe.

Statistical Yearbook of Guangdong (various years), ed. Guangdong Statistical Bureau, Beijing: Zhongguo Tongji chubanshe.

Statistical Yearbook of Shanghai (various years), ed. Shanghai Statistical Bureau, Beijing: Zhongguo Tongji chubanshe.

Sun Jian (1989), 'Guangdongsheng Yasuo Touzi Guimo Jishi' (A Report of Guangdong's Efforts to Contain its Investment Scale), *China Investment and Construction* 8 (Aug.): 17–18.

Sun Yonghong and Geng Qingjun (1990), '1979–88 Nian Woguo Shiji Niandu Touzi Guimo Pingjia' (An Assessment of the Yearly Investment Scale, 1979–88), *Investment Research* 3 (Sept.): 19–24.

Tan Jian (1989), *Zhongguo Zhengzhi Tizhi Gaige Lun* (On China's Political System Reform), Beijing: Guangming Daily chubanshe.

Tang Chunrong (1989), 'Guangdong Caizheng Shouru Zhan Guomin Shouru Bizhong Xiajiang Yuanyin Jianxi' (A Preliminary Analysis of the

Reasons for the Fall of Fiscal Revenue as a Proportion of National Income in Guangdong), *Jihua Yu Fazhan* 5 (Oct.): 38–9.

Tao Changyuan and Lin Weiting (1984), 'Cong Jianmian Shui Kan Shuishou de Jingji Ganggan Zuoyong' (Tax Alleviation: The Leverage Function of Taxes in the Economy), *Shanghai Caishui Yanjiu* 5 (May): 28–30.

Tian Jianghoi (1992), 'Jiushi Niandian Zhongguo Touzi Renwu Ji Hongguan Tiaokong Zhongdian' (Investment Tasks and Major Targets of Macro-Adjustment in China in the 1990s), in Xue Muqiao and Liu Guogang (1992), 84–98.

Tian Yinong *et al.* (1986), *Lun Zhongguo Caizheng Guanli Tizhi de Gaige* (On China's Fiscal System Reform), Beijing: Economics and Sciences Press.

Tu Jimo (1985), 'A Preliminary Deliberation to Improve the Allocation of Shanghai's Fiscal Resources in the Seventh Five-Year Plan Period', *Shanghai Caizheng Yanjiu* 2 (Feb.): 10–13.

—— (1988), 'Shanghai Caizheng "Huapo" Paoxi' (An Analysis of the Fiscal 'Slides' in Shanghai), *Shanghai Jihua Jingji Tansuo* 1 (Feb.): 47–52.

—— (1990), 'Shanghai Difang Touzi Fangshi de Bianhua Yu Duice' (Approaches to Shanghai's Local Investment: Changes and Solutions), *Shanghai Jihua Jingji Tansuo* 1 (Feb.): 26–31.

Wang Fengling (ed.) (1991), *Guoyou Zichan Chanquan Jieding Wenti Yanjiu* (A Study of the Issues concerning the Demarcation of Property Rights of State-Owned Assets), Beijing: Jingji Kexue chubanshe.

Wang Guangzhen *et al.* (eds.) (1993), *Zhujiang Sanjiao Zhou Jingji Shehui Wenhua Fazhan Yanjiu.* (A Study of the Development of Economic and Social Culture in the Pearl River Delta), Shanghai: Shanghai Renmin chubanshe.

Wang Haibo (1981), 'Guanyu Woguo Jilei Yu Xiaofei Bili Guanxi de Chubu Fenxi' (A Preliminary Analysis of the Accumulation–Consumption Ratio in the People's Republic of China), *Zhejiang Xuekan* 1 (Jan.): 13–27.

—— (ed.) (1990), *Zhongguo Guomin Jingji Gebumen Jingji Xiaoyi Yanjiu* (A Study of the Economic Efficiency of the Various Sectors of the Chinese National Economy), Beijing: Jingji Guanli chubanshe.

Wang Hao (1989), 'Sanshuo, Sanbian' (Three 'Sayings', Three Defences), *Zhongguo Jinbao*, 13 Jan.: 2.

Wang Kunwei (ed.) (1989), *Gaige, Kaifang, Fazhan* (Reform, Opening, Development: a collection of essays from the various annual meetings of the Guangdong Planning Society), Beijing: Zhongguo Jingji chubanshe.

Wang Weijian (1990), 'Thoughts on some Issues concerning the Extrabudgetary Enterprises', *Jihua Jingji Yanjiu* 7: 59–62.

Wang Shaoguang and Wu Angang (1993), *Zhongguo Guojia Nengli Baogao* (A Report on the State Capacity of China), Liaoning: Liaoning Renmin chubanshe.

Wang Xinhua and Wang Yipin (1986), 'Difang Touzi Xingwei Yu Kongzhi

Touzi Guimo' (Local Investment Behaviour and Controlling the Scale of
Investment), *Touzi Yanjiu Ziliao* 21/22 (combined issue): 74–7.

Wang Yaming (1989), 'Guanyu Wanshan Caizheng Baoganzhi de Ruogan
Kanfa' (Some Views on How to Improve the Fiscal *Dabaogan* System),
Jihua Yu Fazhan 6 (Dec.): 14–16.

Wang Zhang (1991), 'Zhongguo Jingji Chengzhangzhong de "Shanghai
Xianxiang" ' (The 'Shanghai Phenomenon' in China's Economic Growth),
Shanghai Gaige 4 (Apr.): 16–17; 5 (May): 14–15, 41; 7 (July): 10–11.

Wang Zhu *et al.* (eds.) (1993), *Zouxiang Shichang: Guoyou Dazhongxing Qiye
Gaige Zhilu* (Marching Towards the Market: The Way Out for the Reform
of Medium-Sized to Large State Enterprises), Shanghai: Shanghai Renmin
chubanshe.

Weng Yi Ran (1993), 'Zhiding Yusuanwai Qiye Guanli Zhidu Kebu
Ronghuan' (The Need for Formulating a Management System for Extrabudgetary Enterprises is Imminent), *Shanghai Audit* 6 (Dec.): 18–19.

Wong Guiying (1989), 'Report on the Preparation of the 1989 National Economic and Social Development Plans of Guangdong Province', *Jihua Yu
Fazhen* 1 (Feb.): 6–12.

Wu Jian and Wang Yongjun (1988), 'Touzi Buzu Lun' (The Theory of Insufficient Investments), *Investment Research* 8 (Aug.).

—— (1989), 'Touzi Buzu Bulun' (The Theory of Insufficient Investments: A
Supplementary Argument), *Investment Research* 8 (Aug.): 17–21.

Wu Jianguo (1994), 'Dui Shishi Caizheng "Zhuanyi Zhifuzhi" de Xianshi
Sikao' (Pragmatic Thoughts on Implementing the Fiscal Transfer Payment
System), *Shanghai Caishui* 3 (Mar.): 12–14.

Wu Jinglian (1991), 'Strategic Issues of China's Economic Reform: Diver-
gences and Choices', in Zhang Zhuoyuan and Wang Fanzhang (1991), 1–24.

—— (ed.) (1992), *1989 Nian Zhongguo Jingji Shikuang Fenxi* (An Analysis of
China's Economic Situation in 1989), Beijing: Zhongguo Shehui Kexue
chubanshe.

—— and Wu Ji (eds.) (1988), *Zhongguo Jingji de Dongtai Fenxi he Duice Yanjiu* (An Analysis of the Dynamics of the Chinese Economy and some Solutions), Beijing: People's University of China Press.

—— Zhou Xiaochuan *et al.* (1988), *Zhongguo Jingji Gaige de Zhengti Sheji*
(The Comprehensive Design of Economic Reform in China), Beijing:
Zhongguo Zhanyun chubanshe.

Wu Qi (1984), 'Zhinan Ertui, Nuli Kaichuang Jingji Lianhe Xiezuo de Xinju-
mian' (Marching against Difficulties: Earnestly Working for a New Phase
of Economic Integration and Co-operation), *Shanghai Jingji Kexue* 5
(Oct.): 8–10.

Wu Ruyin (1992), *Di Xiaolu Jingjixue* (The Economics of Inefficiency: The
Theory of Centrally Planned Economy Reconsidered), Shanghai: Shanghai United Bookstore.

Wu Xiaoqiu (ed.) (1991), *Jin Yunxing Lun* (On the Tight Operation), Beijing: People's University of China Press.

Wu Yixin (1990), *Guangdong Shinian Jingji Tizhi Gaige Yanjiu* (Analysing the Ten Years of Economic System Reform in Guangdong), Guangzhou: Zhongshan Daxue chubanshe.

Xia Chenggen (1994), 'Gongxiangshui he Caizheng Buzhu: Caizheng Tizhi Neizai de Zhihengqi' (Sharing Taxes and Fiscal Subsidies: The Built-In Moderator of the Fiscal System), *Shanghai Reform* 6 (June): 31–2.

Xiang Huaicheng (ed.) (1991), *Jiushi Niandai Caizheng Fazhan Zhanlue* (Strategies for Developing Finance in the Nineties), Beijing: Zhongguo Caizheng Jingji chubanshe.

—— (ed.) (1992), *Zhongguo Yusuanwai Zijin Guanli Lilun Yu Shijian* (Theory and Practice of the Management of Extrabudgetary Funds in China), Harbin: Heilungjiang Renmin chubanshe.

—— (1994), 'Shixing Fenshuizhi Shi Dangqian Caizheng Tizhi Gaige de Zhongyao Neirong' (The Tax-Sharing System is a Major Item of the Tax and Fiscal Reform), *Qiushi* (Jan.): 32–6.

Xiao Hongmei and Yang Zheng (1994), 'Shuozuo Caizheng Xingxiang' (Shaping the New Profile of the Finance Department), *Guangdong Caizheng* 2 (Feb.): 12–13.

Xiao Ruchuan (ed.) (1991), *Guangdong Chanye Jiegou Yanjiu* (A Study of Guangdong's Industrial Structure), Guangzhou: Guangdong Renmin chubanshe.

Xie Minggan and Lou Yuanming (eds.) (1990), *Zhongguo Jingji Fazhan Sishi Nian* (Forty Years of Economic Development in China), Beijing: Renmin chubanshe.

Xie Zhijiang and Jia Huajiang (eds.) (1992), *Quanmin Suoyaozhi Gongye Qiye Zhuanhuan Jingying Jizhi Tiaoli: Zhongdian Nandian Jieda 100 Ti* (Regulation to Change the Operation Mechanism of State Enterprises: 100 Questions and Answers), Beijing: Zhongguo Dabaike Quanshu chubanshe.

Xiong Ruixiang (1985), 'Wanshan Caishui Gaige, Wei Shixian Shanghai Jingji Fazhan Zhanlue Fuwu' (To Further Improve the Fiscal Reform in the Service of Shanghai's Economic Development Strategy), *Shanghai Caishui Yanjiu* 8 (Aug.): 4.

Xu Feiqing (ed.) (1988), *Zhongguo de Jingji Tizhi Gaige: Gaige de Huigu yu Zhanwang* (An Appraisal of the Future of China's Economic System Reform), Beijing: Zhongguo Caizheng Jingji chubanshe.

Xu Fengchao and Zhang Tianping (1989), 'Heli Huafen Zhongyang he Difang Shiquan de Sikao' (Thoughts on How Reasonably to Demarcate the Jurisdiction of the Central and Local Governments), *China Administration* 8 (Aug.): 8–10.

Xu Hangdi (1992), 'To Further Change the Functions of the Planning

Commission; To Contribute Towards the Opening of Pudong and the Re-
vitalization of Shanghai', *Shanghai Jihua Jinhgji Tansuo* 1 (Jan.).

Xu Riqing *et al.* (1985), 'Wanshan Shanghaishi Difang Caizheng de Yanjiu'
(A Study on How to Perfect the Local Fiscal System in Shanghai), in Chen
Minzhi (ed. 1985), 243–58.

—— *et al.* (1985), 'Wanshan Difangshui Tixi, Shixing Fenji Caizheng Tizhi'
(Perfecting the Local Tax System, Practising a Stratified System of Fiscal
Finance), *Shanghai Caizheng Yanjiu* 1 (Jan.): 2–5.

Xu Xiangyi (1991), 'Tizhi Biangezhong de Yusuanwai Zijin Wenti' (The Issue
of Extrabudgetary Funds in a Changing System), *Caizheng Yanjiu* 4 (Apr.):
15–19.

Xu Yi (ed.) (1993), *Zouxiang Xinshiji: Zhongguo Caizheng Jingji Lilun Congshu* (Towards a New Century: Volumes on Fiscal and Economic Theories in
China), vol. 2, Beijing: Jingji Kexue chubanshe.

—— and Xiang Jingquan (eds.) (1987). *Diliuge Wunian Jihua Shiqi de Guojia
Caizheng* (State Finance during the Sixth Five-Year Plan Period), Beijing:
Zhongguo Caizheng chubanshe.

—— and —— (eds.) (1993), *1986–1990: Diqige Wunian Jihua Shiqi de Guojia
Caizheng* (1986–1990: State Finance During the Seventh Five-Year Plan
Period), Beijing: Zhongguo Caizheng Jingji chubanshe.

Xu Yunren (1990), 'Jiasu Tuixing Yi Fenshuizhi Wei Zhongxin de Shenceng
Gaige' (Speed Up the Implementation of More Fundamental Reforms around
the Tax-Sharing System), *Shanghai Jihua Jingji Tansuo* 3 (June): 17–20.

Xuan Zhuxi (1992), ' "Jianzheng Fangquan" Wenti Zuotanhui Fayan
Zheyao' (Summary of Discussion of the 'Streamlining Administration and
Delegating Powers' Seminar), *Theory and Practice of the Special Economic
Zone* 5 (Oct.): 57–9.

Xue Muqiao and Liu Guogang (eds.) (1992), *Jiushi Niandai Zhongguo Jingji
Fazhan Yu Gaige Tanzuo* (Economic Development and Reform Attempts in
China in the 1990s), Beijing: Jingji Kexue chubanshe.

Yan Bin (1991), 'Zhengque Chuli Zhongyang Yu Difang Caizheng Guanxi de
Guanjian: Zhubu Shixing Fenshuizhi' (Correctly Handle the Crux of the
Fiscal Relationship between the centre and Local Governments: Imple-
ment the Tax-Sharing System Step by Step), *Caizheng Yanjiu* 4 (Apr.): 3–10.

Yan Jialin *et al.* (1991), 'Zhuanzhe Yu Jiyu' (Swings and Opportunities: a report on the 1991 economic development of Shanghai), *Shanghai Jihua
Jingji Tansuo* 7 (Dec. Special Issue): 2–14.

Yang Linfeng (1989), 'Woguo Guding Zichan Touzi Chanchu Xiaoying' (The
Efficency of Fixed Asset Investment in China), *Touzi Lilun Yu Shijian* 1
(Jan.): 20–2.

Yang Ming (1988), 'Guangdong Guding Zichan Touzi Zongliang Yu Jiegou
Shiheng Fenxi' (An Analysis of Total Scale and Structural Imbalances of
Investment in Guangdong), *Jihua Yu Fazhan* 6 (Dec.): 38–40.

—— (1989), 'Guangdong Shuishou Shouru Liushi Fenxi' (An Analysis of the Haemorrhage of Tax Revenue in Guangdong, *Jihua Yu Fazhan* 2 (Apr.): 28–30.

Yang Sheng (1993), 'Caizheng Xinyong Zhineng Burong Xueruo' (The Credits Function of the Finance Department should not be Weakened), *Shanghai Caishui* 3 (Mar.): 28–9.

Yang Xiaohui (1990), 'Shengji Zhengfu de Zizhu Xingwei: Kaifang Gaige Shiqi di Guangdong Zhengfu' (Discretionary Behaviour of the Provincial-Level Government: The Guangdong Provincial Government in the Reform Period), Chinese University of Hong Kong M.Phil. dissertation.

Yao Dinghai and Wang Yaming (1990), 'Guangdong Caizheng Shouru Liangge Bili Xiajiang de Chubu Fenxi' (A Preliminary Analysis of the Slide in the Two Proportions of Guangdong's Fiscal Revenue), *Jihua Yu Fazhan* 6 (Dec.): 43–6.

—— and Zeng Shunming (1989), 'Guangdongsheng de Yinhang Xindai Guimo Yu Jiegou de Xianzhuang Fenxi' (An Analysis of the Scale and Structure of Guangdong's Bank Loans), *Jihua Yu Fazhan* 6 (Dec.): 52–4.

Yao Zhenyan (1994), 'Build Up an Investment Finance System Commensurate with the Socialist Market Economy', *China Construction and Investment* 1 (Jan.): 5–10.

You Lin *et al.* (eds.) (1993), *Zhonghua Renmin Gongheguo Guoshi Tongjian, 1976–1992* (A History of the People's Republic of China, 1976–1992), Beijing: Hongqiao chubanshe.

Yu Fei (1989), 'Restructuring during the Retrenchment: Developing amidst the Restructuring', *Jihua Yu Fazhan* 1 (Feb.): 1–5.

Yu Xiangnian (1988), 'The Objectives and Strategies of Shanghai's Externally Oriented Economic Development', *Shanghai Jihua Jingji Tanshuo* 2 (Apr.): 8–13.

Yu Xiguang *et al.* (1992), *Dachao Chuqi* (The Rise of the Big Wave: The Prelude and Aftermath of the Southern Tour of Deng Xiaoping), Beijing: Zhongguo Guangbo chubanshe.

Yuan Ming (1994), 'China after Deng Xiaoping: The Road to Constitutional Democracy, *Ming Pao* (Hong Kong), 8 June: D3.

Yuan Shang and Han Zhu (1992), *China after Deng Xiao Ping's Southern Tour*, Beijing: Gaige chubanshe.

Yuan Shouren and Cao Tong (1994), 'Xinde Qipaoxian, Xinde Qifeidian' (The New Starting Point: An Interview with the Director of Guangdong Finance Bureau), *Guangdong Caizheng* (Feb.): 2, 6–8.

Zeng Niansi and Sui Liang (1992), 'Guanyu Shanghai Shiqu Chengzhen Jiti Jingji Zhuangkuang de Tiaocha' (A Survey of the Economic Situation of the Urban Collective Sector in Shanghai), *Shanghai Caishui* 12 (Dec.): 7–10.

Zeng Xianyou (1993), 'A Study of the Financial Management of Extrabudgetary Enterprises in Maoming', *Guangdong Caizheng* 1 (Jan.): 46–8.

Zeng Xiaohong (1994), 'Fenshuizhi, Weini Siliang Weiniyou' (Thinking and Worrying about the Tax-Sharing System), *Guangdong Caizheng* 1 (Jan.): 18–19.

Zeng Zhiwen (1994), 'Fenshuizhi Zhongrentan' (A Collection of Views on the Tax-Sharing System.): *Guangdong Caizheng* 1 (Jan.): 8–9.

Zhang Hanqing (ed.) (1992), *Gaige Kaifang Zai Guangdong* (Reform and Opening in Guangdong: Implementation and Thoughts on the One Step Ahead Policy), Guangzhou: Guangdong Higher Education Press.

Zhang Jinfan (ed.) (1985), *Zhongguo Gudai Xingzheng Guanli Tizhi Yanjiu* (A Study of the Adminstrative System in Ancient China), Beijing: Guangming chubanshe.

Zhang Linghan (1989), Chengli Shenzhen Renda Jigou de Zhanwang (The Prospect of Establishing the People's Congress in Shenzhen), *Theory and Practice of the Special Economic Zone* 2 (Apr.): 16–18.

Zhang Zelu (ed.) (1991), *Zhongguan Touzi Xue* (The Theory of Medium-Level Investment), Beijing: People's University of China Press.

Zhang Zhuoyuan and Wang Fanzhang (eds.) (1991), *Zhongguo Shinian Jingji Gaige Lilun Tansuo* (Theoretical Probes in the Ten Years of Economic Reform in China), Beijing: Zhongguo Jinghua chubanshe.

Zhao Xiaomin (ed.) (1985), *Caimao Jingji Tizhi Gaige Yanjiu* (A Study of Financial and Trade System Reform), Beijing: Zhongguo Zhanyun chubanshe.

Zheng Rujuan (1993), 'Jianghua Caizheng Shenji de Jidian Tansuo' (Several Suggestions for Strengthening Fiscal Audits), *Shanghai Audit* 2 (Apr.): 17–19.

Zhong Chengxun (ed.) (1993), *Difang Zhengfu Touzi Xingwei Yanjiu* (A Study of the Investment Behaviour of Local Governments), Beijing: Zhongguo Caizheng Jingji chubanshe.

Zhong Qijun (1993), 'A Preliminary Study of the Approach whereby the Finance Department Invests Directly in Extrabudgetary Enterprises', *Guangdong Caizheng* 1 (Jan.): 55–6.

Zhonggong Zhongyang Wenxian Yanjiushi (1982), *Sanzhong Quanhui Yilai Zhongyao Wenxian Xuanbian* (Since the Third Plenum: A Compendium of Important Documents), 2 parts, Beijing: Renmin chubanshe.

—— (1986–8), *Shierda Yilai Zhongyao Wenxian Xuanbian* (Since the Twelfth Party Congress: A Compendium of Important Documents), 3 parts, Beijing: Renmin chubanshe.

—— (1991–3), *Shisanda Yilai Zhongyao Wenxian Xuanbian* (Since the Thirteenth Party Congress: A Compendium of Important Documents), 3 vols., Beijing: Renmin chubanshe.

Zhongguo Jihua Guanli Bianji Bu (1988), *Shengji Jihua Guanli Wenti Tansuo* (A Study of Planning Administration Issues at the Provincial Level), Beijing: Zhongguo Jihua chubanshe.

Zhongguo Renmin Yinhang Renshi Ju (1985), *Renshi Gongzuo Wenjian Xuanbian: Ganbu Guanli Bufen* (A Compendium of Documents on Personnel Work: Section on Cadre Management), Beijing: Zhongguo Jinrong chubanshe.

Zhonghua Renmin Gongheguo Minzhengbu (1986), *Zhonghua Renmin Gongheguo Xingzheng Quhua Shouce* (A Handbook of the Boundary Demarcation of Administrative Regions in the Peoples's Republic of China), Beijing: Guangming Ribao chubanshe.

Zhou, Li. (1993), 'Jihua Tizhi Gaige de Sikao' (Thoughts on the Reform of the Planning System), *China Investment and Construction*, 6 (June), 17–18.

Zhou Xiaochuan and Yang Zhiyang (1992), *Zhongguo Caishui Tizhi de Wenti Yu Chulu* (The Problems and Way Out of the Fiscal and Taxation System in China), Tianjin: Tianjin Renmin chubanshe.

Zhou Youdao (1992a), '92 Caishui Gongzuo Tansuo' (Probing the Way of the Fiscal Work of 1992), *Shanghai Caishui* 1 (Jan.): 6–9.

—— (1992b), 'Shanghai Jiang Shixing "Yiti Liangyi" Caizheng Xintizhi' (Shanghai will Implement the 'One System: Two Wings' New Fiscal System), *Shanghai Caishui* 11 (Nov.): 4–7.

—— (1993), 'A Report on the Final Accounts of Shanghai's 1992 Budget, *Shanghai Caishui*, 7 (July), 4.

Zhu Jiangchou (1992), 'Baoshui Shibi' (The Ten Drawbacks of the 'Tax Contracting' Practice), *Guangdong Taxation* 9 (Sept.): 8–9.

Zhu Ronglin (1993), 'Shanghai Dabu Manxiang Xinshiji' (Shanghai Marching toward the New Century), *Economic Forecasting* 4 (Dec.): 43-5.

Zhu Xiaoming (1990), 'Tupo Chuantong Tizhi Moshi, Gaige Zhengfu Guanli Jigou' (Break through the Traditional System Model, and Reform the Management Structure of the Government: an appraisal of the ten years' organizational reform of the Shenzhen Government), *Theory and Practice of the Special Economic Zone* 4 (Aug.): 30-3.

ENGLISH-LANGUAGE MATERIALS

Agarwala, Ramgopal (1992), *China: Reforming Intergovernmental Fiscal Relations* (World Bank Discussion Paper no. 178), Washington, DC: World Bank.

Bachman, David (1990), 'China and Privatization', in Ezra Suleiman and John Waterbury (eds.), *The Political Economy of Public Sector Reform and Privatization*, Boulder, Colo.: Westview Press, 275-92.

Bailey, D. J., and Paddison, R. (eds.) (1988), *The Reform of Local Government Finance in Britain*, London: Routledge.

Barnett, A. Doak (with Ezra Vogel) (1967), *Cadre, Bureaucracy, and Political Power in Communist China*, New York: Columbia University Press.

—— (ed.) (1969), *Chinese Communism in Action*, Seattle: University of Washington Press.

—— (1974), *Uncertain Passage: China's Transition to the Post-Mao Era*, Washington, DC: Brookings Institution.

324 Bibliography

Bennett, Robert J. (ed.) (1990), *Decentralization, Local Governments, and Markets: Towards a Post-Welfare Agenda*, Oxford: Clarendon Press.

Bergère, Marie-Claire (1981). ' "The Other China": Shanghai from 1919 to 1949', in Christopher Howe (ed.), *Shanghai: Revolution and Development in an Asian Metropolis*, Cambridge: Cambridge University Press, 1–34.

—— (1986), *The Golden Age of the Chinese Bourgeoisie, 1911–1937*, Cambridge: Cambridge University Press.

Blecher, Marc (1991), 'Development State, Enterpreneurial State: The Political Economy of Socialist Reform in Xinju Municipality and Guanghan County', in Gordon White (ed.), *The Chinese State in the Era of Economic Reform*, London: Macmillan Press' 265–91.

Burns, John (ed.) (1989), *The Chinese Communist Party's Nomenklatura System: A Documentary Study of Party Control of Leadership Selection, 1979–84*, Armonk, NY: M. E. Sharpe.

—— (1994), 'Strengthening Central CCP Control of Leadership Selection: The 1990 *Nomenklatura*', *China Quarterly* 138 (June): 458–91.

Chang, Maria Hsia (1992), 'China's Future: Regionalism, Federation, or Disintegration', *Studies in Comparative Communism*, 25/3: 211–27.

Chang, Parris (1970), 'Research Notes on the Changing Loci of Decentralization in the Chinese Communist Party', *China Quarterly* 44: 169–94.

—— (1972*a*), 'Decentralization of Power', *Problems of Communism* 21/4: 67–75.

—— (1972*b*), 'Provincial Party Leaders' Strategies for Survival during the Cultural Revolution', in Scalapino (1972), 501–39.

—— (1981), 'Shanghai and Chinese Politics: Before and After the Cultural Revolution', in Christopher Howe (1981), 66–90.

Chapman, Richard A. (ed.) (1971), *Style in Administration: Readings in British Public Administration*, London: Allen & Unwin.

Cheema, G. S., and Rondinelli., D. A. (1983), *Decentralization and Development: Policy Implementation in Developing Countries*, London: Sage Publications.

Cheung, T. Y. Peter (1994), 'Relations between the Central Government and Guangdong', in Y. M. Yeung and David K. Y. Chu (1994), 19–52.

Chung, Jae Ho (1995*a*), 'Beijing Confronting the Provinces: The 1994 Tax-Sharing Reform and its Implications for Central–Provincial Relations in China', *China Information* 9/2–3: 1–23).

—— (1995*b*). 'Studies of Central–Provincial Relations in the People' Republic of China: A Mid-Term Appraisal', *China Quarterly* 142: 487–508.

Clark, Gordon L., and Dear, Michail (1984), *State Apparatus: Structure and Language of Legitimacy*. Boston: Allen & Unwin.

Clarke, Michael, and Stewart, John (1990), 'The Future of Local Government: Some Lessons from Europe', unpub. MS.

Cohen, Paul A. (1984), *Discovering History in China: American Historical Writing on the Recent Chinese Past*, New York: Columbia University Press.

Crane, George T. (1990), *The Political Economy of China's Special Economic Zones*, Armonk, NY: M. E. Sharpe.

—— (1994). '"Special Things in Special Ways": National Economic Identity and China's Special Economic Zones', *The Australian Journal of Chinese Affairs* 32: 61–70.

Datta, A. (1984), *Union-State Relations*, New Delhi: Indian Institute of Public Administration.

Dente, B., and Kjellberg, F. (eds.) (1988), *The Dynamics of Institutional Change: Local Government Reorganization in Western Democracies*, London: Sage Publications.

Dittmer, Lowell (1978), 'Bases of Power in Chinese Politics: A Theory and an Analysis of the Fall of the "Gang of Four"', *World Politics* 31: 26–60.

Donnithorne, Audrey, (1967), *China's Economic System*, London: George Allen and Unwin.

—— (1969), 'Central Economic Control in China', in Ruth Adams (ed.), *Contemporary China*, London: Peter Owen, 151–78.

—— (1972a), 'China's Cellular Economy: Some Economic Trends since the Cultural Revolution', *China Quarterly* 52: 605–19.

—— (1972b), *The Budget and the Plan*, Canberra: Australian National University Press.

—— (1976), 'Comment: Centralization and Decentralization in China's Fiscal Management', *China Quarterly* 66: 328–40.

Duncan, Simon, and Goodwin, Mark (1988), *The Local State and Uneven Development: Behind the Local Government Crisis*, Cambridge: Polity Press.

Dunleavy, Patrick (1980), 'Social and Political Theory and the Issues in Central–Local Relations', in G. W. Jones (1980), 116–36.

—— and O'leary, Brendan (1987), *Theories of the State: The Politics of Liberal Democracy*, London: Macmillan Education.

Elazar, Daniel, (1976), 'Federalism versus Decentralization: The Drift from Authencity', *Publius: The Journal of Federalism* 6/3: 9–19.

Emerson, R. M. (1962), 'Power-Dependence Relations', *American Sociological Review* 27/1: 31–40.

Evans, Peter, Rueschemeyer, Dietrich, and Skocpol, Theda (eds.) (1985), *Bringing the State Back In* New York: Cambridge University Press.

Fairbank, John K., and MacFarquhar, Roderick (eds.) (1987), *The Cambridge History of China. Vol. 14: The People's Republic of China. Part I: The Emergence of Revolutionary China, 1949–1965*, Cambridge: Cambridge University Press.

Falkenheim, Victor C. (1972a), 'Continuing Central Predominance', *Problems of Communism* 21/4: 75–83.

—— (1972b), 'Provincial Leadership in Fukien: 1946–66', in Robert A. Scalapino (ed.) *Elites in the People's Republic of China*, Seattle: University of Washington Press, 199–244.

Falkenheim, Victor C. (1978), 'Political Participation in China', *Problems of Communism* 27/3 18–32.

—— (1979), 'Rational-Choice Models and the Study of Citizen Politics in China', *Contemporary China*, 3/2: 93-101.

—— (ed.) (1987), *Citizens and Groups in Contemporary China*, Ann Arbor: Centre for Chinese Studies, University of Michigan.

Ferdinand, Peter (1984), 'Interest Groups and Chinese Politics', in Goodman (ed. 1984), 10–25.

—— (1990), 'Regionalism', in Gerald Segal (ed.) *Chinese Politics and Foreign Policy Reform*, London: Royal Institute of International Affairs, 135–58.

Feuerwerker, Albert, Murphey, Rhoads, and Wright, Mary C. (1967) (eds.), *Approaches to Modern Chinese History*, Berkeley: University of California Press.

Fewsmith, Joseph (1994), *Dilemmas of Reform in China: Political Conflict and Economic Debate*, Armonk, NY: M. E. Sharpe.

Foley, Michael (1989), *The Silence of Constitutions: Gaps, 'Abeyances' and Political Temperament in the Maintenance of Government*, London: Routledge.

Forster, Keith (1990), *Rebellion and Factionalism in a Chinese Province: Zhejiang, 1966–1976*, London: M. E. Sharpe.

Frey, Frederick W. (1985), 'The Problem of Actor Designation in Political Analysis', *Comparative Politics* 17/2: 127–52.

Goldsmith, Michael (ed.) (1986), *New Research in Central–Local Relations*, Aldershot: Gower.

—— and Page, Edward C. (eds.) (1987), *Central and Local Government Relations: West European Unitary States*, London: Sage Publications.

Goldstein, Avery (1994), 'Trends in the Study of Political Elites and Institutions in the PRC', *China Quarterly* 139: 714–30.

Goldstein, Steven M. (1988), 'Reforming Socialist Systems: Some Lessons of the Chinese Experience', *Studies in Comparative Communism* 21/2: 221–37.

—— (1992), 'Rural Politics in Socialist China: Clientelism and Reform', *Studies in Comparative Communism* 25/4: 419–37.

Goodman, David S. G. (1980), 'Li Jingquan and the South-West Region, 1958–66: The Life and "Crimes" of a "Local Emperor"', *China Quarterly* 81: 66–96.

—— (1981*a*), 'The Provincial Revolutionary Committee in the People's Republic of China, 1967–1979: An Obituary', *China Quarterly* 85: 49–79.

—— (1981*b*), 'The Shanghai Connection: Shanghai's Role in National Politics', in Howe (1981), 125–52.

—— (1984), 'Provincial Party First Secretaries in National Politics: A Categoric or a Political Group?', in Goodman (ed. 1984), 68–80.

—— (ed.) (1984), *Groups and Politics in the People's Republic of China*, Armonk, NY: M. E. Sharpe.

—— (1986), *Centre and Province in the People's Republic of China: Sichuan and Guizhou, 1955–1965*, Cambridge, Mass.: Harvard University Press.

—— (ed.) (1989), *China's Regional Development*, London: The Royal Institute of International Affairs.

—— (1994), 'The PLA and Regionalism in Guangdong', *Pacific Review* 7: 29–39.

—— and Segal, Gerald (eds.) (1994), *China Deconstructs: Politics, Trade and Regionalism*, London: Routledge.

Gottman, Jean (ed.) (1980), *Centre and Periphery: Spatial Variation in Politics*, London: Sage Publications.

Granick, David (1990), *Chinese State Enterprises: A Regional Property Rights Analysis*, Chicago: University of Chicago Press.

Gregory, Paul R., and Stuart, Robert C. (1990), *Soviet Economic Structure and Performance*, 4th edn., New York: Harper Collins.

Griffith, J. A. G. (1966), *Central Departments and Local Authorities*. London: Allen & Unwin.

Griffiths, Franklyn, and Skilling, Gorden (eds.) (1971), *Interest Groups in Soviet Politics*. Princeton: Princeton University Press.

Hague, D. C., Mackenzie, W. J. M., and Barker, A. (eds.) (1975), *Public Policy and Private Interests: The Institutions of Compromise*. London: Macmillan Press.

Harding, Harry (1984*a*), 'Competing Models of the Chinese Communist Policy Process: Towards a Sorting and Evaluation', *Issues and Studies* (Feb.), 13–36.

—— (1984*b*), 'The Study of Chinese Politics: Towards a Third Generation of Scholarship', *World Politics* 36: 284–307.

—— (1993), 'The Evolution of American Scholarship on Contemporary China', in Shambaugh (ed. 1993), 14–40.

—— (1994), 'The Contemporary Study of Chinese Politics: An Introduction', *China Quarterly* 139: 699–703.

Heclo, H, and Wildavsky, A. (1981), *The Private Government of Public Money*, London: Macmillan Press.

Himsworth, Chris (1988), 'The Legal Limits of Local Autonomy', in Bailey and Paddisson (1988), 60–74.

Holt, Robert T, and Turner, John E. (eds.) (1970), *The Methodology of Comparative Research*, New York: The Free Press.

Hood, Christopher (1986*a*), 'Concepts of Control over Public Bureaucracies: "Comptrol" and "Interpolable Balance"', in Kaufman *et al.* (1986), 765–83.

—— (1986*b*), 'The Hidden Public Sector: The "Quangocatization" of the World?', in Kaufman *et al.* (1986), 183–207.

—— and Schuppert, Gunnar Folke . (eds.) (1988), *Delivering Public Services in Western Europe: Sharing Western European Experience of Para-Governmental Organization*, London: Sage Publications.

Hough, Jerry F. (1969), *The Soviet Prefects: The Local Party Organs in Industrial Decision-Making*, Cambridge Mass.: Harvard University Press.

Howe, Christopher (1971), *Employment and Economic Growth in Urban China 1949–1957*, London: Cambridge University Press.

—— (ed.) (1981), *Shanghai: Revolution and Development in an Asian Metropolis*, Cambridge: Cambridge University Press.

Hsiao, Katherine H. (1987), *The Government Budget and Fiscal Policy in Mainland China*, Taipei: Chung-Hua Institution for Economic Research.

Huang Yasheng (1990), 'Webs of Interests and Patterns of Behaviour of Chinese Local Economic Bureaucrats and Enterprises during Reforms', *China Quarterly* 123: 431–58.

Iyer, Ramaswamy R. (1990), 'Public Sector Holding Companies: Relationship with Government and Allied Issues', *Public Enterprise* 10/1: 27–33.

Janos, Andrew C. (1970), 'Group Politics in Communist Society: A Second Look at the Pluralist Model', in Samuel Huntington and Clement H. Moore (eds.), *Authoritarian Politics in Modern Society: The Dynamics of Established One-Party Systems*, New York: Basic Books, 4327–50.

Jia Hao and Lin Zhimin (eds.) (1994), *Changing Central-Local Relations in China: Reform and State Capacity*, Boulder, Colo.: Westview Press.

Joffe, Ellis (1994), 'Regionalism in China', *Pacific Review* 7/1: 17–27.

Jones, George William (ed.) (1980), *New Approaches to the Study of Central-Local Government Relationships*, Aldershot: Gower.

Joseph, William A., Wong, Christine P. W., and Zweig, David (eds.) (1991), *New Perspectives on the Cultural Revolution*, Cambridge Mass.: Harvard University Council on East Asian Studies.

Kaufman, F. X., Majone, G., and Ostrom, V. (eds.) (1986), *Guidance, Control and Evaluation in the Public Sector*, New York: Walter de Gruyter.

Keith, Ronald (1991), 'Chinese Politics and the New Theory of the "Rule of Law"', *China Quarterly* 125: 109–18.

Kojima, Reeitsu (1992), 'The Growing Fiscal Authority of Provincial-Level Governments in China', *The Developing Economies* 30/4: 315–46.

Kornai, Janos (1979), 'Resource-Constrained versus Demand-Constrained Systems', *Econometrics* 47/4: 801–19.

—— (1980), *The Economics of Shortage*, Amsterdam: North Holland Publishing.

Krasner, Stephen D. (1984), 'Approaches to the State: Alternative Conceptions and Historical Dynamics', *Comparative Politics* 17/1: 223-46.

Krug, Barbara (1985), 'Regional Politics in Communist China: The Spatial Dimension of Power', *Issues and Studies* 21/1: 58–78.

Kueh, Y. Y. (1985), *Economic Planning and Local Mobilization in Post-Mao China* (Research Notes and Studies no. 7.), London: Contemporary China Institute, School of Oriental and African Studies.

Kugler, Jacek, and Domke, William (1986), 'Comparing the Strength of Nations', *Comparative Political Studies* 19/1: 39–69.

Kuhn, Philip A. (1975), 'Local Self-government under the Republic: Problems of Control, Autonomy, and Mobilization', in Frederick Wakeman, Jr. and Carolyn Grant (eds.), *Conflict and Control in Late Imperial China*, Berkeley: University of California Press, 257–98.

Lakshmann, T. R., and Chang-i Huao (1987), 'Regional Disparities in China', *International Regional Review* 11/1: 97–104.

Lampton, David M. (1986), *Paths to Power: Elite Mobility in Contemporary China*, Ann Arbor: Centre for Chinese Studies, University of Michigan.

—— (1987), 'Chinese Politics: The Bargaining Treadmill', *Issues and Studies* 23/3: 11–41.

—— (ed.) (1987), *Policy Implementation in Post-Mao China*, Berkeley: University of California Press.

Landau, Martin (1969), 'Redundancy, Rationality and the Problem of Duplication and Overlap', *Public Administration Review* 29/4: 346–57.

Lardy, Nicholas (1975), 'Centralization and Decentralization in China's Fiscal Management', *China Quarterly* 61: 25–60.

—— (1976), 'Reply', *China Quarterly* 66: 340–54.

—— (1978), *Economic Growth and Distribution in China*, Cambridge: Cambridge University Press.

Lattimore, Owen (1980), 'The Periphery as Locus of Innovation', in Gottman (1980), 205–8.

Levenson, Joseph R. (1967), 'The Province, the Nation, and the World: The Problem of Chinese Identity', in Feuerwerker *et al.* (1967), 268–88.

Li Cheng and Bachman, David (1989), 'Localism, Elitism, and Immobilism: Elite Formation and Social Change in Post-Mao China', *World Politics* 62/1: 64–94.

Lieberthal, Kenneth, and Lampton, David M. (eds.) (1992), *Bureaucracy, Politics and Decision-Making in Post-Mao China*, Berkeley: University of California Press.

—— and Oksenberg, Michel (1988), *Policy Making in China: Leaders, Structure and Processes*, Princeton: Princeton University Press.

Lijphart, Arend (1971), 'Comparative Politics and the Comparative Method', *American Political Science Review* 65/3: 682–93.

Lin Sen (1992), 'A New Pattern of Decentralization in China: The Increase of Provincial Powers in Economic Legislation', *China Information* 7/3: 1992–3), 27–38.

Lin Zhimin (1994), 'Reform and Shanghai: Changing Central–Local Fiscal Relations', in Jia Hao and Lin Zhimin, (1994), 239–60.

Lindbeck, John M. H. (ed.) (1972), *China: Management of a Revolutionary Society*, London: George Allen and Unwin.

Loughlin, Martin (1983), *Local Government, the Law, and the Constitution*, London: Local Government Legal Society Trust.

Lyons, Thomas (1987), *Economic Integration and Planning in Maoist China*, New York: Columbia University Press.

Lyons, Thomas (1990), 'Planning and Inter-provincial Co-ordination in Maoist China', *China Quarterly* 121: 36–60.

Manion, Melanie (1985), 'The Cadre Management System, Post-Mao: The Appointment, Promotion, Transfer and Removal of Party and State Leaders', *China Quarterly* 102: 203–33.

March, James G., and Olsen, Johan P. (1984), 'The New Institutionalism: Organizational Factors in Political Life', *American Political Science Review* 78/3: 734–49.

Mawhood, Philip (1983), *Local Government in the Third World*, New York: John Wiley & Sons.

Meny, Yves, and Wright, Vincent (ed.) (1985), *Centre-Periphery Relations in Western Europe*, London: George Allen and Unwin.

Migdal, Joel S. (1988), *Strong Societies and Weak States: State–Society Relations and State Capabilities in the Third World*, Princeton: Princeton University Press.

Moody, Peter R., Jr. (1994), 'Trends in the Study of Chinese Political Culture', *China Quarterly* 139: 731–40.

Narang, A. S. (1985), *Indian Government and Politics*, New Delhi: Gitanjali Publishing House.

Nathan, Andrew (1973), 'A Factionalism Model of CCP Politics', *China Quarterly* 53: 34–66.

—— (1976), 'Policy Oscillations in the People's Republic of China: A Critique', *China Quarterly* 68: 720–33.

Nee, Victor, and Mozingo, David (eds.) (1983), *State and Society in Contemporary China*, London: Cornell University Press.

Newton Kenneth (1980), *Balancing the Books: Financing Problems of Local Government in West Europe*, Beverly Hills, Calif.: Sage Publications.

Oi, Jean (1989), *State and Peasant in Contemporary China*, Berkeley: University of California Press.

—— (1992), 'Fiscal Reform and the Economic Foundations of Local State Corporatism in China', *World Politics* 45/1: 99–126.

Oksenberg, Michel (1968), 'Occupational Groups in Chinese Society and the Cultural Revolution', in Michel Ohsenberg *et al.* (eds.), *The Cultural Revolution: 1967 in Review* (Michigan Papers in Chinese Studies no.2), Ann Arbor: University of Michigan Centre for Chinese Studies Publications, 1–44.

—— (1976), 'The Exit Pattern from Chinese Politics and its Implications', *China Quarterly* 67: 501–18.

—— (1987), 'Politics Takes Command: An Essay on the Study of Post-1949 China', Fairbank and MacFarquhar (1987), 543–90.

—— (1993), 'The American Study of Modern China: Toward the Twenty-First Century', in Shambaugh (ed. 1993), 315–43.

—— and Tong, James (1987), 'The Evolution of Central–Provincial Fiscal Relations in China, 1950–83: The Formal System', unpub. MS.

—— (1991), 'The Evolution of Fiscal Relations in China, 1971–1984: The Formal System', *China Quarterly* 125: 1–32.

Ostrom, Elinor (1991), 'Rational Choice Theory and Institutional Analysis: Towards Complementarity', *American Political Science Review* 85/1: 237–43.

Paddison, Ronan (ed.) (1983), *The Fragmented State: The Political Geography of Power*, Oxford: Blackwell.

Page, Edward C. (1982), 'Central Government Instruments of Influence upon Services Delivered by Local Governments', University of Strathclyde Ph.D. dissertation.

Parsons, Talcott (1969), 'On the Concept of Political Power', in R. Bell, D. B. Edwards and R. H. Wagner (eds.), *Political Power: A Reader in Theory and Research*, New York: Free Press, 251–84.

Perry, Elizabeth J. (1989), 'State and Society in Contemporary China', *World Politics* 41/3. 579–91.

—— (1994), 'Trends in the Study of Chinese Politics: State–Society Relations', *China Quarterly* 139: 704–13.

—— and Wong, Christine P. W. (eds.) (1985), *The Political Economy of Reform in Post-Mao China*, Cambridge, Mass.: Harvard University Press.

Pickvance, Chris, and Preteceille, Edmond, (eds.) (1991), *State Restructuring and Local Power: A Comparative Perspective*, London: Pinter Publishers.

Poggi, Gianfranco (1978), *The Development of the Modern State: A Sociological Introduction*, Stanford, Calif.: Stanford University Press.

—— (1990), *The State: Its Nature, Development and Prospects*, Cambridge: Polity Press.

Ponting, Clive (1985), *The Right to Know: The Inside Story of the Belgrano Affair*, London: Sphere Books.

Pye, Lucian (1975), 'The Confrontation between Discipline and Area Studies, in Lucian Pye (ed.), *Political Science and Area Studies: Rivals or Partners?*, Bloomington, Ind.: University Indiana Press, 3–22.

—— (1981*a*), *The Dynamics of Chinese Politics*, Cambridge, Mass.: Oelgeschlager, Gunn and Hain.

—— (1991*b*), 'Foreword', in Howe (1981), pp. xi–xvi.

—— (1988), *The Mandarin and the Cadre: China's Political Cultures*, Ann Arbor: Centre for Chinese Studies, University of Michigan.

Ranson, Stewart, Jones, George, and Walsh, Kieron (eds.) (1985), *Between Centre and Locality: The Politics of Public Policy*, London: George Allen and Unwin.

Reynolds, Bruce L, and Kim, Ilpyong J. (1988), *Chinese Economic Policy: Economic Reform at Midstream*, New York: Paragon House.

Rhodes, R. A. W. (1979), 'Research into Central–Local Relations in Britain: A Framework for Analysis', in Social Science Research Council, *Central–Local Government Relationships*, London: Social Science Research Council, app. 1.

Rhodes, R. A. W. (1981), *Control and Power in Central–Local Relations*, Aldershot: Gower.

—— (1988), *Beyond Westminster and Whitehall: The Subcentral Governments of Britain*, London: Unwin Hyman.

Riskin, Carl (1991), 'Neither Plan nor Market: Mao's Political Economy', in Joseph, *et al.* (1991), 133–52.

Rondinelli, D. A. (1981), 'Government Decentralization in Comparative Perspective: Theory and Practice in Developing Countries', *International Review of Administrative Sciences* 47/2: 133–45.

Rosenthal, Donald B. (1980), 'Bargaining Analysis in Intergovernmental Relations', *Publius: The Journal of Federalism* 10/2: 5–44.

Ross, Cameron (1987), *Local Government in the Soviet Union: Problems of Implementation and Control*, London: Croom Helm.

Rothenberg, Jerome (1987), 'Space, Interregional Economic Relations, and Structural Reform in China', *International Regional Science Review* 11/1: 5–22.

Rousseau, Mark O., and Zariski, Raphael (eds.) (1987), *Regionalism and Regional Devolution in Comparative Perspective*, New York: Praeger.

Saxena, A. P. (ed.) (1980), *Administrative Reforms for Decentralized Development*, Kuala Lumpur: Asian and Pacific Development Administration Centre.

Scalapino, Robert A. (ed.) (1972), *Elites in the People's Republic of China*, Seattle: University of Washington Press.

Schurmann, Franz (1968), *Ideology and Organization in Communist China*, 2nd ed., Berkeley: University of California Press.

Segal, Gerald (1994), *China Changes Shape: Regionalism and Foreign Policy* (Adelphi Paper no. 287), London: International Institute for Strategic Studies.

Shambaugh, David (1984), *The Making of a Premier: Zhao Ziyang's Provincial Career*, Boulder, Colo.: Westview Press.

—— (1993), 'Losing Control: The Erosion of State Authority in China', *Current History* (Sept.), 253–9.

—— (ed.) (1993), *American Studies of Contemporary China*, Armonk, N Y and Washington, DC: M. E. Sharpe and the Wilson Centre Press.

Sharpe, L. J. (1986), 'Intergovernmental Policy-Making: The Limits of Subnational Autonomy', in Kaufman *et al.* (1986), 159–81.

Shils, Edward (1975), *Centre and Periphery: Essays in Macro-Sociology*, Chicago: University of Chicago Press.

Shirk, Susan (1990), 'Playing to the Provinces: Deng Xiaoping's Political Strategy of Economic Reform', *Studies in Comparative Communism* 23/3: 227–58.

—— (1993), *The Political Logic of Economic Reform in China*, Berkeley: University of California Press.

Shue, Vivienne (1984), 'Beyond the Budget: Finance Organization and Reform in a Chinese County', *Modern China* 10/2: 147–86.

—— (1988), *The Reach of the State: Sketches of the Chinese Body Politic*, Stanford, Calif.: Stanford University Press.

Simeon, Richard (1986), 'Considerations on Centralization and Decentralization', *Canadian Public Administration* 29/3: 445–61.

Siu, Helen (1989), *Agents and Victims in South China: Accomplices in Rural Revolution*, New Haven: Yale University Press.

Skinner, G. William (1964–5), 'Marketing and Social Structure in Rural China', *Journal of Asian Studies* 24/1: 3–43; 24/2: 195–228; 24/3: 363–99.

—— (1971), 'Chinese Peasants and Closed Community: An Open and Shut Case', *Comparative Studies in Society and History* 13/3: 270–81.

—— and Winckler, Edwin A. (1969), 'Compliance Succession in Rural Communist China: A Cyclical Theory', in Amitai Etzioni (ed.), *A Sociological Reader on Complex Organizations*, 2nd edn., New York: Holt, Rinehart and Winston, 410–38.

Smith, Brian C. (1985), *Decentralization*, London: Allen and Unwin.

—— (1986), 'Spatial Ambiguities: Decentralization within the State', *Public Administration and Development* 6/4: 455–65.

Smith, Bruce L. R., and Hague, D. C. (eds.) (1971), *The Dilemmas of Accountability in Modern Government: Independence versus Control*, London: Macmillan Press.

Solinger, Dorothy (1977), *Regional Government and Political Integration in Southwest China, 1949–54*, Berkeley: University of California Press.

—— (1987), 'Uncertain Paternalism: Tensions in Recent Regional Restructuring in China', *International Regional Science Review* 11/1: 23–42.

—— (1996), 'Despite Decentralization: Disadvantages, Dependence and Ongoing Central Power in the Inland—the Case of Wuhan', *China Quarterly* 145: 1–34.

Starr, John Bryan (1976), 'From the 10th Party Congress to the Premiership of Hua Kuo-feng: The Significance of the Colour of the Cat', *China Quarterly* 67: 457–88.

Stewart, John, and Stoker, Gerry (eds.) (1989), *The Future of Local Government*, London: Macmillan Education.

Strassoldo, Raimondo (1980), 'Centre–Periphery and System–Boundary: Culturological Perspectives', in Gottman (1980), 27–61.

Tarrow, Sidney (1977), *Between Centre and Periphery: Grassroots Politicians in Italy and France*, New Haven: Yale University Press.

—— Katzenstein, Peter J., and Graziano, Luigi (eds.) 1978, *Territorial Politics in Industrial Nations*, New York: Praeger.

Teiwes, Frederick C. (1966), 'The Purge of Provincial Leaders, 1957–1958', *China Quarterly* 27: 14–32.

Teiwes, Frederick C. (1972), 'Provincial Politics in China: Themes and Variations', in Lindbeck (1972), 116–92.

—— (1974), *Provincial Leadership in China: The Cultural Revolution and its Aftermath*, Ithaca, NY: Cornell University China–Japan Program.

Theonig, J. C. (1978), 'State Bureaucracies and Local Government in France', in K. Hanf and F. W. Scharpf (eds.), *Interorganizational Policy-Making. Limits to Co-ordination and Central Control*, Beverly Hills, Calif.: Sage Publications.

Tong, James (1989), 'Fiscal Reform, Elite Turnover and Central–Provincial Relations in Post-Mao China', *Australian Journal of Chinese Affairs* 22: 1–30.

Tsou, Tang (1976), 'Prolegomenon to the Study of Informal Groups in CCP Politics', *China Quarterly* 65: 98–114.

—— (1991), 'The Tiananmen Tragedy: The State–Society Relationship, Choices, and Mechanisms in Historical Perspective', in Womack, (1991), 265–327.

—— (1994), *Twentieth–Century Chinese Politics from the Perspectives of Macro-History and Micro-Mechanism Analysis*, Hong Kong: Oxford University Press.

Vogel, Ezra F. (1969), *Canton under Communism: Programs and Politics in a Provincial Capital, 1949–1968*, Cambridge, Mass.: Harvard University Press.

—— (1989), *One Step Ahead in China: Guangdong under Reform*, Cambridge, Mass.: Harvard University Press.

Walder, Andrew (1986), *Communist Neo-Traditionalism: Work and Authority in Chinese Industry*, Berkeley: University of California Press.

Waldron, Arthur (1990), 'Warlordism versus Federalism: The Revival of a Debate?', *China Quarterly* 121: 116–28.

Wang Gungwu (1963), *The Structure of Power in North China During the Five Dynasties*, Kuala Lumpur: University of Malaya Press.

Wang Shaoguang (1995), 'The Rise of the Regions: Fiscal Reform and the Decline of Central State Capacity in China', in Andrew Walder (ed.), *The Waning of the Communist State: Economic Origins of Political Decline in China and Hungary*, Berkeley: University of California Press, 87–113.

White. Gordon (1984), 'Developmental States and Socialist Industrializations in the Third World', *Journal of Development Studies* 21/1: 97–120.

—— (1993), *Riding the Tiger: The Politics of Economic Reform in Post-Mao China*, London: Macmillan Press.

White, Lynn T., III (1971), 'Shanghai's Polity in Cultural Revolution', in John W. Lewis (ed.), *The City in Communist China*, Stanford, Calif.: Stanford University Press, 341–8.

—— (1972), 'Leadership in Shanghai, 1955–69', in Scalapino (1972), 302–77.

—— (1976a), 'Local Autonomy in China during the Cultural Revolution:

The Theoretical Uses of an Atypical Case', *American Political Science Review* 70/2: 479–91.

—— (1976*b*), 'Workers' Politics in Shanghai', *Journal of Asian Studies* 36/1: 99–116.

—— (1978), *Careers in Shanghai: The Social Guidance of Personal Energies in a Developing Chinese City, 1949–66*, Berkeley: University of California Press.

—— (1987), 'Leadership and Participation: Shanghai's Managers', in Falkenheim (1987), 189–212.

—— (1989), *Shanghai Shanghaied? Uneven Taxes in Reform China*, Hong Kong: Centre of Asian Studies, University of Hong Kong.

Whitney, Joseph B. R. (1969), *China: Area, Administration, and Nation Building* (University of Chicago Department of Geography Research Paper no. 123), Chicago: University of Chicago Department of Geography.

Winkler, Edwin A. (1976), 'Policy Oscillations in the People's Republic of China: A Reply', *China Quarterly* 68: 734–50.

Wolman, Harold (1990), 'Decentralization: What It Is and Why We Should Care', in Bennett (1990), 29–42.

Womack, Brantly (ed.) (1991), *Contemporary Chinese Politics in Historical Perspective*, Cambridge: Cambridge University Press.

Wong, P. W. Christine (1985), 'Material Allocation and Decentralization: Impact of the Local Sector on the Industrial Reform', in Perry and Wong, (1985), 253–78.

—— (1986), 'The Economics of Shortage and Problems of Reform in Chinese Industry', *Journal of Comparative Economics* 10/4: 363–87.

—— (1987), 'Between Plan and Market: The Role of the Local Sector in Post-Mao China', *Journal of Comparative Economics* 11/3: 385–98.

—— (1991), 'Central–Local Relations in an Era of Fiscal Decline: The Paradox of Fiscal Decentralization in Post-Mao China', *China Quarterly* 128: 691–715.

—— (1992), 'Fiscal Reform and Local Industrialization: The Problematic Sequencing of Reform in Post-Mao China', *Modern China* 18/2: 187–227.

—— Heady, C., and Woo, W. T. (1995), *Fiscal Management and Economic Reform in the People s Republic of China*, Hong Kong: Oxford University Press.

Wu Guoguang (1994), 'Command Communication: The Politics of Editorial Formulation in the People's Daily, *China Quarterly* 137: 194–211.

Yang, Dali L. (1991), 'Reforms, Resources, and Regional Cleavages: The Political Economy of Coast–Interior Relations in Mainland China', *Issues and Studies* 27/9: 43–69

Yeung, Y. M., and Chu, K. Y. (eds.) (1994), *Guangdong: Survey of a Province Undergoing Rapid Change*, Hong Kong: Chinese University Press.

Zhao Suisheng (1990), 'The Feeble Political Capacity of a Strong One-Party Regime: An Institutional Approach toward the Formulation and

Implementation of Eonomic Policy in Post-Mao Mainland China', *Issues and Studies* 26/1: 47–80, 26/2: 35–74.

Zweig, David (1987), 'Context and Content in Policy Implementation: Household Contracts and Decollectivization, 1977–1984', in Lampton (1987): 255–83.

—— (1991), 'Internationalizing China's Countryside: The Political Economy of Exports from Rural Industry', *China Quarterly* 128: 716–41.

Index

338   Index